KANT AND THE FACULTY OF FEELING

Kant stated that there are three mental faculties: cognition, feeling, and desire. The faculty of feeling has received the least scholarly attention, despite its importance in Kant's broader thought, and this volume of new essays is the first to present multiple perspectives on a number of important questions about it. Why does Kant come to believe that feeling must be described as a separate faculty? What is the relationship between feeling and cognition on the one hand, and desire on the other? What is the nature of feeling? What do the most discussed Kantian feelings, such as respect and sublimity, tell us about the nature of feeling for Kant? And what about other important feelings that have been overlooked or mischaracterized by commentators, such as enthusiasm and hope? This collaborative and authoritative volume will appeal to Kant scholars, historians of philosophy, and those working on topics in ethics, aesthetics, and emotions.

KELLY SORENSEN is Associate Professor of Philosophy and Religious Studies at Ursinus College. His work has been published in numerous journals including *Kantian Review*, *The Journal of Philosophy*, and *Ethical Theory and Moral Practice*.

DIANE WILLIAMSON is the author of *Kant's Theory of Emotion: Emotional Universalism* (2015).

KANT AND THE FACULTY OF FEELING

EDITED BY

KELLY SORENSEN
Ursinus College

DIANE WILLIAMSON
Syracuse University

CAMBRIDGE
UNIVERSITY PRESS

University Printing House, Cambridge CB2 8BS, United Kingdom

One Liberty Plaza, 20th Floor, New York, NY 10006, USA

477 Williamstown Road, Port Melbourne, VIC 3207, Australia

314–321, 3rd Floor, Plot 3, Splendor Forum, Jasola District Centre, New Delhi – 110025, India

79 Anson Road, #06–04/06, Singapore 079906

Cambridge University Press is part of the University of Cambridge.

It furthers the University's mission by disseminating knowledge in the pursuit of education, learning, and research at the highest international levels of excellence.

www.cambridge.org
Information on this title: www.cambridge.org/9781107178229
DOI: 10.1017/9781316823453

© Cambridge University Press 2018

This publication is in copyright. Subject to statutory exception and to the provisions of relevant collective licensing agreements, no reproduction of any part may take place without the written permission of Cambridge University Press.

First published 2018

Printed in the United Kingdom by Clays, St Ives plc

A catalogue record for this publication is available from the British Library.

Library of Congress Cataloging-in-Publication Data
NAMES: Sorensen, Kelly, 1966- editor.
TITLE: Kant and the faculty of feeling / edited by Kelly Sorensen, Ursinus College, Pennsylvania, Diane Williamson, Syracuse University, New York.
DESCRIPTION: New York : Cambridge University Press, 2017. | Includes bibliographical references and index.
IDENTIFIERS: LCCN 2017037810| ISBN 9781107178229 (hardback) | ISBN 9781316630884 (pbk.)
SUBJECTS: LCSH: Kant, Immanuel, 1724-1804. | Emotions. | Emotions (Philosophy) | Senses and sensation.
CLASSIFICATION: LCC B2799.E5 K36 2017 | DDC 128/.37092–dc23 LC record available at https://lccn.loc.gov/2017037810

ISBN 978-1-107-17822-9 Hardback

Cambridge University Press has no responsibility for the persistence or accuracy of URLs for external or third-party internet websites referred to in this publication and does not guarantee that any content on such websites is, or will remain, accurate or appropriate.

Contents

List of Contributors	*page* vii
List of Abbreviations	ix
Introduction *Diane Williamson*	1
1 Rational Feelings *Alix Cohen*	9
2 Two Different Kinds of Value? Kant on Feeling and Moral Cognition *Wiebke Deimling*	25
3 The Practical, Cognitive Import of Feeling: A Phenomenological Account *Jeanine M. Grenberg*	41
4 Feeling and Inclination: Rationalizing the Animal Within *Janelle DeWitt*	67
5 Feeling and Desire in the Human Animal *Allen W. Wood*	88
6 "A new sort of a priori principles": Psychological Taxonomies and the Origin of the Third Critique *Patrick Frierson*	107
7 Between Cognition and Morality: Pleasure as "Transition" in Kant's Critical System *Kristi Sweet*	130
8 What Is It Like to Experience the Beautiful and Sublime? *Paul Guyer*	147

9	How to Feel a Judgment: The Sublime and Its Architectonic Significance *Katerina Deligiorgi*	166
10	The Feeling of Enthusiasm *Robert R. Clewis*	184
11	Sympathy, Love, and the Faculty of Feeling *Kelly Sorensen*	208
12	Respect, in Every Respect *Diane Williamson*	224
13	Is Kantian Hope a Feeling? *Rachel Zuckert*	242

Bibliography   260
Index   272

Contributors

ROBERT R. CLEWIS is a Professor of Philosophy at Gwynedd Mercy University.

ALIX COHEN is Lecturer in Philosophy at the University of Edinburgh.

WIEBKE DEIMLING is Assistant Professor of Philosophy at Clark University.

KATERINA DELIGIORGI is Reader in Philosophy at the University of Sussex.

JANELLE DEWITT is Ruth Normal Halls Postdoctoral Fellow at Indiana University, Bloomington.

PATRICK FRIERSON is Paul Garrett Associate Professor of Philosophy at Whitman College.

JEANINE M. GRENBERG is Professor of Philosophy at St. Olaf College.

PAUL GUYER is Jonathan Nelson Professor of Humanities and Philosophy at Brown University and Florence R. C. Murray Professor Emeritus in the Humanities at the University of Pennsylvania.

KELLY SORENSEN is Associate Professor of Philosophy and Religious studies at Ursinus College.

KRISTI SWEET is Associate Professor of Philosophy at Texas A&M University.

DIANE WILLIAMSON is currently studying law at Syracuse University.

ALLEN W. WOOD is Ruth Norman Halls Professor of Philosophy at Indiana University, Bloomington, Indiana, and Ward W. and Priscilla B. Woods Professor at Stanford University.

RACHEL ZUCKERT is Associate Professor of Philosophy at Northwestern University.

Abbreviations

Citations to Kant's published works follow the table of abbreviations below. Unpublished works by Kant cite the volume and page number of *Kants gesammelte Schriften,* published by the Deutsche (formerly Königlich Preußischen) Akademie der Wissenschaften (Berlin: de Gruyter [and predecessors], 1900–).

A	*Critique of Pure Reason,* 1st ed.
B	*Critique of Pure Reason,* 2nd ed.
AK xx: xxxx	*Kants gesammelte Schriften,* Akademie edition, by volume:page number
APV	*Anthropology from a Pragmatic Point of View*
CB	*Conjectural Beginning of Human History*
CF	*The Conflict of the Faculties*
CJ	*Critique of the Power of Judgment*
CPR	*Critique of Practical Reason*
EH	*Essay on the Maladies of the Head*
G	*Groundwork of the Metaphysics of Morals*
MM	*The Metaphysics of Morals*
MPT	*On the Miscarriage of All Philosophical Trials in Theodicy*
OBS	*Observations on the Feeling of the Beautiful and Sublime*
OT	*What Does It Mean to Orient Oneself in Thinking?*
P	*Prolegomena to Any Future Metaphysics*
PP	*Toward Perpetual Peace*
R	*Religion within the Boundaries of Mere Reason*
Rxxxx	*Reflexionen*
	(When there is no space between "R" and numeric digits, the reference is to numbered passages within Kant's handwritten notes. A citation to the volume and page number of the Akademie edition follows the numbered passage.)

TP	*On the Common Saying: That May Be Correct in Theory, but It Is of No Use in Practice*
UH	*Idea for a Universal History with a Cosmopolitan Aim*
UTP	*On the Use of Teleological Principles in Philosophy*

Introduction

Diane Williamson

According to *Anthropology from a Pragmatic Point of View*, one of Kant's last works and the culmination of lectures given throughout his career, there are three mental faculties: cognition, feeling, and desire. Feeling is a separate mental faculty. Nevertheless, although Kant discusses feelings in his precritical period, as in *Observations on the Feeling of the Beautiful and Sublime*, the first and second *Critiques* omit any reference to feeling as a separate faculty. Additionally, the first and second *Critique* explain their difference in the terms of theoretical and practical reason, implying that there need only be two *Critiques* at all. Yet, Kant wrote a third *Critique*, and in that work, feeling is its own mental faculty worthy of its own *Critique*. Perhaps due to this shift in Kant's philosophy, there is an unfortunate lack of scholarly attention paid to the faculty of feeling. This collection of new research begins to pull the academic helm in that direction.

The fact that Kant makes feeling its own faculty, putting it on equal footing with cognition and desire, is intriguing. This parallelism suggests that there is a relationship among the three faculties and that feeling plays a necessary role in Kant's transcendental psychology. Feeling has a psychological meaning for Kant, not a purely epistemological one, and so the development of his theory of feeling is also the development of his merger between rationalism and empiricism (or moral sense theory, in the practical realm). Kant's philosophy develops these prior schools of thought and leaves us with a comprehensive theory of feeling itself. Since feeling is often thought of as something sui generis, for better or for worse, the fact that Kant attempts to explain its psychological nature and role should be of philosophical interest even to his dissenters.

Still, Kant's term "feeling" is somewhat ambiguous. For one thing, it is unclear whether it is a mental phenomenon or is mixed up with physical sensations – or both. His discussion of feeling in *Anthropology* appears to omit any reference to the five senses, but it is still likely that he believes that feeling and empirical cognition are integrally related. And what about desire? One major, time-honored question of Kant scholarship is whether feelings prompt desires on Kant's account, and, if so, does that leave Kant with a theory of human nature that is deterministic and hedonistic? He writes that the feeling of pleasure has the effect of prompting a desire to remain in the current state and pain prompts an alteration of that state. This effect suggests that pleasure thereby has a connection to desire and also sometimes a connection to cognition, because there can be intellectual pleasures. Additionally, several of the contributors to this volume claim that the faculty of feeling is divided into higher and lower branches, suggesting a variety of types of feelings and ways that feeling can relate to cognition and desire. The precise nature of these myriad connections is the subject matter of this volume.

Kant's theory of feeling also helps us to understand his theory of emotion. While many Kant scholars have devoted attention to Kant's theory of emotion, few focus on Kant's theory of feeling – which is the most natural place to locate his theory of emotion – and even fewer discuss feeling as a faculty. Indeed, Kant's theory of emotion has much to offer contemporary philosophical debates about emotion, but there is unfortunately still little scholarly consensus regarding Kant's take on "emotion." Kant uses a variety of terms, including affects, feelings, and passions, to refer to a variety of psychological experiences that might all be called "emotion" by a modern reader. "Passions" fall under the faculty of desire, but he associates "affects" and "feelings" with the faculty of feeling. The present volume should therefore also find an audience among those scholars of emotion who are attempting to understand historical approaches as well as those who are attempting to popularize Kant's theory of emotion because they recognize its unique value.

Kantians discuss certain feelings time and time again, such as respect, beauty, sublimity, enthusiasm, and hope. These are not the typical feelings one would expect to see at the center of a philosophical account of feeling. Casual readers of Kant often see passages about these feelings as mere side remarks, not as part of a thoroughgoing philosophy of feeling. Perhaps this blindness occurs because, while Kant writes about atypical feelings like respect and the sublime, he has much less to say about normal feelings like sadness and anger. Indeed, it is decidedly strange to a contemporary ear to even consider respect or sublimity as a *feeling* at all. For another example, the feeling of reason's need discussed by Alix Cohen in this volume might strike us as a completely new feeling, not yet given a name. This strangeness should be taken as a sign of the uniqueness of Kant's theory of feeling

Introduction 3

and its philosophical value. Kantian feelings show us that cognition and reason are embodied, and Kant's discussion of them helps us to accept the natural universality of reason. Also, the strangeness of Kantian feelings can help us to see that feelings are in fact strange. Katerina Deligiorgi shows, for example, that the feeling of the sublime involves thoughts about the nature of the subject, but it is the object, not the subject, that we think of as sublime. Perhaps many feelings involve this sort of subreption of subjective effects in the object that appears to cause them.

The authors of this volume have come together to promote Kant's faculty of feeling as an object of study in its own right. Our goal is to focus on key questions relating to this faculty so as to then generate more focused discussion within the field. The editors asked small groups of scholars to research similar topics and share their conclusions with each other, seeking feedback. The goal was not only to push our authors to be more focused and clear, but also to gather individuals willing to work together on the same topic for the sake of collectively developing our understanding of Kant's faculty of feeling.

The book is organized according to, first, a discussion of the faculty of feeling as it relates to the other two faculties and, second, according to those Kantian feelings that are generally recognized as canonical. In the first case, we explore the faculty of feeling in relationship to cognition and desire. Additionally, we explore Kant's comments about feelings from the *Critique of the Power of Judgment*, asking whether judgment and feeling are functionally equivalent. Alix Cohen and Wiebke Deimling discuss the faculty of feeling and its relationship to theoretical reason. Jeanine Grenberg discusses the affective experience of moral cognition, exploring its theoretical and practical aspects. Allen Wood and Janelle DeWitt worked together to advance the current scholarship of Kant's theory of motivation and its relationship to the faculty of feeling. Kristi Sweet and Patrick Frierson discuss the faculty of feeling and its relationship to judgment and the third *Critique*. The discussion of the canonical Kantian feelings includes commentaries by Paul Guyer, Katerina Deligiorgi, Robert Clewis, Diane Williamson, Kelly Sorensen, and Rachel Zuckert.

We begin with a discussion of the relationship between feeling and theoretical reason. In Chapter 1, "Rational Feelings," Alix Cohen explores Kant's references to the feelings associated with theoretical reason, specifically the feeling of reason's need for unity and systematicity. She argues that this feeling is analogous to respect because it is a self-wrought feeling, but one that arises with the a priori functioning of theoretical reason instead of practical reason. Responding to Guyer's concern that this feeling involves little more than the delusion that nature is systematic, she argues that epistemological activity in accordance with this need for systematicity is justified so long as reason operates within the bounds of possible experience.

In Chapter 2, "Two Different Kinds of Value? Kant on Feeling and Moral Cognition," Wiebke Deimling argues that feelings are entirely different than cognition for Kant, but that they track information. After exploring Kant's definition of pleasure as a state that gives rise to the desire to remain in that state, she settles on the related possibility, that pleasure is the feeling of the promotion of life activity, as more informative. Pleasure and pain are natural responses, she holds, and emotions are merely their more complex, human versions. Moral cognition is pleasurable, for Kant, according to Deimling's reading, because it involves consistency, and consistent sensations best promote our faculties.

In Chapter 3, "The Practical, Cognitive Import of Feeling: A Phenomenological Account," Jeanine Grenberg argues that Kantian feeling is both phenomenological and transcendental. She holds that feeling must be understood in the context of Kant's empirical psychology and that in comprehending the moral law we have an experience of ourselves as autonomous, which arouses respect. She argues that our apperception of ourselves as autonomous is the practical analogue of the "transcendental unity of apperception" of theoretical reason. She also clarifies the relationship between feeling and inner sense, arguing that feelings are temporal and that they play a receptive role in practical cognition.

We turn next to the relationship between feeling and desire. In Chapter 4, "Feeling and Inclination: Rationalizing the Animal Within," Janelle DeWitt argues that Kant's account of motivation is cognitive and that portraying it as such ensures that Kant can account for rational desires. Just as sensibility and understanding play two complementary roles in theoretical reason, feeling and reason, she argues, cooperate within practical reason. DeWitt characterizes feelings as "action-initiating evaluative judgments"; hence they determine the faculty of desire by means of pleasure. This interpretation makes the faculty of desire secondary to the faculty of feeling for Kant, and the faculty of feeling is itself always activated by a representation of an object's relationship to the subject. Normative evaluation comes within feeling's characterization of the relationship between the object and the subject: It comes when the desire is being formed, not later. While she holds that propensities and inclinations are proto-desires, DeWitt argues that they also involve an analogue to judgments, but to be free for Kant means to form a judgment that accords with all of the subject's interests, especially moral interests.

In Chapter 5, "Feeling and Desire in the Human Animal," Allen Wood begins his commentary on DeWitt's interpretation by arguing that the judgmental faculties of nonhuman animals are more sophisticated than Kant believes and that they do indeed involve making choices. This argument paves the way for him to then consider the relationship between human rationality and human animality. Wood pushes back against those who hold that Kant's view of animality undergirds our cultural history of ascetic misogyny. The problem, he argues, in agreement with DeWitt, lies in interpreting Kantian empirical desire to be arational or to involve some other form of reason. He characterizes feelings as "value-cognitive" because they, on Kant's account, involve judgments of value. Similarly, on this account, the "higher" faculty of desire is merely the perfection of the "lower" through the further working of reason and feeling. Wood adds to DeWitt's thesis by accounting for the clash between inclination and reason in terms of the human predisposition to "unsocial sociability" and the passions it engenders. Also, Wood objects that pleasure itself does not make choices.

We next turn to the third *Critique* and its focus on feeling as a separate faculty. In Chapter 6, "'A new sort of a priori principles': Psychological Taxonomies and the Origin of the Third Critique," Patrick Frierson points to the division of Kant's tripartite psychology into lower and higher faculties in order to make sense of Kant's decision to write a third *Critique*. While in the second *Critique* Kant holds that there are no a priori principles of feeling, he reversed his thinking in a matter of months, holding that another *Critique* was in fact necessary to outline the a priori realm of feeling. Frierson argues that it is the aligning of feeling with judgment that provoked the discovery of its a priori principles, and he demonstrates that Kant posits an extremely close connection between feeling and teleological judgment. What changes after the publication of the second *Critique*, Frierson argues, is Kant's definition of judgment. Before the third *Critique*, Kant assumes that it is the faculty of applying pregiven concepts, but in the third *Critique*, we see that these concepts can in fact be generated from particulars. In other words, Frierson shows that Kant comes to realize that judgment can be either determinate or reflective.

In Chapter 7, "Between Cognition and Morality: Pleasure as 'Transition' in Kant's Critical System," Kristi Sweet shows the way that the third *Critique* completes Kant's philosophical and psychological systems because it creates a connection between his theoretical and practical philosophy (or between scientific and moral cognition). She examines the geographical and geopolitical metaphors Kant uses to describe this connection, and she argues that in order for feeling to be a passage between cognition and desire it must share something with each. With cognition, judgment (the feeling of beauty) shares the role of seeking out an object for apprehension. With pure practical reason, judgment shares the feature of universality. Sweet additionally argues that Kant's theory of judgment unites the two ways in which the notion of the sensus communis was previously understood (theoretically and practically).

The next section of the book explores the canonical Kantian feelings. In Chapter 8, "What Is It Like to Experience the Beautiful and Sublime?" Paul Guyer argues that the physiological differences between pleasures need not be included in Kant's rather simple definition of pleasure, which is merely the disposition to remain in a particular state. The disposition, along with the context in which it arises, gives us the essence of the sensation. In the context of a beautiful object, this account of pleasure preserves the insight that one's aesthetic judgments could be mistaken. Additionally, Kant's account of pleasure suggests that there may be some overlap between the beautiful and the sublime. Guyer concludes that the disposition to remain (or the mixed feelings of wanting to stay and wanting to leave) characterize the beautiful and the sublime better than the attempt to delineate specific physiological sensations for each.

In Chapter 9, "How to Feel a Judgment: The Sublime and Its Architectonic Significance," Katerina Deligiorgi observes that the feeling of the sublime is difficult to categorize given Kant's taxonomy of feeling and that it offers a bridge between phenomenological embodiedness and moral self-knowledge. It combines pleasure and displeasure as well as purposiveness and contrapurposiveness. Noting that the sublime is determined a priori, she combines the thought content of the feeling with its subreption under its outer cause (such as the view from a high mountain peak). She emphasizes that the feeling of the sublime only arises out of a relationship between a certain kind of object (grand, natural) and a certain kind of subject (rational, moral). Ultimately, the content of the feeling is the subject's moral vocation, and it provides the subject with a moral orientation.

Demonstrating that Kant devoted a considerable amount of philosophical attention to the feeling of enthusiasm, in Chapter 10, "The Feeling of Enthusiasm," Robert Clewis explores the various valences of this uniquely Kantian feeling. Stemming from an imaginative representation of a moral idea, the feeling of enthusiasm can be both morally useful and morally dubious. Enthusiasm, for Kant, can be either an affect or a passion. The latter is the case when the imaginative representation of a moral idea (like freedom) leads to immoral ideas and immoral means of pursuit. When enthusiasm is an affect, it can itself be aesthetically sublime. Clewis describes enthusiasm as involving a free play between imagination and reason, thereby giving the subject a feeling of the expansion of her mental capacities. Similarly, there are interested and disinterested variants of the feeling. Kant describes the public interest in the French Revolution as an important sign of progress in the world, demonstrating the moral concern of many people not themselves affected by the outcome. In any case, according to Clewis, Kant is clear that it ought not to play a role in moral education. Enthusiasm, while related to moral ideas, stems from an imaginative representation of them. The content is too mixed with non-moral ideas to play a guiding role in moral thought. Or, as Clewis speculates, it may be the case that reason does properly identify moral ideas, but its free play with the imagination leads to false ideas.

Similarly, in Chapter 11, "Sympathy, Love, and the Faculty of Feeling," Kelly Sorensen shows that Kant has good reasons to be both suspicious and praising of love and sympathy. After outlining Kant's reasons for opposing sympathy, which Sorensen shows are premonitory of Nietzsche's account of pity, and those in favor of cultivating it, Sorensen helps us understand the reason for the different accounts by making a distinction between two kinds of sympathy. Feeling, like each of the faculties, has a higher and lower form, as does sympathy. The lower form of sympathy may be an immediate response, what Sorensen calls "ur-sympathy," and it may be mixed with self-conceit. The higher form, on the other hand (although it might actually be what Kant calls an "affect" because of its ability to overpower prudential reason when morally necessary), is nevertheless brought about through morally legitimate cognition. While highlighting Kant's positive account of sympathy has become popular, Sorensen shows that his critical remarks are just as important.

In Chapter 12, "Respect, in Every Respect," Diane Williamson turns to the most widely discussed Kantian feeling. She exhibits the variety of ways in which Kant uses the term "respect" and defends the thesis that ultimately Kant has a single, coherent account of this feeling. She suggests that a different type of respect relates to the four types of Kantian duties: positive self-respect, negative self-respect, positive other-respect, and negative other-respect. She then argues that respect for the moral law is at base the same phenomenon as respect for persons. Williamson defends the position that respect is indeed a feeling for Kant, but it is unusual in that it arises from pure moral comprehension. She suggests that the insight that reason can cause feelings was developed by Kant in the second *Critique*, and this insight then led to his characterization of other intellectually wrought feelings.

Lastly, in Chapter 13, "Is Kantian Hope a Feeling?" Rachel Zuckert explores one of the least-known Kantian feelings. She asks whether hope is a feeling on Kant's account, concluding in the affirmative. Zuckert holds that hoping is part of being a healthy, rational animal, and she gives hope for the Highest Good as an example. As a positive feeling, hope has the natural tendency to reproduce itself. Rational reflection can then verify the permissiveness of this feeling or even strengthen it. She demonstrates that hope has an intentional content, but she argues that that content causes the feeling, which is itself passive. Even still, hope is rationally guided. Similarly, as a feeling, she argues that hope has a quasi-motivational character: it is not itself the motivation for action but is an important support for moral motivation.

Overall, the authors do not all agree on what constitutes the nature of feeling for Kant. Even still, together we have identified many pillars of concurrence as well as areas that call out for further research and debate. With this volume we have set the stage for a lively symposium on a central Kantian topic that continues to be of central importance for our theoretical and moral lives every day.

I

*Rational Feelings**
Alix Cohen

While it is well known that Kant's transcendental idealism forbids the transcendent use of reason and its ideas, what had been underexplored until the last decade or so is his account of the positive use of reason's ideas as it is expounded in the appendix of the *Critique of Pure Reason*.[1] The main difficulty faced by his account is that, while there is no doubt that for Kant we need to rely on the ideas of reason in order to gain knowledge of the empirical world, the justificatory grounds for our use remain unclear. Commentators have suggested various ways of addressing this worry. Some emphasize that reason's demand for systematicity is purely methodological. Others stress that the assumption that nature itself is systematically unified is transcendentally necessary.[2] Some simply deem Kant's account "extremely self-contradictory."[3] What is clear is that if neither the presupposition of nature's systematic unity nor the command to seek this unity have any justification, reason's regulative function, which plays a crucial role in Kant's account of cognition, also lacks justification. This would be a disastrous result, for it would threaten the very possibility of cognition and its progress.

This chapter proposes to tackle this problem from a new angle by exploring the role of reason's feelings in Kant's account. While the relationship between practical reason and feeling has been explored at length in the literature, the relationship between theoretical reason and feeling has not, and my aim is to suggest that doing so can shed new light on reason's

---

* Unless otherwise indicated, all translations are from *The Cambridge Edition of the Works of Immanuel Kant: Practical Philosophy*, translated and edited by Mary J. Gregor. Cambridge: Cambridge University Press, 1996.
[1] See "Transcendental Dialectic," *Critique of Pure Reason*.
[2] For the first, see for instance Paul Guyer, "Reason and Reflective Judgment: Kant on the Significance of Systematicity," *Noûs* 24, no. 1 (1990): 17–43. For the second, see for instance Michelle Grier, *Kant's Doctrine of Transcendental Illusion* (Cambridge: Cambridge University Press, 2001), 286.
[3] Norman Kemp Smith, *A Commentary to Kant's Critique of Pure Reason* (New York: Palgrave Macmillan, 2003), 547. See also Thomas E. Wartenberg, "Reason and the Practice of Science," in *The Cambridge Companion to Kant*, ed. Paul Guyer (Cambridge: Cambridge University Press, 1992), 231.

cognitive activity. For focusing on the fact that theoretical reason's need manifests itself as a feeling will enable me to reassess how this need is met through reason's regulative use of its ideas.

Following a summary in Section 1.1 of Kant's account of the regulative use of the ideas of reason, Section 1.2 turns to reason's feelings. After spelling out the function of feeling in the general economy of the mind, I put forward an account of the genesis of theoretical reason's feelings that defines them as affective manifestations of reason's activity. To support the claim that these feelings can play a legitimate role in cognition, Section 1.3 argues that we should think of them on the model of the feeling of respect for the moral law. They are both rational feelings in the sense that they are effects of reason on feeling – affective manifestations of reason and its activity. On this basis, Section 1.4 shows that the function of the feeling of reason's need allows us to vindicate the regulative use of the ideas of reason, although it does so for the sole purpose of enabling our cognitive activity.

1.1 The Cognitive Function of the Ideas of Reason

Although Kant defines reason's ideas as concepts to which no corresponding object can be given in experience, they nevertheless have a legitimate role to play in it.

> [I]n regard to the whole of possible experience, it is not the idea itself but only its use that can be either **extravagant** (transcendent) or **indigenous** (immanent), according to whether one directs them straightway to a supposed object corresponding to them, or only to the use of the understanding in general regarding the objects with which it has to do. (A643)

In its more general form, the positive function of reason is to project the idea of systematic unity as the regulative principle of cognition: "what reason quite uniquely prescribes and seeks to bring about concerning it is the systematic in cognition, i.e., its interconnection based on one principle" (A645). By turning its ideas into heuristics, reason provides orientation within the empirical world by commanding us "to seek out the necessary and greatest possible unity of nature" (A679). It enables the progress of cognition by demanding that we structure and unify our cognition of the world – Kant talks about "the systematic connection that reason can give to the empirical use of the understanding" (A680).[4]

---

[4] While I cannot get into the details of these principles here, note that each corresponds to an idea of reason. They consist in looking for homogeneity (by searching for "sameness of kind"), variety (by "distinguish[ing] subspecies") and continuity (by looking for the "affinity of various branches").

Rational Feelings 11

Although the complete systematization of knowledge can never be realized, reason can nevertheless be successful in enabling the concrete unification of certain laws, in particular by bringing heterogeneous laws of nature under higher ones. For instance, "under the guidance of those principles we come to a unity of genera in the forms of these paths [i.e., orbits of planets], but thereby also further to unity in the cause of all the laws of this motion (gravitation)" (A663). The regulative use of the ideas of reason thus plays a crucial role in Kant's account of cognition, its condition of possibility, and its progress.

Though the preceding claims have been much discussed in the literature, what is often left out is that the ground of reason's demand for systematicity is its need for it: "this guiding thread [i.e., the principle of systematicity] is not an objective principle of reason, a principle of insight, but a merely subjective one [i.e. a maxim] of the only use of reason allowed by its limits – *a corollary of its need*" (OT 140; emphasis added).[5] While reason cannot presuppose the objective reality of its ideas in the empirical world, it can orient itself in the sensible world on their basis as long as this orientation is based on its need. Yet how are we to make sense of the status of this need? As Paul Guyer first noted, adopting regulative principles seems to amount to "merely postulating or presupposing that an object will meet one's needs, rather than obtaining evidence that it does." Thereby, we merely "transform our own need for systematicity into a self-serving delusion that nature is systematic."[6] In other words, neither the presupposition of nature's unity nor the command to seek unity on which it is based seem to have any justification. If true, this would entail that reason's regulative function, which plays a crucial role in Kant's account of cognition, its condition of possibility, and its progress, also lacks justification.

(A660). For illuminating discussions of how the regulative use of the ideas of reason furthers the progress of cognition, see Frederick Rauscher, "The Appendix to the Dialectic and the Canon of Pure Reason: The Positive Role of Reason," in *The Cambridge Companion to Kant's Critique of Pure Reason*, ed. Paul Guyer (Cambridge: Cambridge University Press, 2010), 290–309, and Nicholas Rescher, *Kant and the Reach of Reason: Studies in Kant's Theory of Rational Systematization* (Cambridge: Cambridge University Press, 2000), esp. 64–98.

[5] See also: "The second regulative idea of merely speculative reason is the concept of the world in general. For nature is really the single given object in regard to which reason *needs* regulative principles" (A685; emphasis added). "[I]n relation to that which is given to the senses as existing, we *need* the idea of a being which is **necessary** in itself, but can never have the least concept of this being and its absolute **necessity**" (A679; emphasis added).

[6] Paul Guyer, *Kant and the Claims of Taste*, 2nd ed. (Cambridge: Cambridge University Press, 1997), 44, 42.

Commentators have suggested various ways of addressing this worry with mixed degrees of success.[7] What has not been explored, however, is the role the feeling of reason's need plays in Kant's argument. While this feeling does not appear in the first *Critique*, it figures prominently in the essay, "What Does It Mean to Orient Oneself in Thinking?" where Kant talks about "reason's feeling of its own need [*Bedürfnis*]," "a felt* *need* of reason" [*gefühltes Bedürfnis der Vernunft*] (OT 136, 139). The few commentators who do discuss this feeling suggest that it should be interpreted metaphorically. According to Pauline Kleingeld, for instance, the conative terms in which Kant describes reason should be understood as cases of "symbolic exhibition" so as to avoid "confounding [Kant's] distinction between reason and feeling."[8] Similarly for John Zammito, "*Bedürfnis* must not be read too literally as itself a feeling or need."[9] These metaphorical interpretations are largely based on the footnote that claims that "[r]eason does not feel" (OT 139n). By contrast with these interpretations, I will argue that they are rational feelings in the full nonmetaphorical sense of the term. To support this claim, the following section will put forward an account of the genesis of theoretical reason's feelings that defines them as affective manifestations of reason's activity.

1.2 Theoretical Reason's Feelings: The Pain of Reason's Need vs. the Pleasure of Systematization

The argument I defend here starts from a conception of feeling that I began to develop in previous work.[10] In this chapter I simply lay out features of that view, without trying to defend them in any detail. As I see it, making sense of the function of feeling in the general economy of the

---

[7] See the commentators mentioned in notes 3 and 4. As Hannah Ginsborg succinctly puts it, "Either way, it might seem, to adopt the principle of judgment is to presuppose something factual about nature, some objective feature in virtue of which it meets our cognitive needs. And, either way, Guyer's problem arises: what justification do we have for presupposing *a priori* something whose obtaining is discoverable – at least to some extent – by empirical enquiry?" (Ginsborg, "Why Must We Presuppose the Systematicity of Nature?" in *Kant and Laws*, ed. Michela Massimi and Angela Breitenbach [Cambridge: Cambridge University Press, forthcoming]).

[8] Pauline Kleingeld, "The Conative Character of Reason in Kant's Philosophy," *Journal of the History of Philosophy* 36, no. 1 (1998): 84. She argues that "Kant's talk of the needs, striving, and satisfaction of reason ... can be understood as based on an analogy ... An organism (1) is to the object of its needs (B) as reason (C) is to the regulative ideas or postulates (D)" (Kleingeld, "The Conative Character of Reason in Kant's Philosophy," 96).

[9] John H. Zammito, *The Genesis of Kant's Critique of Judgment* (Chicago: Chicago University Press, 1992), 238.

[10] See Cohen, "Kant on Emotions, Feelings and Affectivity," in *The Palgrave Kant Handbook*, ed. Matthew C. Altman (London: Palgrave Macmillan, forthcoming).

mind will enable me to determine the role of rational feelings in Kant's account of theoretical reason's activity.

According to Kant, our mental powers are constituted by three faculties: the faculty of cognition, which generates cognitions; the faculty of desire, which generates volitions; and the faculty of feeling.[11] Without getting into the detail of Kant's account, what is crucial for the purpose of my argument is that each faculty gives rise to different kinds of mental states and has a distinct function in the general economy of the mind.[12] While the faculty of cognition is cognitive and the faculty of desire conative, Kant defines the feelings of pleasure and pain in terms of the promotion and hindrance of life: "Pleasure is *the representation of the agreement of an object or of an action with the subjective conditions of life*" (CPR 9n). What this means in my view is that the faculty of feeling enables the agent to track and evaluate his mental activity and its conditions – its function is orientational.[13] On this basis, we can make sense of the painfulness of feelings of pain and the pleasantness of feelings of pleasure in light of the fact that they manifest the negative or positive effects of a representation upon the subject and his potential for activity. Anything that inhibits his potential for activity is painful while everything that facilitates it is pleasurable. The function of feeling is thus to make the subject aware of what promotes and what hinders his activity: "Life is the inner principle of self-activity. . . . Only active beings can have pleasure and displeasure. Subjects that are active according to representations have pleasure and displeasure" (AK 28:247–48).

According to Kant, feelings can be oriented either toward objects or toward the subject. This is due to the fact that each faculty of the mind has a higher and lower subfaculty. Whereas the lower faculties passively receive

---

[11] These faculties are distinct in kind, so that contrary to common misconceptions, the faculty of cognition does not include "all the faculties of the mind" ... "We can trace all faculties of the human mind without exception back to these three: the faculty of cognition, the feeling of pleasure and displeasure, and the faculty of desire" (CJ 206). For a comprehensive map of the different faculties, their subfaculties, and their interrelations, see Julian Wuerth, *Kant on Mind, Action, and Ethics* (Oxford: Oxford University Press, 2014), 221–34.

[12] "To every faculty of the mind one can attribute an *interest*, that is, a principle that contains the condition under which alone its exercise is promoted" (CPR 120). For detailed discussions of Kant's account of the faculties and their functioning, see in particular Alfredo Ferrarin, *The Powers of Pure Reason: Kant and the Idea of Cosmic Philosophy* (Chicago: University of Chicago Press, 2015), 25–57.

[13] Kant hints at this definition of feeling in the following passage: "Here the representation is related entirely to the subject, indeed to its feeling of life, under the name of the feeling of pleasure or displeasure, which grounds *an entirely special faculty for discriminating and judging* that contributes nothing to cognition but only holds the given representation in the subject up to the entire faculty of representation, of which the mind becomes conscious in the feeling of its state" (CJ 204; emphasis added).

representations from objects, the higher faculties are themselves sources of representations. In the case of the faculty of feeling, its higher faculty is concerned with the subject, its lower faculty with objects.

> The *lower* faculty of pleasure and displeasure is a power to find satisfaction or dissatisfaction in the objects which affect us. The *higher* faculty of pleasure and displeasure is a power to sense a pleasure and displeasure in ourselves, independently of objects. (AK 28:228–29)

Insofar as lower feelings are object based, when a sensible feeling of pleasure is triggered by the representation of an object, it gives rise to a sensible desire: "inclination is thereby aroused" (CJ 207). By contrast, higher feelings are subject based in the sense that they manifest the state of the subject's mental agency. The feeling of reason's need is one of these higher feelings.

While Kant does not offer an account of the genesis of the feeling of reason's need, his clearest statement asserts that "Reason does not feel; it has insight into its lack and through the *drive for cognition* it effects the feeling of a need" (OT 139n). This suggests that the feeling of reason's need already presupposes cognitive activity. The gap between reason's ideal for cognition and the current state of cognition gives rise to a feeling of need when it is combined with a drive to cognize.

To make sense of this claim, recall that, as spelled out in Section 1.1, while reason's aim is the systematization of knowledge, it is incapable of fully achieving its end. The world can never be fully cognized and thus our knowledge of it can never be fully unified. The incompleteness of our knowledge takes the form of an unbridgeable gap between reason's ideal for cognition as it is presented by the ideas of reason and cognition in its current state. Although reason has a conception of what the complete conditions of appearances should look like, it is unable to provide them. The feeling of reason's need is the effect of the incompleteness of the agent's theoretical framework on feeling. In order to avoid potential misunderstandings, note that this feeling is not the effect of the recognition or judgment of incompleteness, but rather the affective manifestation of reason's incapacity to achieve the complete systematization of knowledge.[14]

Furthermore, as already noted, although the complete systematization of knowledge can never be realized, reason can nevertheless be successful in the concrete unification of certain laws, in particular when it brings

---

[14] I would like to thank Yoon Choi for helping me clarify this point.

heterogeneous laws of nature under higher ones. What is often overlooked, however, is that this epistemic success gives rise to a feeling of pleasure.

> [T]he discovered unifiability of two or more empirically heterogeneous laws of nature under a principle that comprehends them both is the ground of a very noticeable pleasure, often indeed of admiration, even of one which does not cease though one is already sufficiently familiar with its object. (CJ 187)[15]

This pleasure manifests the achievement of a distinct kind of cognition, systematized cognition, which alone fulfills the end of reason.[16] For as Kant notes, "The interest of [reason's] speculative use consists in the *cognition* of the object up to the highest a priori principle" (CPR 120). When this interest is fulfilled and cognition is unified according to general a priori principles, no matter how partially, it gives rise to what I would like to call the pleasure of systematization. This feeling manifests the effective realization of the ideas of reason in the form of systematic knowledge – although of course, this realization can only ever be partial.

In this sense, the activity of speculative reason is the cause of two distinct feelings: a positive one, the pleasure of systematization, and a negative one, the feeling of reason's need. Crucially for my account, they are intrinsically connected to each other, for there is a loop from the pain of reason's need to the pleasure of systematization. Insofar as the feeling of reason's need is a negatively valenced feeling, it triggers a desire to dispose of it and thus of what has caused it, namely the gap between reason's ideal for cognition and its current state.[17] This gap is thus filled by using the

---

[15] See also: "It thus requires study to make us attentive to the purposiveness of nature for our understanding in our judging of it, where possible bringing heterogeneous laws of nature under higher though always still empirical ones, so that if we succeed in this accord of such laws for our faculty of cognition, which we regard as merely contingent, pleasure will be felt" (CJ 187–8).

[16] This type of cognition corresponds to what Kant calls the act of "comprehension." It consists in making sense of something by means of the general principles and grounds that determine it as well as other instances of the same kind, by contrast with "conception," which consists in understanding something by means of concepts: "to *understand* something (*intelligere*), *i.e.*, to cognize something *through the understanding by means of concepts*, or to *conceive* ... to *comprehend* [*begreifen*] something (*comprehendere*), i.e., to cognize something through reason or a priori to the degree that is sufficient for our purpose" (AK 9:65). See also AK 24:135 and 24:845–46. For an account of the distinction between understanding and comprehension, see Angela Breitenbach, "Understanding, Knowledge, and the Touchstone of Truth," in *Proceedings of the 12th International Kant Congress*, ed. Violetta L. Waibel and Margit Ruffing (Berlin: de Gruyter, forthcoming).

[17] As Kant writes, "Pleasure is a state of the mind in which a representation is in agreement with itself, as a ground, either merely for preserving this state itself (for the state of the powers of the mind reciprocally promoting each other in a representation preserves itself), or for producing its object" (AK 20:230–31). Conversely for pain: "What directly (through sense) urges me to leave my state (to go out of it) is disagreeable to me – it causes me pain" (APV 231). For a discussion of the motivational function of feeling in this context, see Rachel Zuckert, "A New Look at Kant's Theory of Pleasure," *The Journal of Aesthetics and Art Criticism* 60, no. 3 (2002): 239–52.

ideas of reason as a regulative guide for cognition so as to further the unification of knowledge. When reason's need is fulfilled through the progress of the empirical systematization of cognition, it occasions a feeling of pleasure – the pleasure of systematization.[18] Thus the loop from the pain of reason's need to the pleasure of systematization effects the ongoing and never-ending progress of systematized cognition.

However, assigning a cognitive role to the feeling of reason's need goes against Kant's account of cognition, which prohibits feelings from providing any cognitive content, epistemic standard, cognitive ground, or epistemic guidance. As he repeatedly claims, "pleasure and displeasure in general ... is something merely subjective, which yields no cognition" (MM 400).[19] Let me briefly spell out what this claim entails.

First, in feelings, "nothing at all in the object is designated" (CJ 204), for they "involve what is *merely subjective* in the relation of our representation and contain no relation at all to an object for possible cognition of it (or even cognition of our condition)" (MM 211–12). No knowledge can be attained through them: they "can never produce a cognition" (AK 24:730). This is because they do not yield objective but merely subjective certainty:

> [F]requently we take something to be certain merely because it pleases us, and we take something to be uncertain merely because it displeases or annoys us. This certainty or uncertainty is not objective, however, but instead subjective. (AK 24:198)

Second, feelings cannot be used to justify or validate beliefs in any way. Epistemic justification is only a matter of evidence, judgment, and logical inference, and affective states are thus irrelevant.

> Someone can be aesthetically certain if he holds the opposite of a thing or cognition that he has to be impossible merely because it does not please him. Thus, e.g., if his cognition is to believe in a divine being, eternal government, a future world, reward for good actions, punishment for bad

---

[18] My account of the genesis of the feeling of reason's need can be used to address a potential objection raised by Kleingeld. She notes that "nowhere does Kant discuss the anthropological structures that would account for the genesis of the feeling of the 'need of reason' in a manner parallel to this discussion of the feeling of respect" (Kleingeld, "The Conative Character of Reason in Kant's Philosophy," 85–86). Yet I have shown that Kant's remarks in "What Does It Mean to Orient Oneself in Thinking?" can be interpreted so as to provide such an account.

[19] See also: "Through sensation, good feeling, pain – one does not cognize an object" (AK 24:904); and "Feelings can never produce a cognition" (AK 24:730). As Sherman notes, "Kant's own official theory of the emotions leaves out the conceptual connection of emotion with cognition" (Nancy Sherman, *Making a Necessity of Virtue: Aristotle and Kant on Virtue* [Cambridge: Cambridge University Press, 1997], 178).

ones, etc. Certainty here rests merely on feeling[;] as something gives someone pleasure or displeasure, so accordingly does he accept it or reject it. In this way the human mind is actually subjected to very many illusions and deceptions. (AK 24:198)

When we use feelings in such ways, they produce illusions, unwarranted beliefs, and false cognitions; they give rise to illegitimate epistemic procedures: wishful thinking, unreliable grounds, warped standards, bias, and partiality. They introduce a subjective dimension into what should be wholly objective. For instance, if a belief that is unjustified gives me pleasure and induces me to accept it as true, or if I take a mere hypothesis to be true on the basis that it comes together with a feeling of certainty, I bring non-epistemic concerns to bear onto epistemic ones, thereby leading to unjustified beliefs. Thus feelings should not be used to provide any cognitive content, epistemic standard, cognitive ground, or epistemic guidance.

If this claim is correct, the justification of the regulative use of the ideas of reason now seems even more problematic than Guyer originally thought. For if it operates through what is in effect an affective feedback loop from the pain of reason's need to the pleasure of systematization, it seems to give rise to a vicious circle that turns cognition into a futile exercise of "self-serving delusion."[20] However, I will argue that it does not, since Kant's rejection of the cognitive role of feeling only applies to sensible feelings. The feeling of reason's need, by contrast, is a rational feeling, and as such, it can play a legitimate role in cognition. To support this claim, I will show that, although Kant does not say much about the feeling of reason's need, it should be thought of as belonging to a distinctive category of feeling, rational feeling, modelled on the feeling of respect for the moral law.

1.3 Reason's Feelings: The Feeling of Need vs. the Feeling of Respect

There is a vast literature on Kant's account of the feeling of respect, and I cannot even begin to make a dent in it here.[21] However, what is crucial

---

[20] Guyer, *Kant and the Claims of Taste*, 42.
[21] The literature on the feeling of respect for the law is usually divided into two camps: affectivists who argue that the feeling of respect is necessary for dutiful action, and intellectualists who acknowledge it is present, but argue all motivational work is on the part of reason. For the former, see for instance Richard McCarty, "Kantian Moral Motivation and the Feeling of Respect," *Journal of the History of Philosophy* 31, no. 3 (1993): 421–35. For the latter, see Andrews Reath, "Kant's Theory of Moral Sensibility: Respect for the Moral Law and the Influence of Inclination," *Kant-Studien* 80 (1989): 284–302. What these interpretations have in common is that they fail to appreciate that the feeling of respect belongs to the distinctive category of "rational feeling." As such, on my reading, it

for my present purpose is to note that what makes respect for the moral law a feeling is the following:

(1) It "is an effect on feeling." (CPR 76)
(2) It is a "subjective ground of activity." (CPR 79)
(3) It is "the subjective determining ground of the will" (CPR 71) – an incentive (*Triebfeder*).

Yet Kant also points out that the feeling of respect is of "a peculiar kind" (CPR 76):

(1R) It is a feeling that "is not of empirical origin." (CPR 73)
(2R) It is a subjective ground of activity that is "produced solely by reason." (CPR 76)
(3R) It is an incentive that "can be cognized a priori." (CPR 78)

The features that set respect apart from other feelings are meant to avoid a contradiction between, on the one hand, Kant's rejection of heteronomous forms of motivation based on sensible feelings and, on the other, his need to account for an incentive that impels us to act for the sake of the moral law. For, by contrast with the feeling of respect, other feelings have the following features:

(1S) They are effects on feelings that are "*received* by means of influence." (G 401n)
(2S) They are subjective grounds of activity that are "sensible" and "pathologically effected." (CPR 75)
(3S) They are subjective determining grounds of the will that "always belong to the *order of nature*" (MM 377) – inclinations (*Neigungen*).

Notwithstanding their fundamental differences, the feeling of respect and sensible feelings have a feature in common, which Kant repeatedly emphasizes. Namely, both the feeling of respect and sensible feelings generate a "drive"; they have a conative dimension.

> [R]espect as consciousness of direct necessitation of the will by the law is hardly an analogue of the feeling of pleasure, although in relation to the faculty of desire *it does the same thing* but from different sources. (CPR 117; emphasis added)[22]

functions neither as an inclination, as affectivists believe, nor as a cognition, as intellectualists believe; rather, it has the unique features of a rational feeling insofar as it manifests the conditions of moral agency.

[22] See also: respect "is something that is regarded as an object neither of inclination nor fear, though it has something analogous to both" (G 401n).

Rational Feelings

While this analogy emphasizes what the feeling of respect shares with sensible feelings (i.e., its motivational aspect), Kant also draws another analogy, an analogy between theoretical reason's feeling of its need and moral feeling.

> [Theoretical reason] does not feel . . . it effects the feeling of a need. It is the same way with moral feeling, which does not cause any moral law, for this arises wholly for reason; rather, it is caused or effected by moral laws, hence by reason, because the active, yet free, will needs determinate grounds. (OT 139n)

What this analogy suggests is that theoretical reason's feeling of its need and moral feeling share three features that set them apart from all other feelings:

A. They are both called "feeling" in a sense that needs to be qualified.
   a. For theoretical reason's feeling, "[r]eason does not feel," and yet there is "a felt *need* of reason." (OT 139)
   b. Practical reason's feeling is a "singular feeling which cannot be compared to any pathological feeling." (CPR 76)
B. They are both caused by reason alone.
   a. Theoretical reason's feeling "arises wholly from reason." (OT 139n)
   b. Practical reason's feeling is "produced solely by reason." (CPR 76)
C. They both supply grounds for rational activity.
   a. Theoretical reason's feeling provides "a subjective ground for . . . *orienting* itself in thinking." (OT 137)
   b. Practical reason's feeling is a "subjective ground of activity." (CPR 79)

The analogy between the feeling of reason's need and moral feeling is not only apt but remarkably enlightening. For in both cases the notion of feeling has been qualified so that the features that make them feelings are preserved while those that make them sensible are replaced with rational features. Unlike ordinary sensible feelings, the feeling of reason's need and the feeling of respect do not have a sensible cause. As Kant notes repeatedly concerning the feeling of respect, what distinguishes it from all feelings "*received*" by means of influence" is that it is "a feeling *self-wrought*" (G 401n). While "every influence on feeling and every feeling in general" is "*pathological*," the feeling of respect is "*practically effected*" rather than "sensibly effected": "the incentive of the moral disposition must be free from any sensible condition . . . on account of its origin, [respect] cannot be called pathologically effected" (CPR 75). It is because the feeling of reason's need and the feeling of respect "find their source in reason itself" that they are "specifically different from all feelings of the first kind" (G 401n). They are what we could call 'autonomous feelings,' in reference to Kant's distinction between the autonomous form of motivation, in which the will determines itself through the moral law, and heteronomous forms of motivation, in which the will is determined by sensible feelings and natural impulses.[23] They are autonomously generated as well as rationally determined since they are only conditioned by the agent's own rational capacities rather than external conditions over which he has little or no control. It is in this sense that they are feelings like no others – rational feelings, caused by reason and thus independent from any sensible cause.

There is thus a crucial difference between reason being motivated by nonrational, sensible feelings, and it being motivated by rational feelings.

> [W]e could not allege a need *of reason* if we had not before our eyes a problematic but yet unavoidable concept of reason [i.e., an idea of reason] ... Without such prior necessary problems there are no *needs*, at least *not of pure reason*; the rest are needs of inclination. (CPR 142)[24]

Only sensible feelings fall prey to Kant's claim that feelings are not capable of providing epistemic guidance. By contrast, we can legitimately use the ideas of reason regulatively on the basis of theoretical reason's feeling insofar as it is a *rational* feeling.[25] As a rational feeling, the feeling of reason's need can be used as a ground for our cognitive activity. Insofar as it originates in reason, it is rationally determined and provides us with a legitimate guide to a cognitive task – an affective response that can play a justificatory role, by contrast with other kinds of affective responses (e.g., wishful thinking, discussed in Section 1.2).

To make sense of the nature of the cognitive function that is thereby vindicated, however, we need to focus on its role as a rational *feeling*. As the following section will show, by applying my account of feeling to the

---

[23] See G 433.
[24] For a clear and detailed account of the nature of inclinations in Kant's psychology, see Patrick R. Frierson, *Kant's Empirical Psychology* (Cambridge: Cambridge University Press, 2014), esp. chap. 2.
[25] As Willaschek notes, "even the interest of speculative reason is practical in so far as it is based on a *need* of reason and also in so far as it directs us to *do* something (namely to inquire into a priori principles)" (Marcus Willaschek, "The Primacy of Practical Reason and the Idea of a Practical Postulate," in *Kant's Critique of Practical Reason: A Critical Guide*, ed. Andrews Reath and Jens Timmermann [Cambridge: Cambridge University Press, 2010], 185).

case of theoretical reason's feelings, we can determine their function vis-à-vis reason's activity and thereby vindicate reason's regulative use of its ideas. Yet crucially, this vindication is restricted to the sole purpose of enabling cognitive activity.

1.4 The Vindication of the Regulative Use of the Ideas of Reason

On my reading, when we rely on theoretical reason's feelings, we act, to borrow Kant's idiom, for reason's sake, to promote rational agency and its conditions. And in this respect, we do so legitimately. To make sense of this claim, recall that, as spelled out in section 1, without reason's demand for unity through its ideas, the activity of the understanding would have no guidance: "the law of reason to seek unity is necessary, since without it we would have no reason, and without that, no coherent use of the understanding, and, lacking that, no sufficient mark of empirical truth" (A651).[26] The regulative use of the ideas of reason makes it possible for reason to guide the understanding in the ongoing production of systematic knowledge: reason "gives a principle for the progression according to empirical laws, through which the investigation of nature becomes possible" (AK 20:204–5). Reason's feelings, qua feelings, contribute to this ongoing progress by manifesting the conditions of rational agency – a feeling of pleasure when its conditions are fulfilled and rational agency is furthered, and a feeling of pain when its conditions are unfulfilled and rational agency is hindered.

> [H]ence we are also delighted (strictly speaking, relieved of a need) when we encounter such a systematic unity among merely empirical laws, just as if it were a happy accident which happened to favor our aim, even though we necessarily had to assume that there is such a unity, yet without having been able to gain insight into it and to prove it. (CJ 184)[27]

---

[26] For a similar claim that without the assumption of systematicity the use of the understanding and thus the possibility of experience itself will be undermined, see A653–54. For a discussion of this claim, see Guyer, *Kant and the Claims of Taste*, 35–47. Although I cannot defend this part of the claim here, I would argue that theoretical reason ought to rely on its feelings. Otherwise, it can never progress and realize its ends, as Kant suggests when he writes that "the most common experience would not be possible without it" (CJ 187).

[27] Kant notes that "Conversely, a representation of nature that foretold that even in the most minor investigation of the most common experience we would stumble on a heterogeneity in its laws that would make the unification of its particular laws under universal empirical ones impossible for our understanding would thoroughly displease us; because this would contradict the principle of the subjective-purposive specification of nature in its genera" (CJ 187–88). This feeling of displeasure should be interpreted as the affective effect of our cognitive failure to systematize our cognitions.

Yet crucially for my account, it is not because the regulative use of reason's ideas gives rise to successful systematization that it is justified.

Of course, our ideas as regulative guides do work, and we do feel pleasure from their success. There is thus a sense in which the ongoing empirical realization of the ideas of reason through the unification and systematization of our knowledge of the natural world serves as a retroactive and ongoing confirmation that we were not in the wrong in relying on them.[28] Or to put it slightly differently, if they did not work, we would know it. If cognition was not progressing by doing so, it would not make sense for reason to carry on using its ideas regulatively. Yet it is merely an empirical and incomplete confirmation. The fact that the regulative use of the ideas of reason occasions actual systematized cognition only provides us with grounds for thinking that this use is not obviously illegitimate, but it is not sufficient to justify the regulative use of reason's ideas.

On my reading, the justification of the regulative use of the ideas of reason is grounded on the function of rational feelings. Insofar as they manifest the conditions of rational agency and motivate us to act accordingly, what they justify is the use reason makes of its ideas in order to enable cognitive activity. In this respect, a crucial difference between theoretical and practical reason is that, in the case of the latter, the feeling of its need justifies the belief in the existence of the object of its ideas whereas, in the former, it only justifies our regulative use of the ideas themselves: "the principle that determines our judgment about it, though it is *subjective* as a need, is yet, as the means of promoting what is *objectively* (practically) necessary, the ground of a maxim of assent for moral purposes, that is, *a pure practical rational belief*" (CPR 146). The ultimate justification of our reliance on the ideas of reason is practical, which confirms the fact that it is essentially connected to the needs of rational activity. While this broader claim falls beyond the limits of this chapter, let me make sense of the narrower claim about the justification of the use theoretical reason makes of its ideas by considering what goes on when relying on the feeling of reason's need is not justified, what Kant calls the transcendent use of reason.

In this case, reason's feeling of its need pushes reason beyond the legitimate bounds of experience.

> [H]uman reason, without being moved merely by the idle desire for extent and variety of knowledge, proceeds impetuously, driven on by an inward

---

[28] As Kant writes, "one is thereby neither prescribing a law to nature nor learning one from it by means of observation (although *that principle can be confirmed by the latter*)" (CJ 186; emphasis added).

need, to questions such as cannot be answered by any empirical employment of reason, or by principles thence derived. (B21)[29]

Thereby, reason produces dialectical inferences whose conclusion illegitimately asserts the objective reality of the ideas of reason. When reason addresses its needs by making a transcendent use of its ideas, its mistake is to think that its feelings can contribute to cognition by the mere fact of assigning objective reality to the content of its ideas. The transcendent use of reason is really just reason's wishful thinking for its ideas to generate their own content. By contrast, recall that when reason uses its ideas merely regulatively, their function is not (or at least not directly) to generate content but merely to enable cognitive activity: "reason really has as object only the understanding and its purposive application" (A644). Reason is thus only indirectly conducive to cognition. As Kant repeatedly notes, the purpose of reason's demand for unity is "for the provision of our understanding," "to bring the understanding into thoroughgoing connection with itself" (A305). It is in this sense that reason's ideas are the condition of possibility of cognitive activity.[30] Owing to reason's guidance, the understanding can get on with its activity, which does give rise to knowledge. However, it is the regulative use of the ideas of reason rather than their objective validity (i.e., the fact that they are true of nature itself) that is necessary for the cognitive activity of the understanding.

As a result, to go back to Guyer's original worry, the regulative use of reason's ideas is in some sense "self-serving" insofar as it serves theoretical reason's purpose. However, it is certainly not "a delusion" since it does not entail any belief that nature is systematic.[31] As I have argued, by relying on reason's regulative function on the basis of the feeling of reason's need, what we are committed to is neither the presupposition of nature's systematic unity nor the duty to seek this unity; rather, we are committed to the activity of cognizing, and ultimately, to rational agency and the improvement of its condition. On my reading, this commitment alone is justified, which is all that cognition needs to keep going.

---

[29] Cf. also our "inextinguishable desire to find firm footing somewhere beyond the limits of experience. Reason has a presentiment of objects which possess a great interest for it" (A796).
[30] To formulate this claim slightly differently, although there is no space to defend it here, the regulative use of the ideas of reason is transcendentally necessary in the sense that it is the condition of possibility of theoretical rational agency. In a similar vein, Sasha Mudd talks about the "transcendental conditions on *how* we know" rather than "*what* we know": "It conditions our cognitive activity without directly conditioning the objects we grasp through our activity" (Mudd, "Rethinking the Priority of Practical Reason in Kant," *European Journal of Philosophy* 24, no. 1 [2016]: 88).
[31] Guyer, *Kant and the Claims of Taste*, 42.

1.5 Conclusion

This chapter set out to shed new light on the notion of reason's need by emphasizing the fact that this need manifests itself as a feeling. As I have argued, the function of the feeling of reason's need allows us to vindicate our reliance on the regulative use of the ideas of reason, although it does so for the sole purpose of enabling our cognitive activity. Of course, a lot more work needs to be done to offer a complete picture of theoretical reason's activity in relation to its ideas. However, what I hope to have shown is that focusing on rational feelings suggests a new way in Kant's account of rational agency and its conditions. Insofar as we can only express our commitment to reason through its activity (theoretically through the attempt to systematize knowledge according to the regulative ideas of reason, and practically through universalizable willing for the sake of the moral law), rational feelings enable us to cognize and will as we ought to. Recall the analogy Kant draws between the feeling of reason's need and moral feeling: just as the feeling of respect plays the role of determining ground for the will, the feeling of reason's need provides a determining ground for our regulative use of the ideas of reason.[32] In this sense, rational feelings reflect the transcendental conditions of agency: they are concerned with the subject as transcendental a priori legislator of nature and freedom.[33]

---

[32] OT 139.
[33] For helpful feedback on earlier drafts of this chapter, I would like to thank Yoon Choi and Diane Williamson.

2

Two Different Kinds of Value?
Kant on Feeling and Moral Cognition*
Wiebke Deimling

How does Kant understand the relationship between feeling and moral cognition? This chapter explains why Kant (1) often presents feeling and moral cognition as pulling us in different directions, and (2) nevertheless takes feelings such as respect, love, and sympathy to be supportive of morality. The opposition between feeling and desire on the one hand and moral cognition and action on the other has been in the foreground through much of the history of Kant scholarship. We often portray it as central to his system. The canonical reading is something like the following: Kant leaves behind his early sympathies for moral sense theory and makes pure practical reason central to his ethics. This involves being suspicious toward our emotions. But the scholarship has evolved, aided by a growing interest in a wider body of Kant's work: for example, in the *Metaphysics of Morals* and in the student notes we have from Kant's lectures on ethics, anthropology, metaphysics, and pedagogy. Scholars have reconsidered the opposition between feeling and morality and called it into question. They have pointed us to feelings that support the demands of practical reason, have stressed the positive role of feeling in Kant's theory of moral motivation and virtue, and some have suggested that emotions play an important cognitive role.[1]

---

* I owe thanks to the faculty and the graduate students at Indiana University Bloomington for comments on an early version of this paper. Special thanks go to Sandra Shapshay, Curtis Sommerlatte, and Allen Wood. I would also like to thank the philosophy department at the University of Pennsylvania for helping me develop some of the thoughts expressed here. Paul Guyer's help was invaluable and so was the help of Reed Winegar.

[1] To name only a few scholars pointing to feelings that support practical reason on Kant's account see, e.g., Marcia Baron, "Love and Respect in the Doctrine of Virtue," in *Kant's Metaphysics of Morals: Interpretative Essays*, ed. Mark Timmons (Oxford: Oxford University Press, 2002), 391–407; Elizabeth Anderson, "Emotions in Kant's Later Moral Philosophy: Honour and the Phenomenology of Moral Value," in *Kant's Ethics of Virtue*, ed. Monika Betzler (Berlin: de Gruyter, 2008), 123–46; Melissa Seymour Fahmy, "Active Sympathetic Participation: Reconsidering Kant's Duty of Sympathy," *Kantian Review* 14, no. 1 (2009): 31–52; and Jeanine Grenberg, *Kant's Defense of Common Moral Experience: A Phenomenological Account* (Cambridge:

This research program has given us a more accurate and more complete understanding of Kant's ethics and moral psychology. And it has been important to developing compelling Kantian arguments in the contemporary philosophical debate about emotion. But it also leaves a tension with the fact that Kant presents feeling and moral cognition as pulling us in different directions. He warns that our feelings can tempt us to act contrary to what we know is the right thing to do. They are an unreliable basis for moral motivation. And they can lead us to rationalize – to deceive ourselves and others about our obligations. The happy philanthropist, as Kant describes him in the *Groundwork*, might be struck by misfortune and lose the joy he takes in helping others (G 398).[2] Sympathy might lead us to give too much of ourselves and drive us to resent those we are helping, deeming them unworthy of help (MM 457). And even the moral feeling can turn into an affect, make us lose the composure necessary for virtue, and make us unable to judge what is and is not morally relevant (Kant calls this phenomenon *Enthusiasm* [MM 408f.]).[3] Even in those works where

---

Cambridge University Press, 2013). For scholars stressing the role of feeling in moral motivation and Kant's theory of virtue see Mary J. Gregor, *Laws of Freedom* (Oxford: Blackwell, 1963); Barbara Herman, *The Practice of Moral Judgment* (Cambridge, MA: Harvard University Press, 1993); Nancy Sherman, *Making a Necessity of Virtue: Aristotle and Kant on Virtue* (Cambridge: Cambridge University Press, 1997); Allen W. Wood, "The Final Form of Kant's Practical Philosophy," *Southern Journal of Philosophy* 36 (1997): 1–20; Marcia Baron, *Kantian Ethics Almost without Apology* (Ithaca, NY: Cornell University Press, 1999); Jeanine Grenberg, "Feeling, Desire, and Interest in Kant's Theory of Action," *Kant-Studien* 92, no. 2 (2001): 153–79; Robert B. Louden, *Kant's Impure Ethics: From Rational Beings to Human Beings* (Oxford: Oxford University Press, 2002); Andrea Esser, *Eine Ethik für Endliche, Kant's Tugendlehre in der Gegenwart* (Stuttgart: Frommann-Holzboog, 2004); Melissa Zinkin, "Respect for the Law and the Use of Dynamical Terms in Kant's Theory of Moral Motivation," *Archiv für Geschichte der Philosophie* 88, no. 1 (2006): 31–53; Maria Borges, "Physiology and the Controlling of Affects in Kant's Philosophy," *Kantian Review* 13, no. 2 (2008): 46–66; Alix Cohen, *Kant and the Human Sciences: Biology, Anthropology, and History* (New York: Palgrave Macmillan, 2009); and Paul Guyer, "Moral Feelings in the Metaphysics of Morals," in *Kant's Metaphysics of Morals: A Critical Guide*, ed. Lara Denis (Cambridge: Cambridge University Press, 2010), 131–50. And finally, for readings stressing the cognitive role of feelings, see Jeanine Grenberg, *Kant's Defense of Common Moral Experience*; Janelle DeWitt, "Respect for the Moral Law: The Emotional Side of Reason," *Philosophy* 89, no. 1 (2014): 31–62; and Diane Williamson, *Kant's Theory of Emotion: Emotional Universalism* (New York: Palgrave Macmillan, 2015).

[2] I am using the translations in the Cambridge edition of Kant's works where available. Some translations of the student notes on Kant's anthropology lectures are my own.

[3] All of these examples can be read as the emotions in question posing both a motivational problem and a problem of moral cognition. The section I cite to point to the case of enthusiasm is the section on apathy in the beginning of the "Doctrine of Virtue": "Only the apparent strength of someone feverish lets a lively sympathy even for *what is good* rise into an affect, or rather degenerate into it. An affect of this kind is called *enthusiasm*, and the *moderation* that is usually recommended even for the practice of virtue is to be interpreted as referring to it … That is the state of health in the moral life, whereas an affect, even one aroused by the thought of *what is good*, is a momentary, sparkling phenomenon that leaves one exhausted. – But that human being can be called fantastically virtuous

Kant clearly assigns a positive role to the emotions, for example in the *Metaphysics of Morals* and in his anthropological theory, he is firm in recommending caution. In the *Groundwork* he famously claims that we should wish to be free of inclinations altogether (G 428). In the treatment of emotions in his anthropological theory Kant is equally harsh, if not harsher, in expressing his suspicion. In the published *Anthropology*, for example, he says that affects are "illnesses of the mind" (APV 251) and that "Passions are cancerous sores for pure practical reason, and for the most part they are incurable because the sick person does not want to be cured" (APV 266). The student notes on his lectures report him claiming that "All inclinations put us in slavery" (AK 25:208) and that we should "have inclination to nothing" (AK 25:1529).[4]

This chapter argues that understanding the relationship between feeling and cognition helps us resolve the tension: it can help us explain how feelings play a positive role in Kant's account while also deserving our suspicion. I start with a discussion of Kant's theory of feeling. Section 1 gives an exposition of the contrast Kant draws between feeling and cognition: cognition characteristically refers to an object while this is not the case for feeling. In section 2 I look at how feeling and desire relate on Kant's account: in a few places Kant uses desire to explain the nature of feeling. He seems to give a definition of feeling in terms of desire. But he also stresses that our ability to explain feeling is limited. Kant's account of the relationship between feeling and desire shows that we cannot define feeling through its content, that is, through what it represents. Section 3 returns to thinking about the relationship between feeling and cognition. While Kant contrasts feeling and cognition and argues that feeling is a peculiar kind of representation, he nevertheless understands feeling as tracking information: all feelings are a form of the feeling of life (*Lebensgefühl*). Feelings track the promotion and hindrance of life activity. Section 4 continues spelling out how feeling and cognition relate and focuses specifically on moral cognition. There are parallels between the ways in which moral cognition on the one hand and feeling on the other track value. I show that understanding his theory of feeling explains his seemingly contradictory attitudes toward the

---

who allows *nothing to be morally indifferent* (*adiaphora*) and strews all his steps with duty, as with mantraps; it is not indifferent to him whether I eat meat or fish, drink beer or wine, supposing that both agree with me" (MM 408f.).

[4] It is of course important to assess the scope of these claims. "Inclination" (*Neigung*) is *not* a general term that Kant uses to refer to everything we call "emotion" today. Instead, inclination is a specific type of emotion for Kant, namely habitual desire, a "desire that serves the subject as a rule (habit)" (APV 265).

emotions. Having a complete picture of Kant's theory of feeling reveals an interesting perspective on the role of emotions, which is fruitful to consider for contemporary philosophical work on the emotions.

2.1 Feeling and Cognition

Kant distinguishes three basic human faculties. We get a particularly clear statement of the division in the first introduction to the third *Critique*: "We can trace all faculties of the human mind without exception back to these three: the faculty of cognition, the feeling of pleasure and displeasure, and the faculty of desire" (CJ 245). The division structures Kant's discussion in the anthropology lectures. In the published *Anthropology* he devotes one book to each faculty.[5] I discuss the relationship between feeling and desire below. But first I want look at what Kant has to say about feeling and cognition. They are presented as standing in contrast with one another. In the introduction to the *Metaphysics of Morals*, describing the "Relation of the Faculties of the Human Mind to Moral Laws," he puts it as follows:

> The capacity for having pleasure or displeasure in a representation [*bei einer Vorstellung*] is called *feeling* because both of these involve what is *merely subjective* in the relation of our representation and contain no relation at all to an object for possible cognition of it (or even cognition of our own condition). While even sensations, apart from the quality (of e.g., red, sweet and so forth), because of the nature of the subject, are still referred to an object as elements in our cognition of it, pleasure and displeasure (in what is red or sweet) expresses nothing at all in the object but simply a relation to the subject. They are ideas that do not represent objects but refer to sensations within us. (MM 211–12)[6]

All feelings for Kant are feelings of pleasure and displeasure. And what is characteristic of pleasure and displeasure when compared to other mental states is that they are subjective. The main point of contrast here is cognition. Cognition refers to objects while feeling does not. Kant's thoughts that there is a pipe ready to smoke after getting up in the morning and that he should smoke no more than one pipe a day are about

---

[5] In the very early lecture sets the distinction between feelings of pleasure and displeasure and the faculty of desire is not yet fully developed (see the lecture notes from his students Collins and Parow dated 1772–1773). But he seems to have worked out the division only three years later and becomes more and more explicit in making use of it (see the lecture notes from Friedländer AK 25:1775).
[6] See also CJ 206f. and AK 25:1499.

the world in a way that his enjoyment of the pipe is not.[7] Kant draws a similar contrast between cognition and sensation (*Empfindung*) in the first *Critique* in what has come to be known as the *Stufenleiter* passage (because it lays out the different steps, *Stufen*, of cognition). He introduces cognition as an "objective perception" (B376/A320f.). And both intuitions and concepts are introduced as cognitions. The main contrast in the *Stufenleiter* passage is between cognition (*Erkenntnis*) and sensation (*Empfindung*). A sensation there is defined as "a perception that refers to the subject as a modification of its state" (B376/A320f.). The fact that Kant introduces both feeling and sensation as subjective suggests that Kant thinks of feeling as a kind of sensation. But it also poses questions about sensation. In the *Stufenleiter* passage Kant presents sensations as characteristically subjective. But in the passage from the introduction to the *Metaphysics of Morals* quoted above, he suggests that they are objective at least in some sense: "even sensations ... because of the nature of the subject, are still referred to an object as elements in our cognition of it" (MM 212). In other places, Kant suggests that sensation is objective. In the "Analytic of the Beautiful" of the third *Critique* Kant points out that we use the term "sensation" (*Empfindung*) in two different ways.

> If a determination of the feeling of pleasure or displeasure is called sensation, then this expression means something entirely different than if I call the representation of a thing (through sense, as a receptivity belonging to the faculty of cognition) sensation. For in the latter case the representation is related to the object, but in the first case it is related solely to the subject, and does not serve for any cognition at all, not even that by which the subject cognizes itself. (CJ 206)

In contrast to his remarks in the first *Critique*, it looks like Kant weakens the contrast between cognition and sensation when he stresses the special role of feeling in his later works. But on a closer look we can see that the claims he makes in the "Analytic of the Beautiful" and in the introduction to the *Metaphysics of Morals* are compatible with the division he presents in the *Stufenleiter* passage. In the *Metaphysics of Morals* Kant qualifies his remark that sensations are objective. Sensations are objective "apart from the quality (of e.g., red, sweet and so forth)" and he introduces them as "*elements* of cognition" (*Erkenntnisstücke*) (MM 212; emphasis added). The latter stresses that they are more objective than feeling. But it also implies that they are not cognitions on their own. They can refer to objects

---

[7] For Kant's smoking habits see Manfred Kühn's biography: Kühn, *Kant: Eine Biographie* (München: C. H. Beck, 2003), 258.

given other conditions of cognition. But by themselves they do not have intentionality or are at least not fully intentional. In short, Kant explains the subjectivity of feelings by pointing out that, unlike sensations, feelings are not even elements of cognition.

Giving a good reading of the role Kant ascribes to sensation and of how he sees the relationship between sensation and feeling is challenging.[8] What is clear is that he wants to characterize feeling as especially subjective even when compared to other already subjective mental states. We might think that the contrast between feeling and cognition is about content: Kant is making a distinction between a mental state about a subject and a mental state about an object. But this is not the case. The passage from the introduction to the *Metaphysics of Morals* quoted above notes that feeling does not enable "even cognition of our own condition" (MM 212). The difference between feeling and cognition is not a difference in *what* they represent but in the *way* they represent if feeling can be said to represent at all. In sections 2 and 3 I focus more closely on the nature of feeling. Even from what I have said so far we can see the following: if we were to locate his theory of feeling within the contemporary debate about the nature of emotions, the opposition between feeling and cognition suggests that we should characterize his account as noncognitivist. On a cognitivist account feelings centrally involve thoughts or judgments. Kant's claims rule this out.

Reading Kant as a noncognitivist is in tension with some recent readings, especially of Kant's accounts of the moral feeling and aesthetic experience. Scholars have argued that what makes moral feelings differ from other kinds of feelings is their content.[9] There is a similar debate about the content and intentionality of feeling in Kant's account of aesthetic experience. Paul Guyer has suggested that pleasure in the beautiful is non-intentional or "internally opaque with regard to their diverse causal histories or relations to the objects."[10] Richard Aquila, on the

---

[8] For different positions on whether and how sensations for Kant have intentionality see, e.g., Rolf George, "Kant's Sensationism," *Synthese* 47 (1981): 229–55; Richard E. Aquila, "Is Sensation the Matter of Appearances?" in *Interpreting Kant*, ed. Moltke S. Gram (Iowa City: University of Iowa Press, 1982), 11–29; Lorne Falkenstein, "Was Kant a Nativist?" *Journal of the History of Ideas* 51, no. 4 (1990): 573–97; and Apaar Kumar, "Kant's Definition of Sensation," *Kant Studies Online* (2014): 262–311.

[9] See, e.g., Chapter 3, "The Practical, Cognitive Import of Feeling: A Phenomenological Account," by Grenberg in this volume; Grenberg, *Kant's Defense of Common Moral Experience*; DeWitt, "Respect for the Moral Law"; Ina Goy, "Immanuel Kant über das moralische Gefühl der Achtung," *Zeitschrift für philosophische Forschung* 61 (2007): 337–60; and Rachel Zuckert, "A New Look at Kant's Theory of Pleasure," *The Journal of Aesthetics and Art Criticism* 60 (2002): 239–52.

[10] Paul Guyer, *Kant and the Claims of Taste*, 2nd ed. (Cambridge: Cambridge University Press, 1997).

contrary, has argued that we should think of feelings in aesthetic experience as having content. More recently, Hannah Ginsborg, Henry Allison, and Rachel Zuckert have advocated readings similar to Aquila's.[11] Ascribing a cognitive role to feelings makes it harder to explain how Kant describes the relationship between feeling and cognition. And it is harder to distance Kant's theory from theories he wants to reject, namely theories that analyze moral feelings as kinds of perception both in a rationalist framework and as a moral sense theory (mainly as they are put forth by Wolff and Hutcheson).[12] But, as we see below, I take it that Kant's account also does not fit neatly into a noncognitivist framework.

2.2 Feeling and Desire

Although Kant talks about feeling frequently and in different contexts, he does not say much about the nature of feeling. If we look beyond the core texts, we find a few places where he justifies this silence. In the lecture notes we have from Busolt (1788–1789), for example, Kant is reported to claim that "feeling" is primitive: "It is not further explicable if one does not want to proceed tautologically. One always has to rely on what is already known. Feeling of pleasure and displeasure is a faculty of receptivity, by which we can be affected" (AK 25:1499). He makes a similar remark in the first introduction to the third *Critique* while again drawing a contrast between feeling and cognition:

> It can be readily seen here that pleasure or displeasure, since they are not kinds of cognition, cannot be explained by themselves at all, and are felt, not understood; hence they can be only inadequately explained through the influence that a representation has on the activity of the powers of the mind by means of this feeling. (CJ 232)

---

[11] Richard E. Aquila, "A New Look at Kant's Aesthetic Judgment," in *Essays in Kant's Aesthetics*, ed. Ted Cohen and Paul Guyer (Chicago: University of Chicago Press, 1982), 87–114; Hannah Ginsborg, "Reflective Judgment and Taste," *Noûs* 24, no. 4 (1990): 63–78; Ginsborg, "Aesthetic Judging and the Intentionality of Pleasure," *Inquiry* 46 (2003): 164–81; Henry Allison, *Kant's Theory of Taste: A Reading of the Critique of Aesthetic Judgment* (Cambridge: Cambridge University Press, 2001); and Zuckert, "A New Look at Kant's Theory of Pleasure."

[12] See Christian Wolff, *Psychologia Empirica*, § 536 (Frankfurt and Leipzig: Renger, 1738, second edition) as well as Francis Hutcheson, *An Inquiry into the Original of Our Ideas of Beauty and Virtue*, (1725), edited by Wolfgang Leidhold. Rev. ed. (Indianapolis, IN: Liberty Fund, 2008), treatise II, section I (and arguably Shaftesbury depending on how we understand second-order affections arising according to his account: see Anthony Ashley Cooper [3rd Earl of Shaftesbury], *Inquiry Concerning Virtue, or Merit*, book 1, part 2, section 3). In contrast, we can argue that Hume too is best read as rejecting the claim that emotions play a cognitive role.

Seemingly in conflict with the general silence about what feelings are and with the above claims that feeling is primitive, Kant makes a few remarks that look like a definition of feeling. We find one such remark in the published *Anthropology* where he gives us a criterion for distinguishing between pleasure and displeasure: "What directly (through sense) urges me to leave my state (to go out of it) is disagreeable to me – it causes me pain; just as what drives me to maintain my state (to remain in it) is agreeable to me, I enjoy it" (APV 231). This criterion appeals to the faculty of desire. When we feel hot, for example, we have a desire to move to the shade or to have a cold drink. If we feel pleasantly warm basking in the sun, we have no desire to move. The passage from the first introduction to the third *Critique* quoted above makes the same reference to desire, when it claims that feeling can be (inadequately!) explained through the "influence that a representation has on the activity of the powers of the mind by means of this feeling" (CJ 232). Two pages earlier he gives a similar analysis to the one we get in the published anthropology: "Pleasure is a state of the mind in which a representation is in agreement with itself, as a ground, either merely for preserving this state itself ... or for producing its object" (CJ 230f.). When we feel pleasantly warm basking in the sun the state we desire is the same as the state we are currently in. There is harmony between the representation of our situation now and our representation of the desired state. When we feel hot and desire to move to the shade, which is more pleasant to us, we seek to bring about that harmony.[13] In the first introduction to the third *Critique* Kant refers to this definition as a "transcendental" definition. He describes it as transcendental because he thinks that we can know about the connection between feeling and desire a priori.[14]

---

[13] I am explaining the harmony Kant points to in terms of a mind-world match. This suffices for the purposes of the argument I am making here. But my explanation is obviously problematic for aesthetic pleasure. Kant denies that aesthetic pleasure is crucially tied to wanting to bring about an external state in CJ, § 2 of the "Analytic of the Beautiful."

[14] The line of reasoning for why we know this connection a priori is something along the following lines:

(1) A desire (as opposed to a mere wish) will take into account the possibility of following through with an action considering the necessary means. (G 394)
(2) Our empirical natures, in one way or another, require a feeling in order to put our desires into action (ascribing this to Kant is controversial; but we find it clearly expressed at least in the *Metaphysics of Morals* at 399).
(3) Therefore, there is a necessary connection between feeling and desire.

In the first introduction to the third *Critique* Kant stresses that transcendental definitions are valuable even though they do not provide satisfactory definitions of empirical concepts: "It is useful to attempt a transcendental definition of concepts which are used as empirical principles, if one has cause to suspect that they have kinship with the pure faculty of cognition *a priori*" (AK 20:230).

We have to be cautious in assessing the role this definition plays. As we have just seen, Kant points to its inadequacy right when *and* right after he provides it in the first introduction. So we have textual reasons for caution and the definition is in direct conflict with the claim that feeling is unanalyzable. Why does Kant want to limit the definition's role and what work can it still do? A closer look suggests that it lacks substance. Compare the claim (1) that feeling gives rise to the desire to leave or remain in a state to another claim (2) that a trapezoid is a four-sided flat shape with straight sides that has at least one pair of parallel opposite sides. Claim (1) does not provide descriptive content for the concept "feeling" in the same way that (2) provides content for the concept "trapezoid." The definition also raises circularity worries. Kant points to feeling in his analysis of desire. Desire is "the self-determination of a subject's power through the representation of something in the future as an effect of this representation" (APV 251) or, put differently, "to be, by means of one's representations, the cause of the objects of these representations" (MM 211). This self-determination either presupposes a feeling (in the case of a sensual desire) or gives rise to a feeling (in the case of an intellectual desire).[15] Because Kant feels joyful and relaxed eating in good company, he has a desire to go out to eat with friends. But he might also feel joyful eating in good company because he desires it as fulfilling the duty to promote our health since "[e]ating alone (solipsismus convictorii) is unhealthy for a scholar who *philosophizes*; it is not restoration but exhaustion (especially if it becomes solitary *feasting*); fatiguing work rather

---

[15] See MM 212 as well as some places in the students' notes on the anthropology lectures, e.g., AK 25:207 and AK 25:578. There is debate about whether *intellectual* desires to do what is morally right *have to* involve feeling. Some argue that on Kant's account feeling does *not* have to play a role in moral motivation. See Andrews Reath, "Kant's Theory of Moral Sensibility: Respect for the Moral Law and the Influence of Inclination," *Kant-Studien* 80 (1989): 284–302; Henry Allison, *Kant's Theory of Freedom* (Cambridge: Cambridge University Press, 1990). Others hold that feeling is always part of moral motivation even though it of course does not ground it (see Alexander Broadie and Elizabeth M. Pybus, "Kant and Direct Duties," *Dialogue* 20, no. 1 [1981]: 60–67; Kelly Sorensen, "Kant's Taxonomy of the Emotions," *Kantian Review* 6, no. 1 [2002]: 109–28; Anderson, "Emotions in Kant's Later Moral Philosophy"; and Guyer, "Moral Feelings in the Metaphysics of Morals"). I assume here that there is convincing textual evidence for the latter reading. As indicated in the previous note, in the introduction to the "Doctrine of Virtue" Kant states that "[e]very determination of choice proceeds from the representation of a possible action to the deed through the feeling of pleasure or displeasure" (MM 399). And there is further evidence that Kant held this view for a long time, that it is not just a view he came to in his later works. In his early lectures on ethics Kant is reported to stress that the intellect does not by itself have the motive force to move the will. "When I judge by the understanding that the action is morally good, I am still very far from doing this action of which I have so judged. But if that judgment moves me to do the action, that is the moral feeling" (AK 27:1428; see also AK 27:275).

than a stimulating play of thoughts" (APV 280).[16] Based on this analysis of desire, the pair of definitions would look as follows. According to the transcendental definition of feeling discussed above, we have a feeling if and only if we have a desire to remain in or to leave a state. And, as we have just seen, we have a desire if and only if our representation of something is tied to a positive feeling. The circularity worries about the transcendental definition are intuitively plausible, too. Explaining pain to someone who does not feel pain by pointing them to the desire they would have if a horse was standing on their foot is not helpful. We understand the desire in terms of being in agony in the first place. For the pointer to be helpful we have to have felt pain and have a sense of what it is like. Or, to put it in terms of what Kant, according to Busolt, said in his lecture: "one always has to rely on what is already known" (AK 25:1499).

What is Kant trying to achieve with the transcendental definition? We can make sense of the restrictions Kant puts on it if we understand it as a pointer to our phenomenology. Pleasure is the kind of feeling that we typically have when we are in a state that we want to remain in: when we are comfortably basking in the sun, for example. Thinking about basking in the sun gives us an opportunity to reflect on our experience of pleasure. Understanding the definition in this way addresses the problems mentioned above. We are acknowledging that feeling is unanalyzable, that there is no more to feeling than its phenomenology. Desires can help us reflect on this phenomenology but they do not provide feeling with content. Circularity too is no longer a problem. Thinking about a desire can guide our attention to a feeling exactly because feeling is central to our desires. On the flip side of course understanding the definition in this way means that, if we do not have access to the relevant experience, the definition does not help us understand pleasure and displeasure. We can explain pleasure and displeasure only to those who are already acquainted with it.

2.3 Feeling and Life

Besides the transcendental definition Kant gives us a further criterion for understanding feeling and the distinction between pleasure and displeasure. In the published *Anthropology* he puts it as follows: "Enjoyment is the

---

[16] For more on Kant's eating habits see the preceding pages (APV 278ff.). And see Alix Cohen, "The Ultimate Kantian Experience: Kant on Dinner Parties," *History of Philosophy Quarterly* 25, no. 4 (2008): 315–36.

feeling of promotion of life; pain is that of hindrance of life" (APV 231). In his notes Kant puts the same thought more strongly in the apparent form of a definition of feeling: "Feeling is the sensation of life" (AK 19:187). This criterion is more closely related to the transcendental definition just discussed than it might at first appear. This is because Kant understands life in terms of the faculty of desire. Having a faculty of desire is characteristic of all living beings in general: "the faculty of a being to act in accordance with its representations is called *life*" (MM 211) and "living beings do something according to the faculty of desire, and lifeless beings do something then when they are impelled by an outside force" (AK 25:577). Kant provides us with some examples illustrating this general point:

> If we compare all cases, which provide us pleasure and displeasure, we find generally that everything being in accord with making life palpable to us gives us pleasure and that everything that binds our faculties of life [*Lebens-Fähigkeiten*] arouses pain. The principle of all pleasure and pain lies thus in the facilitation or binding of our faculties of life. Our eye feels the greatest pleasure when it is put into the greatest activity by objects. But when the sight of objects is such that our eye is blurred and one impression lifts the other, or if it does not have any impressions, then it feels pain, if not another sense is entertained or put into activity. We experience pleasure and pain as life being promoted or hindered. Whatever makes the greatest impression on our taste buds [*GeschmacksDriesen*] tastes the best. Music gives our ear simultaneous impressions, and these cause in the organ the greatest agitation. (AK 25:167)

Kant understands life activity in terms of the activity of our faculties. When our senses, and here in particular our eyes and the like, are active, we feel pleasure. When their activity is inhibited we feel pain.

At a first glance this passage seems problematic. It strikes us as wrong that activity as such is pleasurable to us. There are many situations in which we find ourselves in discomfort because there is too much activity. Our eyes can be overstimulated. Film, for example, makes use of this. It gives us more frames per second than we can process, which can convey discomfort, insecurity, or panic. When Kant is reported to say that "our eye is blurred and one impression lifts the other" he himself is suggesting overstimulation can cause discomfort. In later lecture notes he is reported to use drinks as an example: gradually increasing their strength will not gradually increase the pleasure we get from them because at some point our nerves will become overstrained (AK 25:567). Kant takes pleasure to be tied to *successful* activity of our faculties and not to how much demand is put on them. When we are watching a scene in a film that gives us too many frames for us to process our faculties are less active in the relevant sense than if there were fewer frames.

Feeling can respond to life activity more widely or more narrowly. Some pleasures respond to the activity of one particular faculty being promoted, as in the example of the eye above. Kant marks other pleasures as characteristically based on the activity of multiple faculties. Pleasure in beauty responds to the activity of the imagination and the understanding being promoted in their interplay. More complex feelings such as joy and sadness will involve activity across different faculties and over a longer period of time. In the notes on his anthropology lectures Kant is reported to suggest that more complex feelings like these are particular to human beings and I have argued elsewhere that these complex feelings are similar to the states that we today refer to as emotions.[17] Inappropriate feelings are often described as being too narrowly focused and therefore unreliable in tracking life activity. Kant notes that this happens, for example, in our response to opium.

> Often something produces a feeling of the promotion of life, through which life is actually diminished. It is like this with opium, which at first seems promotive to life since it makes the blood very liquid and thin, such that it can spread through the veins fast, but ultimately it has sad consequences. (AK 25:768)

According to Kant opium overall hinders life activity. But since we are focused exclusively on the immediate effect it has on our circulation, it still feels pleasurable. He also uses his own hypochondria as an example.

> I myself have a natural disposition to hypochondria because of my flat and narrow chest, which leaves little room for the movement of the heart and the lungs; and in my earlier years this disposition made me almost weary of life ... The oppression has remained with me, for its cause lies in my physical constitution. But I have mastered its influence on my thoughts and actions by diverting my attention from this feeling, as if it had nothing to do with me. (CF 104)

Kant feels displeasure, he is "weary of life," because he is focused on the diminished activity in his heart and lungs. But the feeling is inappropriate and hence a case of hypochondria because it is too narrow. Joy in life and

---

[17] "All animals are capable of pleasure [*Vergnügen*] and pain, but not of joy and sadness; because the latter can only spring from a comparison of the current situation with our previous situation; but an animal is not capable of making such a comparison" (AK 25:422). And similarly: "Animals are able to experience neither real joy nor sadness; because these presuppose reflecting on the state after which one is conscious of the current and the preceding state" (AK 25:1082). See Deimling, "Kant's Pragmatic Concept of Emotions," in *Kant on Emotion and Value*, ed. Alix Cohen (New York: Palgrave Macmillan, 2014).

weariness about life should not be a response merely to the activity of one faculty if its activity does not have a broader impact on our life overall. And when Kant broadens his focus, when he treats the original response to the activity in his heart and lungs as having "nothing to do with me," his feelings become more appropriate.

Feelings for Kant track life activity. The way Kant phrases his thoughts about this might suggest that it makes feelings cognitive, that they contain thoughts or judgments *that* life is being promoted or hindered. We have a "feeling *of* [the] promotion of life" (APV 231; emphasis added) and a feeling is a "sensation of life" (AK 19:187). This is again in tension with the contrast Kant sets up between feeling and cognition and with his claim that feelings are primitive. But we can understand feelings as tracking life activity without saying that they are cognitions of life activity. They are reliable indicators of it: whenever we feel pleasure or displeasure there is some change in the activity of our faculties underlying it.

2.4 Feeling and Practical Cognition

Based on what I have laid out in section 3, we can see that Kant understands emotions as value tracking: they respond to the promotion and hindrance of life. But it is not obvious what, if anything, this has to do with moral value. Does Kant's theory of feeling help us explain the tension between the positive role Kant ascribes to the emotions and the suspicions he expresses against them? Life and life activity are not central to Kant's moral theory. So even though feelings and moral judgments are both value tracking, they track different kinds of values. The kind of value tracking involved also differs. Moral judgments express moral cognitions. They are based on recognizing the moral law and what it requires us to do. Our feelings do not involve cognitions. We might in a weaker sense be able to say that feelings are *about* the promotion and hindrance of life activity. But that would be similar to saying that the quicksilver in the thermometer rising is about it getting warmer in the garden.

Despite the differences between moral judgments and our felt responses there are important similarities, too. What I want to show in this section is that there is a structural similarity between them that can help us explain Kant's evaluation of our emotions. Feeling and moral cognition do not track the same values but they track value analogously.

At the level of complex feelings that have a comparatively broad scope in tracking life activity as described above, consistency and inconsistency become important. And the role consistency and inconsistency play is similar to the role they play in moral judgments. To go back to the examples used above: when we experience pleasure in beauty we experience the activities of our imagination and our understanding to be in harmony with one another, that is to be consistent. When Kant is sad about his ill health, he experiences the inhibited activity in his lungs as inconsistent with the general healthy functioning of his body and with his daily activities.

Emotions that Kant introduces as supportive of morality tend to be comparatively complex while those he introduces as obstacles tend to be comparatively narrow. Kant introduces "Love of human beings" (MM 401), "sympathy" (MM 448ff.) and "respect for oneself (self-esteem)" (MM 399 and MM 402) as supportive and worthy of cultivation. All of them track complex values. They are responses to ourselves and others as a whole person. When we feel love for someone we are sensitive to what promotes and hinders the activity of her faculties, to which things are going well and to which things are going not so well in her life. Feeling self-respect means being similarly sensitive to the activities of our own faculties and to how these activities interact. In contrast to that jealousy and pity are obstacles to moral action. When we are jealous we are taking into account only very specific traits of another person, namely those traits that make the other person seem superior to us (AK 27:436f.). When we feel pity as opposed to sympathy we focus only on a person's suffering (MM 457). We are unable to take a broader perspective on the other's ends and are unable to take an active stance in promoting her happiness. As we have seen above, Kant introduces affects and passions in general as hindrances to morality (APV 251 and 266). He introduces both as narrow. Affects and passions are feelings and desires that constrain the scope of our attention. An affect "compels us to direct our attentiveness to it alone and to nothing else" (AK 25:1340). And a passion "prevents reason from comparing it with the sum of all inclinations" (APV 265). Jealousy, as discussed above, is introduced as a passion. And anger is an affect, which makes us disregard the broader context of a situation (APV 254).

Moral judgments often concern maxims that are about the very activities grounding our emotional responses. The feelings of illness and regret we might have on a hungover morning respond to the same inconsistencies that we need to take into account at night to judge that we should not have another beer (if we want to fulfill the Kantian duty to refrain from "stupefying" ourselves [MM 427]). And our love for a friend is sensitive to her facing the same obstacles we need to take into account when judging that our help is morally required.

The moral feeling or feeling of respect is a special case of an emotion supporting morality. I cannot give an adequate account of its role in the framework of this paper but only sketch how it fits into the picture.[18] What kind of life activity does it respond to? From what Kant says about the moral feeling the most obvious answer is: the activity of practical reason. The moral feeling arises directly from our reflection on the moral law and from our reflection on determining our will and actions in accordance with it (G 442n; G 460; CPR 71ff.; MM 399f.). But the activity of practical reason in turn is responsive to all of our life activities and has an effect on them. It, for example, tells us to take care of our bodies and to provide them with the right kind of nourishment. It also tells us to keep our faculties active in order to train them for future applications (see Kant's discussion of duties to self [MM 427f.]). The activity of practical reason causing the feeling of respect goes along with the promotion of other life activities. The moral feeling de facto tracks a broad range of activities and responds to the consistency or inconsistency between them.

Kant explicitly construes felt responses as analogous to the judgment of practical reason when he compares how humans and animals guide their behavior. He claims that animals have an "analog to reason" (see the note to § 90 at CJ 464). We find a longer pointer to this claim in the student notes on Kant's anthropology lectures.

> For animals all instincts are brought into harmony through an *analogon rationalis*. For the human being this is not so: the harmony among the instincts is up to him, and as long as he does not make it, he is the most erratic among all animals. But when he just starts achieving purposiveness then he acts such that he becomes a harmonizing automaton. (AK 25:1150)[19]

Kant claims that the feelings and desires of animals track life activity accurately because they are brought into harmony by an analog to reason. This means that for animals feelings ensure that life is preserved and promoted through their behavior. Their having an analog to reason presumably is to be explained through teleological considerations. Human beings are in a different situation. We need practical reason to step in to

---

[18] I take Kant to use the terms "moral feeling" and "feeling of respect" interchangeably. Saying that the moral feeling supports morality is understating its role. I take it that Kant wants to claim that the moral feeling is always necessary for putting what we know is our duty into action.

[19] This claim also appears in the lectures on metaphysics (see, for example, AK 28:689f.). In developing this idea Kant draws on Hermann Samuel Reimarus's work (Reimarus, *Allgemeine Betrachtungen über die Triebe der Thiere* [Bohn: Hamburg, 1760], § 15 and § 16, 23ff.; §§ 27–29, 47ff.; and § 33, 54ff.).

ensure harmony among our feelings and desires. But some of our emotions, the complex responses, are at least able to track life activity across different faculties and over a longer period of time. They display some aspects of the analog to reason that Kant ascribes to animals.

2.5 Conclusion

This paper has provided an analysis of how Kant understands the relationship between feeling and cognition. He presents feeling and cognition as opposed to one another: what is characteristic of feeling is that it does *not* function in the way cognition does. But he also takes feelings to track information. They track value in that they are responses to the promotion and hindrance of life activity. For this tracking of life activity universality and consistency are central in the same way that they are central for moral judgments.

Taking a close look at Kant's theory of feeling can help us with a puzzle we face in the scholarship. It can help us understand his seemingly ambiguous attitudes toward the emotions. We can understand why he suggests both that we should be suspicious of the emotions and that they play an important role in his theories of the particular duties and moral motivation. From a moral point of view emotions deserve our suspicion because moral judgments and feelings track different kinds of values. Life activity, which is central to our felt responses, does not play a role in Kant's moral theory. But the parallels between our felt responses and our moral judgments explain why emotions provide important feedback. And they provide us with pointers about how practical reason and feeling interact to guide our behavior.

Kant's theory of feeling is intriguing from the point of view of contemporary theories of emotion. It bridges the divide between cognitivist and noncognitivist theories of emotion in similar ways that promising contemporary accounts do. He provides an interesting perspective on the role emotions play and on how they relate to moral deliberation and action. He shows why being attuned to our emotional lives is worthwhile. Because feelings track value they carry wisdom. But he also shows why our emotions are sources of risk. The way they respond to value is often inscrutable to us and it can be in conflict with practical reason's response to value.

3

The Practical, Cognitive Import of Feeling
A Phenomenological Account

Jeanine M. Grenberg

It is difficult to articulate a specifically cognitive role for feeling in any of Kant's works. One easily looks to a feeling–judgment connection in the *Critique of the Power of Judgment*, the exact nature of which is disputed among scholars. Or, in the practical realm, one easily finds much discussion of a feeling–moral motivation connection, again, the exact nature of which is disputed among scholars.[1] It is, however, difficult to find a practical but specifically cognitive (i.e., knowledge-related) role for feeling in Kant's works. This is, perhaps, because Kant does, at points, seem to advocate a pure, feeling-less cognition of the moral law. According to so-called intellectualist interpreters, then, were feeling to be involved in practical cognition, we would not accomplish a truly a priori appreciation of the authority of the moral law.[2]

Yet Kant does assert a practical and specifically cognitive role for feeling.[3] I have already argued elsewhere that this is the case, suggesting

---

[1] See, e.g., Richard McCarty, *Kant's Theory of Action* (Oxford: Oxford University Press, 2009); Andrews Reath, "Kant's Theory of Moral Sensibility: Respect for the Moral Law and the Influence of Inclination," *Kant-Studien* 80 (1989): 284–302.

[2] The term "intellectualist" (as opposed to "affectivist") for interpreters of Kant's moral motivation was coined by McCarty, *Kant's Theory of Action*. The clearest example of an intellectualist interpreter is Reath, "Kant's Theory of Moral Sensibility." Even Patrick Frierson (*Kant's Empirical Psychology* [Cambridge: Cambridge University Press, 2014]), who would describe himself as an affectivist not an intellectualist – because he welcomes third-personal analysis of feeling within the realm of moral psychology – insists that the "from within space of reasons" (his language for that transcendental space within which practical cognition emerges) does not involve feeling; the space of reasons is, for him, a space within which reason recognizes the authority of the moral law without appeal to feeling.

[3] The clearest point at which Kant suggests that feeling plays a practical cognitive role in our moral lives is at CPR 91–92: "[T]he justification of moral principles as principles of a pure reason could also be carried out very well and with sufficient certainty by a mere appeal to the judgment of common human understanding, because anything empirical that might slip into our maxims as a determining ground of the will *makes itself known* at once by the feeling of gratification or pain that necessarily attaches to it insofar as it arouses desire, where pure practical reason directly *opposes* taking this feeling into its principle as a condition. The dissimilarity of determining grounds (empirical and rational) is made known by this resistance of a practically lawgiving reason to every meddling

41

that the moral feeling of respect, as a temporal but non-intuitional sensible experience, constitutes our felt, first-personal "phenomenological" (as opposed to empirical) experience of the authority of the moral law.[4] In this chapter, I revisit a particular section of my book to respond to a potential objector: because all feeling is experienced in time, it seems that moral feeling would have to be a third-personal, empirical experience of the self as an object via inner sense, and hence, not a first-personal phenomenological experience of oneself as subject.[5]

This chapter shall proceed as follows. I first present the objection and consider two possible responses to it: rejecting that feeling is temporal, or accepting that feeling is temporal but affirming a determination of time that is not the empirical determination of time in inner sense. Having chosen the second of these options because it better respects Kant's limits on reason, I then explore practical cognition grounded in a nonempirical determination of time. First, I dwell on sections in both the first and second *Critiques* wherein Kant defends a rational-phenomenal causation within which our awareness of the moral law is understood as the effect of a rational cause and thus takes on a practical cognitive role akin to receptivity to intuitions. I then consider how such receptivity to and awareness of the moral law is possible in time without being an empirical awareness. We discover that awareness of the moral law occurs not in empirical, but phenomenological, time: it is the result of a schematism of the intelligible moral law, wherein time is determined by this intelligible law and the concept of causality as freedom, all guided by the transcendental imagination. The result of this schematism is thus not an empirical object or event determined by the pure concept of natural causality, but instead a practically determined will. The relation of this will to the moral

---

inclination, by a special kind of *feeling*, which, however, does not precede the lawgiving of practical reason but is instead produced only by it and indeed as a constraint, namely, through the feeling of a respect such as no human being has for inclinations of whatever kind but does have for the law; and it is made known so saliently and so prominently that no one, not even the most common human understanding, can fail to see at once, in an example presented to him, that he can indeed be advised by empirical grounds of volition to follow their charms but that he can never be expected to *obey* anything but the pure practical law of reason alone."

[4] See Grenberg, *Kant's Defense of Common Moral Experience: A Phenomenological Account* (Cambridge: Cambridge University Press, 2013).

[5] The section I refer to is Grenberg, *Kant's Defense of Common Moral Experience*, 40–46. I note that while felt experience is "not an empirical experience of objects," it is an experience of "myself as an agent" (Grenberg, *Kant's Defense of Common Moral Experience*, 43–44). The idea that feeling must be explored exclusively as a part of our empirical psychology wherein I encounter myself as an object is defended most thoroughly by Frierson, *Kant's Empirical Psychology*. Although I do not seek here to respond directly to his project, I am indebted to it and to him for helping me think through these ideas more deeply.

The Practical, Cognitive Import of Feeling 43

feeling of respect is then revisited, confirming that the phenomenological expression of this intelligible causality is indeed this feeling, which can now be confirmed as a phenomenological awareness of ourselves as legislating subjects of the moral law. Through moral feeling, I thus gain access to my self-as-practical-subject, clothing the bare bones of that theoretically accessed self-as-subject, the Transcendental Unity of Apperception, with an apperceptive cognition of merely practical content: I know myself as subject not only as the locus of all my thoughts but also as a being who is the source of all moral obligation.

3.1 The Problem and Two Possible Resolutions of It

Here, then, is our problem: if the moral feeling of respect occurs in time, does it *really* escape being an aspect of our empirical experience? Isn't it, rather, an experience that occurs (as any temporal experience does) within inner sense and hence as an empirical psychological experience of oneself third personally as an empirical object? Indeed, within Kant's worldview, it seems that first-personal experience of oneself – including experience of one's feelings – is impossible. The only point at which I encounter myself as subject, first personally (instead of as object, third personally) is when I admit that I must be the subject of all my thoughts in the Transcendental Unity of Apperception.[6] But such recognition of self-as-subject allows no appeal to any particular content of that self, only the admission that this bare, formal transcendental "I" must be the subject of all my thoughts.[7] Temporal, felt experience must thus be understood as third-personal experience, a topic to be explored not via phenomenology but only via empirical psychology.

Third-personal reflection on feeling – and especially on the moral feeling of respect – has been emphasized in recent literature by Patrick Frierson, who suggests that the best way to make sense of the importance of moral feeling is to explore it third personally within the discipline of moral psychology.[8] According to him, the moral feeling of respect is best

---

[6] "The **I think** must **be able** to accompany all my representations; for otherwise something would be represented in me that could not be thought at all, which is as much as to say that the representation would either be impossible or else at least would be nothing for me... Thus all manifold of intuition has a necessary relation to the **I think** in the same subject in which this manifold is to be encountered" (B131–32).

[7] Because the I think "in all consciousness is one and the same," it "cannot be accompanied by any further representation" (B132).

[8] Frierson, *Kant's Empirical Psychology*.

understood not as a first-personal phenomenological experience, but as an empirical experience of oneself as an object within empirical psychology.[9]

Frierson does not explicitly reject the idea that one could experience feeling first personally.[10] Nonetheless, the problem remains for anyone (including Frierson) who would want to welcome even the very possibility of first-personal felt experience within Kant's moral philosophy: how can we make sense of the very possibility of first-personally felt experience if the only framework within which we can speak of the experience of feeling is the third-personal framework of inner sense? I present this problem as follows:

1) Although feeling is not (like sensible intuition is) involved in the construction of empirical objects of experience in space and time, felt phenomenological experience does occur in time.
2) But time, as a form of sensible intuition, *is* involved in the construction of objects of empirical experience. Any experience in time is an experience in inner sense.
3) If feeling is temporal, its involvement in the construction of a cognition must result in an empirical object of cognition (i.e., the

---

[9] When Frierson makes his initial distinction between transcendental critique and empirical psychology, he relies heavily upon H. J. Paton's conception of distinguishing these two realms. Here are some excerpts from Paton, which Frierson himself quoted: "[W]e regard actions from two different points of view ... First of all we can take an external and scientific view of action ... But ... we have also a very different point of view, the point of view of the agent acting, a point of view which sees the action from within, not from without ... Hence it may be the case from an external or psychological point of view our motive is the feeling of [respect], whereas from the internal or practical point of view our motive is simply the moral law, the law of our own free and rational will, without the intervention of any kind of feeling. We may perhaps say that from one point of view [respect] is the *cause* of our action, but from another point of view the moral law is its *ground*" (H. J. Paton, *The Categorical Imperative: A Study in Kant's Moral Philosophy* [London: Hutchinson and Co., 1947], 67) (quoted at Frierson, *Kant's Empirical Psychology*, 121). This is essentially a summary not only of Paton's but also Frierson's distinction between empirical psychological and transcendental critical points of view. Note here the way that feeling is handled in these two perspectives: we can give only a third-personal scientific account of the role of feeling in events (it seems we cannot speak of "actions" as such from this external, scientific perspective); but we allow no room for feeling from the transcendental "from within" space of giving reasons for actions. What is notable here is that we find no meaningful room for the exploration of feeling first personally.

[10] Frierson has in fact suggested that one can speak of feeling first personally (see Frierson, "Kantian Feeling: Empirical Psychology, Transcendental Critique, and Phenomenology," *Con-textos Kantianos* no. 3 [2016]: 353–71). Even here, though, Frierson does not grant that experience of feeling any transcendental import. Feeling can provide merely subjective information about "what it is like" to experience something but can do nothing to point us toward any objective cognition. So, although we can infer a priori that moral reasons and our freedom to act on them will show up to us via feeling, "our freedom does not need to show up subjectively as a particular sort of feeling" (Frierson, "Kantian Feeling," 10). To the contrary, it is still the case that the from-within space of reasons is just that: a space of reasons involving no appeal to feeling.

4) But an object of inner sense does not grant me knowledge of myself as agent or subject, but only knowledge of myself as object via empirical psychology.
5) First-personal, felt phenomenological experience of myself as agent or subject is thus impossible.

I have indeed admitted that the moral feeling of respect is a temporal experience, and also that, in feeling it, we experience ourselves first personally as subjects and agents. Is there any way of responding to this objector?

It is worthwhile, before turning to my own resolution of the matter, to consider what options are available at this point. Essentially, this objector challenges me to think more about what exactly the relationship of feeling is to time. There are at least two different directions I could go here. I could, on the one hand, bite the bullet and retract my claim that the moral feeling of respect is a temporal experience. This would be to give a very strong reading of Kant's claim in *Metaphysics of Morals* that feeling gives us only "a relation to the subject" (MM 211–12). This reading is strong in that one would not only be rejecting the idea that feeling is involved in the construction of empirical objects; one would also be saying that somehow feeling gets around time entirely and is a truly atemporal, even quasi-mystical experience. Indeed, on the strongest of readings, one might say that feeling itself becomes a third form of intuition. Such an intuition would not need to rely upon time at all, but would have status as its own form of sensibility with its own capacity to be the sensible basis of the construction of its own (mystical) experience, and ultimately (because intuition as such would be involved in the cognition) the construction of a quasi-theoretical or speculative cognition of morality, now relying on this new form of intuition.[11]

On the other hand, I could insist that feeling is temporal, but not temporal in the sense of being an object of empirical inner sense. This would be to admit that there is a determination of time that is not an empirical determination of time via pure concepts of the understanding.

---

[11] I am indebted to Ryan H. Wines of Stockholm, Sweden, for helping me to think about this first option. He gave a paper, unpublished, at the 2015 Kant Seminar at the University of Oslo that opened my mind to this option. The various details of this option I go on to discuss are not ideas I explicitly attribute to him, but I am indebted to him for inspiring me to think in these directions generally.

To take this route would be a less strong approach, since I would not be denying feeling a temporal status, only insisting that time as determined empirically in the first *Critique* is not the only way of determining time. This route would also have less of a mystical quality about it because, although we would need to admit that time has a relationship to something intelligible and thus atemporal (i.e., a relationship to that noumenal moral law that is determining my will as a morally obligated will), we would still insist that, given our nature as sensible beings, we could access that relationship to things noumenal only temporally. But now this temporal relation would be in phenomenological time, not empirical time.

There are interpretive advantages to each of these approaches. There is, after all, something tempting about suggesting that feeling could be an intuition, thus allowing a rather straightforward parallel between theoretical and practical cognition. We have already suggested that determination of feeling produces a more determined practical subject, and this is a would-be cognition that seems to require something weighty like intuition to do the job of construction on the receptive side.

But there are clear disadvantages to this approach as well. To claim that the feeling of respect is timeless would be to assert a mystical, outside-of-space-and-time experience every time I felt the feeling. This would suggest that when we experience this feeling we are in fact completely entering into an experience of the noumenal realm as such. But, in fact, we have only two intuitions (space/time), and the moral feeling of respect is not an intuition, but a *feeling*. Kant makes a clear *distinction* between feeling and intuition in which each plays clearly different roles. He asserts that while feeling is not involved in the construction of empirical objects, intuition is: "While even sensations, apart from the quality (of, e.g., red, sweet, and so forth) they have because of the nature of the subject, are still referred to an object as elements in our cognition of it, pleasure or displeasure (in what is red or sweet) expresses nothing at all in the object but simply a relation to the subject" (MM 212).

So, admitting feeling as intuition would violate both Kant's epistemic categories and the bounds of human experience itself, literally taking us beyond the "human standpoint" (A26/B42) defined by our sensible intuitions of space and time, thereby suggesting some nonhuman, mystical experience of the moral law and ourselves as its author. Indeed, it would be to fall into a "fanaticism" of the sort Kant mentions at the end of his highest-good discussion when he envisions those who would try to apply reason not only "negatively" to affirm practical cognitions but also positively to reach actual theoretical or speculative cognition of the

The Practical, Cognitive Import of Feeling

supersensible. According to him, "speculative reason" should, when given the practical datum of obligation to the moral law, "go to work with these ideas in [only] a negative way (really, only to secure its practical use) . . . so as . . . to ward off . . . *fanaticism*, which promises such an extension [of pure concepts to supposed experience] by means of supersensible intuition or feelings" (CPR 135–36). To appeal to feeling as its own kind of intuition would be equivalent to asserting that we have a "supersensible intuition or feeling" that yields not merely practical but actual theoretical or speculative cognition of the moral law, and that would be mere moral fanaticism.

Finally, such an approach even violates Kant's constraints on the bounds of *practical* cognition as discussed in *Groundwork III*. There, Kant insists that we must admit something wondrous and incomprehensible in our practical lives: "[W]e do not indeed comprehend the practical unconditional necessity of the moral imperative, but we nevertheless comprehend its *incomprehensibility*; and this is all that can fairly be required of a philosophy that strives in its principles to the very boundary of human reason" (G 463). But to admit a mystical experience of the moral law would erase this incomprehensibility; we do not take a clear object of theoretical cognition to be incomprehensible. To suggest that in fact we do simply have an experience of the moral law is no longer to take it as an object of wonder or mystery. Perhaps it would be hard to describe in time and via empirical means what one's mystical experience was. But once one had a direct mystical experience of the moral law, it would no longer have that wondrous, incomprehensible quality as such. It would be something that we simply knew.

Having said all this, Kant already suggests, very early in the first *Critique* discussion of theoretical cognition, that we *will* get beyond the limits of theoretical cognition to *some* extent when we turn to the practical. As early as the "B Introduction" to the first *Critique*, Kant claims that "even if we cannot cognize . . . objects as things in themselves, we at least must be able to think them as things in themselves" (Bxxvi), and that such thinking of intelligible objects, in order to achieve the status of "objective validity" "need not be sought in theoretical sources of cognition; it may also lie in practical ones" (Bxxvin). As such, having *some* merely *practical* cognition of things intelligible is not out of order, and, indeed, we have already suggested that some receptivity to the authority of the moral law is precisely this practical encounter that will assure such practical cognitions of things noumenal. But it would be beyond the scope of Kant's promise here to admit a practical cognition that had absolutely everything a theoretical cognition did (especially a claim that sensible intuition itself could expand to a third type of intuition, viz., feeling).

But welcoming the second option of time being determined differently in practical moral experience has clear advantages. First, because the result of the construction of phenomenological experience will be only via feeling (not intuition) and only for practical (not theoretical) purposes, it respects both the constraints of the second *Critique* about the construction of a cognition of the moral law and also of Kant's *Groundwork III* claim that the moral law itself will remain an object of wonder and mystery. We will not know the moral law intimately and internally as one who experienced it mystically would; we will only get to know enough of the moral law and ourselves as author of it to know what we must do. Further, by admitting a determination of time that is not an empirical determination of time or of any intuition, we avoid a model of practical cognition that essentially would become a fanatical theoretical or speculative cognition instead. Finally, in that same appeal to time that is not an empirical but instead a phenomenological determination, we find and affirm in Kant's works the beginning of a long tradition of taking time and temporality as being central to the exploration of phenomenology.

One might worry that the forthcoming account in which we appeal to feeling playing a receptive and quasi-intuitive role in practical cognition would also be a form of moral fanaticism, since, as we have just seen, Kant does speak of how fanaticism would appeal to "supersensible intuition *or feelings*" (CPR 135–36; emphasis added). But the forthcoming account does not present moral feeling as a "*supersensible* feeling" (i.e., a feeling the experience of which is entirely within the supersensible realm and which as a mode of supersensible intuition grounds theoretical or speculative cognition of some object in that supersensible realm). Instead, it is a *phenomenological* feeling (i.e., a feeling that is experienced in time, and thus within the human standpoint, but which is also recognized as the effect of a supersensible cause). Furthermore, appeal to this feeling will not ground theoretical or speculative knowledge of some object in the supersensible realm (and not even practical cognition of some *object* in the supersensible realm) but instead practical cognition of myself as a *subject* influenced by a still mysterious and only hinted-at object in the supersensible realm (viz., the intelligible moral law).

Indeed, welcoming feeling as playing a meaningful role in the construction of practical cognition actually respects the constraints that Kant places on cognition generally. Even as we enter into the realm of practical cognition, we still face the challenge of revealing the authority of an intelligible law to beings who require *two* roots for cognition (receptivity and activity), and who, further, have access only to sensible, not

The Practical, Cognitive Import of Feeling

intelligible, receptivity or intuition. These are the famous limits to knowledge Kant laid out for us in the first *Critique*. Versus Leibniz and other rationalists who would assert that sensibility is just confused concepts, Kant asserts that sensibility and understanding are two distinct roots of cognition, one receptive the other active, and that both must work in conjunction with each other to produce cognition.[12] Further, one cannot expect thought to do the work of sensible intuition, or vice versa; rather, each has its own capacity and its own role in cognition that cannot be accomplished otherwise.[13] This insistence upon two roots of cognition, and especially the limitation of human cognition to what can be given in space and time, constitutes what Kant has called the "human standpoint" on cognition (A26/B42).

The challenge, then, is to affirm a way epistemically to admit that we have some practical inkling, hint, or trace of the noumenal realm that is a genuine practical cognition, but which respects the contours of the human standpoint or way of knowing that demands appeal to both receptive and active elements of cognition. Let us turn, then, to consideration and defense of a new role for time in phenomenological experience that respects these constraints.

3.2 The Phenomenological Determination of Time

3.2.1 The Determination of Time in the Practical Cognition of the Moral Law

What, then, is it about a temporal experience of moral feeling that makes it a *special* temporal experience, one that respects the receptive-active structure of cognition from the human standpoint, but which also succeeds in providing a new epistemic framework within which to cognize things practical? In short, in the experience of moral feeling, a different

---

[12] "Our cognition arises from two fundamental sources in the mind, the first of which is the reception of representations (the receptivity of impressions), the second the faculty for cognizing an object by means of these representations (spontaneity of concepts); through the former an object is given to us, through the latter it is **thought** in relation to that representation (as a mere determination of the mind). Intuition and concepts therefore constitute the elements of all our cognition, so that neither concepts without intuition corresponding to them in some way nor intuition without concepts can yield a cognition" (A50/B74).

[13] "[T]hese two faculties or capacities cannot exchange their functions. The understanding is not capable of intuiting anything, and the senses are not capable of thinking anything. Only from their unification can cognition arise" (A51/B75–76).

determination of time yields not an empirical object determined by pure concepts but instead a phenomenological experience that reveals a schematism of the moral law and, with that, a trace or hint of one's own intelligible and legislating subject through the determination of both time and feeling by the transcendental imagination. Ultimately, we discover a felt moment *in* time that points us to an intelligible object *outside* of time. This determination of feeling in time is caused by the intelligible moral law and the causality of freedom (instead of by the pure concept of natural causality) whose influence is transmitted through the transcendental imagination, and results not in cognition of an object as such (since noumenal objects are beyond our ken) but instead in a felt indication or trace of the moral law encountered as the phenomenological (instead of empirical) effect of a noumenal cause that can show itself in phenomenological experience of the subject thereby affected.

To tell this story, however, we need first to welcome a framework within which the receptive-active framework of theoretical cognition can find a parallel in practical cognition. We can indeed find, in Kant's discussion of the highest good, his willingness to suggest that appeal to the "practice of the moral law" (CPR 137) allows us to make practical claims about God, an appeal in which this practice of the moral law plays a role for practical cognition not unlike that receptive role of intuition in a theoretical cognition. That is, in theoretical cognition, sensible intuition is the means via which we receive the "content" that gives objective validity to the mere form of thought provided by concepts. As Kant reminds us, "[w]ithout sensibility no object would be given to us," and "thoughts without [this sensible] content are empty" (A51/B75).[14] So, Kant's suggestion in his discussion of the highest good is that when the stuff or "content" of space and time falls short, our awareness of a practical law steps in to allow our cognition to continue to have reference to objects beyond space and time, but now only for practical purposes. As Kant notes, even though the purported "object" of would-be theoretical speculators of the object of God turns out to be nothing but a "mere word" and offers no "hope for an extension of *theoretical* cognition" (because there is no content upon which our concepts could work here) (CPR 138; emphasis added), the possibility for *practical* cognition of such an object is more promising:

---

[14] See also A95: "It is entirely contradictory and impossible that a concept should be generated completely *a priori* and be related to an object although it neither belongs itself within the concept of possible experience nor consists of elements of a possible experience. For it would then have no content, since no intuition would correspond to it though intuitions in general, through which objects can be given to us, constitute the field or the entire object of possible experience."

[W]ith respect to the practical there still remains to us, of the properties of understanding and will, the concept of a relation to which the practical law ... furnishes objective reality. Once this is done, reality is given to the concept of the object of a morally determined will (that of the highest good) and with it to the conditions of its possibility, the ideas of God, freedom, and immortality, but always only with reference to the practice of the moral law (not for any speculative purpose). (CPR 138)

The "practice of the moral law" thus plays the receptive role of providing the stuff or content upon which concepts previously used in the construction of empirical objects can now act to produce practical cognitions (or postulates) of God, freedom, and immortality.

But *how* is this moral law, which assures this practical determination of these concepts (now understood as the "categories of freedom" [CPR 65]) "given" to us in the first place? This is, after all, the previous condition of content necessary in order for us to be able actively to use our concepts specifically as concepts of freedom. By what human capacity can we take in this practical object? We have already gone beyond the limits of what could be given to us in space and time, and we know from the first *Critique* that a capacity for receiving something or being given something cannot be taken up by our capacity for understanding, because the role of these two roots of knowledge cannot be exchanged. This is just not the sort of thing that understanding can do.

The ultimate answer to this question is, of course, appeal to that fact of reason that is given to us. And, as I have argued previously,[15] this ability to be given the most basic fact of morality (viz., to be given an awareness of the authority of the moral law over my will) must be taken up by the only other capacity within us for taking things in: our capacity for feeling. Where the sensible, receptive intuitions of space and time fall short, the receptive (but not intuitive) capacity for feeling must enter the scene. Feeling thus plays what I have called an enabling instead of an evidential role in facilitating practical cognition.[16] It is the intelligible moral law itself that will affirm the objective validity of a practical cognition of the authority of the moral law over my will. But to take in or receive this object from the human standpoint, we need some sort of capacity for receptivity that would receive it. By process of elimination, we realize that only the capacity of feeling could play this role of giving me a practical

---

[15] See Grenberg, *Kant's Defense of Common Moral Experience*, chap. 8, where I argue that only feeling could be the receptive vehicle for the fact of reason.
[16] See Grenberg, *Kant's Defense of Common Moral Experience*.

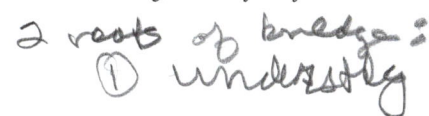

cognition of an intelligible object, viz., a cognition of the authority this intelligible moral law has for my will.

But now the challenge of our objector returns: we have said that the experience of this moral feeling is a phenomenological experience of myself as legislating subject, and is not an experience of myself as an empirical object in inner sense. But *how* could I experience a feeling in time that is not an empirical experience of myself in inner sense? We need, essentially, to have a framework within which an intelligible and noumenal cause has a phenomenal and temporal but merely practical (and not empirical) effect.

Initial textual support for taking just this route for understanding the determination of time in the experience of moral feeling can be found in Kant's resolution of the Third Antinomy. There, Kant resolves the thesis and anti-thesis oppositions of the antinomy by appealing to the idea, entirely possible within the realm of transcendental idealism, that the effects of an intelligible cause can be present in the chain of empirical experience:

> If ... appearances do not count for any more than they are in fact, namely, not for things in themselves but only for mere representations connected in accordance with empirical laws, then they themselves must have grounds that are not appearances. Such an intelligible cause, however, will not be determined in its causality by appearances, even though its effects appear and so can be determined through other appearances. Thus the intelligible cause, with its causality, is outside the series; its effects, on the contrary, are encountered in the series of empirical conditions. The effect can therefore be regarded as free in regard to its intelligible cause, and yet simultaneously, in regard to appearances, as their result according to the necessity of nature. (A536–37/B564–65)

What, then, is Kant's claim here? Essentially, the suggestion is that, although a noumenal cause cannot present itself as an object of experience or as a theoretical cognition, it is nonetheless possible that what would otherwise seem a mere phenomenal experience is in fact a special phenomenal effect of a noumenal cause. And while the noumenal cause cannot appear in the chain of phenomenal causes, the effect of that cause can.

Kant suggests later in the Third Antinomy that these phenomenal effects with noumenal causes are, essentially, indications, traces, or hints of our noumenal heritage in the phenomenal world. The intelligible cause cannot be presented as an empirical object; indeed, it "is passed over as entirely unknown *except* insofar as it is *indicated* through the empirical character as only its sensible sign" (A546/B574; emphasis added). Nonetheless, Kant is confident enough in these traces or indications of the intelligible in the phenomenal even to define intelligible things through this sensuous expression: "I call intelligible *that in an object of sense* which is not itself appearance" (A538/B566; emphasis added). When an aspect of our phenomenal experience can be granted this status as an indication of its intelligible causal heritage, that aspect of our phenomenal experience is more precisely called, in my terms, a "phenomenological" experience.

Kant's concern in this text of the Third Antinomy is to suggest that we can encounter a trace of the intelligible notion of *freedom* (not the moral law as such) present in the empirical realm; but we can bring the same structure of the relationship of intelligible and phenomenal things to our understanding of the impact of the authority of the moral law being given through a temporal, felt experience. Let us thus take this picture of intelligible cause/phenomenological effect as a guide for thinking of our practical cognition of the moral law as enabled by the moral feeling of respect. We can, first, find passages in the second *Critique* that encourage us to bring just this model of intelligible-phenomenal causality specifically to our cognition of the moral law. Consider first Kant's claim that making sense of those "determinations of a practical reason" that affirm the validity of the moral law must take place "in the sensible world" and not just on some distant intelligible plane:

> [S]ince actions *on the one side* indeed belong under a law which is no law of nature but a law of freedom, and consequently belong to the conduct of intelligible beings, but *on the other side* as also events in the sensible world yet belong to appearances, the determinations of a practical reason can take place only with reference to the latter and therefore, indeed, conformably with the categories of the understanding, but not with a view to a theoretical use of the understanding, in order to bring a priori the manifold of (sensible) *intuition* under one consciousness, but only in order to subject a priori the manifold of *desires* to the unity of consciousness of a practical reason commanding in the moral law, or of a pure will. (CPR 65)

The "determinations of a practical reason," or the moral law, must have their effect in this "sensible world" and specifically upon the "manifold of desires" found in sensible, human wills; as such, Kant welcomes the thought that the noumenal moral law is able to find its sensible expression in our sensibly affected wills not through "a theoretical use of the understanding," but only via "practical reason."

In the following section ("Of the Typic of Pure Practical Judgment," CPR 67–71), Kant struggles with the question of *how* one could do this; that is, how we could "find in the sensible world a case which, though as such ... stands only under the law of nature, yet admits of the application to it of a law of freedom and to which there could be applied the supersensible idea of the morally good, which is to be exhibited in it *in concreto*" (CPR 68). In other words, just as he did in the Third Antinomy, Kant is here seeking a way in which "supersensible" things – here, the moral law itself – could be made tangible – *in concreto* – within the phenomenal world, since that is, after all, the world in which moral decisions and actions must be taken.

Kant then makes an interesting move: he suggests that schemas produced by the transcendental imagination – that faculty which, in the first *Critique*, played the crucial role of allowing otherwise heterogeneous concepts and intuitions to have an affinity to each other for the production of theoretical cognition – can now be utilized to connect these two new heterogeneous things (viz., a supersensible moral law and a sensibly affected will):

> Physical causality, or the condition under which it takes place, belongs among concepts of nature, whose schema transcendental imagination sketches. Here, however, we have to do not with the schema of a case in accordance with laws but with the schema of a law itself (if the word schema is appropriate here), since the *determination of the will* (not the action with reference to its result) through the law alone without any other determining ground connects the concept of causality to conditions quite other than those which constitute natural connection. (CPR 68–69)

Kant's suggestion here is that an intelligible-phenomenal causal structure akin to what we have just seen articulated in the resolution to the Third Antinomy can in fact, with the assistance of "transcendental imagination," reveal a "schema of a [moral] law" in the phenomenal world. That schema of the law would be a "determination of the will ... through the law alone," in other words a causal determination of my phenomenal will by a supersensible law, a determination through which I recognize myself as obligated to that law (since, as Kant notes parenthetically, we are not yet concerned with that "action" that would be the "result" of my taking up this law).

Let us dwell on this important move for a moment. First, it makes sense that Kant would appeal to a "schematism" produced by the power of the "transcendental imagination" in making sense of how to connect two such varied things as an intelligible moral law and a sensibly affected will. Kant had first appealed to such a faculty in the A Deduction of the first *Critique*, and assigned it a role there that he later retracted in the B Deduction. But his fullest discussion of the role of the transcendental imagination in relation to schemata comes in a later section of the *Critique* present in both editions, "On the Schematism of the Pure Concepts of the Understanding" (A137ff./B176ff.). To appreciate Kant's second *Critique* appeal to the schema of the moral law, and to appreciate how it is that the transcendental imagination has something in it of both concepts and intuitions, it will be important for us to dwell for a moment upon this first *Critique* articulation of schemas.

According to Kant, a schema, which "is in itself always only a product of the imagination" (A140/B179) is what really does the work of resolving otherwise heterogeneous things into an agreeable "homogeneity" that is experience:

> Now it is clear that there must be a third thing, which must stand in homogeneity with the category on the one hand and the appearance on the other, and makes possible the application of the former to the latter. This mediating representation must be pure (without anything empirical) and yet **intellectual** on the one hand and **sensible** on the other. Such a representation is the **transcendental schema**. (A138/B177)

Kant thus appeals here to a sort of bridge faculty of the transcendental imagination to do the work of assuring an affinity between otherwise heterogeneous concepts and intuitions.

Kant furthermore uses the language of "a transcendental *time*-determination" (emphasis added) to describe this activity of the transcendental schemata, and this depiction clarifies his meaning when he suggests that the imagination expressed in the schemata has within itself something both of concepts and intuitions to help mediate the two:

> [A] transcendental time-determination is homogeneous with the **category** (which constitutes its unity insofar as it is **universal** and rests on a rule *a priori*). But it is on the other hand homogeneous with the **appearance** insofar as **time** is contained in every empirical representation of the manifold. Hence an application of the category to appearances becomes possible by means of the transcendental time-determination which, as the schema of the concept of the understanding, mediates the subsumption of the latter [i.e., appearances] under the former [i.e., the category]. (A138–39/B177–78)

Because a schema is a rule (like a category) but a rule expressed in time (as an intuition), it has something of both otherwise heterogeneous elements within itself, thus making it the most appropriate faculty for resolving the heterogeneity of concepts and intuitions into something "homogeneous."

It is important, though, not to think that a schema is simply an image, or an empirical product of the imagination in which I produce an image in time in my head of whatever concept it is that I am trying to understand (like a triangle). Rather, Kant gives an example of schemata produced by *transcendental* imagination ~~in order~~ to distinguish them from mere empirical "images" (the usual thing that the imagination, in its empirical use, would produce):

> In fact it is not images of objects but schemata that ground our pure sensible concepts. No image of a triangle would ever be adequate to the concept of it. For it would not attain the generality of the concept, which makes this valid for all triangles, right or acute, etc., but would always be limited to one part of this sphere. The schema of the triangle can never exist anywhere except in thought, and signifies a rule of the synthesis of the imagination with regard to pure shapes in space." (A140–41/B180)

Kant's point here is that this product of the imagination has an affinity with concepts because it provides a rule that applies generally to all cases of its kind, yet also has an affinity with intuition because this rule is a rule in concreto that tells us something about the determination of things in space and/or time. But a merely empirical image would not truly have the former, viz., universal applicability to all appropriate "pure shapes in space." As such, we recognize the schema as something short of this full empirical image, a connection of the promise of appearances to the universal concept in question, but one that must not and cannot be a specific empirical image or object. Kant thus starts using the language in this section of a "sensible concept" to make sense of this strange intermediary notion of a schema: "Hence the schema is really only the phenomenon, or the sensible concept of an object, in agreement with the category" (A146/B186).

Given this account of the transcendental imagination in producing schemata, it makes perfect sense that Kant would return to schemata produced by the transcendental imagination when, in his practical philosophy, he faces a challenge with exactly the same contours as the challenge he was facing in his theoretical philosophy. The need to provide a bridge between the intelligible moral law and a sensibly affected will provides exactly the same challenge of assuring affinity between heterogeneous things that we have just reviewed. As such, it makes sense to appeal to the transcendental imagination and the "sensible concept" of schemata here, instead of to bare concepts, to make sense of that faculty that would allow a sensible, temporal determination or schema of the moral law to appear.

But how exactly would this determination of the will by the transcendental imagination, resulting in a schematism of the moral law, work? The connection here between the schematism and *time*-determination guides us here. The work of a schema is to determine time in a way that connects the intuition of time to the activity of thought. And although Kant does not explicitly mention time as that aspect of the usual constructs of sensibility that is being determined by the moral law, his reference to a "schema" of the moral law encourages just that claim. The *schematism* of the moral law is, then, an expression of the moral law *in time*. And this makes sense, for, surely, the sensibly affected will that this intelligible law is seeking to determine is indeed something that exists in time.[17]

This is the crucial point at which to appreciate, however, that, although our sensibly affected will is determined in time by the moral law, this does not mean that my ultimate experience of that determination (which we will eventually understand as the moral feeling of respect) is an empirical experience in "inner sense" as such. Kant does indeed, in the Transcendental Aesthetic, equate determinations in time with determinations in inner sense.[18] But all of this is with the assumption that the contents of the intuition of time will eventually be determined as complete empirical objects and events, and theoretical cognition thereof, through the pure concepts of the understanding. The Transcendental Aesthetic brackets the role of concepts in the production of inner sense, so that point is not made evident there, and the entire first *Critique* is devoted to theoretical cognition, so he is not concerned at this point with the determination of time for practical cognitions. But when he turns to things practical in the second *Critique*, none of these constraints is in place; there is thus more room for him to dwell on time determinations not explicitly related to the production of empirical products, but instead of practical products. Indeed, Kant's appeal to the transcendental imagination as being the means by which an intelligible moral law determines the will of a being in the sensible world as a schematism of that intelligible law provides us with just what we need for that alternative, nonempirical determination of time that we have been seeking.

---

[17] It is clear that these passages are making sense of a will that exists within the sensible world: the moral law is seeking a *sensible* expression or schema, and we finite beings have only two forms of sensibility, space and time. To think that the moral law would find its sensible schema spatially is, however, to say too much: a determination of space by the moral law would seem to demand some observable, perceivable "object" of the moral law in front of us, and this does not seem Kant's point here. Though it might be his point in the "Beauty as a Symbol of Morality" section of the *Critique of the Power of Judgment*. That is, it may be that the moral law could be the source of a determination of both space and time in beautiful works of art or nature that succeed in symbolizing that law. But that is not Kant's task here. Here, he is instead seeking a more internal, but still sensible, determination of our wills. Once put that way, it seems obvious that time must be the form of sensibility connecting an intelligible law to sensibly affected wills.

[18] "[Since] all representations, whether or not they have outer things as their object, nevertheless as determinations of the mind themselves belong to the inner state, while this inner state belongs under the formal condition of inner intuition, and thus of time, so time is an *a priori* condition of all appearance in general, and indeed the immediate condition of the inner intuition (of our souls) … [S]o from the principle of inner sense I can say entirely generally: all appearances in general, i.e., all objects of the senses, are in time, and necessarily stand in relations of time" (A34/B50–51).

It is especially important at this point to recall that Kant insisted in the first *Critique* that a schemata is not an empirical image. When we envision the schema of the moral law, then, we are not encountering an empirical image or object of the moral law in time. In other words, it is not a complete, full-fledged empirical object in inner sense. The importance of this point is the same for practical application as it was for theoretical application: a fully empirical image of the moral law would not have the universality of application that we are seeking. Just as a mere image of the triangle could only be of acute or isosceles triangles and not of triangles in general, an empirical image of the moral law could only be of obligation to this or that action, not to action generally.

As such, time is indeed determined in the schematism of the moral law, but, as with theoretical schemata, the product of this time determination is not an empirical object. Instead, the intelligible moral law via the transcendental imagination acts here to produce an intellectual but temporal schema of itself as a morally obligated will. It is true that when Kant speaks of the activity of this intelligible law, he connects it with the concept of causality: "the determination of the will ... through the law alone ... connects the concept of causality to conditions quite other than those which constitute natural connection" (CPR 68–69). But this is not a reference to the pure concept of natural causality (i.e., the notion of causality that assures that every empirical event has a cause). Rather, this is an indirect reference to that causality as freedom that is the reciprocal flip side of the intelligible moral law and that we saw referenced previously as the concepts of freedom. That this is the case is clear when Kant warns the reader not to assume that causality is playing a role here as it would in the construction of an empirical event. Rather, as he notes, "the determination of the will [by the moral law] ... connects the concept of causality to *conditions quite other than those which constitute natural connection*" (CPR 68–69; emphasis added).

We are thus not seeking a determination of time by the natural concept of causality that affirms the construction of natural objects and events but rather a determination of time by the concept of causality as freedom and the intelligible moral law that affirms the construction of a sensibly affected will as morally obligated. A successful determination of time by the transcendental imagination in conjunction with an intelligible cause (and not in conjunction with pure concepts of the understanding in their usual role) thus yields not an empirical experience as such, but instead, as we have been saying, a phenomenological experience, now understood as a nonempirical schematism of the moral law in time.

Let us dwell on the differences between the two. Both of these experiences are in time; the difference between them, though, comes down to the question of what it is that determines the contours of the temporal experience for each. The temporal aspect of empirical experience is something that is determined directly by pure concepts of the understanding, and the result (if it be only time that is involved) is an object in what Kant calls "inner sense" (A22/B37). But now Kant turns to the intelligible moral law and its concept of causality as freedom in conjunction with the transcendental imagination to explain the determination in time of the sensibly affected will. These two heterogeneous elements (an intelligible law with its concept of freedom, and a sensibly affected will) need to be brought *together*, but *not* to produce objects or events.

The crucial point to appreciate here is this: since the concept of causality is operating very differently in this initial phenomenological experience of the givenness of the moral law than it would in the construction of an empirical object of inner sense, the result of this construction not only *is* not but *cannot* be empirical experience in inner sense: a merely empirical image of anything would require the activity of the pure concept of natural causality to be operative. That is, the pure concept of causality understood as the notion of natural causality in which every event has a cause would have to be operative for the product of this time determination to be one of inner sense. But were that concept operative, the result would be a merely empirical image of the moral law in time, and this empirical image would not contain the universality required for the schema. So, as we have been suggesting, the concept of *natural* causality is absent here. The concept of causality operative in the determination of a sensibly affected will by the moral law is not the concept of natural causality but instead the causality of freedom, and that is not a determining force that would result in the production of an empirical object in inner sense. So, Kant's appeal to the work of the transcendental imagination in producing a schema of the moral law makes it reasonable for us to see him as providing the epistemological basis for a kind of temporal experience that is not empirical, but instead, is a phenomenological temporal experience that is a trace or indication of a supersensible fact.

3.2.2 The Determination of Feeling in the Practical Cognition of the Moral Law as Practical Apperception

We thus appreciate the distinctive determination of time as a schema of the moral law by the transcendental imagination, which is at the basis of phenomenological experience. But we have been saying that this phenomenological experience is a *felt* phenomenological experience, and, as such, we must also make sense not just of a distinctive determination of time but also of a special determination of *feeling* to explain the givenness of the moral law. Recall, though, that Kant said that this determination of the will by the law is, essentially, a determination by which one "subject[s] *a priori* the manifold of desires to the unity of consciousness of a practical reason commanding in the moral law, or of a pure will (CPR 65; emphasis added). It thus makes perfect sense that this schematism of the moral law *in concreto* expresses itself as a phenomenological experience of feeling: if what the moral law is doing when it determines a will is to order the desires of that will toward a "unity of consciousness" in which one recognizes the untrumpable authority of the moral law that orders and organizes one's desires in general, then clearly the felt experience of the "special" (CPR 92) moral feeling of respect that constrains all our inclinations and desires is precisely the phenomenological felt experience one would *expect* when this moral law acts as it does![19] The schema, or time determination, of the moral law produced by the transcendental imagination is thus the background first step that makes possible the temporal experience of a feeling that is "a special kind of feeling" (CPR 92) precisely because it has this special intelligible causal heritage, and thus this special time determination, of which we have been speaking. One could not experience this sort of feeling unless the transcendental imagination were doing the schematism work that it does.

There is a further point to make about the nature of this causal framework within which an intelligible moral law determines a sensibly affected will, resulting in the phenomenological experience of the moral feeling of respect: this rational causality is, in fact, a causal influence of my supersensible self upon my phenomenal self. To see this, consider Kant's *Groundwork* description of the moral feeling of respect as a feeling that is "*self-wrought* by a rational concept":

> Even though respect is a feeling, it is not one *received* by influence, but one *self-wrought* by a rational concept, and therefore specifically different from all feelings of the former kind ... [Respect] signifies merely the consciousness of the *subordination* of my will to a law, without mediation of other influences on my sense. (G 401n)

---

[19] See CPR 92: "The dissimilarity of determining grounds (empirical and rational) is made known by this resistance of a practically lawgiving reason to every meddling inclination, by a special kind of *feeling*, which, however, does not precede the lawgiving of practical reason but is instead produced only by it and indeed as a constraint, namely, through the feeling of a respect such as no human being has for inclinations of whatever kind but does have for the law."

One might worry that Kant is here suggesting that the experience of moral feeling is not a receptive experience; but, in fact, he is saying just the opposite. Consider: other feelings we have (of fear, attraction, and so forth) are indeed "received by influence." That is, they are caused by something external to the feeling person; hence, we experience the feeling entirely passively as the receptor of the influence of this external object. But, as we have been saying, the moral feeling of respect is caused by the moral law. But the moral law, as autonomously legislated, is just my own intelligible nature. Moral feeling is, therefore, caused by my own intelligible nature. But, surely, my *empirical* self will *experience* this as "received by influence" in a certain limited sense: my empirical, conscious self is not the cause of this feeling, so one does not experience moral feeling as if one's empirical conscious self had *chosen* to feel it. To this extent, it resembles other feelings with external causes: my empirical self experiences the feeling as if having a cause outside itself through which that empirical self feels passively the influence of one's own intelligible self. But deeper reflection on this feeling reveals to an attentive mind the true cause of the feeling as one's true intelligible self. As such, indirectly (and as a mere indication or trace), one does feel this feeling as a "special" one with a distinctive causal history, "not … received by influence." What I cognize in the moral feeling of respect is thus some glimpse or indication of myself as a practically legislating subject of morality (and not just of myself as passively or receptively receiving that legislation).

As such, even though the intelligible moral law cannot be present as an *object* of phenomenological experience, we can still welcome this further determination of oneself as a practical experiencing *subject* that *is* part and parcel of this phenomenological experience. I cannot encounter myself as an intelligible object (i.e., some odd noumenal version of myself in inner sense) and I cannot experience the moral law as an intelligible object (since the cause of this phenomenal effect does not itself appear in experience). But I can claim a further "relation to the *subject*" (MM 212; emphasis added) that is accomplished in this phenomenological effect of the moral law that is my experience of moral feeling. The practical cognition of oneself that is accomplished as an aspect of the practical cognition of the moral law through feeling is thus not the empirical psychological self of inner sense wherein one does indeed become an empirical object to oneself. We know this to be the case because of the special form of determination of time by the transcendental imagination that is operative in this determination. Instead, it is a further determination not of a phenomenological object as such but of my phenomenological self-as-subject. We thus have an experience in time wherein time is determined, via imagination and feeling, to reveal the traces of our practical destiny as legislators of morality.

In affirming the cognition of the moral law as revealing something to us about ourselves as intelligible subjects we have, furthermore, discovered an epistemic account of how it is that we come to have a practical cognition of our intelligible selves as author of the moral law that is more satisfying than what Kant initially proposed when he first introduced the idea of intelligible-sensible causal interaction in the Third Antinomy. There, just after presenting the feasibility of this causal structure, he suggests further that one can have a cognition of oneself as an "intelligible object" via the implausible route of "pure apperception":

> In the case of lifeless nature and nature having merely animal life, we find no ground for thinking of any faculty which is other than sensibly conditioned. Yet the human being, who is otherwise acquainted with the whole of nature solely through sense, knows himself also through pure apperception, and indeed in actions and inner determinations which cannot be accounted at all among impressions of sense; he obviously is in one part phenomenon, but in another part, namely in regard to certain faculties, he is a merely intelligible object, because the actions of this object cannot at all be ascribed to the receptivity of sensibility. We call these faculties understanding and reason. (A546–47/B574–75)

Kant suggests here that we can "know" ourselves as intelligible beings – and indeed as "objects," not merely as acting subjects – in a way that thoroughly avoids the involvement of anything sensible or receptive. It is strange that Kant speaks here of us knowing ourselves as objects through apperception, since the language of apperception, at least when referenced in the Transcendental Unity of Apperception, refers specifically to awareness of oneself as subject. It is even stranger that he suggests we access ourselves as "intelligible objects" without any reference to intuition, receptivity, or anything sensible. That is, after all, precisely what is "pure" about this assertion of "pure apperception": I know myself as an "intelligible object" that "cannot at all be ascribed to the receptivity of sensibility" and I know this object that is myself entirely without reference to that sensibility.

This route is implausible for many reasons, but central among them for our purposes is the thought that one could escape the receptive-active model of cognizing when one cognizes one's intelligible self. The idea that we could have a simple, direct, and complete active apperception of ourselves as intelligible beings violates just the limits of cognition we have been seeking to respect. Indeed, it seems almost a trace of that Cartesian confidence in the pure access to one's noumenal soul that Kant heartily rejects in the Paralogisms. We cannot accept, even for things practical, that one could acquire a true cognition of any sort without both receptive and active components being involved. The thought of succeeding in cognition of an "intelligible *object*" also seems too strong: even when the practice of the moral law is introduced as datum upon which our concepts can operate, we have not concluded that we know ourselves as objects. To the contrary, we gain only hints or indications of ourselves as practical subjects.

And yet, even as we thus reject both cognition of intelligible objects and this "purity" of pure apperception, we simultaneously welcome the language of "*ap*perception" to describe what we have just asserted in the felt, phenomenological cognition of oneself as a legislating subject. That is: in identifying one's supersensible self as the legislating source of a truly categorical imperative, one perceives oneself as the practical subject of all moral demands, just as in theoretical terms, one perceives oneself as the subject of all one's thoughts. Just as the "I think" is the unity of theoretical cognition, the "I-am-obligated" is the unity of practical cognition.

To appreciate this point, compare the following quotes. We have already seen Kant describe the determination of a morally obligated, sensibly affected will in these terms:

> [T]he determinations of a practical reason can take place ... not with a view to a theoretical use of the understanding, in order to bring a priori the manifold of (sensible) *intuition* under one consciousness, but only in order to subject a priori the manifold of *desires* to *the unity of consciousness of a practical reason commanding in the moral law, or of a pure will*. (CPR 65; emphasis added)

Now consider very similar language noted in Kant's B Deduction description of the Transcendental Unity of Apperception:

> The **I think** must **be able** to accompany all my representations; for otherwise something would be represented in me that could not be thought at all, which is as much as to say that the representation would either be impossible or else at least would be nothing for me ... Thus all manifold of intuition has a necessary relation to the **I think** in the same subject in which this manifold is to be encountered. (B131–32)

What we see here are practical and theoretical versions of apperception. On the one hand, the manifold of desires is brought under "the unity of consciousness of a practical reason"; on the other, the manifold of intuition must be brought under the unity of consciousness that is the "I think."

We can thus describe experience of the moral feeling of respect as a practical apperception to complement the theoretical apperception of oneself in the Transcendental Unity of Apperception. Essentially, this practical cognition reveals our practical vocation that defines one's intelligible self as a particular kind of rational being (viz., one who is author of and therefore subject to moral principles). This parallel between theoretical and practical apperception holds because in both we encounter one's self-as-*subject*, not one's self-as-inner-sense-object. In the theoretical realm, I encounter myself as the subject of all my thoughts; in the practical realm, I encounter myself as the subject (or author) of all moral legislation. Whenever I experience sensuous objects and events, I can refer back to the implicit awareness that I am the subject perceiving these things; whenever I experience the moral feeling of respect, I can refer back to the implicit awareness that I am the legislator of the law that constrains me.

One might worry at this point that introducing so thick a claim as moral obligation into the realm of the I think is illicit. After all, as we noted at the beginning of this chapter, the Transcendental Unity of Apperception must be a bare, formal recognition of ourselves without any content. In Kant's words, because the I think "in all consciousness is one and the same," it "cannot be accompanied by any further representation" (B132). That is, the apperception that affirms all thoughts as my own would need to be the same in every case; otherwise, each representation would not be "my" own in the same way. As such, apperception cannot welcome other content along with it sometimes though not at others. To do so would, essentially, be to say that I have as many selves as I have contents associated with this basic apperception. Or, as Kant puts it, "I would have as multicolored, diverse a self as I have representations" (B134).

But this is not a problem for us. It is surely the case that this practical apperception – precisely for its being practical – *seems* to have more content to it than the bare, merely formal apperception of oneself as the subject of all one's thoughts. And yet, this recognition of oneself as the locus of all moral constraint contains a similar notion of being the bare unifying locus of morality, just as theoretical apperception is the bare unifying locus of thought. We are not cognizing ourselves as objects but only recognizing ourselves as the implicit underlying subject of practical demands. Indeed, one can even say that this practical consciousness is a consciousness that accompanies *all* our thoughts, at least implicitly. That is not to say that we are always feeling the moral feeling of respect. But the fact that is at the foundation of the sensible schema of the moral law is always present: just as we are always the locus of all our thoughts (even though we do not always make this conscious to ourselves), we are also always the locus of all moral obligation (even though we do not always make this conscious to ourselves). Self-consciousness, as understood through the Transcendental Unity of Apperception, is thus implicitly moral self-consciousness of the authority of the moral law, an implicit fact that experience of the moral feeling of respect brings to consciousness. This felt conscious experience affirms who I am, indeed, the *kind* of rational being I am.[20]

We thus have found, in our feeling-based, practical appeal to how we know imperatives, a preferable alternative to achieving this hint of our noumenal selves. Pure apperception of this noumenal self, like the "fanaticism" Kant worries about (at CPR 141), *would* be a violation of the human standpoint, because it illicitly avoids the need for receptivity in cognition and asserts too much when it claims cognition of an intelligible object. But felt practical apperception of ourselves as legislators of the moral law avoids these problems. We finally have a mode of practically cognizing our supersensible selves that respects the limits of cognition of sensibly affected rational beings.

3.3 Conclusion

We have thus most fully defended the idea that the moral feeling of respect is a first-personal, phenomenological – not a third-personal, empirical – experience by focusing upon the relationship of an experience of the feeling to a special determination of time; and we have done so in a way

---

[20] I am thus deeply sympathetic with the work of Julian Wuerth (*Kant on Mind, Action, and Ethics* [Oxford: Oxford University Press, 2014]), who suggests that Kant interpreters have been wrong to think that the Paralogisms of the first *Critique* are the last word on Kant's interest in the rational soul. Wuerth insists that if we read Kant's corpus overall (starting before the first *Critique*, then turning to the first *Critique*, and finally moving to post-*Critique* thoughts), we will find that the discussion of the Paralogisms in the *Critique of Pure Reason* is only his negative project of rational psychology, providing only hints of the positive account of rational psychology that Kant wants to retain after ridding it of its metaphysical excesses. According to Wuerth, in his negative account of rational psychology, Kant rejects the excessive claim that immortality of the soul can be concluded from reflection upon the soul as substance. But once that excessive claim is rejected, there is still much more to say about the substantial soul. The rationalists' failure to recognize the virtues of transcendental idealism prevented them from being able to cling to notions of "permanence, incorruptibility, and personality" (Wuerth, *Kant on Mind, Action, and Ethics*, 116) of the soul in any but the most heavy handed of metaphysical ways. But transcendental idealism gives Kant a new way to understand the applicability of such ontologically significant notions of the soul. In the claims I have made in this chapter, I take a similar tack, suggesting that practical cognition allows us to move beyond the merely negative claims about the rational soul (from the Paralogisms) to a genuinely positive, though only practical, claim about the nature of our intelligible soul, accessible only as subject.

that does not violate but instead respects the receptive-active limits of the human standpoint from which cognition is acquired. Time's normal role is to be involved in the construction of empirical experience; but it here has a second role in being determined not toward the construction of an empirical object but toward the cognition of oneself as a morally obligated subject via a now also particularly determined feeling (viz., the moral feeling of respect, as a felt phenomenological effect of a supersensible cause). Our experience of moral feeling is thus in time, but not in the empirical time sequence of inner sense as such; it is instead in phenomenological time, which has its own causal line distinct from the causal line that moves merely empirical time. This experience does not have the same intuitive structure as empirical time: time (and, ultimately, my will) is not determined by the pure concept of natural causality here; instead, time (and, ultimately, my will) is determined by the pure rational principle of the moral law and the concept of causality as freedom via the activity of the transcendental imagination and the vehicle of feeling.

Finally, I am happy to recognize Kant's phenomenological determination of time and feeling as the beginning of a tradition in phenomenology of non-empirical determinations of time. Interestingly though, Kant's pursuit of such thought was inspired by and limited to a merely practical project, whereas both nineteenth-century and contemporary phenomenology seem to have lost that practical grounding. Perhaps we can take this review of eighteenth-century practical phenomenology as a call to arms to return phenomenology to its practical roots.

4

Feeling and Inclination
*Rationalizing the Animal Within**

Janelle DeWitt

One bedrock feature of Kant's moral psychology is his description of humans as *sensibly affected rational beings*. Implicit in this description is a duality of nature that gives rise to distinct forms of motivation – reason, stemming from our "higher," rational nature, and inclination, stemming from our "lower," animal/physical nature. However, what remains unclear from this division is how these two natures, and their relationship to each other, should be characterized.

Many commentators believe that Kant intends them to be understood as *entirely* distinct, in part because they stem from opposite sides of the metaphysical divide (the rational and the natural orders) and in part because reason, as the source of moral motivation, must remain unadulterated by its associated lower nature. Since these natures remain distinct, their characterizations are thought to proceed straightforwardly. Our higher nature, considered independently of its associated lower nature, shares the same basic characteristics as purely rational beings. The result is a nature entirely absent of any visceral experiences such as emotions, feelings, wants, or needs. In contrast, our lower nature, considered independently of its associated higher nature, shares the same basic characteristics as nonhuman animals. The result is a nature entirely devoid of reason, where inclinations take the form of blind, impulsive, instinctual urges. The suggestion then is that these two natures could be separated and little would change in how each, in itself, functions. As a result, the purpose of rational nature in human beings must be to govern their unruly, animalistic side. But because these natures remain distinct, it must do so from the outside – i.e., as a nature that stands *above* the animal as an independent ruler.[1]

---

* I would like to thank Melissa McBay Merritt, Krista Thomason, Rachel Zuckert, Ariel Zylberman, and most of all Allen Wood and Barbara Herman for their helpful comments and discussions on this chapter.
[1] Tamar Schapiro provides one of the clearest examples of this view in Schapiro, "Foregrounding Desire: A Defense of Kant's Incorporation Thesis," *Journal of Ethics* 15, no. 3 (2011): 147–67. She states that

This understanding of the structure of motivation is most clearly revealed in how those same Kantians describe the incorporation thesis. A rough version of this account generally begins with the experience of pleasure in some object. This pleasure then elicits, through blind causal processes, an unreflective attraction to the object in the form of a felt urge or inclination. When the urge is strong enough, it immediately moves the animal to act. As a result, animals have only a mechanistic, instinctual form of agency. But humans, in contrast, have a genuine form of agency, one that involves *free* choice, and somehow this must be accounted for. Since we share the same animal natures, the difference cannot lie in the form of our inclinations. Instead, it lies in the addition of a rational nature that can act as a gatekeeper. Inclinations now must first "propose" the action to reason for its approval. Reason, because of its standpoint above inclination, must then assess the proposal, and endorse (or reject) it before the inclination is allowed to move the subject to act. When this subject, *from the point of view of reason*, endorses the proposed action, he is said to "incorporate" it into his maxim. This incorporation thus provides him space between the inclination and the action for normative reflection. Without this normative distance, he would have no opportunity to exercise control over his agency, leaving him entirely subject to the mechanical forces of his animal nature.

Though this "distinct natures" view is able to give an explanation for how reason can generate a form of agential control (via the incorporation thesis), it unfortunately seems to come at the high price of a unified psychology. Because the subject's two natures are *entirely* distinct, reason can *only* exercise control as an alien force external to his lower nature. The result of this, however, is a deep rupture between fundamental parts of the subject's psychology – of who and what he is – because he can identify with only one of his two natures at any given time. In other words, it creates a Dr. Jekyll/Mr. Hyde–type persona, one in which the subject will be constantly alternating between these two natures, never succeeding to identify with both from a single agential perspective. This is not to deny that there can, at times, be tension between elements of our psychology. But the view in question leads to a radical form of alienation – one in which the subject *never* experiences himself as unified. So unless he can take on the perspective of his rational *and* animal natures at the same time, he will continue to have a fractured psychology, and thus a fractured sense of what it is to be human.

"the non-rational form of agency exercised by our inclining part is structurally analogous to the type of agency that is exercised by nonhuman animals, creatures of instinct. The suggestion is that our capacity to incline has its source in our animal nature" (155). Because of this, she identifies the source of our inclinations, i.e., our lower nature, as our "inner animal," and our higher, rational nature as our "outer human." See also Schapiro, "The Nature of Inclination," *Ethics* 119, no. 2 (2009): 229–56.

The noncognitive or nonrational characterization of our lower nature thus leads us into an intractable dilemma – either we preserve our agency by fracturing our psychology or we maintain a unified psychology by conceding our agency.[2] Any satisfactory escape from this dilemma will require a different form of agential control, one in which reason can govern from *within* our lower nature, as a symbiotic force. And it is precisely the noncognitive characterization of our lower nature that is preventing reason from functioning in this way. In other words, without this noncognitive assumption, it becomes possible for our rational nature in the practical domain to take on the same characteristic function that it has in the theoretical domain – structuring and ordering input from our lower nature in a way that produces a unified experience of the world – but in this case, it will be a unified *practical* experience. In fact, I believe that our rational nature will cross the metaphysical divide and structure our animal nature all the way down to sensations of pleasure and pain – not for theoretical cognition, but for practical cognition, i.e., for cognition "having to do only with the determining grounds of the will" (CPR 20). The result will be a sophisticated, *cognitive* account of nonmoral motivation, one in which reason serves to both unify and guide our lower nature *through* the structure that it provides. In the end, when we realize how deeply our rationality is infused into our lower nature, we will see that, on Kant's view, even the animal within us becomes rational.

4.1 The Noncognitive Account of Feeling and Inclination

Nonmoral motivation, for Kant, is largely thought to be the result of an interplay between two basic elements of our psychology – feelings of pleasure and pain, and the desires they arouse. Since neither of these elements is thought to involve reason, human motivation will initially take

---

[2] When characterizing theories of emotion in general, as I do here, I will use the set of terms 'cognitive/noncognitive' and 'rational/nonrational' interchangeably – the first set is commonly used by contemporary emotion theorists, while the second set is more closely associated with Kant. (However, in order to prevent confusion, when discussing the details of Kant's own theory, I will restrict the use of the related term 'cognition' to its traditional Kantian sense.) By 'cognitive/rational,' I thus mean only the most minimal claim that emotion is at least *partially* constituted by reason, in the form of an appraisal or evaluation of the significance or worth of an object, circumstance, or event. (I.e., to be a cognitive theory at all, emotion must have at least some cognitive content. But the theory can also be thought of as strongly or weakly cognitive depending on how that content is spelled out. The strongest version, originating with the Stoics, specifies that the evaluative judgment must take a conscious, propositional form. Weaker versions allow for perceptual (or nonpropositional) judgments as well – i.e., merely *seeing* or *perceiving x as good*.) By 'noncognitive/nonrational,' then, I mean the complete denial of reason's involvement in the constitution of the emotion itself (as found in causal, mechanistic, or brute sensation theories of emotion).

the same basic form as that found in animals. To see how this interplay works, consider the act of drinking water. As a finite being, an animal will eventually come to feel a certain sort of pain we call thirst. Whether through a hardwired instinct, following the lead of its parents, or trial and error, the animal soon discovers that drinking water alleviates this pain, resulting in a sensation of pleasure at having satisfied its thirst. Through mechanisms of association, the animal then begins to expect pleasure (or alleviation of pain) from drinking water. This expectation of future pleasure manifests itself in the present by affecting the animal's perception. When the animal is in a state of thirst, past associations of pleasure with water will make it appear more attractive or pleasant – i.e., as something "to be drunk." The pull that this attractiveness exerts on the attention of the animal is thus felt as an unreflective urge to drink. Now, the more often the animal experiences pleasure from drinking, the more attractive water will appear to be, and the stronger and/or more consistent the urge will become – a reinforcing pattern that will eventually result in an inclination, or habitual desire, to drink water.

In the human case, little is thought to change. Because of past associations, whenever I am thirsty, I will likewise experience an urge for something to drink (usually coffee). But since I am also a rational creature in possession of a more advanced cognitive life, I can conceptualize the objects of pleasure and pain in ways that animals cannot. As a consequence, I might strongly associate pleasure with coffee generally (i.e., as *coffee*), yet still associate displeasure with the particular coffee available on campus. I will then feel an urge to avoid any campus location and desire coffee from the nearby café instead. However, despite the involvement of reason in conceptualizing the object of pleasure, this object still functions no differently than it does in animals – as the *causal* source of the pleasure. The pleasure itself remains nothing more than a purely subjective sensation. So when it elicits a desire (i.e., motivates), it does so simply because of the inherent pleasant (or painful) aspect of the sensation itself. In other words, Kant is thought to have held a noncognitive, sensation-based account of our emotions and appetites. And since, according to the picture above, there can be no desire without a feeling preceding it, these feelings take on a prominent role in nonmoral motivation – i.e., they are the determining grounds of the will (MM 212; AK 29:894).

However, despite the widespread acceptance of this basic view of feeling, and the account of motivation that it gives rise to, few arguments have been offered in support of it. This is likely due, in large part, to the fact that Kant never explicitly offers a systematic account of feeling in any of his major texts, so there seems to be little material with which to work. Instead, the source for this view seems to be little more than his highly suggestive terminology. Considering that Kant not only describes them as feelings of *pleasure* and *displeasure*, but also appears (through most of his work) to use the terms translated as 'feeling' (*Gefühl*) and 'sensation' (*Empfindung*) interchangeably, it would be natural to assume that a brute noncognitive or sensation theory is operating in the background.[3] Noncognitive views, as opposed to their cognitive counterparts, characterize feelings in terms of their felt, experiential or affective quality. And as a very simplistic view of emotion and appetite, it would lack the degree of sophistication required to warrant much attention, thus explaining the absence of an explicit account in his work.

Additional support for the noncognitive assumption is thought to be found in Kant's generally negative attitude toward emotion. Whether it was due to his Pietist upbringing or his Stoic influences, Kant has long been thought to have been, at best, highly skeptical of the value of emotion in human life, earning him the title of "cold-hearted" from the very beginning. But more often than not, he is portrayed as having been outright contemptuous of them. After all, they have the unwelcomed ability, through the interplay discussed above, to charm, distract, and distort our rational activity. In even darker moments, they are alien influences, rising up from our animal nature, that seek to overturn reason's authority by clouding the force of its pure moral law, all so that they can sow the seeds for vice-breeding passions. Because emotions have this tendency, Kant is thought to have insisted that reason must remain independent so that it can fully guard against their destructive influence. The consequence is a wholesale rejection of any theory in which emotion is even partially constituted by reason, because this would be tantamount to an invitation for the corruption of reason to its very core. A noncognitive view, in contrast, would be a highly attractive alternative, because it would maintain a strict barrier between our higher and lower natures and thus help to limit the negative influence of emotion on reason.

4.2 The Possibility of a Cognitive Alternative

At this point, however, I believe we should step back and ask, "Is this *really* Kant's view?" Though it is classically attributed to him, I believe its basic

---

[3] It is for this reason that I will use 'feeling' and 'emotion' interchangeably. Though both are ordinary senses of *Gefühl*, the use of *feeling* strongly, and in my view, misleadingly predisposes the reader to a sensation view.

structure and character should actually strike us as being rather *un*-Kantian. In it, our two basic natures are characterized in a way that excludes any type of union or synthesis, resulting in a radical divide between them. And because they are also both sources of motivation, they are now pitted against each other in perpetual opposition. Our lower nature is worrisome because, as pure animality, it can be dangerous and unpredictable. Yet reason has no control over it other than the ability to suppress it through force.

The problem is, we find *nothing* like this on the theoretical side – not in how the function of our rational nature is understood, nor in how it is thought to relate to our lower nature. In fact, what we see is the exact opposite. Rather than being the object of contempt, sensibility is regarded as essential to the cognitive life of humans because it provides the matter for cognition (among other things). Nor is reason set the task of merely filtering the raw input from sensibility, approving some of it and rejecting the rest. Instead, its essential function is to shape and organize this sensory input, and it does so in part by providing the very structure for the experience itself. The result is a single, highly conceptualized, and thereby *unified* experience of the world, one in which both the understanding and sensibility play crucial and harmonious roles.

So if *this* is how he conceives of the function of our higher, rational nature and its relation to sensibility on the theoretical side, why would he view the practical side any differently? Would we not expect instead that the same essential character of our rational nature, and its relation to our lower nature, would be manifest in *both* its theoretical and practical forms? If so, then Kant would be more likely to value our lower nature as part of a practical life that is essentially human, because it provides the matter to the will required for us to engage in particular actions in the world. The task of practical reason would then be to govern, in the sense of unifying and harmonizing, by giving shape and structure to this matter. The result would be a single, unified, highly conceptualized and richly textured practical engagement with the world – one in which our rational nature is expressed *through* its structuring of the emotions and appetites of our lower nature. In other words, given his broad theoretical commitments, we should actually expect a strongly *cognitive* account of feeling, one that allows our lower, animal nature to be transformed by reason, thus elevating it to the more dignified status of *humanity*.[4]

---

[4] "A human being has a duty to raise himself from the crude state of his nature, from his animality, more and more toward humanity, by which he alone is capable of setting himself ends" (MM 387).

Feeling and Inclination: Rationalizing the Animal Within 73

And as it turns out, numerous passages found throughout his work are highly suggestive of just such a theory. That is, though he often uses the language of sensation in relation to our feelings, he also refers to them frequently as *estimations* (*Schätzungen*), *appraisals* (*Beurteilungen*), and even *judgments* (*Urteile*). Consider, for example, his discussion of self-love in the *Lectures on Ethics*, where he says, "The love that takes pleasure in others is the judgment that we delight in their perfection" (AK 27:357). In his various notes and fragments, he states that "Feeling makes distinctions only for oneself; the judgment is not valid for others" (R1850 AK 16:137). In the *Anthropology*, he defines admiration as "a judgment in which we do not grow weary of being astonished" (APV 243). And finally, the most striking of all is Kant's description of respect as an "estimation of worth that far outweighs any worth of what is recommended by inclination" (G 403). From these passages, it is clear that feelings of pleasure (and displeasure) can take the form of an evaluation or appraisal of the worth of some object or action. But in order to uncover what their particular structure might be, we need to consider Kant's own answer to the question, "What, exactly, are feelings?"[5]

4.3 The Cognitive Structure of Feeling and Desire

In the *Lectures on the Philosophical Doctrine of Religion*, Kant makes the following statement: "But here I do not want to know *in what* I take pleasure, but rather *what* pleasure itself is." He answers by explaining that "pleasure itself does not consist in the relation of my representations to their object; it consists rather in the relation of my representations to the subject, insofar as these representations determine the subject to actualize the object" (AK 28:1060 and nearly identically at CPR 21). A similar description, in a somewhat more condensed form, is found in an early footnote of the second *Critique*. There he defines pleasure as "*the representation of the agreement of an object or of an action with the subjective conditions of life*," i.e., with the faculty of desire (CPR 9n).[6] According to these definitions, pleasure cannot be, as commonly assumed of Kant, a nonrepresentational or purely

---

[5] In this section, I am merely highlighting Kant's use of cognitivist language in his description of various emotions. In DeWitt, "Respect for the Moral Law: the Emotional Side of Reason," *Philosophy* 89, no. 1 (2014): 31–62, I give a full defense of this claim by showing that Kant's tripartite theory of the mind, among other things, necessarily commits him to a cognitive theory.
[6] Similar descriptions of pleasure as a *representation of an agreement* or *of a relation* can be found scattered throughout Kant's writings. See MM 212, CJ 209, AK 29:894, AK 28:247, and R1021 AK 15:457 for examples.

subjective sensation. Why? Because first and foremost, pleasure is defined *as a representation*.[7] But more specifically, it is a representation, not of the object itself (a theoretical cognition), but of the object's *agreement* with the subject's faculty of desire – the source of his life or activity. And it is through this representation of agreement that we confer value onto objects, because "the value of things always comes down to their concordance with subjects" (R715 AK 15:317; see also R823 AK 15:367, G 428). So feelings, in representing this relation, are the determinations of value, and it is in virtue of this that they motivate. That is, they are action-initiating evaluative judgments. And it is with this understanding of feeling in mind that Kant says the faculty of desire is determined by a pleasure in an object.

To see how this view of feeling works, consider the act of drinking coffee. That coffee is hot and caffeinated does not in itself motivate me to drink it. But when I recognize that I am currently cold, tired, and with still more writing to do, consideration of these properties *does* motivate me. The warmth and caffeine will alleviate my current discomfort and help me to continue working. Kant describes this relationship between the coffee and my subjective condition as a sort of "fit" that promotes my life or activity – in this case, my philosophical writing. The representation of this fit is the pleasure that determines my will. Furthermore, when I judge the coffee in this way, as positively fitting (or *agreeing*) with my needs and activities, then I am at the same time judging the coffee to be *good* (i.e., to be *pleasing or agreeable*). These pleasures, then, are a type of judgment that involves attributing to the object the subjective/evaluative predicates of *good/bad*, or more precisely, of *agreeable/disagreeable* (a subset of the general category of good/bad) (AK 28:245).[8]

The same holds for displeasure. If instead I were ready for bed, then the caffeine in the coffee would hinder my ability to sleep (i.e., negatively fit with my needs/activities). I would then judge it to be *bad* (i.e., *displeasing* or *disagreeable*), and so would avoid drinking it. Any object that neither pleases

---

[7] In fact, it appears that pleasure can even take the form of an *unconscious* representation. In the *Anthropology*, Kant strongly implies as much when he writes, "The feeling that urges the subject to remain in the state he is in is *agreeable*; but the one that urges him to leave it is *disagreeable*. Combined with consciousness [emphasis added], the former is called *enjoyment*, the latter *lack of enjoyment*" (APV 254). If a feeling can be combined with consciousness, then it stands to reason that it can be found without it – i.e., that there can be unconscious pleasures as well. If so, then an unconscious pleasure is a pleasure, not in virtue of its consciously felt qualities (as the sensation view claims), but in virtue of its representational content.

[8] The *beautiful/ugly* and the moral *good/evil* are the remaining two subsets of subjective predicates falling under the general category of *good/bad*. But since the beautiful/ugly, as aesthetic pleasures, are not determining grounds of the will (i.e., not predicates of *practical* pleasures), I will not discuss them here. The good/evil, as the basis of *moral* motivation, are addressed in DeWitt, "Respect for the Moral Law."

nor displeases me in this way (i.e., neither promotes nor hinders my activity) is motivationally inert. It leaves me *indifferent* to it because it would have *no* connection to my will at all, the source of my activity (AK 28:253).

We now have the basic structure of feeling in hand. With these feelings, there is a sensible need, stemming from my animal nature, that drives the judgment – e.g., the alleviation of my fatigue. Certain objects are considered in relation to these needs, some of which are judged to fit. When there is a positive fit, the principle of self-love is determined to hold between the object and the subject. And since a need stemming from our finite, animal nature is the basis of this judgment, the resulting pleasure will determine *choice* (the *lower* faculty of desire) to make the object actual. Finally, when an object is determined to fit in this way, it is judged to be *agreeable* (AK 28:248).

This basic structure of feeling also determines *how* it motivates. That is, its motivational power stems from the fit it represents. I judge that the coffee fits with my needs because the caffeine it contains *will wake me up*. Implicit in this representation of fit, then, is the *expectation of a need being satisfied* by the coffee. It is this expectation that is the source of my *interest* in the coffee, and so is what ultimately motivates me to drink it (CJ 204). Now, Kant distinguishes the representation of the actual satisfaction of my need, i.e., the alertness I come to feel, as a second type of pleasure – what he specifically refers to as sensations of *gratification (Vergnügen)* or *enjoyment* (*Genuß*) and *pain* (*Schmerz*).[9] These two types of pleasure (what I will call judgments and sensations of pleasures, respectively) must work together to

---

[9] It is important to note here that even *sensations* of pleasure take the form of a representation of fit, but in their case, it is of an *actual* fit between the object and the need of the subject. More specifically, it represents a need having been *successfully* satisfied by an object (while *pain* represents a failure). For this reason, I believe that Kant thinks of these sensations as the practical analogue of empirical/theoretical intuition. That is, a sensation of pleasure is a singular, immediate, but *subjective* rather than *objective* representation – i.e., a representation not of the object itself (which would be an empirical intuition), but of the object's relation to the subject. And just as an empirical intuition results from the organization of raw sensory data (the matter of the senses) by the forms of intuition (space and time), so too does a sensation of pleasure. But with pleasure, the form is instead the *interior sense*, a sense explicitly distinguished from the inner sense of time in the *Anthropology* (APV 153). And as with intuition, it is also the matter that gives these sensations their characteristic qualitative feel (the particular aspects we commonly associate with pleasure). Finally, just as we can cognize an object *as being in space* or *as being in time*, we can (practically) cognize an object *as being enjoyable/gratifying* – i.e., *as presently satisfying an existing need*. This is one of the points at which, however, the language of contemporary emotion theory pulls apart from Kant. Sensations of pleasure, as form/matter composites, do qualify as (practical) cognitions in the strict Kantian sense, but not as judgments. Yet in the contemporary sense, they would still be considered judgments, just of the weaker *perceptual* variety. Kant appears to include this weaker sense when he describes feelings more generally as "relations of fit," only some of which are judgments properly speaking (because they involve practical *concepts*).

motivate. That is, the judgments of pleasure can motivate only because of the expectation of gratification (the actual satisfaction of a need) they represent. This follows because it is only through the gratification of a need that our animal life is furthered. The ability to gratify is thus the *condition* of the coffee being able to determine the will.[10] Because of this condition, I am said to drink it *for the sake of* the expected gratification. So when I judge the coffee as agreeable, I am judging it to be *good for* satisfying my needs (AK 28:252; AK 29:891; CPR 59; CPR 62; CJ 207). This is why Kant calls all empirical pleasures forms of self-love – because they are all ultimately directed toward satisfying one's own needs.

What, then, of desire? On the commonly assumed bipartite model of the mind, where mental functions are divided between cognition and desire, desires tend to be thought of as inherently intentional or fully determinate states – e.g., hunger is characterized not as a blind urge, but as a desire *for food*. But Kant has a tripartite model, one in which the main division of mental labor includes the faculty of feeling. Given this difference in the conception of the mind, we should expect desire to take on a different form, one that is shaped in relation to his conception of feeling.

In the second *Critique*, just before his definition of pleasure, Kant defines the faculty of desire as "a being's *faculty to be by means of its representations the cause of the reality of the objects of these representations*" and shortly after, as "the faculty of the *causality of a representation with respect to the reality of its object*" (CPR 9n; see also MM 211). Two things are notable about this definition. First, it is essentially defining the faculty of desire as the *source of our causality* for making the object of certain representations actual (AK 25:576–77; MM 356). And second, it is not, itself, the source or cause of those representations. (Neither is the faculty of cognition, as I have shown elsewhere.) So their source must lie in a third faculty – the faculty of feeling. More specifically, the faculty of feeling must first represent an object to be good (i.e., judge it to fit with the needs or condition of the subject) before the faculty of desire can become the cause of the object represented. Therefore, the function of pleasure is to judge an object to be good in relation to the needs and circumstances of the subject, and the function of desire, in turn, is to be the cause of the object once it has.[11]

---

[10] Clearly, neither coffee nor its caffeine is agreeable to everyone. Kant notes this by pointing out that the expected gratification that serves as the basis for my judging the coffee as agreeable is dependent on the privately valid grounds of my own senses (i.e., in relation to my particular subjective condition) (AK 28:248–49; CJ 212). So this judgment holds *only for me* – i.e., it is *merely* subjective.

[11] With this distinction between feeling and desire, the point of normative reflection can now be found here, at feeling's approval of an object for desire, rather than downstream, at reason's approval of the desire itself. The difference is significant. When we step back and judge an object

To understand how this conception of desire works, we must begin with its source. Kant states that "it is true of every created being that the desire for something always presupposes a need, and it is because of this need that I desire it. But why is this? *Simply because no creature is self-sufficient*, and so each one always has a need of many things" (AK 28:1062). All (sensible) desire thus originates in our particular subjective condition registered by the faculty of desire (the source of one's life or activity) – i.e., with one's particular needs, wants, or activities due to one's individual circumstances and constitution. In the example discussed above, it begins with my current condition of being cold, tired, and having more work to be done.[12] But, desire only *begins* here, because merely feeling tired and needing to wake up, or feeling cold and needing to warm up, cannot yet bring about any action. At this stage, these needs, or what we might call *proto-desires*, are more like action potentials that must first be engaged before they can move the subject to action.[13] They have this status because at this point they are indeterminate. There is no intentional object yet toward which to direct their causality. To put this point another way, the faculty of desire is considered to be a source of causality because it can determine the *means* for making the object of a representation actual (CPR 58–59). But these means cannot be determined until one has a representation of a particular object (e.g., coffee vs. tea) to be brought about. So in order for the latent causality of a proto-desire to be unleashed, something needs to provide it with an intentional object. In Kant's terminology, the *elater* (proto-desire) needs an *elater animi* (incentive or *Triebfeder*).[14]

---

in relation to our need, our practical/evaluative stance is turned outward toward the world with which we are engaging, rather than inward toward our own desires (a problem often noted with the distinct natures view).

[12] What this means, in essence, is that the pain I am feeling in being cold and tired is telling me something about the state of my body (or mind) in relation to its environment that needs attention – i.e., that I have a need to both warm up and wake up. It is in this sense that sensations of pain can be the way in which we represent unsatisfied needs (because they represent the failure of any presently existing object to satisfy that need).

[13] I call these basic needs and wants proto-desires because Kant's terminology is not always consistent. In the *Anthropology*, he seems to refer to them as undetermined desires or peevish wishes. "The undetermined desire, in respect of the object, which only impels the subject to leave his present state without knowing what state he then wants to enter, can be called the peevish wish (one that nothing satisfies)" (APV 251). In the *Religion*, he seems to describe them as propensities, or the "subjective ground of the possibility of an inclination (habitual desire, *concupiscentia*)" (R 29). I believe it is also to these that Kant is referring in his description of concupiscence. "*Concupiscence* (lusting after something) must also be distinguished from desire itself, as a stimulus to determining desire. Concupiscence is always a sensible modification of the mind but one that has not yet become an act of the faculty of desire" (MM 213).

[14] "The causality of the representation with regard to (*later addition*: oneself is pleasure) the actuality of the object (*later addition*: objects in general) is desire (*later addition*: life; the *consensus* with life: pleasure). The representation must hereby, however, have a relation to the subject of determining it

This is where judgments of feeling come into the account of desire. When a feeling judges an object to be good for satisfying a particular need, it is, at the same time, setting that object as an end of the faculty of desire to be brought about (i.e., it is providing matter to the will). So through a determination by feeling, a proto-desire is transformed into a fully determinate desire that moves the subject to action. Such a determinate desire is thus a *Begierde*, or desire in the "narrow sense" – i.e., a desire that is "necessarily *preceded* by" a pleasure. When this interplay becomes habitual, it results in an inclination (MM 212).[15] So when my faculty of feeling judges coffee to be good for satisfying my particular needs, I then become (more or less) *inclined to* the coffee – i.e., motivated to make the existence of coffee a reality. Feeling is thus the *elater animi* needed to activate the *elater*. In addition, because my desire is made determinate by feeling in this way, it will be an expression of the value I judge coffee to have given my current needs and circumstances. This overall conception of feeling and its relation to the faculty of desire is reflected in a dense passage of the second *Critique* where Kant states that "satisfaction with one's whole existence ... is a problem imposed upon him by his finite nature itself, because he is needy and this need is directed to the matter of his faculty of desire, that is, *something related to a subjective feeling of pleasure or displeasure underlying it by which is determined what he needs in order to be satisfied with his condition*" (CPR 25; emphasis added).

4.4 Agency and the Rational Structure of Practical Experience

One of the virtues of this basic structure of feeling and its relation to desire is that it can account for a wide range of appetite and emotion, from basic instinctual responses on the one end, to purely rational, moral emotions on the other, with ordinary human emotion and appetite falling in between. It can produce this wide array because it allows reason to have varying degrees of involvement, from ways of conceptualizing the subject and the

---

to action. This relation is pleasure, and indeed in the reality of the object, i.e., an interest (interest does not belong to judging). The interest rests on the satisfaction with our condition, which depends on the reality of the object. (That which carries an interest with it is called the *causa impulsiva*). An *elater* is the subjective receptivity to be moved to desire. ... An *elater* is the capacity of a *causa impulsiva* to determine the desire to a deed, insofar as it rests on the constitution of the subject" (R1021 AK 15:457–58). He then describes the *elater animi* as "The possibility of a representation being a *causa impulsiva*" (R1056 AK 15:470–71), i.e., as a judgment of feeling.

[15] "As for practical pleasure, that determination of the faculty of desire which is caused and therefore necessarily *preceded* by such pleasure is called desire [*Begierde*] in the narrow sense; habitual desire [*Begierde*] is called *inclination*" (MM 212). Desire in the wide sense, or *Begehren*, suggests the general category that includes the full range of desire – proto-desires, fully determinate desires, wishes, passions, etc.

object of the judgment, to providing different principles by which to judge the fit between the two. Perhaps even more importantly, however, is that, when reason becomes involved in these ways, we begin to set our own ends rather than have nature set them for us. In other words, the more rational/cognitive a feeling becomes, the more *self*-determined, and hence freer, we will be.[16] Reason's involvement in feeling thus allows for a very different form of agential control to take shape. It no longer governs (as it did on the previous view) as an alien force, standing above our lower nature as an independent ruler. Instead, it now governs by guiding and directing feeling from within, thus shaping the very structure of our practical engagement with the world.

This general view clearly reveals itself when we consider the contrast between the simpler forms of human feeling discussed earlier and our basic instinctual responses. To be a feeling of any kind, an object must be judged to fit with the subject (i.e., his condition) in a way that furthers the subject's life or activity. General categories of feeling are thus individuated on the basis of variations within this basic structure. The primary point of departure between simple feelings and instinctual responses is in the two forms of need the subjective condition can take – *propensity* and *instinct*.

Most human feeling begins with a propensity. This might be best described as a state of *potential* fit with one or more objects.[17] For example, my being cold and tired is a state that can potentially fit with a slew of caffeinated beverages. But it can also fit with a nap, or even a bout of brisk exercise. Because this state potentially fits with a number of objects, it is thus indeterminate between them. So in order to act, I must first judge which of these objects will *best* satisfy my needs. I happen to like the taste

---

[16] "The capacity to set oneself an end – any end whatsoever – is what characterizes humanity (as distinguished from animality) ... [because of this] the human being has a duty to cultivate the crude predispositions of his nature, by which the animal is first raised into the human being" (MM 392; see also MM 387 quoted earlier). As this passage suggests, I believe that this is a gradual transformation that takes place through cultivation. In the case of our emotions, this cultivation serves to increase reason's involvement in their constitution (through its ability to generate and refine the concepts operative in the judgment itself). It is not surprising, then, that the more reason becomes involved, the more it will displace the surrogacy of nature (thereby increasing our freedom).

[17] "Propensity is the inner basis of all possible desires" (AK 25:580). "Propensity is distinct from actual desire. It is the possibility of desiring something, and is a predisposition of the subject to desire" (AK 25:796–97). "By *propensity* (*propensio*) I understand the subjective ground of the possibility of an inclination (habitual desire, *concupiscentia*), insofar as this possibility is contingent for humanity in general" (R 29n). In this footnote, Kant describes propensity as the lowest (the most indeterminate in relation to an object) state of the faculty of desire. Above it is instinct, then inclination, and finally passion (a relationship to an object so strong that it excludes mastery over oneself).

of both coffee and tea, but when I am very tired, I will judge the higher caffeine content of coffee to be a better option. Yet when I am sick, I will judge tea to be better instead. And after several cups of either, I know to expect diminishing returns, so the alternatives to caffeine will then take on more value (in the form of a better fit with my need). Through this comparison of possible objects in relation to the current status of my needs, my actions will be highly adaptable and fine-tuned to the ever changing circumstances I find myself in. In other words, when I drink coffee, I am not acting unreflectively on an urge resulting from a physiological adaptation to caffeine. Instead, I am acting from a recognition of the value coffee has in relation to my current needs and activities, and the greater value it might have than sleep or exercise.

Finally, when I judge coffee to be good in this way, it is still considered to be a general form of self-love because it is still directed at satisfying my own needs. But because it requires comparison among several potential objects, Kant calls it a form of *nonmechanical* self-love, or more specifically, a "self-love which is physical and yet *involves comparison* (for which reason is required)" (R 27). These propensities, and the judgments of feeling in relation to them, thus comprise the predisposition to *humanity*, a predisposition we have in virtue of being "a living and at the same time a *rational* being" (R 26).[18] It is thus a predisposition rooted in prudential reason – the form of reason subservient to our needs and natural ends (R 28).

However, in addition to these propensities, the subjective condition of *all* animal life must have another form, that of instinct. With the general feelings of self-love above, the needs are indeterminate, often potentially fitting with several objects. So before one can act, reason (in the form of a judgment of feeling) must first select one of the objects to pursue, thereby making the proto-desire determinate. But if this was the only form that our subjective condition could take, we would be in trouble. Until reason had gained some strength and had a fairly substantial amount of experience to draw from, the indeterminate nature of our propensities would make action impossible. A newborn infant could not judge that his mother's milk would satisfy his hunger, and so would soon starve. As a consequence, nature must be able to act as a surrogate for reason, providing directly for the needs most essential to the individual's survival. In other words, it must be able to "prejudge" a minimal set of objects that will reliably and

---

[18] The feelings discussed here are the most primitive form of humanity. As the comparison involved in the judgment becomes more complex, we will move from simple feelings in relation to particular needs, to the more complex feelings of happiness and the passions. These are the two types of feeling/inclination that Kant was most concerned with in this passage of the *Religion*.

consistently satisfy these needs for all members of its species. And it can do this because the sensibility of our lower/animal nature possesses what Kant calls an *analogue of reason*.[19] This analogue, in turn, has its own "principles," the innate rules of sensibility (likely connected to the interior sense), which can generate what I call analogue judgments of feeling. More specifically, through an innate principle of association, the animal is predetermined or hardwired to expect pleasure from certain objects, an expectation that then underlies a relationship of fit (an analogue judgment) without ever having experienced the object. So as it turns out, even instincts are determined by a "judgment" of feeling. It is just one that is innate and so makes our instincts determinate with respect to their objects from the moment of birth. This is how nature sets our ends for us.

When these analogue judgments determine the subject's essential needs, the result is a set of instincts, or natural drives responsible for self- and species preservation (i.e., drives for nourishment, protection, and propagation). They function as natural drives because they have, in effect, an intentional object built into them by nature, and so are operational from the moment of birth (unlike propensity). This is how a baby can suckle without having been taught, why a chick will flee from a hawk even though it has never seen one before, and why even adult humans can sense beforehand whether something is fit to be eaten (AK 28:254; CB 111). But because the subject has no experience of the object yet, and so no particular, conscious representation of it, instincts are experienced as *blind* urges, i.e., as a "felt need to do or enjoy something of which we still do not have a concept" (R 29n; see also AK 25:796–97, AK 28:255–56). To put this another way, analogue judgments of feeling present themselves in a strongly perceptual way. The hawk will just *look* dangerous to the chick, triggering an urge to flee even though the chick has no experience and so no conscious recognition of the hawk as a predator.[20] So instinct is a state of the faculty of desire that is more determinate than

---

[19] "[F]or, if they are lacking consciousness, then they are also missing understanding and reason, and sensibility alone reigns. With animals one calls this an analogue of reason and there is an instinct of sensibility whereby they need no reason, but rather which an external being placed in them for acting, or for working according to instinct; the analogue of reason is the summation of all lower powers [i.e., of sensation, imagination, reproduction, and anticipation]" (AK 28:450; see also AK 28:594, CJ 464).

[20] Kant believes that all sensible emotion can alter perception. Consider his discussion of hatred in the *Lectures on Anthropology*. "If one feels hatred, then the imagination shows everything from its most detestable side" (AK 25:1260). It is for this reason that I believe we should think of these judgments of feeling as being built into the perception or experience itself. That is, they help to structure our practical point of view by enabling us to experience the world as value-laden, an experience that helps to shape our deliberative field and guide our actions.

propensity, because it does have an intentional object. But it is not yet an inclination, because nature only provides it an obscure representation of that object, rather than the fully conscious or determinate representation that reason provides human inclination (R 29n; AK 25:583–84).

Finally, the analogues of judgment responsible for instinct are also considered to be a general form of self-love, because they are still directed toward satisfying the needs of the subject. But because reason is *not* involved, Kant calls them a form of *physical*, or merely *mechanical* self-love, that is, "a love for which reason is not required" (R 26). These instincts, and the analogue judgments of feeling in relation to them, are thus the specific elements of lower nature that comprise the predisposition to *animality*, a predisposition we have simply in virtue of being "*a living being*" (R 26).

Now, though nature can stand in as a surrogate for reason in animals and the very young, at least giving these creatures *some* form of agency, the type it can produce is very limited. Obviously, not all movement can be characterized as an *action*. A Venus flytrap is capable of movement toward an object, but because no representations are involved, it can only be characterized as a mechanical *reaction* to a physical stimulus according to the laws of nature. Plants, therefore, have no agency at all. But when an animal acts from instinct, it *does* act from a representation of an object as good or bad (an analogue judgment of an object as being fit or unfit to satisfy a need), so it does have at least a minimal form of agency. However, nature is limited from producing anything more robust. For genuine agency, the subject's response to an object must be able to take into account his own particular needs and circumstances, because it is only in doing so that he can act with a conception of *his own* individual well-being in mind. And this is where nature fails the individual. When reason is not involved, the animal cannot conceptualize the object, its own needs, or the relationship between the two. So the subject's need is in a fixed and relatively rigid relationship with the object set for it by nature. For the most part, a chick will always judge a hawk to be dangerous, whether or not the hawk is caged. Because of this, instinct only produces coarse-grained, stereotyped actions characteristic of all members of the species. And this is the problem. Because these are innate drives, nature must design them to provide for individual members of the species *on the whole*. That is, instincts are macro-level response mechanisms oriented toward the preservation and promotion of the *species*, and they do so by providing for the *average* member of the species in the *most likely* circumstances. As a result, instincts can lead to unproductive and even highly detrimental behavior in some individuals, because they cannot take their *particular* circumstances into account. A lame animal, for example, might be better off hiding from a predator, but its instinct will drive it to flee anyway. So at this point, nature can only provide for a form of agency that reflects the *general* needs and constitution of the average member of its species. In order to move closer to genuine agency, the subject's response to his environment needs to be adaptable, or capable of fine-tuning. Now, it is true that some nonrational animals are capable of moderating their instinctual responses through the associations they form from experience, allowing them to become a little more adapted to their particular environments. As Kant notes, the more a dog participates on hunts, the more it will learn to expect patterns of behavior from a hare and alter the manner of its chase (AK 29:949). But even so, the animal's judgment will still be between unconceptualized particulars, which then limit how it can respond. So without reason, animals can only expand the boundaries of instinct, never fully succeeding in stepping outside of them. They are thus limited to a mechanical form of agency.

Therefore, in order for any sort of genuine agency to take shape, the subjective conditions that action originates in must become open ended, or indeterminate. Otherwise, the actions they produce cannot be closely tailored to the individual – how he conceives is best for his own life to go given his unique needs, goals, talents, and circumstances. Kant describes this sense of freedom grounded in an indeterminate way of life in the *Conjectural Beginning of Human History*.

> [Through experimenting with objects he was not directed to by instinct] he discovered in himself a faculty of choosing for himself a way of living and not being bound to a single one, as other animals are. ... He stood, as it were, on the brink of an abyss; for instead of the single objects of his desire to which instinct had up to now directed him, there opened up an infinity of them, and he did not know how to relate to the choice between them; and from this estate of freedom, once he had tasted it, it was nevertheless wholly impossible for him to turn back to that of servitude (under the dominion of instinct). (CB 112)[21]

---

[21] Glimpses of this conception of freedom in an indeterminate form of life can be seen throughout Kant's work. "The characterization of the human being as a rational animal is already present in the form and organization of his *hand*, his *fingers* and *fingertips* ... By this means nature has made the human being not suited for one way of manipulating things but undetermined for every way, consequently suited for the use of reason" (APV 323).

So until we can break free of the determinate life of instinct, where nature essentially structures our lives for us, there can be no room for *self*-determination, and so no freedom. This is where reason becomes crucial. It not only helps to make our original condition more indeterminate, but it also provides us the tools to then determine ourselves. It achieves both by helping the subject to produce a rich, conceptualized understanding of himself, his environment, and the relationship between the two.

Now, this conceptualization can vary in degree in each of the elements of the judgments of feeling, which then accounts for their cognitive range (from the nonrational/noncognitive analogue judgments of instinct, to the empirical/cognitive judgments of ordinary emotion, to the purely rational/cognitive judgments of moral emotion).[22] One of the first places this conceptualization has an impact is with the subject's representation of the object. The natural drive for sex, for example, is generally directed toward other members of the same species. But a man, as the object of this drive, can be thought of under more than one aspect. As the object of *instinct*, he will be judged to fit the needs of the subject *qua* member of the human species. When the object is represented in this way, the resulting instinctual drive is then relatively indiscriminate among members of the species. But when the subject can also represent him *qua* spouse, the relationship of fit will take on new complexity. In valuing him *as her spouse*, she will also value, e.g., the various activities and commitments that are constitutive of married life. As a result, the subject now has two ways to value her spouse, and so two ways in which she can determine her need (even with respect to the same object) – instinct and spousal love (AK 27:384–85; AK 25:1361; APV 269–70).

The subject can also conceptualize himself and his own needs differently, both in more specific and more general ways. When he understands in greater detail the particular circumstances in which he finds himself, and has a better understanding of himself and his own constitution, his relation to the object will again take on more complexity. Anyone confronted by a knife-wielding mugger has reason to fear. But whether it is better to fight,

---

[22] Kant often gives detailed conceptual analyses of specific emotions, analyses that I cannot do full justice to here. (A quick look at any one of his discussions of envy, jealousy, or *Schadenfreude* shows just how detailed these analyses can be, analyses that I believe are yet more evidence of his cognitivism. See MM 458, AK 27:437–43, AK 27:347, AK 27:693–95, and AK 27:709 for examples.) Instead, I have the less ambitious plan of setting out a few rough sketches in order to show how Kant's framework could be used to account for a wide range of emotions, as well as their ability to generate finely tuned, context-sensitive responses.

flee, or give in will depend in large part upon the subject's own particular constitution, such as his temperament, size, athletic ability, or training. If he is small, fast, or a bit timid, flight might be the best course of action. But if he is a little slow, yet confident and well trained in self-defense, he should probably resist instead. Mere instinct, in contrast, elicits a one-size-fits-all, stereotyped response.

Seeing his needs and circumstances in a more general way also greatly expands the possible range of his responses beyond that of animals. He can come to see some of his own needs as shared, which then helps to bring him into community with others (a form of sympathy). He can consider his subjective condition in the context of societal norms, leading to emotions of pride, shame, or resentment. Or he can consider his needs and their potential satisfaction in relation to others, which can form the basis for jealousy and envy.

And finally, the subject can act from a conception of his own happiness – i.e., of his long-term, overall well-being and the value particular objects have in relation to it. It is only in taking this most general stance on his own subjective condition that he can begin to bring his needs into harmony, thus helping to maximize the satisfaction of the whole (R 58; A800/B828; G399; R 6610; AK 19:107). Why? Because the feelings discussed earlier, in judging an object to fit with a *particular* need, enable the subject to value, e.g., the taste of coffee independently of its ability to wake him up (and so independently of his need for sleep as well). The problem, however, is that the satisfaction of a single need, like a late-night craving for coffee, often comes at the expense of potentially more important needs, like sleep. So what the subject needs is the ability to value coffee, not just in relation to a single need (for something tasty to drink), but in relation to *all* of his needs, including his need for sleep. In other words, he needs the ability to consider how the coffee will impact his long-term, overall well-being. And it is his feelings of happiness that enable him to do this. With these feelings, an object is judged to fit with the subject only when it furthers his life or activity *as a whole* – i.e., increases his happiness by positively contributing to the maximal satisfaction of his needs overall. So if the coffee, in satisfying one need at the expense of another, is determined to have a negative impact on the satisfaction of his needs overall, then the subject will judge it to be (what I call) *disagreeable in general*. In doing so, he will then be motivated, for the sake of his own happiness, to abstain for the night (despite still finding the taste of the coffee to be agreeable). It is through these feelings of happiness, then, that the subject has the greatest control over the direction his life will take.

Thus, as reason becomes more involved, we begin to see a genuine form of agency take shape. The more richly textured the subject's conception of himself and his circumstances becomes, the more indeterminate and open ended his subjective condition will be. This then makes room for him to act, not from nature's generic conception of his well-being, but from *his own* conception. In other words, through reason's involvement in feeling, he begins to set his own ends by judging objects to be good in relation to his needs and circumstances as he himself understands them. And this ability to *self*-determine is what makes him free.

So in the end, we see that, through the judgments of feeling and their associated desires, reason generates a complex evaluative framework that structures our practical point of view. That is, this faculty enables us to evaluate the world and our relation to it according to our current sensible needs (particular feelings), our long-term or overall well-being (feelings of happiness), and even morality (moral feelings), all from *the very same practical perspective*. More specifically, I can judge that extra cup of coffee to be good for satisfying my current need, but at the same time as negatively affecting my health and well-being, and so also as potentially violating an indirect duty. The result is a complex but unified deliberative field, and thus a unified psychology. And when coffee is judged in this complex manner, we see that practical reason thus governs by giving shape and structure to the matter of my will. To put this another way, my rational nature is expressed through the appetites and emotions of my lower nature, and in doing so, it transforms my animality into humanity.[23]

Finally, it now becomes possible for there to be varying degrees of freedom in relation to the varying degrees of reason's involvement in feeling. We are most free when we determine ourselves in a way that is *entirely* independent of our sensible needs, i.e., when we determine ourselves according to the moral law through the feeling of respect for it. (Kant designates this form as "inner freedom" (CPR 161; MM 418).) And we are the least free when we are entirely determined by our sensibility, i.e., when nature determines our actions for us through the analogue judgments of instinct. However, as we saw above, there is a wide range

---

[23] "The result of this presentation of the first history of human beings is that the departure of the human being from the paradise which reason represents to him as the first abode of his species was nothing other than the transition from the crudity of a merely animal creature into humanity, from the go-cart of instinct to the guidance of reason – in a word, from the guardianship of nature into the condition of freedom" (CB 115).

of feeling that extends between morality and instinct. In humans, freedom from the natural drives of instinct reaches its maximum (short of morality) only in happiness. By it we fully become the authors of our own actions, and so of our own lives.

> The first and most important observation that a human being makes about himself is that, determined through nature, *he is to be the author of his happiness and even of his own inclinations and aptitudes, which makes this happiness possible* [emphasis added]. ... As a freely acting being, indeed in accordance with this independence and self-rule, he will thus have as his foremost object that his desires agree with one another and with his concept of happiness, and not with instincts; and the conduct befitting the freedom of a rational being consists in this form. (R7199 AK 19:272–73)

5

Feeling and Desire in the Human Animal
Allen W. Wood

Human beings are a species of animal. Yet there can be no denying that they are a species unique in nature. One undeniable difference – according to some philosophers (such as Ludwig Feuerbach) the chief difference – is that human beings are the only animals that can form a concept of their own species and ask how their species differs from others. But we have a hard time figuring out what our species is, and how it differs from others.

The difficulty lies partly in our conception of other animals. Many philosophers, Kant among them, seem to me to have grossly underestimated the cognitive and agential capacities of nonhuman animals. Kant denies animals the faculty of *understanding* (intellect or intelligence) and therefore denies them the logical capacities to *think* or to *judge*.[1] Regarding theoretical cognition, the representations of nonhuman animals are all particular mental occurrences that relate only to particular objects. As regards practical capacities, Kant ascribes to all animals the capacities he calls "life" and a "faculty of desire": "*to be by means of its representations the cause of the reality of the objects of these representations*" (CPR 9n; cf. APV 251) and also a power of choice (*Willkür, arbitrium*). But Kant holds that nonhuman animals do not *choose* at all in our sense of the word because for an animal there are never real alternatives between choices. The *arbitrium brutum* of nonhuman animals is simply a mechanism causally necessitated by particular impulses or stimuli (*Antriebe*) – that is, representations accompanied by feelings of pleasure or displeasure (A533–34/B561–62; A802/B830). If an animal acts against one stimulus, this is only because that stimulus is overpowered by another, stronger one, just as a physical force acting on a body might be overpowered by a force acting in the opposite direction (AK 29:611). This in turn is because animal choices are

---

[1] These claims about Kant on animal cognition have recently been convincingly argued by Curtis Sommerlatte, "Empirical Cognition in the Transcendental Deduction: Kant's Starting Point and His Humean Problem," *Kantian Review* 21, no. 3 (November 2016): 437–63.

not guided by judgments about what is good and bad or even pleasant and unpleasant. As Kant also puts it, unlike our human world, the animal's world *contains no value* (AK 27:344).

In a lecture I once heard, Patricia Churchland described the behavior of most nonhuman mammals as falling into four categories that she aptly characterized as *"the four Fs*: feeding, fighting, fleeing and uh – reproduction." Can these familiar forms of animal behavior be adequately accounted for, as Kant thought, by causal necessities operating through instinct plus mechanical habituation? I doubt it. I don't see any way of making sense of behavior that fits these patterns without attributing to animals certain value judgments about various items in their environment: as potential meals, enemies, dangers or mates. I therefore think our commonsense view of nonhuman animals is quite different from Kant's view. Objects whose behavior is describable and explainable in purely mechanical terms – planets in their orbits, billiard balls careening on felt surfaces, swinging pendulums, and spheres rolling down inclined planes – are different, and the difference is not merely that the forces determining animals are *mental* or *conscious* attractions and repulsions rather than physical or material pushes and pulls.

Animals do seem to make *choices*. They may not be *free* choices, made with the capacity to follow a self-given rational principle (G 448; CPR 33), but they are genuine choices nonetheless. A feeding animal decides to eat this leaf or chase this hare because it judges the leaf to be succulent and the hare to be catchable. Nothing forces animals to do precisely what they do in the way that a billiard ball is mechanically forced by the cue ball to go off in precisely the direction from which it was struck. A feeding, fighting, fleeing, or mating animal decides to move in this or that direction, where there are clear options open to the animal about whether and exactly how to attack or retreat, dodge or hide, mount or be mounted. Animals respond to both inner needs and outer circumstances that give them reasons (of some sort) for choosing as they do based on the kinds of value that their world presents to them.

5.1 What Kind of Animal Are We?

How similar is the human species to other animal species, and how different? There is no simple way of answering such a question. All we can say is that we are exactly as much like any other animal species, and exactly as different from it, as our faculties, and our use of them, shows us to be. The question may seem to be susceptible to a simple answer chiefly because some superstitious religious views hold that human beings are metaphysically or supernaturally different from all other animals – they have a "spiritual" nature (an immaterial or immortal soul, and special nonnatural capacities) that other animals lack. Kant seems at times to endorse such talk, especially in his popular lectures, but on metaphysical questions he remains austerely agnostic about the nature of the human soul and its relation to the body. As a confirmed religious nonbeliever who wants to reject these superstitions, I squint skeptically when I hear talk about the "spirituality" of human nature. Or at least I used to – until I realized that such talk, though it may endorse a supernaturalist metaphysics or various backward religious dogmas, need not do so. In my favorite philosophers, the German idealists, it can instead be merely a way of referring to what we all know is distinctive about human animals. It can express an ethical rather a metaphysical stance – one that resists reductive scientistic imperialism when it tries to denigrate our reason and impoverish our humanity.

It is no doubt true that human beings are animals, but we clearly do have certain capacities – traditionally summed up under the term "rationality" – that no other animal has. The big question always remains: In what does this "reason" consist? Kant thought that this basic characteristic of our species entails *freedom*. It says less about how we behave than about what we *can do*. The human being is not so much an *animal rationalis* as an *animal rationabilis* (APV 321–22). Human beings are free to modify and even create their own nature. This means the character of our species is that this character itself is always incomplete and something to be self-made through our own (collective) actions in history (UH 18–20). But how close do certain other animals come to having rationality? And how, in us, does our rationality relate to our own animal nature? How does our rational nature determine the character of our own animality? These are difficult questions.

Determining how animal cognition and behavior resemble, and how they differ from, human cognition and behavior is the subject of ongoing empirical research by people who do *ethology* and *comparative psychology*. The question *Do animals think?* is still much debated. Some researchers defend mechanistic views of animal mentality fairly close to Kant's, while others hold that animals think in much the same sense that human beings do and attempt to determine empirically the degree and kind of similarity and difference.[2] If I may kibitz on these discussions, which are outside my field of expertise, it seems to me that researchers may be asking the wrong

---

[2] A recent anthology of articles on these issues is Randolph Menzel and Julia Fischer, eds., *Animal Thinking: Contemporary Issues in Comparative Cognition* (Cambridge, MA: MIT Press, 2010).

question if they wonder only *whether* or *how far* concepts we apply to our own mentality (such as "thinking") also apply to nonhuman animals. As Thomas Nagel long ago showed us, the perceptual experience of bats that orient themselves in dark caves through echolocation must be conceptualized differently from the perceptual experience of human beings who do the same things in lighted spaces through sight.[3] In a similar way, I suggest, the word "thinking" might be applied to chimpanzees or dolphins, or even of moles, ostriches, frogs, or fish, but *thinking* might be a different thing for each species, requiring a different concept.[4]

These are clearly empirical issues, and it seems initially plausible that empirical research should decide them. In this event, however, it turns out to be devilishly difficult to devise experiments that genuinely bear on empirical issues with philosophical implications. When some empirical finding is taken to settle a philosophical dispute, it is usually the case that either the design of the experiment or the interpretation of the evidence has smuggled in some dubious philosophical thesis that is then alleged to have been empirically verified. I think any experienced person with an understanding of the *philosophical* issue is more likely to make correct calls on philosophically significant empirical questions than are experimental psychologists who often seem not to understand what is at stake philosophically.

5.2 The Meaning of Our Animal Nature for Kantian Morality

Whether or not we accept Kant's psychologically determinist account of nonhuman animal mentality, his extreme views raise difficult questions for his own views about the animal nature of human beings. These difficulties are enhanced by the fact that Kant inherited from Baumgarten, Tetens, and others a highly mechanistic conception of *human* empirical psychology that depicts human cognition and action as causal processes conforming to psychological laws of nature distinct from laws of physics but conceived as just like them. It is difficult to reconcile such an account with the theory of free agency employed in both his moral philosophy and

---

[3] Or at least that is one conclusion – admittedly not a conclusion often emphasized – that I would draw from Nagel's arguments in this much-discussed article. Thomas Nagel, "What Is It Like to Be a Bat?" *Philosophical Review* 83, no. 4 (1974): 435–50; reprinted in Nagel, *Mortal Questions* (Cambridge: Cambridge University Press, 1979).

[4] Tad Brennan, who seems to me to know as much about the Stoics as anyone I have ever met, once told me that they held the view I am pushing here. One rather obvious but currently unfashionable conclusion we might draw from this Stoic position is that we would learn more about human beings from studying human beings than from studying our near evolutionary relatives, such as baboons, chimpanzees, or bonobos.

his pragmatic anthropology. Kant thinks freedom and natural necessity can be shown to be logically compatible, but no more than that. This is the only point he is making by distinguishing the sensible or phenomenal concept of our action from the intelligible or noumenal concept (A557–58/B585–86). It is sadly common, however, to saddle Kant with the positive metaphysical doctrine that down here in the phenomenal world we are just as causally determined as planets and billiard balls, but we are as free as angels up there in the (unknowable) noumenal stratosphere.[5] That misinterpretation naturally invites a criticism first put forward by Reinhold, later made even more famous by Sidgwick: only actions proceeding from pure reason are free, while those proceeding from inclination are causally necessitated and we are not responsible for them.

Kant's views about animal mentality also raise difficulties for those moral philosophers, such as Christine Korsgaard, who defend a "Kantian" conception of moral agency that views human beings as free agents standing in relation to their own animal nature conceived as essentially the same as the nature of nonhuman animals.[6] Korsgaard tries to wriggle out of these difficulties by adopting a conception of nonrational animality that is clearly not Kantian – by which I mean, it is clearly different from *Kant's*. Her conception of animality is closer to the way I have said our common sense views nonhuman animals. She holds, for example, that animals have *intelligence*: they form *concepts* and have *beliefs* (in other words, they make *judgments*), whereas Kant denied all of this. Korsgaard, however, still thinks our animality is the same as the animality of other animals. That sharpens the question: How do we as free and rational agents stand in relation to the "inner animal" from which, on this view, our empirical inclinations proceed? For Korsgaard our inner animal is not a rational agent. But it is also not an animal outside us, trotting along next to us like a pet dog, offering external facts for our observation to which our rational deliberations might pay attention. It is inside us; it is part of us. The beast within us is supposed

---

[5] A recent attempt to take seriously the mechanistic aspects of Kant's empirical psychology is found in Patrick R. Frierson, *Kant's Empirical Psychology* (Cambridge: Cambridge University Press, 2014). This is not the place to say why I think his attempt fails, but he carries on with his project of reading Kant's anthropology as involving mechanistic causality in the phenomenal world and saving our freedom only in the intelligible world: see Frierson, *Freedom and Anthropology in Kant's Moral Philosophy* (Cambridge: Cambridge University Press, 2003). I have had my say on these issues in several places, notably *Kantian Ethics* (Cambridge: Cambridge University Press, 2008), chap. 7, §§ 5–6, and "The Antinomies of Pure Reason," in *The Cambridge Companion to Kant's Critique of Pure Reason*, ed. Paul Guyer (Cambridge: Cambridge University Press, 2010), 245–65.

[6] See Christine Korsgaard, "Fellow Creatures: Kantian Ethics and Our Duties to Animals," in *The Tanner Lectures on Human Values*, ed. Grethe B. Peterson, Vols. 25/26 (Salt Lake City: University of Utah Press, 2004).

to have some direct involvement in our rational deliberations about what to do while nevertheless remaining only a nonrational animal. How can we think of these necessarily nonrational contributions to our rational deliberations? This problem has been explored in a series of thoughtful and probing articles by Tamar Schapiro, who, to her credit, seems to find more puzzlement than satisfaction in dealing with the topic.[7] We will consider some of her suggestions a bit later.

In Chapter 4, "Feeling and Inclination: Rationalizing the Animal Within," in this volume, Janelle DeWitt champions a very different approach to these issues by calling into question the separateness of our humanity from our animal nature in Kant's anthropology and moral psychology. She does not deny that Kant distinguished our predisposition to animality from our predispositions to humanity and personality, since those distinctions are undeniable (R 26–28; APV 321–25). What she questions is their meaning in the context of Kant's theory of human nature. To frame DeWitt's view in my own terms: our animal nature is already a human and rational animal nature – just as, I would suggest, the animal nature of a cat is a distinctively cat-animal nature and the animal nature of a bat is a distinctively bat-animal nature. The *human* inner animal is already a *rational* animal – "all the way down."

One controversy closely relates to these issues about Kant's view of human nature, a view commonly portrayed as not merely mistaken but even unhealthy and pernicious. As DeWitt points out, Kant is often criticized for holding moral views that are hostile to emotion, hostile to our animal nature, even hostile to "the body." These criticisms are almost never merely expressions of a scholarly interpretation of Kant. Their real target is always something larger and more important. Kant is being brought in only as an object lesson, cautionary tale or scapegoat (depending on how you look at it). The view is that our entire culture is beset with unhealthy attitudes toward the senses, toward nature, toward vitality, toward sexuality. This has been a persistent theme in many feminist critiques of Kant.[8] The idea is that this deeper part of

---

[7] Tamar Schapiro, "The Nature of Inclination," *Ethics* 119, no. 2 (2009): 229–56; "Desires as Demands: How the Second-Person Standpoint Might Be Internal to Reflective Agency," *Philosophy and Phenomenological Research* 81, no. 1 (2010): 229–36; "On the Relation between Wanting and Willing," *Philosophical Issues* 22, no. 1 (2012): 334–50; "Foregrounding Desire: A Defense of Kant's Incorporation Thesis," *The Journal of Ethics* 15, no. 3 (2011): 147–67; "What Are Theories of Desire Theories Of?" *Analytic Philosophy* 55, no. 2 (2014): 131–50.

[8] One clear example: Robin May Schott, *Cognition and Eros: A Critique of the Kantian Paradigm* (Boston: Beacon Press, 1988).

Kant's philosophy both expresses and contributes to these deplorable attitudes by its "disdain for the body."

For my own part, so far I agree – as regards our cultural traditions. There is still much in our sexual morality, at least on the side of moral and political conservatives, and some religious moralists, that is ignorant, backward, and pernicious. This strain in popular morality also plays a significant role in the oppression of women. I also agree that some of Kant's attitudes about sex and about women are deeply opposed to those of enlightened people today. His view of women was at least mildly misogynistic even in the context of his own time; it is less often appreciated, however, that Kant was also more concerned than most people at the time with protecting the dignity of women, especially in the area of sex.[9] Common images of Kant, however, often go well beyond cataloging his deplorable attitudes and outdated political views. They attempt to see these as rooted in a still-deeper pathology regarding the human body and our animality. That is where I stop agreeing and want to push back. I think it is better for our cultural attitudes to understand Kant correctly than to distort his teachings so as to make him a suitable whipping boy for people of goodwill.[10]

5.3 Kant's "Dualisms"

Kant's conceptions of reason and feeling, rightly understood, do not involve an alienation of the intellect from the senses, or the mind from the body, or an attitude of "disdain" directed at feeling, the senses, or the body. In support of a better understanding, DeWitt appeals to the parallel

---

[9] I have discussed these topics at greater length in Wood, *Kantian Ethics*, chaps. 1 § 4 and chap. 13.

[10] How far has the influence of Kant's philosophy actually contributed to what we deplore in our culture's attitudes toward morality, feelings, the body, or women? I doubt that it has contributed very much. However prevalent they may be, the common images of Kant as hostile to natural feeling and human emotion are based on fairly obvious distortions and misreadings. These caricatures, however, are usually put in service of *attacking* the views he is portrayed as holding. The object of these attacks is not anyone who ever existed. It is "Kant" – that prune-faced Prussian ogre, whose deserving backside the misreadings offer for our righteous chastisement. But discussions of this grotesque "Kant" surely contribute more to the *criticism* of unhealthy attitudes than to their perpetuation. I doubt that academic criticism, whether of Kant or of "Kant," is going to do much to alter our cultural attitudes – either for better or worse. It is usually consumed only by intellectuals, most of whom are already hostile to the unhealthy ideas being attributed to "Kant." I would argue that, on the whole, Kant's actual philosophy, however strong or weak its influence has been, has tended to favor the other side of these issues – the "good" side. It is an undeniable fact that a clear majority of the most distinguished scholars now working on Kant's (or Kantian) ethics and related topics are women, and most of these scholars are also feminists. A good discussion of the relation of Kant's philosophy to feminism is presented by Marcia Baron, "Kantian Ethics and the Claims of Detachment," in *Feminist Interpretations of Immanuel Kant*, ed. Robin May Schott (University Park: Pennsylvania State University Press, 1997), 145–72.

between the theoretical side of Kant's philosophy and the practical side in arguing that, in the latter, we should not expect a discontinuity or disharmony. It is true that Kant's theoretical philosophy is based on the idea that we must both sense and think, and that the understanding must cooperate with sensible intuition to make possible cognition of the objective world. Students of Kant in recent years have devoted much effort, and with success, to showing how this is possible. But she may be overestimating the force of this argument, or at least estimating its force based on relatively recent discussions of Kant's theoretical philosophy. For one of the chief themes in the early reception of Kant's philosophy was the worry that Kant's "dualism" of sense and intellect threatens the possibility of theoretical cognition. This was a major theme in the skeptical attacks on Kant by Jacobi, Schulze, and Maimon. The early response to these attacks by Reinhold and Fichte conceded more to the critics than most recent interpreters of Kant's philosophy would allow.

Moreover, in the view of many of these critics, the "dualism" of sense and understanding in theory was paralleled by other dualisms in Kant – of reason and inclination in the practical sphere, and of the theoretical and the practical within the system of Kant's philosophy as a whole. Since I tend to look at Kant from the perspective of his German idealist appropriators, this means that I see DeWitt's contribution a bit differently from the way she sees it. She sees her account as bringing our account of the practical in Kant into line with the theoretical. But I see her arguments for the harmony and continuity of reason and feeling as direct, frontal responses to a long line of criticism raised against Kant from the beginning. They complement the work of recent interpreters of Kant's account of theoretical cognition by showing how the "dualism" in practice does not lead to an untenable or "alienated" conception of feeling, desire, and action.

The most basic claim DeWitt makes is that, for Kant, feeling is cognitive in the realm of practice (or value) in something like the way that sensible intuition is cognitive in the realm of theory. She is right to question the coherence of any view that would represent feeling, in relation to desire, choice, and action, as merely blind impulse or brute sensation. For this would make it impossible to understand how our "lower" animal or sensible nature could contribute even to desire, still less to rational choice. Kant does, as I have already said, represent the *arbitrium brutum* of nonhuman animals as operating through psychic causal processes that are mechanistic in conception, devoid of anything like cognitions of value.

The common interpretation of Kant against which she is arguing seems based on the assumption that Kant regarded the lower or animal side of our desiring nature as being just like his account of the *arbitrium brutum* of nonhuman animals. That leads directly back to the Reinhold-Sidgwick objection. I have already mentioned how it also creates a problem for Kant interpreters such as Korsgaard and Schapiro. For them, the desires of the "inner animal" are supposed to offer us direct, though resistible, incentives to act. But what could these incentives be like? We are supposedly free to resist the impulses and desires of the inner animal, yet they still exert influence on us.

Schapiro has suggested several different models for this influence. In most of her papers, the idea seems to be that the inner animal "nominates" courses of action and then urges or pressures us to follow them. As rational agents, we stand back, detached from this pressure, consider these nominations, and decide, whether well or badly, which ones to accept and which not. We get the final say. But how a nonrational animal can make "nominations" a rational agent can understand is not easily explained. How an inner brute could exert nonrational "pressure" on a rational agent is also deeply obscure. In one of Schapiro's papers, the suggestion seems to be that the inner animal is more like a child begging a parent for candy. Our rational self must play the role of the adult, deciding when to indulge the child and when to say no. But that model transforms the animal not only into a valuing being but even into a *human* being, albeit an immature and imperfectly rational one. None of these models is particularly convincing. Schapiro even suggests that our relation to our inner animal is unique, not capable of being modelled on anything else. But what I see here is clear evidence not of a phenomenon sui generis, but rather of an unsolved problem, even one that is bound to be insoluble as long as we see empirical desire – our "lower faculty of desire" – as a sort of nonrational self, and our rational self – our "higher faculty of desire" as a *different* (rational) self. For that leaves us alienated from our animality in just the ways the critics (from Kant's day down to our own) rightly regard as problematic.

5.4 Reflective Detachment and Our Moral Life

Something like Korsgaard's picture seems inevitable if we take the view that rational agency consists essentially in "standing back," reflectively disengaged from something else (whatever it might be), where the job of the rational self is to test this other thing for permissibility.[11] This picture

---

[11] See Christine Korsgaard, *The Sources of Normativity* (Cambridge: Cambridge University Press, 1996), 34–37, 92–100; cf. Korsgaard, *Self-Constitution: Agency, Identity, and Integrity* (Oxford: Oxford University Press, 2009), 10–11.

seems harmonious with the conception of Kantian ethics that was made fashionable in the late twentieth century through the work of Rawls and O'Neill. On this conception, moral agency consists in starting with "maxims" (based on empirical desires) and then testing them using a rigorous four-step "CI-Procedure." This too offers us a conception of Kantian ethics in terms of a rational agent standing back reflectively from something given to it "from outside" and testing it – that is to say given from outside its rational activity of judging and deciding, but not from outside itself, since the maxims to be tested come from desires and projects "inside" the agent (perhaps ultimately from its "inner animal").

This is not the place for me to say why I regard the universalizability procedure as a misunderstanding of the way Kant in fact uses the Formulas of Universal Law and the Law of Nature in the *Groundwork* and elsewhere.[12] But we can observe that it clearly gets fundamentally wrong the way Kant thinks about the moral life. On this picture, an agent's main business in life is represented by its "maxims"; these originate outside morality. Moral reflection consists in testing these maxims for permissibility from an abstract, impartial standpoint of universal legislation, imposing side constraints on our loves and commitments, and saying a stern "No!" when our desires or our projects violate standards of pure impartiality. This looks more like what we get from certain utilitarian views, rightly criticized by philosophers such as Bernard Williams, who worry that the impartial standpoint of morality threatens our authentic selfhood and even our integrity.[13]

For Kant, all our ends ought to be expressions of our *moral vocation*.[14] Morality is not a mere side constraint imposed by impartial reason on a set of maxims coming from outside it. Morality does forbid, in particular cases, making exceptions of ourselves, or our inclinations, to principles valid equally for all persons who are ends in themselves. But Kant's duties of virtue – the duties to include among our ends our own perfection and the happiness of others – involve partiality in an essential way. We are partial to ourselves in making our own perfection an end of morality; duties of love involve partiality toward those particular others whose happiness we make our ends. This partiality is especially noticeable in the duty of friendship, to which Kant gives more prominence than is

---

[12] The place where I do say this is: Wood, *Formulas of the Moral Law* (Cambridge: Cambridge University Press, 2017).
[13] Bernard Williams, *Moral Luck* (Cambridge: Cambridge University Press, 1981), chap. 3.
[14] This is not the place to show how Kant is in this respect like his idealist followers, such as Fichte. But see Wood, *Fichte's Ethical Thought* (Oxford: Oxford University Press, 2016), 193–94, 242–44.

usually appreciated. Morality for Kant cannot threaten our integrity. On the contrary, the self-government of a morality of autonomy is the only legitimate protection our integrity has. That is one big reason I do not see how Kant's actual views can be reconciled with a "Kantian" ethics whose essence is a reflective disengagement from our desires or maxims that rules on their permissibility using a universalizability procedure to insure impartiality. Such an ethics is not "Kantian," or at least not *Kant's*.[15]

In fact, the conception of the rational agent beginning with "maxims" that are based on empirical desire and feeling, then testing these maxims for permissibility, is not at all the way Kant actually pictures moral action. On the contrary, our moral vocation is the vocation of rational beings whose capacity for self-government simply *is* their *rational* "faculty of desire." For Kant, moral action involves the application of general principles or duties to individual cases by practical judgments that are made effective *through* desire and feeling.

5.5 Kant on Feeling and Desire

DeWitt's reading of Kant begins by looking carefully at what Kant actually says about the concepts of feeling and desire. Kant emphasizes that feelings – pleasure and displeasure (*Lust und Unlust*) – are noncognitive in the sense that they provide us with no objective theoretical cognition of the properties of the objects in which we find pleasure or displeasure. But as DeWitt convincingly shows, all feeling for Kant is essentially cognitive in a different sense. Pleasure is a representation (*Vorstellung*) of an object as suited to the conditions of life for the subject, and in this way it involves – or else it simply *is* – a subjective judgment (*Urteil, Beurteilung*) of value. Feeling is essentially *value cognitive*.

A striking example of the way feeling involves judgments of value is Kant's account of aesthetic pleasure in connection with the pure judgment of taste. Kant notes that such judgments of taste involve both pleasure in the object and the judgment that this pleasure is communicable – that it can be

---

[15] Nor is abstract disengagement from desire and feeling the way Aristotle thinks of rational choice or decision (*prohairesis*). For him, deliberation through right reason (*orthos logos*) draws practical conclusions according to the virtue of prudence or practical wisdom (*phronesis*), and choice occurs not in abstraction or disengaged from and over against the nonrational elements of wishing for the good – opinion about the good, desire, pleasure, and pain – but through them and by means of them. See Aristotle, *Nicomachean Ethics* III/5, trans. Terence Irwin, 2nd ed. (Indianapolis, IN: Hackett, 1999). See also Terence Irwin, *The Development of Ethics*, vol. 1 (Oxford: Oxford University Press, 2007), 175–77.

expected of everyone. He asks whether the pleasure or the judgment comes first, and he answers that the judgment comes first (CJ 216–19). This should surprise and perplex anyone who thinks pleasure for Kant is a mere noncognitive sensation. It becomes perfectly intelligible to us when we realize that, for Kant, *all* feelings necessarily involve subjective judgments of value. In the case of a pure judgment of taste, the universal communicability of our feeling of pleasure is something we necessarily value (in which we take an interest), both empirically and intellectually (CJ 293–303).

The judgments of value involved in feeling are *subjective*: they are judgments only of the *apparent good for me*. More specifically, they are judgments of an anticipated agreeableness (or in the case of displeasure, disagreeableness) of an object in relation to the conditions of my life. They are also *fallible* judgments: first, because what is anticipated may not come to pass (what attracted us through pleasure may in the event be disagreeable); but second, even what I find agreeable may not satisfy my true needs or belong to my true welfare or happiness. Nevertheless, Kant's theory of desire and inclination in general would be impossible without the subjective judgments of value found in feeling. Because this is so, we never need to view our animal nature as something alien to our rational nature. The "inner animal" is never an inner beast or child standing outside our rational nature and exerting nonrational "pressure" on it. Our inclinations are habitual (but subjective and fallible) judgments of value, internal to our rational nature, which we may then reflect on and judge according to rational principles. Inclinations themselves already present us with reasons, because even the animality from which they proceed is always already a human animality, that is, a rational animality.

We all know, of course, that Kantian ethics does see a conflict between duty and inclination as central to our moral life. But this is *not* correctly seen as a conflict between our "rational part" and our "animal part." Our animality is at most an occasion for the conflicts. We will return to this point presently, and explain how the conflict is entirely *within our rational nature*.

DeWitt gives us a careful and detailed examination, based on Kant's explicit statements, of the way feeling operates in us and how it leads to desire and inclination in us as fully rational beings. The starting point, present in our predisposition to animality, is *instinct*. Instincts are preconceptual tendencies to desire something even before we become acquainted with it. On Kant's account, this occurs even in nonrational animals, and it, together with mechanical conditioning or habituation, is how all nonrational animals desire and act. In us, however, instincts are different. They give rise to *valuations*. They result in propensity (*Hang*) and *concupiscence*, which is the subjective possibility of a (human) desire. Desire first makes its appearance in the form of an indeterminate wish – an "empty" or "idle" (*müßig*) wish, hence "peevish" or "moody" (*launisch*) wish – a wish nothing satisfies (APV 251). Such a wish is our experience of the pressure of a need for which we can as yet assign no determinate object. It is not indeterminate because it is mechanically particular (as for Kant the impulse of an *arbitrium brutum* must be), but only because it has *not yet* been conceptualized. Such needs or wishes can acquire determinate objects only through our rational agency, which judges that our needs should be satisfied in determinate ways through determinate objects.

We are rational animals, capable of judging and choosing – but also condemned to judge and choose – the means by which our natural needs are to be satisfied.[16] It is only through such judgments that our natural needs become determinate (human) desires. Even our most animal desires already have the value-cognitive form of reasons. When these desires become habitual, through our adoption of the maxim of satisfying a determinate need through a determinate kind of object, they become *inclinations*. Inclination, therefore, is already something in which we are rationally complicit and for which we are responsible. It is a distortion of Kant's theory to represent inclinations as brute presentations from our "inner animal nature" to our rational faculty, as though our reason were wholly disengaged from them.

Kant's view here is echoed (though in somewhat different terminology) by his two great followers, Fichte and Hegel. For Fichte, our empirical, bodily, or animal nature manifests itself as a drive (*Trieb*). When this drive has no determinate object, we experience it as "longing" (*Sehnen*). It is then differentiated by reflection into a plurality of drives, the satisfaction (*Befriedigung*) of each of which is a form of enjoyment (*Genuß*) (SL 122–32).[17] In Hegel, the assignment of determinate objects to a drive is called "resolve" (*Entschließen*) and the identification of ourselves with the pursuit of such an object is called "choosing" or "electing" (*Wählen*)

---

[16] This for Kant is the symbolic significance of the biblical story of our first parents' liberating act of eating from the tree of the knowledge of good and evil (Genesis 3:1–7). The "voice of God" commanding them to eat only from the tree of life is the voice of instinct; their choice to eat from a different tree opens their eyes to good and evil by confronting them with the anxiety-provoking and abysmal prospect of henceforth having to devise their own way of life for themselves according to judgments and choices made by their own reason (CB 112).
[17] Johann Gottlieb Fichte, *System of Ethics*, trans. Daniel Breazeale and Günter Zöller (Cambridge: Cambridge University Press, 2005). Cited in the text as SL, according to the volume: page number of Fichte, *Sämmtliche Werke*, ed. I. H. Fichte (1845–1846) (Berlin: Walter de Gruyter, 1971).

(PR §§ 10–14).[18] In all three philosophers, our empirical desires emerge from our embodied rational animality. They are never presented to us as coming entirely from outside our rational agency, even when we experience a conflict between what we desire and what reason tells us to do. This is perhaps clearest in Fichte, for whom our natural drive is only one aspect of an original or fundamental drive (*Urtrieb*), which becomes separated by reflection from a "pure drive" for freedom. The ethical drive, through which we prosecute our moral vocation, is a *mixed* drive, combining the natural and pure drives and thereby reuniting through reason the two sides of our nature as rational yet also embodied (animal) beings (Fichte SL §§ 11–12, 4:132–53).

Thus for the great German idealists, including Kant, our animal nature or "lower power of desire" is never viewed as alien to our rational nature. It is only a "lower" function of it; conversely, our rationality or "higher power of desire" is always nothing but the "higher" perfection of our distinctively human animality. For this reason, the relation of reason to inclination, though one of "(inner) constraint" (*Zwang*) or necessitation (*Nötigung*) (G 398; MM 379), is always *inner* constraint – not only in the obvious sense that it is not exercised by a being outside us (such as a police officer) but also in the deeper sense that it is exercised through our own desires and feelings, and *not* by a rational arbiter: a mere yea- and naysayer that stands outside, above, or over against them. We need to constrain ourselves because we have certain feelings and desires, but the constraint itself is also carried out through feelings and desires.

5.6 The Radical Propensity to Evil and Unsociable Sociability

DeWitt's account in Chapter 4 needs to be supplemented in a couple of ways. I do not think that the supplement I am about to sketch is opposed to what she says, and I suspect that at least part of what I am about to say is something with which she agrees. I look forward to her developing it in her own way in future writings.

First, our inclinations, arising out of our human animality, do pose some sort of resistance to our reason, but these inclinations are also expressions of our rational nature and not something alien or external to it. As I said a bit ago, we need some account of how this conflict occurs. Kant's account of it takes several interrelated forms. One is his discussion in the *Religion* of the radical propensity to evil in human nature (R 19–44).

---

[18] G. W. F. Hegel, *Elements of the Philosophy of Right*, ed. Allen W. Wood, trans. H. B. Nisbet (Cambridge: Cambridge University Press, 1991). Cited in the text by paragraph (§) number.

This propensity, as Kant repeatedly emphasizes, is not fully explicable even in principle (R 25, 34–36, 78). It is clear, however, that this source is *not* our natural inclinations themselves, which are entirely innocent and even good (R 34–35, 57–58). The source lies in our own misuse of our rational faculty, occasioned by social competitiveness (R 36, 93–94).

This gives a special meaning to Kant's claim (quoted by DeWitt) that our rational predisposition to humanity "involves comparison, for which reason is required" (R 27). Not only does reason compare different objects and judge their comparative goodness for us, but it also involves comparison of *ourselves* with *other human beings*, involving a desire that the comparison should be to our advantage and their disadvantage. "It is only in comparison with others that we regard ourselves happy or unhappy" (R 27). Our only natural measure of happiness, welfare, or prosperity is therefore a viciously competitive one. A human being "is poor (or considers himself so) only to the extent that he is anxious that other human beings will consider him poor and will despise him for it" (R 93). Our propensity to evil is thus rooted in what Kant elsewhere calls "self-conceit" (CPR 73). Kant provides an account of this propensity in *Idea for a Universal History* when he argues that nature's device for developing our species' predispositions is "unsociable sociability" – the desire to have your own way in everything and to seek a superior rank among your fellow human beings (UH 20–21).

It is this distinctively human, distinctively rational social and competitive tendency in us that, according to Kant, gives rise to the *passions*: inclinations that reason finds it difficult or impossible to restrain (R 94; APV 265–75). Passions, whether "natural" or "social," are always directed at other human beings and seek superiority over them (APV 268). The power of the passions to resist reason does *not* come from outside our rational nature, as by some sort of "pressure" on our rational nature exerted by an inner animal. On the contrary, it is rooted in a delusion (*Wahn*) that makes us overestimate the value of some objects of inclination that are seen as sources of social superiority. The delusion incapacitates us for making rational comparisons between this value and other values. A passion is a mania or addiction (*Sucht*) (APV 266). The delusion it involves is not innocent; it is *chosen*; it is a self-deception (APV 274–75).[19] A passion is thus "an illness that abhors all medicine... an enchantment that refuses all recuperation" (APV 266).

---

[19] Kant does not deny that we can fall into devilish vices, in which we *seem* to adopt evil itself as our principle (AK 27:632; AK 27:440). But we cannot really adopt such a principle, or will evil *as evil*:

5.7 Rational Feelings, Empirical Feelings, and Moral Virtue

The second theme that needs development in order to complete DeWitt's account is the role of feeling and desire in moral agency itself. Some accounts of Kant's moral psychology proceed as if Kant attributes to reason a kind of supernatural power to constrain inclinations from entirely outside them – perhaps by the power of a purely theoretical or contemplative judgment of what morality commands. Perhaps those who read Kant in this way think of the constraining power of reason metaphysically, as a supernatural lightning bolt descending upon our animal nature from out of the intelligible world. Such readers of Kant naturally find his doctrines, so interpreted, to be off-putting, even odious, or perhaps simply absurd. But to read Kant in that way is also profoundly to misunderstand him.

Kant holds that there can be no action whatever without a *desire* to act – to pursue an end and follow a maxim. Desire, moreover, always involves feeling: a desire for an object is the representation of the object connected with a feeling of pleasure (MM 211). But the connection between pleasure and desire can come about in either of two distinct ways. Either the pleasure comes first, in which case the desire is an empirical desire, impulse, or inclination. Or alternatively, the desire comes first, as when our will responds to a technical instruction, prudential counsel, or moral command of reason and chooses to obey it (CPR 9n; MM 211). The choice to follow instrumental reason or prudence then produces in us a pleasure in the representation of the chosen action. The same thing occurs in moral action or action from duty. In instrumentally, prudentially, or morally rational action, feeling and desire play different roles from the ones they play in action from immediate inclination. But the role of feeling and desire is equally essential. In neither case is it *pleasure* that directly produces the action as its cause. It is *desire* – the combination of the representation of an object with pleasure – through which the action of the subject causes the object (CPR 9n; MM 211; APV 251).

The feelings associated with rational action, and especially with moral action, are essential to Kant's moral psychology. Kant began his journey as

---

we cannot have a "diabolical will" or "evil reason," since to choose is by its concept to choose what we represent as good (R 35; cf. MM 46; cf. CPR 59). We can, however, choose evil as evil in the sense that we can represent evil to ourselves as good as the result of an "inner lie" (MM 430–31). Willing evil *as evil* could never be done honestly, as an innocent error; it always involves self-deception. See Wood, "The Evil in Human Nature," in *Kant's Religion within the Boundaries of Mere Reason: A Critical Guide*, ed. Gordon Michalson (Cambridge: Cambridge University Press, 2014), 34–38.

a moral philosopher in his prize essay, "Inquiry concerning the Distinctness of the Principles of Natural Theology and Morality" (1764). There he seemed to be a follower of Francis Hutcheson's moral sense theory, which made moral feeling the foundation of morality. Kant soon abandoned this view in favor of a rationalist position he came to identify with the phrase "metaphysics of morals." But it is a mistake to think that Kant ever abandoned the concept of moral feeling. He always thought of the concept of moral feeling that he found in Shaftesbury and Hutcheson as the first form in which an ethics of principles established itself in the modern period (AK 29:620–26).[20] Though no longer viewed as the foundation of ethics, moral feelings remained throughout his life essential to Kant's moral psychology, and he always made a special place for them.

In the *Groundwork*, the only feeling Kant specifically identifies is the feeling of *respect* for the moral law (G 401n). But it plays an indispensable role in his account of acting from duty and in the derivation of the first formula of the moral law (G 400–2).

In the second *Critique*, Kant says that "respect for the moral law is not the incentive to morality; instead, it is morality itself [or] pure practical reason subjectively considered as an incentive" (CPR 76). But a mere two pages later, he declares: "Respect for the moral law is therefore the sole and also the undoubted moral incentive" (CPR 78). How could Kant make these two apparently mutually contradictory claims within the space of only two pages? I submit that, in an earlier article, DeWitt provided the solution to this puzzle.[21] The key to her solution is the same thesis as the one she defends in her essay in this volume: namely, that for Kant all feeling is essentially value cognitive. Thus to say that the moral law itself, or pure practical reason, is the moral incentive is not different from saying that the feeling of respect is the moral incentive. We could deny the latter claim only if we mistakenly failed to see that this feeling is itself the apprehension (or value cognition) of a reason. The feeling of respect is, as Kant formulates a bit later, the "practical estimation [*Schätzung*] of the law itself" (CPR 79). In the two pages intervening between the two apparently contradictory claims, Kant argues for that crucial proposition.

---

[20] See Wood, "Kant on the History of Ethics," in *Kant's Lectures on Ethics: A Critical Guide*, ed. Lara Denis and Oliver Sensen (Cambridge: Cambridge University Press, 2015), 120–37.

[21] Janelle DeWitt, "Respect for the Moral Law: The Emotional Side of Reason," *Philosophy* 89, no. 1 (2014): 31–62.

In the *Metaphysics of Morals*, Kant's account of the rational feelings essential to moral motivation is enriched and further developed. He now explicitly distinguishes four such feelings:

(a) *Moral feeling*: pleasure or displeasure, i.e. approval or disapproval, directed to deeds or actions.
(b) *Conscience*: feelings of contentment or condemnation directed to oneself before the inner forum in which we pass judgments of guilt or innocence on ourselves and our actions.
(c) *Love of human beings* (*philanthropia*): feelings of pleasure in the perfection – that is, in the humanity or rational nature of persons as ends in themselves and beings having dignity – that motivates us both to respect them and promote their well-being.
(d) *Respect* for oneself or for other persons. (MM 399–403)

All four feelings are predispositions of the mind belonging essentially to our rational nature as moral persons. "Consciousness of them is not of empirical origin; it can instead follow only from consciousness of a moral law, as the effect this has on the mind" (MM 399). Without them one could not be subject to duties at all. I submit that the above list is only a selection from, or perhaps it sketches the taxonomy for, the many rational feelings there might be. Each duty, and each virtue, carries with it an end, and a desire for the end. This means it carries with it a susceptibility to the feeling of pleasure that belongs to the desire for the end or of displeasure belonging to the aversion to its opposite.

The rational feelings necessary for moral agency must encompass all the pleasures essential to the possession of moral virtue. But virtues and vices, as Kant conceives them, also involve *empirical* feelings. Our duty of sympathetic participation (*Teilnehmung*) is the duty actively to sympathize with others, and elicit in ourselves the empirical feelings of love and sympathy that will result from doing this. Thus the "friend of humanity" whose beneficence Kant says involves no true or genuine moral worth, because it is not done from duty, may nevertheless conspicuously exemplify a moral virtue, and that is why such beneficence is to be regarded as dutiful, amiable, and deserving of praise and encouragement (G 398).[22]

---

[22] The wildly erroneous thought (one that many readers take away from this discussion in the *Groundwork*) that Kant *disapproves* of beneficence from sympathy is probably the most common starting point for the deplorable misunderstandings of the basic spirit of Kantian ethics that still prevail among many moral philosophers. For my own more full discussion of this topic, see Wood, *The Free Development of Each: Studies on Freedom, Right, and Ethics in Classical German Philosophy* (Oxford: Oxford University Press, 2014), chap. 1.

A careful look at what Kant says about duties, virtues and vices in the "Doctrine of Virtue" reveals that they consist at least as much in feelings and attitudes as in actions and omissions. Love and respect for others, and the virtues associated with duties of love and respect, are attitudes associated with feelings. The opposed vices, such as malice and envy (which are opposed to virtues of love) and ridicule or defamation (opposed to virtues of respect), also consist in feelings of pleasure or displeasure as much as in deeds. The vice of envy consists in *being distressed at* the successes of those we envy and not only in actively diminishing their well-being (MM 458–59); the vice of ridicule consists in *being amused by* the mockery to which others are subjected and not only in directly exposing them to derision (MM 467). For Kant, every bit as much as for Aristotle, virtues and vices consist partly in feeling pleasure and displeasure in the right or the wrong things.[23]

Accordingly, the cultivation of virtue and the combatting of vice will involve cultivating certain feelings and desires, both rational and empirical, as well as doing the right deeds and pursuing the right ends. Cultivating moral perfection will involve not only the strengthening of desires connected to rational moral feelings, but also the gradual bringing about of a harmony between the commands of morality and our *empirical* desires. This is for Kant a difficult and even an endless task, due to the obstacles we ourselves have placed in its way through the competitiveness of social life. The resulting conflict between nature and culture that belongs to the human condition thus involves the struggle to reform our practical sensibility as much as our external conduct. "Our natural predispositions, since they were aimed at the purely natural [rather than the social] condition, suffer injury from progressing culture and injure culture in turn, until perfect art again becomes nature, which is the ultimate goal of the moral vocation of the human species" (CB 117–18).

---

[23] Aristotle, *Nicomachean Ethics*, 1104b3–1105a16.

6

"*A new sort of a priori principles*"
Psychological Taxonomies and the Origin of the Third Critique

Patrick Frierson

In *Early German Philosophy*, Lewis White Beck lays out a clear and straightforward account of the nature and origin of Kant's commitment to a distinct faculty of feeling and a corresponding third *Critique* for that faculty.[1] For Beck, Kant holds that "Art [has] its own rules," so he is committed to offering "a phenomenological examination of art and ... a transcendental justification of its conditions," which requires "the establishment of a *third faculty of the mind*, with its own a priori principles and its own operations which supply an a priori form to aesthetic and critical judgments."[2] In order to provide a priori principles for art, "Kant [becomes] the first author to maintain clearly and consistently the three-faculty theory."[3] On Beck's account, then, Kant's commitment to a distinct faculty of feeling coincides with and even follows from his key insight that a priori normative principles govern aesthetic judgment. In contrast to this view, Paul Guyer has recently drawn attention to the wide range of features from Kant's *Critique of the Power of Judgment* that were present in anthropology lectures as early as 1772 – including Kant's early commitment to a three-faculty theory of soul – and has rightly focused attention on the question of what *changed* in Kant's thought to explain his sudden shift from pessimism about any possible Critique of Taste to writing and publishing one. For Guyer, the key to this change is Kant's concern with "teleology" as a way of bridging the gap between nature and freedom.[4] In this chapter,

---

[1] A full discussion of the origin of Kant's three-faculty theory of the soul would require discussion of Tetens, but that is beyond the scope of this chapter. For some discussion of the influence of Tetens on Kant, see Lewis White Beck, *Early German Philosophy: Kant and His Predecessors* (Cambridge, MA: Harvard University Press, 1969); Corey W. Dyck, *Kant and Rational Psychology* (New York: Oxford University Press, 2014); and Thomas Sturm, *Kant und die Wissenschaften vom Menschen* (Münster: Mentis Verlag, 2009).
[2] Beck, *Early German Philosophy*, 497.   [3] Beck, *Early German Philosophy*, 497.
[4] See Paul Guyer, "Beauty, Freedom, and Morality: Kant's *Lectures on Anthropology* and the Development of his Aesthetic Theory," in *Essays on Kant's Anthropology*, ed. Brian Jacobs and Patrick Kain (Cambridge: Cambridge University Press, 2003), 135–63.

I defend (against Guyer) a close connection between Kant's psychological commitment to a three-faculty theory of soul and his *Critique of the Power of Judgment*, but argue (against Beck) that it was precisely insights *from* his psychology that made possible his transcendental insights, rather than vice versa. In particular, Kant's psychological taxonomy of mental powers provoked consideration of the possibility that there could be a special connection between judgment and aesthetic feeling, and the realization of this possibility led to Kant's focus on teleology and ultimately to the *Critique of the Power of Judgment*.

Recent commentators rightly point to the central place in any story of the origin of the third *Critique* that must be given to the letter Kant wrote at the end of December 1787 to Carl Leonhard Reinhold.[5] In this letter, Kant describes how he came to write the "manuscript" that became the *Critique of the Power of Judgment*:

> Without becoming guilty of self-conceit, I can assure you that the longer I continue on my path the less worried I become that any individual or even organized opposition (of the sort that is common nowadays) will ever significantly damage my system. My inner conviction grows, as I discover in working on different topics that not only does my system remain self-consistent but I find also, when sometimes I cannot see the right way to investigate a certain subject, that I need only look back at the general picture of the elements of knowledge, and of the mental powers pertaining to them, in order to discover elucidations I had not expected. I am now at work on the critique of taste, and I have discovered a new sort of a priori principles, different from those heretofore observed. For there are three faculties of the mind: the faculty of cognition, the faculty of feeling pleasure and displeasure, and the faculty of desire. In the Critique *of Pure* (theoretical) *Reason*, I found a priori principles for the first of these, and in the Critique *of Practical Reason*, a priori principles for the third. I tried to find them for the second as well, and though I thought it impossible to find such principles, the analysis of the previously mentioned faculties of the human mind allowed me to discover a systematicity, giving me ample material at which to marvel and if possible to explore, material sufficient to last me for the rest of my life. This systematicity put me on the path to recognizing the three parts of philosophy, each of which has its a priori principles, which can be enumerated and for which one can delimit precisely the knowledge that may be based on them: theoretical philosophy, teleology, and practical philosophy, of which the second is, to be sure, the least rich in a priori grounds of determination. I hope to have a manuscript on this completed though not in print by Easter; it will be entitled "The Critique of Taste." (AK 10:514–15)

[5] Guyer, "Beauty, Freedom, and Morality," and Julian Wuerth, *Kant on Mind, Action, and Ethics* (Oxford: Oxford University Press, 2014).

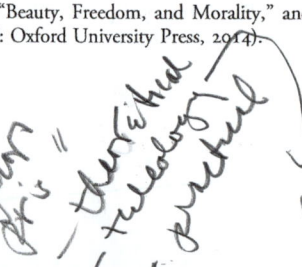

"*A new sort of a priori principles*" 109

As Paul Guyer has rightly noted, this account of the origin of the third *Critique* involves three key claims.[6] First, Kant claims to have discovered an unforeseen fertility in his general account of humans' "mental powers." By reflecting on that general account, he "discovered a new sort of a priori principles." Somehow, his psychological taxonomy of mental powers helped him see a possibility he had not previously seen and thereby helped him solve a problem he had not previously solved. Second, Kant makes clear what precisely this problem was, that is, to find "a priori principles" for "the faculty of feeling pleasure and displeasure." His failure to find such principles had prevented him from writing such a *Critique* earlier, but his psychological taxonomy "put [him] on the path" to find them. Finally, he claims that "teleology" was the key to such a priori principles.

In this chapter, I argue that the most important factor for bringing Kant to the insights of the third *Critique* is the discovery of a new way to make use of his psychological taxonomies to open a path to further philosophical discovery. In focusing on this point, my interpretation differs from that recently offered by Guyer, who claims that the only really important new element is the connection between aesthetics and teleology. I argue, in fact, that it was precisely by drawing on his psychological taxonomy of mental powers that Kant was able to make this connection. In laying out this story, I start with the second point, Kant's effort to find an a priori principle governing aesthetic feeling. I then turn to a brief explanation of Kant's psychological taxonomy of mental powers, highlighting in particular the key insight to which Kant alludes in his letter to Reinhold, a parallel between the tripartite structure of the soul as a whole and a corresponding tripartite structure of the higher faculty of cognition. Finally, I show how this parallelism with its consequent focus on judgment could have inspired several features of the third *Critique*, including the emphasis on teleology; relatedly, I discuss the important way that Kant unifies three formerly distinct critical projects under the single banner of a critique of *judgment*. I conclude with some remarks about the implications of this story for the relationship between psychology and philosophy in Kant's work.

6.1 A Priori Principles for Feeling and the "Universal Validity" of Aesthetic Judgment

One of the key claims of the letter to Reinhold is that, after having "thought it impossible to find any such principles," Kant suddenly "discovered a new

---

[6] Guyer, "Beauty, Freedom, and Morality," 136–37.

sort of a priori principles, different from those heretofore observed" (AK 10:514). Guyer argues that nothing is particularly new in this discovery: "the lectures on anthropology make it clear as no other sources do that Kant had in fact long considered the possibility and sometimes even asserted that there are *a priori* principles for the feeling of pleasure and displeasure in the form of principles of taste."[7] Or, as he puts it later,

> At the beginning of the 1770s, Kant had already arrived at the idea that a judgment of taste is based on an immediate yet universally and necessarily valid feeling of pleasure in an object, a response that in some sense could even ground an *a priori* judgment.[8]

The possibility of a priori principles for feeling cannot have been the basis for the third *Critique*, Guyer's argument claims, because Kant held that such principles were possible twenty years before the *Critique*.

But Kant's claim to have "thought it impossible to find any such principles" is well supported by his published works from the decade preceding the third *Critique*, as well as from notes and lectures during that period. In the *Critique of Pure Reason*, Kant describes as a "failed hope" the desire of "bringing the critical estimation of the beautiful under principles of reason and elevating its rules to a science," contrasting this with what he then took to be the case, which is that "the putative rules or criteria are merely empirical as far as their sources are concerned, and can therefore never serve as *a priori* rules according to which our judgment of taste must be directed" (A21/B35–36). At the time of the first *Critique*, Kant had not yet considered the possibility of an a priori transcendental critique of *judgment* that would be neither empirical nor subsumed under reason, and thus he despaired of any transcendental analysis of the feeling of the beautiful.

The impossibility of such a priori principles for feeling is confirmed throughout Kant's notes and lectures during this period. In lectures on metaphysics from the mid-1770s, Kant reportedly says, "Taste has its rule, for every universal agreement in a feature is the ground of rules. These rules are not *a priori*, and not in and for themselves, but rather they are empirical, and sensibility must be cognized *a posteriori*" (AK 28:251). And in notes from the late 1760s through the late 1780s, he repeatedly emphasizes that taste is "not to be cognized *a priori*" (R1851 AK 16:137; also see R1787, 1821–23, 1928; AK 16:114, 128–29, 159).

Strikingly, throughout the lectures and notes of the 1770s and 1780s, this emphasis on empirically grounded rules persists alongside Kant's consistent

---

[7] Guyer, "Beauty, Freedom, and Morality," 136.
[8] Guyer, "Beauty, Freedom, and Morality," 138; also see 140–42.

reaffirmation of the "universal validity" of aesthetic feeling (e.g., AK 25:179, 1316, 1325, 28:248–49). Unlike merely private (agreeable) feelings, "the beautiful pleases universally" so that "with the beautiful, we believe and demand that it is pleasing to others as well" (AK 25:1316). Kant even raises the central question of the third *Critique*, "how can a human being pass a judgment according to the universal sense, since he still considers the object according to his private sense?" (AK 28:248). But rather than seeking a priori grounds for this validity, Kant's dominant strategy during the 1770s and 1780s explains rules of taste "borrowed from experience" (AK 25:1326) in terms of pleasures that are "general" within communities. Thus Kant parses the term "*allgemein*" – "universal" or "general" – in terms of what is "social" (*gesellschaftlich*, e.g., AK 25:179, 25:1509) or "communal" (*gemeinschaftlichen*, e.g., AK 28:249) and explains that "out of the intercourse among human beings a communal sense arises which is valid for everyone" (AK 28:249). He distinguishes between "what satisfies ... according to private grounds of the senses of a subject" and taste, which "moderates what is produced [by appetite so] that it please all"; and he emphasizes that "only in the community of others does one have taste" (AK 28:251; also see AK 25:1325–26).

During this period, Kant also experiments with grounding the unique status of taste in the distinction between formal and material features of a sensible representation (e.g., R1891 AK 16:150) or in the basic "laws of sensibility" (R1908 AK 16:154; AK 28:892), and he introduces several key elements of the eventual account of aesthetic pleasure in the third *Critique*, such as the distinctions between agreeable, aesthetic, and moral pleasure, and the notion that "free play" of mental faculties is the source of aesthetic pleasure (CJ 217; AK 25:559–60). Kant's claims that taste is something fundamentally social, based on formal features, and related to a play among faculties, could be combined with belief in an a priori principle, and Kant unites all of these commitments in the third *Critique*. But during the 1770s and 1780s, the notion of a set of *empirical* principles that specify what brings social satisfaction seems to be the focus of Kant's aesthetics. In none of his earlier lectures does one find the appeal to "universal validity *and necessity*" that Kant defends in the third *Critique* (AK 20:225; emphasis added).[9] Even in that third *Critique*, moreover, Kant explains that universality need not imply necessity:

---

[9] Thus it is misleading to claim, about the passage at AK 20:225, that "this claim was part of Kant's view on judgments of taste from the outset of his lectures on anthropology in 1772–73" (Paul Guyer, "Editorial Notes," in *The Cambridge Edition of the Works of Immanuel Kant: The Critique of the*

One says of someone who knows how to entertain his guests with agreeable things (of enjoyment through the senses), so that they are all pleased, that he has taste. But here the universality [*Allgemeinheit*] is understood only comparatively, and in this case there are only **general** [*generale*] rules (like all empirical rules are), not **universal** [*universale*] ones. (CJ 213)

Whereas his early notes and lectures allow for a universality of aesthetic judgment that could be merely general, this passage from the third *Critique* goes on to *contrast* mere empirical generality with true universality, "which the judgment of taste about the beautiful ventures or claims" (CJ 213). Aesthetic feeling is an *exception* to a general prohibition on a priori rules of feeling. The evidence from lectures, notes, and the first *Critique* thus supports Kant's claim that the key shift that made a *Critique of Taste* possible was that he "discovered a new sort of a priori principles."

Further confirmation of Kant's pessimism about a priori principles for aesthetic feeling as late as 1787 comes from the *Critique of Practical Reason*, in which he exposes both his interest in a priori principles for feeling *and* his continued pessimism about finding such principles for taste. Kant's *Critique of Practical Reason*, which focuses on establishing "that there is pure practical reason" (CPR 3), reiterates the first *Critique*'s pessimism about a priori principles of feeling: "pleasure or displeasure cannot of themselves be connected a priori with any representation of an object" (CPR 58). But what is arguably the longest single section of the book (CPR 71–89), titled, "The Incentives of Pure Practical Reason" (CPR 71), actually shows "not the ground from which the moral law . . . supplies an incentive but rather what it effects (or, to put it better, must effect) in the mind insofar as it is an incentive" (CPR 72). And what the moral law effects is a *feeling*. This section of the second *Critique* thus provides a detailed transcendental critique that establishes a priori the necessity, and we might even say the "universal validity," of a certain feeling. And Kant emphasizes, no fewer than eight times in the first eight pages of this section, the fact that through this analysis there is a feeling that we can "show a priori" (CPR 72) or "see a priori" (CPR 73, 74, 80) or "cognize

---

Power of Judgment, ed. Paul Guyer [Cambridge: Cambridge University Press, 2000], 360n17). Guyer's reference to the 1772 Collins lectures (AK 25:181, see Guyer, "Editorial Notes," 360n17, 368n17) does include the aforementioned a priori claim, but neither there nor elsewhere before the *Critique of the Power of Judgment* does Kant use the language of necessity. In fact, in one important early lecture, Kant specifically endorses the view that, while taste judges satisfaction "according to . . . *universally valid* sense," still "the beautiful does not please everyone *necessarily*" (AK 28:249; emphasis added).

completely a priori" (CPR 73, 78) or "know a priori" (CPR 79) or "discover a priori" (CPR 80). Crucially, Kant's claim here is *not* about the moral law itself, the a priori status of which he has emphasized throughout his practical philosophy. Rather, what we discover or cognize or know a priori is "a feeling that is positive" (CPR 79) or the fact "that the moral law can exercise an effect on feeling" (CPR 74). And – crucially for understanding the origin of the third *Critique* – Kant insists that "respect for the moral law is a feeling that is produced by an intellectual ground, and this feeling is *the only one that we can cognize completely a priori* and the necessity of which we can have insight into" (CPR 73; emphasis added). Kant's emphatic concern with giving an a priori proof of the necessity of a particular feeling shows that he has not *lost* his interest in a priori principles for feeling. But the fact that he so decisively limits the scope of this ambition shows that his early hopes about an a priori principle for taste have been abandoned. Moral feeling is his consolation prize for having failed to discover an a priori principle of taste.[10]

In apparent refutation of this argument that Kant's discovery of a priori principles for feeling was genuinely new, Guyer quite rightly draws attention to an important passage from lecture notes in Kant's first anthropology course in 1772, one in which Kant seems already to have the key insight he emphasizes in the third *Critique* – the insight that there is a sort of aesthetic judgment that has a priori principles. Kant reportedly says, "With regard to actual taste I must make the judgment about what pleases universally on the basis of experience, but in regard to ideal taste one can make it a priori" (AK 25:179). As Guyer notes in relation to this passage:

> The early Kant often seems to suppose that all judgments of taste are merely empirical observations about what happens to please people ... The present passage shows that matters are not quite that simple, that Kant recognized as early as 1772–3 that there is at least some sense in which judgments of taste are a priori, and that the innovation of the *Critique of Judgment* cannot lie simply in this assertion, as a hasty reading of the letter to Reinhold might suggest.[11]

Guyer may be over-reading the reference in this set of lecture notes. Lecture notes are not entirely reliable, and in this particular case, variant notes from the same set of lectures transcribed the key term differently

---

[10] Thus when the *Critique of the Power of Judgment* considers and rejects moral arguments for genuinely *affective* a priori principles (see CJ 213; AK 20:206–7), Kant is identifying his earlier efforts in the second *Critique* as insufficient.
[11] Guyer, "Beauty, Freedom, and Morality," 141.

(Parow has "a posteriori" rather than "a priori"; see AK 25:376). Moreover, even if the Collins transcription is reliable (as I think probable), we need not take Kant to claim that taste is "a priori" in the sense relevant to transcendental critique. In the first *Critique*, Kant pointed out that "it is customary to say of many a cognition derived from experiential sources that we are capable of it ... *a priori*, because we do not derive it immediately from experience, but rather from a general rule that we have nevertheless itself borrowed from experience" (B2). And Kant makes precisely the same distinction, with reference to taste in particular, in lectures on empirical psychology from the mid-1770s:

> One could say that some rules of taste are *a priori*; but not immediately *a priori*, rather comparatively, so that these *a priori* rules are themselves grounded in universal rules of experience. E.g., order, proportion, symmetry, harmony in music are rules which I cognize *a priori* and comprehend that they please all; but they are again grounded on universal *a posteriori* rules. (AK 28:251)[12]

Thus Kant says in one fragment from 1776–1778 that with "taste ... one can judge *as it were [gleichsam]* a priori what will please all others," and in another, when he says that "by means of taste something can be judged *a priori* with universal validity," he adds that this is so only for someone with "the ability to perceive that which is touching for all sorts of sensitivities *by means of frequent practice*" (R818 AK 15:365; R856 AK 15:378; emphases added). In these early writings, including the Collins lectures, Kant might well claim for taste merely a comparative sense of "a priori," one ultimately grounded in experience. In that sense, his claim in the third *Critique* that aesthetic feeling has rules that are "*universale*" rather than "*generale*" could represent a shift from seeing feeling as susceptible to a priori rules in a very loose sense (*generale*) to seeing it as susceptible to rules that are a priori in the strict sense (*universale*).

Nonetheless, despite the ambiguity about the term "a priori" in these early lectures, Guyer may be right that, in 1772, Kant held out hope for an a priori principle of taste, one that would justify the universal validity that we take aesthetic feelings to have. Strikingly, this lecture was given about a year after Kant's claim that he was "busy on a work ... [that] will work out in

---

[12] Even in the Collins notes themselves, Kant emphasizes that "one can arrive at [the rules of taste] only through experience" (AK 25:179); what it means that they are "a priori" is that "taste is grounded in humanity" in that "the grounds of judgment are not merely abstracted from experience, but lie in humanity" (AK 25:179, 180). Whether the relevant anthropological claims about humanity will themselves be a priori is left undetermined.

"A new sort of a priori principles" 115

some detail the foundational principles and laws that determine the sensible world together with an outline of what is essential *to the Doctrine of Taste*, of Metaphysics, and of Moral Philosophy" (to Herz, June 7, 1771; AK 10:123; emphasis added). The early 1770s thus represent a period of optimism on Kant's part about the possibilities of *both* a priori principles for feeling *and* a philosophical doctrine of taste. Over the next decade, the attempt to work out "foundational principles" blossomed into the *Critique of Pure Reason*, but during that same period, Kant gave up on the possibility of a corresponding Critique of Taste precisely because no a priori principles for feeling can be found. Guyer might be correct that Kant had an early confidence about finding such a priori principles, which would explain both his optimism in 1771 about a "Doctrine of Taste" and why that *Critique* described his pessimism about such an a priori principle as a "failed hope" (A21/B35). As of 1787, however, this hope for such a priori principles had given way to empirical principles of socially sharable satisfactions.

6.2 From Psychological Taxonomy to Philosophical Insight

In September 1787, Kant delivered to his publishers the *Critique of Practical Reason*, in which he argued that respect for the moral law was the *only* feeling for which there could be an a priori principle.[13] Two months later, he announced to Reinhold the discovery of a "new sort of a priori principles," from which would grow the *Critique of the Power of Judgment*. What brought about this new discovery? Kant claims that the key to his discovery came from "looking back at the general picture of the elements of knowledge and of the mental powers pertaining to them" and in particular something about the "three faculties of mind: ... cognition, ... feeling ..., and ... desire" (AK 10:514). And his first introduction seems to rest his entire confidence about a third *Critique* on this three-faculty theory:

> [S]ince in the analysis of the faculties of the mind in general a feeling of pleasure which is independent of the determination of the faculty of desire ... is incontrovertibly given, the connection ... with the other two faculties in a system ... requires that this feeling of pleasure, like the other two faculties, not rest on merely empirical grounds but also on *a priori* principles. (AK 20:207)

---

[13] See AK 10:494, and Mary J. Gregor, "Critique of Practical Reason: Introduction," in *The Cambridge Edition of the Works of Immanuel Kant: Practical Philosophy*, ed. Mary J. Gregor (Cambridge: Cambridge University Press, 1996), 136.

And so, Kant argues, "a critique of feeling" is both required and possible (AK 20:207). But Guyer rightly claims that "the lectures on anthropology as well as those on logic and metaphysics make it clear that there was nothing new in Kant's tripartite division of the power of the human mind," and Kant had – just a few months earlier – despaired of finding any a priori principle for feeling.[14] So what precisely was new? What did Kant suddenly "look at" that had been implicit but unseen in his psychological taxonomy?

Importantly, Kant does not claim in his letter that anything is new in his psychology as such; what is new is a way of *using* that psychology to find a path to a new a priori principle. But this cannot be the mere fact that there are three faculties and thus three possible domains for normative principles, for Kant had long held that. Fortunately, Kant's letter to Reinhold refers not only to his "three faculties of mind" but also to the "general ... elements of knowledge and ... the mental powers pertaining to them." Given that Kant did not say which "mental powers" he had in mind, one might think "mental powers" and "faculties" refer to the same thing, and that what Kant is claiming to have insight into is the three-faculty conception of soul. But there is another possible referent for "mental powers" here. Throughout his lectures on empirical psychology and anthropology, Kant had long held not only that there are three basic mental faculties, but that each of these – and especially the faculty of cognition – is divided into a lower and a higher faculty, where the "higher" faculties are "self-active" or "spontaneous" (AK 28:228, 584, 29:880). Kant had also long held that the higher faculty of cognition "is threefold: *understanding, power of judgment,* and *reason*" (AK 28:241; also see AK 25:537, 773–74, 1032f., 1296, 1476, 28:863–65, 29:888–90).[15] Thus there are really two different "tripartite" conceptions of mind in Kant. There is a tripartite structure to the soul as a whole, divided into cognition, feeling, and desire, and there is a tripartite conception of the "spontaneous" higher cognitive faculties, divided into understanding, judgment, and reason. Kant's unpublished first introduction to the *Critique of the Power of Judgment* shows how his new insight arose from "looking back" at this *pair* of trichotomies.

---

[14] Guyer, "Beauty, Freedom, and Morality," 136.
[15] Note, too, that Kant often uses the terms "reason" or "the understanding" to refer to the higher mental faculty as a whole, such that reason or the understanding in the broad sense includes reason in the narrow sense, understanding in the narrow sense, and judgment. Kant's placement of the power of judgment (*Urteilskraft*) in the higher cognitive faculty is a notable departure from Baumgarten, who places it in the lower cognitive faculty (see *Metaphysica* §§ 606–9).

"A new sort of a priori principles" 117

> Now the **faculty of cognition** in accordance with concepts has its *a priori* principles in the pure understanding (in the concept of nature), the **faculty of desire**, in pure reason (in its concept of freedom), and there remains among the properties of the mind in general an intermediate faculty or receptivity, namely the **feeling of pleasure and displeasure**, just as there remains among the higher faculties of cognition an intermediate one, the power of judgment. What is more natural than to suspect that the latter will also contain *a priori* principles for the former? (AK 20:207–8)

Kant had never lined up the three powers of higher cognition with the three faculties of the soul in order to find in the former the source of a priori principles for the latter.[16] It was the sudden albeit "natural" suspicion that there might be such a correspondence that provoked the discovery of new a priori principles of judgment that could regulate feeling.

A few developments may have prompted Kant to attend to the connection between his three cognitive powers and his three faculties of soul. For one thing, Kant had moved beyond his early view that understanding and judgment differ from reason in that "reason is the faculty of a priori rules" (AK 28:242; also see AK 25:147, 537), replacing this with a conception of *all* higher faculties as having a priori principles. In the first introduction, Kant makes this strong connection between a priori principles and the higher faculties plain in a particularly salient way:

> [I]f the aesthetic judgment carries [a "universally valid and necessary"] claim with it, then . . . its determining ground must lie **not merely in the feeling** of pleasure and displeasure in itself alone, but **at the same time in a rule** of the higher faculty of cognition, in this case, namely, in the rule of the power of judgment, which is thus legislative with regard to the conditions of reflection *a priori*. (AK 20:225)

A priori principles, Kant now sees, must come from higher cognitive powers, but there is one such power – judgment – that has not yet been

---

[16] Admittedly, Kant had occasionally connected the power of judgment with aesthetic feeling in earlier notes (see especially R1844, 1847; AK 16:135, 136; c. 1776–78), but he had not done so in any systematic way. Even in 1772, when Kant says that "Taste is rare, for to it belongs the power of judgment" (AK 25:178), he is clearly using "judgment" in a colloquial rather than a technical-psychological sense since he shortly thereafter refers to the rules of taste as rules, not of judgment, but of "sensibility" (AK 25:181). There is one important note (R806 AK 15:351–55) in which Kant both connects taste with the power of judgment rather than sense *and* develops the first recorded distinction in his notes between reflecting and determining judgment. Unfortunately, the dating of this note is a complete mess, with a range of possible dates from 1773 to 1788–89. Given the thesis of this chapter, I am in agreement with the editors of the *Cambridge Edition* of the notes and fragments that the presence of these ideas in this note "could [and I would add should] argue for a late dating of this note" (Paul Guyer, "Notes," In *The Cambridge Edition of the Works of Immanuel Kant: Notes and Fragments*, ed. Paul Guyer [Cambridge: Cambridge University Press, 2005], 617n87).

exploited for any such principles. Moreover, for Kant, just such a connection with a higher cognitive power is what would make it possible for aesthetic feeling to be properly a priori, where this now brings both universality *and necessity*:

> [Insofar as aesthetic] judgment ... carries with it a universality and necessity which qualifies it for derivation from a determining ground *a priori* ... the judgment would certainly determine something *a priori* by means of the sensation of pleasure or displeasure, but it would also at the same time determine something *a priori*, through the faculty of cognition (namely, the power of judgment), about the universality of the rule for combining it with a given representation. If, on the contrary, the judgment contained nothing but the relation of the representation to the feeling (without the mediation of a cognitive principle), as is the case in the aesthetic judgment of sense (which is neither a cognitive judgment nor a judgment of reflection), then all aesthetic judgments would belong merely to the empirical department. (AK 20:229)

That is, it is only by being linked with a higher *cognitive* faculty that the faculty of feeling can have an *a priori* principle and thus both universality *and necessity*; for this, his previous "laws of sensibility" (R1908 AK 16:154; AK 25:181, 28:892) simply would not do. And so when Kant opens his published version of the third *Critique* with the apparent repetition of the claim that "the faculty of cognition from *a priori* principles can be called **pure reason**" (CJ 167), he makes clear that what he really means here is a "critique of the [entire] higher pure faculty of cognition" (AK 20:243), which higher faculty is made up of understanding, reason in the narrow sense, and judgment, such that "a critique of pure reason, i.e., of our faculty for judging in accordance with *a priori* principles, would be incomplete if the power of judgment, which also claims to be a faculty of cognition, were not dealt with as a special part of it" (CJ 168). Thus "the present [third] critique ... is concerned" with the question of "whether the **power of judgment** ... also has *a priori* principles" (CJ 168), a question Kant comes to answer solidly in the affirmative.

In addition to opening the sphere of "a priori principles" to include the whole higher faculty, a few months before writing the letter to Reinhold, Kant finished his second *Critique* and completed a major revision of the first. In his new preface to the revised *Critique of Pure Reason*, he emphasized that metaphysics is "secure in its first part, where it concerns itself with concepts *a priori* to which ... objects corresponding to them can be given in experience," that is, when it limits itself to "experience" as a "cognition requiring *the understanding* [emphasis added], whose rule I have to presuppose ... *a priori*" (Bxviii, xvii), but that in terms of theoretical cognition, "we can never get beyond the boundaries of possible experience" despite what "*reason* [emphasis added] necessarily and with every right demands" (Bxx). That is, as he puts it in his preface to the third *Critique*, "the [first] critique, which looks to the faculties of cognition as a whole ... is left with nothing but what the **understanding** prescribes *a priori* as law for nature" (CJ 167). At the same time, in his *Critique of Practical Reason*, he establishes the universal validity of the moral law precisely by grounding this law in *reason*. Moreover, he establishes "the primacy of pure practical reason in its connection with speculative reason" (CPR 119), or as he puts it in the third *Critique*, the fact that "**reason** ... contains constitutive principles *a priori* nowhere except strictly with regard to the **faculty of desire**" (CJ 168). The completion of these two projects thus provided a natural backdrop for Kant to notice the peculiar parallel between the cognitive powers and the faculties of the soul: understanding lays down a priori principles for cognition while reason lays them down for desire. And this could well have prompted the "susp[icion]" (AK 20:208) of a "systematicity" that could "put [him] on the path to recognizing the three parts of philosophy, each of which has its a priori principles" (AK 10:514–15).

What Kant obliquely reports in his letter to Reinhold and makes clear in his first introduction is his new appreciation of the potential fruitfulness of his faculty psychology. In particular, by recognizing the parallel between his tripartite conception of soul and the tripartite structure of the higher cognitive faculty, he comes to see the power of judgment as a possible locus for a priori principles for feeling, corresponding to the ways in which the understanding in the narrow sense provides such principles for cognition and reason provides them for volition (or what Kant calls "the faculty of desire"). This hunch that the power of judgment could prescribe rules for feeling catalyzed a series of further insights that gave rise to the third *Critique*.

6.3 Feeling, Teleology, and Reflective Judgment

Once Kant suspected a parallel between the three higher powers of cognition and his three basic faculties of the soul, he needed to figure out how judgment could have an a priori principle of its own. This problem seemed particularly intractable given Kant's standard definition of judgment as "the faculty of applying concepts in a given case" where "the understanding is the faculty of rules [and] the power of judgment the faculty of applying rules" (AK 25:537, see too A132/B171; AK 28:242, 29:888–89).

On this account of judgment, it looks as though any rules governing judgment will come from the understanding; there is no room for a priori rules of judgment as such. The case here is similar to that Kant describes for hypothetical imperatives in the *Groundwork*, that "when I think of a *hypothetical* imperative in general I do not know beforehand what it will contain; I do not know this until I am given the condition" (G 420). So too it seems that judgment cannot have an a priori principle "beforehand" but can only apply whatever principle it takes from the understanding. Kant specifically highlights this problem in the *Critique of the Power of Judgment*, pointing out that what he there calls "determining" judgment "operates only ... under laws of another faculty (the understanding)" (AK 20:248).[17] Moreover, insofar as judgment is the faculty of applying rules, it seems that there can be no further *rule* for judgment because "in that case one would have to have rules of application, but these would again have to have new rules since their application always presupposes the power of judgment, and it would progress like this to infinity" (AK 25:1297). Judgment must be a mental power that does not have its own rules but applies rules given by the understanding.

In the *Critique of the Power of Judgment*, however, Kant shifts from defining judgment as the faculty of subsuming particulars under given concepts or rules to a subtly more general definition: "the faculty for the **subsumption of the particular** under the universal" (AK 20:201) or "the faculty for thinking of the particular as contained under the universal" (CJ 179). The key move here, particularly subtle in the first introduction and a bit clearer in the published introduction, is a deliberate ambiguity about whether or not the relevant universal is *given*. Thus Kant immediately adds:

> If the universal (the rule, the principle, the law) is given, then the power of judgment, which subsumes the particular under it ..., is **determining**. If, however, only the particular is given, for which the universal is to be found, then the power of judgment is merely **reflecting**. (CJ 179)

The search for an a priori principle of judgment led Kant to see that judgment really has *two* functions, the application of universals to particulars and the discovery *of* universals *from* particulars. While the first takes its

---

[17] There is another problem with taking determining judgment as a source of a priori principles *for feeling*. Kant's rejection of the Wolffian-Baumgartenian identification of aesthetic pleasure as a sort of cognition precluded an account of taste according to which the proper application of a universal (a concept) to a particular could be the source of aesthetic pleasure.

principles from elsewhere and thus cannot properly have a priori principles of its own, the second can, and does, have its a priori principle:

> The reflecting power of judgment, which is under the obligation of ascending from the particular in nature to the universal, therefore requires a principle that it cannot borrow from experience, precisely because it is supposed to ground the unity of all empirical principles ... The reflecting power of judgment, therefore, can only give itself such a transcendental principle as a law, and cannot derive it from anywhere else. (CJ 180)

Kant's recognition of the parallel between the three faculties of soul and the three higher powers of cognition led him to search for a priori principles of judgment. From this search, he discovered not only a new kind of judgment ("reflecting") but also, as he put it in the letter to Reinhold, "a new sort of a priori principles" (AK 10:514).

In the context of his search for an a priori principle of judgment, Kant drew from and revised an important discussion from his recently revised *Critique of Pure Reason*. His discussion of the "hypothetical use of [speculative] reason" (A647/B675) has been widely seen as anticipating the roles Kant eventually assigned to reflecting judgment.[18] There, he strikingly anticipates his distinction between determinative and reflecting judgment:

> If reason is the faculty of deriving the particular from the universal, then: Either the universal is **in itself certain** and given, and only **judgment** is required for subsuming, and the particular is necessarily determined through it. This I call the "apodictic" use of reason. Or the universal is assumed only **problematically**, and it is a mere idea, the particular being certain while the universality of the rule for this consequent is still a problem; then several particular cases, which are all certain, are tested by the rule, to see if they flow from it ... This I will call the "hypothetical" use of reason. (A646–47/B674–75)

As in the *Critique of the Power of Judgment*, it is this hypothetical use of reason that brings with it "a priori ... heuristic principles" (A663/B692). Of course, in the first *Critique*, Kant specifically identifies "judgment" exclusively with what he later calls determining judgment, and the

---

[18] See, e.g., R.-P. Horstmann, "Why Must There Be a Transcendental Deduction in Kant's *Critique of Judgment*?" and Reinhard Brandt, "The Deductions in the *Critique of Judgment*," both in *Kant's Transcendental Deductions*, ed. Eckhart Forster (Stanford, CA: Stanford University Press, 1989); but cf. Rudolf A. Makkreel, *Imagination and Interpretation in Kant: The Hermeneutical Import of the Critique of Judgment* (Chicago: University of Chicago Press, 1990). Note, too, that Kant elsewhere assigned the function of reasoning from the particular to the universal to the "understanding" in contrast to judgment and reason – "understanding draws the general from the particular" (AK 29:890) – and also to "wit" as a distinct cognitive power (see APV 201; A654/B682; for interesting connections between wit, judgment, and aesthetic feeling, cf. AK 25:760, 1262–72).

function of the hypothetical use of reason is not exactly identical to the later roles of reflecting judgment.[19] But the general structure of the account in the third *Critique* is already present. Kant distinguishes between two ways in which particulars are subsumed under universals, in one of which the universal is given and in the other not, and the latter requires its own a priori regulative principles. And in his *Prolegomena* (1783) Kant emphasizes this incompleteness of his arguments in this section, noting that "I have indeed presented this problem as important, but have not attempted its solution" (P 364) and leaves it to the "discretion" of "experts" to decide "how far [each] will take his investigation, when he has been just apprised of what may still need to be done" (P 364n). Kant thus left as an unfinished task of the first *Critique* the job of working out the precise status of the regulative principles that take one from particulars to universals, and this unfinished task provided just the resources he needed to articulate a new a priori principle, albeit now a principle of *judgment* rather than reason.

Moreover, in the second section of this same appendix, when Kant goes on to offer a detailed "transcendental deduction" of the ideas of pure reason, not only does he emphasize their merely regulative status (see A671–72/B699–700) but he describes the function of bringing unity to diverse particulars in terms of "the purposive unity of things" and in particular the "systematic unity, order, and purposiveness of the world's arrangement" (A686/B714; A697/B725). These themes relate directly to the third key point alluded to in Kant's letter to Reinhold: teleology. That letter was sent along with Kant's essay, "On the Use of Teleological Principles in Philosophy" (UTP 158–84), in which he anticipates his argument for an a priori principle of reflective judgment in defending "a need to start from a teleological principle where theory abandons us" (UTP 157) in order to engage in "*methodically* conducted experience" as opposed to "mere empirical groping without a guiding principle" (UTP 161). Strikingly, that essay does not discuss the power of judgment at all. Like the first *Critique*, Kant there describes teleology as one of the "claims of *reason*" or a "demand to which *the understanding* submits only reluctantly" (UTP 160, 159; emphasis added). He even treats teleology as a reluctantly accepted but not merely regulative principle of natural explanation, built into "the concept of an organized being" (UTP 179; also see UTP 169), and he entertains the notion that teleology would be explained with "metaphysics" (UTP 179). During the 1780s, particularly in his race theory and his philosophy of history, Kant

---

[19] Makkreel, *Imagination and Interpretation in Kant*, 57–58.

made use of teleological principles as organizing principles of empirical investigation into human beings.

As Kant sought to articulate the nature of reflecting judgment, it was natural to draw on these other contexts in which he had discussed a priori teleological principles governing the investigation of nature. The teleology that made possible methodical observation (UTP 161), the "purposive unity of things" (A696/B714), and the "presupposed" "sameness... in the manifold of possible experience" (A654/B682) could all be seen as different articulations of the a priori principle governing reflecting judgment, a teleological "principle [that] can be nothing other than this: that ... particular empirical laws ... must be considered in terms of the sort of unity they would have if an understanding ... [had] given them for the sake of our faculty of cognition, in order to make possible a system of experience" (CJ 180).

But even if the third higher power of cognition – judgment – had its own a priori principle (teleology), Kant needed to connect this principle – and this cognitive power – with the faculty of *feeling*. As Guyer notes in the context of his own emphasis on teleology, it is precisely the "intimate connection between aesthetics and teleology" that is "unprecedented."[20] On my account, what is really new is a systematic connection between (aesthetic) feeling and judgment. The initial *provocation* to this connection came from an analogy, that just as there are three faculties, there are three higher powers.[21] Kant emphasizes this analogy throughout both introductions to his *Critique of the Power of Judgment* (see CJ 176–77; AK 20:207–8). But a mere analogy is insufficient to *justify* the claim that judgment's a priori principle is a principle *for the faculty of feeling*. In fact, the arguments from both the first *Critique* and his "Teleological Principles" essay suggest that the relevant principle governs the *cognitive* faculty – albeit regulatively – rather than feeling per se. But in the third *Critique*, Kant goes so far as to say that "the power of judgment's concept of a purposiveness of nature" is "a constitutive principle with regard to the feeling of pleasure or displeasure" (CJ 197) and that "[t]he representation of a subjective purposiveness of an object is even *identical with* the feeling of pleasure" (AK 20:228; emphasis added). How can Kant philosophically justify such a tight connection between reflecting judgment and the faculty of feeling?

---

[20] Guyer, "Beauty, Freedom, and Morality," 136.
[21] Kant also draws on another important analogy, that just as feeling is the "intermediary" between cognition and desire, so too judgment is intermediate between the understanding and reason.

Judgment closely relates to feeling in at least three important ways. First, both judgment and feeling are "subjective." Second, judgment is an activity that aims for an end (subsumption of the particular under the universal), and "the attainment of every end is combined with the feeling of pleasure" (CJ 187). Finally, the relevant power of judgment is *reflecting*, and not only had Kant long associated aesthetic feeling with reflection, but the notion of reflecting implies *activity* of cognitive powers; as such, it would be intrinsically linked to the feeling of pleasure, which Kant identifies with the "feeling of the promotion of life" (AK 28:586; cf. CPR 9n; CJ 204; APV 231; AK 15:246, 15:252, 16:133, 25:167–68, 181, 1501, 28:247, 586, 29:891).

First, then, reflecting judgment is uniquely well suited to govern feeling because, like feeling, it is subjective. In the first *Critique*, Kant had already insisted that the hypothetical uses of reason were merely "subjective" (A680/B708), and judgment had long been considered subjective, at least in the sense that it "cannot be learned" but "merely exercised" (AK 25:1297). Kant had long treated the faculty of feeling as the subjective faculty par excellence, that wholly "subjective representation" (AK 28:247). And aesthetic feeling was *particularly* subjective: "The beautiful is thus not the relation of cognition to the object, but rather to the subject" (AK 28:247). Kant rejected Baumgarten's placement of the faculty of feeling *within* his general account of the cognitive faculty (§ 655, Fugate 237) by insisting that "the faculty of pleasure and displeasure is no faculty of cognition, but rather is wholly distinguished from it" (AK 28:245) because "with pleasure and displeasure what matters is not the object, but rather *how* the object affects the mind" (AK 28:246). He picks up this theme in the third *Critique* to argue that this "purely subjective" nature of feeling ensured that any a priori principle of judgment, even if "constitutive" for feeling, would be "only ... a regulative principle of the faculty of cognition" (CJ 197). Even more importantly, in his first introduction to the *Critique of the Power of Judgment*, Kant argues that what primarily indicates "a certain suitability of the power of judgment to serve as the determining ground for the feeling of pleasure" is that "the power of judgment is related solely to the subject" and the "feeling of pleasure and displeasure is only the receptivity of a determination of the subject" (AK 20:208; cf. CJ 189). Precisely because judgment is the only purely subjective cognitive power and feeling is the only purely subjective faculty, "if the power of judgment is to determine anything for itself alone, it could not be anything other than the feeling of pleasure, and conversely, if the latter is to have an *a priori* principle at all, it will be found only in the power of judgment" (AK 20:208).

In the published introduction, Kant takes this argument further, showing how reflecting judgment in particular relates to the faculty of feeling precisely through its teleological principle:

> [T]he subjective aspect in a representation **which cannot become an element of cognition at all** is the **pleasure or displeasure** connected with it ... Now the purposiveness of a thing, insofar as it is represented in perception, is also not a property of the object itself ... Thus the purposiveness that precedes the cognition of an object ... is the subjective aspect of it that cannot become an element of cognition at all. The object is therefore called purposive in this case only because its representation is immediately connected with the feeling of pleasure. (CJ 189)

The a priori principle of *reflecting* judgment is a teleology that *precedes* any cognition of the object, a teleological suitability of the object *for us* and our faculties of cognition, that is, subjectively. But then this teleological principle cannot regulate any *objective* faculty. Purposiveness, properly speaking, is *felt* rather than cognized or desired. So the a priori principle of reflecting judgment, teleology, can only be a principle for the faculty of feeling.

Moreover, and this takes us to the second justification for connecting judgment with feeling, reflecting judgment has a goal-directed character in that it directs the understanding toward "an end that is necessary for it, namely to introduce unity of principles into [the multiplicity of nature]" (CJ 187). But for Kant, "the attainment of every end is combined with the feeling of pleasure" (CJ 187), so if reflective judgment gives an a priori aim valid for everyone, "then the feeling of pleasure is also determined through a ground that is a priori and valid for everyone" (CJ 187). The a priori principle of reflective judgment that makes possible the search for systematicity in our understanding of nature thus provides the first guide to a transcendental anthropology of feeling, since it proposes a necessary *end* for all human beings – unifying particulars under increasingly general laws – the attainment of which is a necessary and universal basis of pleasure for human beings. The presumption of purposiveness in nature grounds a necessary pleasure in actually discovering such purposiveness.

Paul Guyer takes this argument for a connection between pleasure and reflecting judgment to be the primary basis for Kant's posited connection: "Essentially, Kant finally connects pleasure to the faculty of reflective judgment by the theory that all pleasure results from the fulfillment of some aim of the subject."[22] But Henry Allison has rightly shown serious

---

[22] Paul Guyer, *Kant and the Claims of Taste*, 2nd ed. (Cambridge: Cambridge University Press, 1997), 70.

problems with this view, including the fact – acknowledged by Guyer – that Kant nowhere here says that all pleasure requires the attainment of an end (but rather that all attainment of an end brings pleasure) and especially that reading *aesthetic* pleasure under this rubric conflicts with Kant's core claim that such pleasures are "disinterested."[23] Allison then reads this discussion of pleasure as the attainment of a necessary end as a "transitional section" in the introduction, "intended as a bridge between the initial discussion of logical ... purposiveness ... and the central concerns with judgments of taste."[24]

My own suspicion is that this argument is transitional in another sense as well. As Kant sought a priori principles for the faculty of feeling, he first – in the second *Critique* – settled for respect for the moral law as the only possible feeling that could have an a priori basis. Once he decided that judgment might provide for a priori principles and developed the notion of reflecting judgment, he (relatively) quickly discovered a new feeling of pleasure for which he could give a new a priori argument, one closely akin to that in the second *Critique*. Just as the morally necessary subordination of our faculty of desire to a priori principles of reason can prompt feelings of pleasure (and displeasure), so too the epistemically necessary subordination of our faculty of cognition to an a priori principle of judgment can prompt feelings of pleasure. And because both principles are a priori necessary, so too are the respective feelings. What we have in the introduction to the *Critique of the Power of Judgment* is yet another consolation prize, one closer to the ultimate goal of an a priori principle for *aesthetic* feeling, but not quite there yet.

What finally took Kant all the way was a third important connection between reflecting judgment and (aesthetic) feeling. The reflecting power of judgment is specifically a judgment involved in *reflection*, and Kant had long associated reflection with the aesthetic pleasure distinctive of taste: "In everything beautiful, the object must please through reflection in itself, not through impression" (R851 AK 15:376). Connecting judgment with (aesthetic) reflection allowed Kant to move from a concept of the hypothetical use of reason as a relation among concepts of the understanding (subsuming more particular ones under more general ones) to a broader notion of reflecting judgment as a subsumption of particulars, including those that may be preconceptual. And this allowed him to integrate the

---

[23] Henry E. Allison, *Kant's Theory of Taste: A Reading of the Critique of Aesthetic Judgment* (Cambridge: Cambridge University Press, 2001), 56–57.
[24] Allison, *Kant's Theory of Taste*, 57.

sort of reflection involved in the (successful) efforts to bring systematic unity to particulars with the reflection involved in aesthetic judging. And it allowed him to incorporate the notion of a "free play" among faculties, which he had used to make sense of aesthetic pleasure, into his account of reflective judgment. Thus Kant transforms earlier claims that aesthetic judgment is a matter of "intuition" or "laws of sensibility" into the claim that in aesthetic pleasure "the pleasure can express nothing but the suitability [of the form of an object of intuition] to the cognitive faculties that are in play ... and thus merely a subjective purposiveness" (CJ 189–90; also see 20:223–25). The effort to bring a given representation under a concept employs the a priori principle of reflective judgment according to which manifold particulars *can* be so subsumed, and the very same a priori principle allows for taking aesthetic pleasure in the conformity of given "forms in the imagination" to one's "faculty for relating intuitions to concept" (CJ 190). Hence is born a free play between the imagination – as the locus of "intuitions" or "sensibility" – and the understanding, which play is regulated by an a priori principle of reflective judgment.

Once Kant sees that judgment can provide an a priori principle governing the activity of reflection, he can straightforwardly tie judgment to pleasure. He standardly gives two related definitions of pleasure, both of which are evident in the activity of reflection. Pleasure is, on the one hand, "[t]he consciousness of the causality of a representation with respect to the state of the subject, **for maintaining** it in that state" (CJ 220; cf. AK 20:230, 15:241; 25:459, 785, 28:247, 586, 29:890; MM 212; APV 231).[25] Reflecting judgment, governed by its a priori principle, sustains a state of interaction among imagination and the understanding. And in the case of properly aesthetic reflection, there is no limit to how long this state can be maintained. On the other hand, pleasure is also "*the representation of the agreement of an object or of an action with the subjective conditions of life*" (CPR 9n; cf. CJ 204; APV 231, 15:246, 15:252, 16:133, 25:167–68, 181, 1501, 28:247, 586, 29:891). "Life" – the feeling of which frames the whole project of the third *Critique* (see CJ 204) – is synonymous with the activity of "the entire power of the

---

[25] Melissa Zinkin ("Kant and the Pleasure of 'Mere Reflection,'" *Inquiry* 55, no. 5 (2012): 433–53) has rightly emphasized this definition of pleasure, and she also provides an excellent overview of recent accounts of the relationship between judgment and feeling in the third *Critique* (also see Hannah Ginsborg, "Kant's Aesthetics and Teleology," *Stanford Encyclopedia of Philosophy*, February 13, 2013), though my account differs from hers in seeing pleasure as the consciousness *of* a state that continues rather than a consciousness by which a state continues.

mind" (AK 28:247) and in particular a power of spontaneity by which "something... determines itself from inner grounds" (AK 28:765). Reflection consists precisely in an intense activity of free play among powers of mind. Thus it is the "purposiveness of the object with regard to the cognitive faculties of the subject," in that the object gives rise to the spontaneous activity of those powers, that justifies the "universal validity" of aesthetic feeling, the judgment that "pleasure is ... necessarily combined" with reflection on such an object (CJ 190).[26] Because pleasure involves consciousness of a mental state that is both self-perpetuating and involves the activity of one's powers, the ongoing activity of mental powers in reflection necessarily brings a feeling of pleasure. And because this ongoing activity is governed by an a priori principle of purposiveness, that principle governs the faculty of (aesthetic) feeling.

Once Kant turned to judgment as a possible source for a priori principles governing the faculty of feeling, he drew on the resources of the first *Critique* and his essays on teleology, along with his earlier conjectures about the role of reflection and the free play of faculties as grounds of taste, to articulate a new sort of "reflecting" judgment. Unlike what he came to call "determining judgment," reflective judgment has rules of its own. These rules are subjective and thus particularly well suited to govern the faculty of pleasure. And they are rules of *reflection*, that ongoing activity of mental powers the consciousness of which just *is* a sort of pleasure.

6.4 Conclusion

In his 1787 letter to Reinhold, Kant bears witness to an important role for his faculty psychology in generating the insights that led to the third *Critique*. For as long as he held a three-faculty theory of the soul, Kant sought normative principles governing the faculty of feeling, and at some periods he held out hope for *a priori* normative principles. At the time of the first edition of the first *Critique*, he had given up on any such principles. While writing the second, he took moral feeling to be the only feeling one could argue for a priori. But having completed those *Critiques*, and particularly given his recognition that the understanding governs cognition while reason governs volition, Kant saw in his faculty psychology

---

[26] I thank Kristi Sweet for comments in which she rightly pointed out both the prominence of the *Lebensgefühl* for the whole *Critique* and the role that *freedom* plays in Kant's account of life. These comments enriched this paragraph and helped me see afresh how the pleasure of a judgment of taste is a feeling of our own cognitive freedom.

a possible new route to a priori principles for aesthetic feeling. By lining up the three powers of higher cognition with his three faculties, he was invited to consider whether the power of *judgment* might provide the a priori principles for (aesthetic) feeling. This invitation bore fruit in a new kind of judgment – reflecting – and a "new sort of a priori principles."

This story of the origin of the third *Critique* also suggests a new sort of way in which systematicity at the level of psychology can bear fruit in philosophy. On the one hand, philosophical naturalisms of various kinds engage in "philosophical investigations [that] are not superior to ... investigations in the natural sciences but ... [that] clarify and unify the often warring [natural scientific] perspectives into a single vision of the universe."[27] On the other hand, I have argued that, for Kant, and particularly in his pragmatic anthropology, "transcendental analyses provide a priori normative principles for our human powers, and empirical [psychology] shows how to cultivate powers that conform to these norms."[28] What Kant's letter to Reinhold suggests is a more fluid interaction between empirical psychology and transcendental philosophy, according to which normative concerns can prompt psychological claims and these psychological claims in turn inspire fruitful philosophical reflection, but where each requires *justification* within the terms of its own sphere. In this particular case, the "universal validity" of aesthetic feeling, a properly philosophical concern, helped Kant carve out a place for a separate faculty of feeling, a claim that was justified empirically in part through the empirical possibility of human beings having (aesthetic) feelings that are neither merely cognitive nor volitional (see especially AK 29:877–78). This empirical taxonomy of mental powers in turn provided a path for transcendental critique, even though this critique could not be justified *merely* on empirical-psychological grounds.

---

[27] Daniel C. Dennett, *Freedom Evolves* (New York: Penguin, 2004), 15.
[28] Patrick R. Frierson, *Kant's Empirical Psychology* (Cambridge: Cambridge University Press, 2014), 128–29.

7

Between Cognition and Morality
Pleasure as "Transition" in Kant's Critical System

Kristi Sweet

Pleasure can be said in many ways. At least, the pleasure we take in the beautiful can. Kant's "Critique of Aesthetic Judgment" offers an extended meditation on the pleasure involved in a judgment of taste; in so doing, Kant develops many ways to examine, define, explain, and name this pleasure. The four moments of the "Analytic" are discrete, yet obviously interrelated, investigations into aspects of this feeling; Kant's analysis exceeds even this, however. The multiplicity of ways of attending to this pleasure is a function not only of how it is constituted, but also the distinctive relation we have to it, and the unique place it occupies in our system of cognition and moral life. That this is so is evidenced not only in the text itself and its myriad engagements with and approaches to delineating this pleasure, but also in the diversity of scholarship that treats the topic. This diversity is not solely disagreement; rather, the diversity also stems from the varied legitimate angles from which one can get at the structure of or role of this pleasure.

I will not, then, pretend to have something like the final word on the pleasurable feeling we find in ourselves in a judgment of taste. I will, however, suggest a way to understand this feeling that situates it in Kant's larger philosophical project. To this end, I take up pleasure insofar as it can be seen to fulfill Kant's promise that in the third *Critique* he provides for us the necessary "transition" between the theoretical and practical spheres. It is in the third *Critique* that Kant announces that the "[f]eeling of pleasure and displeasure" constitutes a faculty of the mind with its own principle, thus finally admitting of a critique at all (a proposition he had earlier rejected).[1] With this, he expressly conceives of the third *Critique* in relation to its role in his philosophical system and in relation, then, to the principal two spheres of philosophical inquiry.

---

[1] In Chapter 6, Patrick Frierson offers an excellent account of how this came to be for Kant.

While Kant is explicit *that* a transition is needed, he is less clear about what is actually required to effect the transition he has in mind. In this essay, I develop what I take to be necessary for a transition to be possible between the theoretical and practical spheres, between nature and freedom. I argue that Kant has in mind an independent and autonomous sphere that, in virtue of a kind of kinship – what I call a homology – with each of the other two spheres, can mediate between them. Even more than this, Kant suggests that this mediating role is played in virtue of forming a kind of ground common to the other two spheres. To show this, I turn to the underappreciated sections on territory and domain in the introduction to the text. I then turn to how the feeling of pleasure in the beautiful functions as a grounding and mediating sphere of experience. It does this, I suggest, because it is constituted by the *mere* or *pure form* of the other two spheres; this is to say that the pleasure in the beautiful bears the same essential structure as both cognition and morality. Pleasure in the beautiful bears the mere form or structure of cognition insofar as it announces a general accord between an object represented and our faculties of cognition. Pleasure in the beautiful bears the mere form or structure of morality insofar as it presents itself as a kind of universality – one that comes with a demand that involves taking account of all human beings. This comes out most forcefully in Kant's nomination of the feeling of pleasure in the judgment of taste as a *sensus communis*. That the feeling of pleasure in a judgment of taste embodies the pure form or basic structure of *both* cognition and morality is what allows it to offer a transition between these two otherwise heterogeneous spheres.

7.1 On the Need for a Transition

We can motivate the import of pleasure as a transitional feeling if we first understand Kant's own insistence on the importance of a transition for his critical philosophy. Kant introduces the third *Critique* by announcing the need for a transition between the practical and theoretical spheres – between freedom and nature, respectively. This need has a twofold resonance. In one regard, the transition is one in which we have a practical interest: the transition between freedom and nature is one on which the realization of the ends of freedom depends. In another regard, the transition is one of even broader existential and philosophical significance. In this latter regard, the issue is one not driven by some arcane or abstract desire for systematicity. It is, as Kant's contemporaries and immediate successors rightly discerned, a matter of whether the human being is a unified or an irretrievably fractured subject.[2] If our spheres of experience remain intractably disconnected, and even at odds, then the human being remains permanently split between two worlds. As Kant delineates these spheres of experience by way of the faculties that govern them, his account of judgment and the pleasure constituting it thus predictably focuses on the relations of the faculties at stake in this very issue. Kant's emphasis on the question of philosophical systematicity, then, is consanguine with the issue of a fractured or unified subject and cannot be dissociated from its existential import.

Much of the literature that addresses the transitional character of the third *Critique* and the matter it treats takes its point of entry as the practical interest that Kant announces.[3] The need Kant identifies in this vein is this: human freedom has ends that reason demands it realize in the natural order. Freedom, though, has a causality fundamentally different from that we find in nature. While nature operates under the auspices of a mechanistic or conditioned causality, freedom is unconditioned and teleological. Whether freedom can then have effects in the natural order – and specifically, whether the natural order can be transformed into a rational world that is fit for us, as reason demands, becomes a serious issue for the rational consistency of pursuing the good. We need to think, Kant argues, that nature is capable of being transformed by our free activity. Hence, the famous and oft-quoted passage from the introduction to the text on the "incalculable gulf":

> Now although there is an incalculable gulf fixed between the domain of the concept of nature, as the sensible, and the domain of the concept of freedom, as the supersensible, so that from the former to the latter (thus by means of the theoretical use of reason) no transition is possible, just as if

---

[2] We can think here in particular of Schiller, whose concern with this problem in Kant's philosophy led him to develop his aesthetic conception of *Bildung*. The worry can be put this way: "But man can be at odds with himself in a double fashion: either as savage if his feelings rule his principles, or as barbarian if his principles destroy his feelings." While Kant's concern for the holism of the human being does not take shape likes Schiller's will, Schiller's concern nevertheless picks up the dissatisfactory account of a human being whose constitutive parts remain unconnected to each other. Friedrich Schiller, *On the Aesthetic Education of Man* (Mineola, NY: Dover Publications, 2004), 34.

[3] See especially Henry E. Allison, *Kant's Theory of Taste: A Reading of the Critique of Aesthetic Judgment* (Cambridge: Cambridge University Press, 2001), 195–235. While Paul Guyer's work also addresses the issue of systematicity with regard to the systematicity of nature, his larger concerns are articulated clearly throughout *Kant's System of Nature and Freedom: Selected Essays* (Oxford: Oxford University Press, 2005); see esp. 279–81. Klaus Düsing's seminal essay, "Beauty as the Transition from Nature to Freedom in Kant's *Critique of Judgment*," *Noûs* 24, no. 1 (March 1990): 79–92, also forwards the idea that the practical drives the interest in transition. See also Michael Rohlf, "The Transition from Nature to Freedom in Kant's Third *Critique*," *Kant-Studien* 99, no. 3 (2008): 339–60.

there were so many different worlds, the first of which can have no influence on the second: yet the latter **should** have an influence on the former, namely the concept of freedom should make the end that is imposed by its laws real in the sensible world; and nature must consequently also be able to be conceived in such a way that the lawfulness of its form is at least in agreement with the possibility of the ends that are to be realized in it in accordance with the laws of freedom. (CJ 176)

From the perspective of this practical interest, too, we can outline two principal ways we find scholars forwarding how the judgments in the *Critique of Judgment* speak to the problem of "nature ... [being] able to be conceived in such a way that lawfulness of its form is at least in agreement" with the ends of freedom. These are speculative and productive. In the speculative vein, we find authors noting that the third *Critique* bridges the gulf between freedom and nature insofar as we have an encounter with nature that yields something in the neighborhood of knowledge – at the very least, a suggestion that the form of nature is not merely mechanical, but purposive or teleological.[4] In the productive vein of interpretations, we find suggestions that the feeling of pleasure we take in the beautiful actually works in the service of our moral ends. Judgments of taste accomplish something insofar as they actually work on us – on our affective states, primarily – in a way that prepares us for or contributes to the sovereignty of reason in the morally good will.[5] In this, it is our inner nature that is transformed.

While the transition necessitated by the practical interest we have in nature conforming to the demands of freedom is a key part of Kant's interest in transitions, another, perhaps more global need for a transition has largely been underdeveloped in the literature on the third *Critique*. This is the systematic need that is present both with respect to the coherence of our cognitive faculties as well as the system of philosophy (whose two parts are governed by the faculties of understanding and reason). While one may ultimately suggest that since Kant argues for the

---

[4] Two of the most influential books that emphasize the cognitive aspects of how the third *Critique* may complete Kant's system are Paul Guyer, *Kant and the Claims of Taste*, 2nd ed. (Cambridge: Cambridge University Press, 1997) and Rachel Zuckert, *Kant on Beauty and Biology: An Interpretation of the Critique of Judgment* (Cambridge: Cambridge University Press, 2007).
[5] In this vein, see in particular writings that address Kant on culture. Nathan Rotenstreich, "Morality and Culture: A Note on Kant," *History of Philosophy Quarterly* 6, no. 3 (1989): 303–16; Richard Velkley, *Being After Rousseau: Philosophy and Culture in Question* (Chicago: Chicago University Press, 2002); Yirmiyahu Yovel, *Kant and the Philosophy of History* (Princeton, NJ: Princeton University Press, 1980). In addition to this literature, we should note too that crucial to understanding the moral import of the third *Critique* is John H. Zammito, *The Genesis of Kant's Critique of Judgment* (Chicago: University of Chicago Press, 1992).

primacy of practical reason all interest in systematicity is governed by practical interests, we would do well, I think, to acknowledge the apparently independent reasons Kant has for insisting on systematicity for its own sake; such focus will allow the need for transition and the nature of this transition to come out more clearly. Kant writes, "Our cognitive faculty as a whole has two domains, that of the concepts of nature and that of the concept of freedom.... Philosophy is also divided accordingly into the theoretical and the practical" (CJ 174). Both introductions to the text begin with the question of the system and its parts – and both address a philosophical system as well as the system of cognitive faculties. Now, it may be that we come ultimately to think that the systematic consideration is necessary to explore only for the sake of a practical interest. But the way in which the systematic problem is articulated and ultimately solved, for Kant, is independent from its articulation out of the needs of practical reason.

The systematic need for a transition is driven by the demand that the "powers of the mind" should not "constitute only an aggregate" but rather a system (CJ 206). "Such a system," Kant writes, is "highly important for the use of reason in all respects" (CJ 168). Kant has already made his case for a system elsewhere. In the first *Critique* he writes, "Under the government of reason our cognitions cannot at all constitute a rhapsody but must constitute a system, in which alone they can support and advance its essential ends" (A832/B860). Kant's idea of a system is that all of the parts must be related not only to the "unity of the end" but also to each other under the auspices of this end. Kant's description of the relation of the parts of a system will echo his account of an organism later in the third *Critique* – each of the parts work for the sake of the ends of the organism; more than this, each part is connected to the others and cannot be understood or function properly without reference to the entire organism. True understanding of the human being – of our faculties, their uses, and their limits – requires that our faculties be not merely "heaped together" but "articulated" (A836/B864). Indeed, Kant himself makes analogy to an "animal body," and invokes an "organized unity," which he designates as "*articulatio.*" Kant is here borrowing the medical use of the term; "articulate" refers to the connecting of bones at a joint. For a systematic whole, then, the parts must be joined together as bones at a joint. We might even say that the task of a transition between the theoretical and practical spheres is that they must become "jointed" (*gegliedert*). At stake, in any case, in whether there is a transition between the theoretical and practical, between cognition and morality, is whether the human being makes sense or is simply an aggregate of cognitive functions.

Kant suggests that a system becomes articulated – put together – once a transition is discovered between the otherwise heterogeneous spheres of the theoretical and practical. Without a clear picture of how these two spheres can be brought into some kind of relation, philosophy cannot be a science and the human being cannot be thought of as a unified whole. But how exactly these two well-defined spheres can be brought into relation remains elusive – Kant clearly insists on the need for a system and the need for a transition, but he is less clear about how such a transition is effected. Indeed, it may be more accurate to say that he holds a number of things about the transition but develops and explores none of them with any real lucidity or depth.

What Kant does offer is an extended geographical metaphor that allows us to discern how he conceives of the way that the theoretical and practical may be connected to one another through another sphere – the sphere of judgment. While I will not go into great detail analyzing this discussion here, we can see that Kant conceives of the sphere of judgment – specifically, reflective judgment – as occupying a liminal space out beyond the two clearly delineated spheres of cognition and morality, and nature and freedom, and also enabling the success within each of these spheres. Kant delineates his conception of the third *Critique* as providing a transition most elaborately in his discussion of territory and domain in the opening sections of the text.

Kant describes the transitional sphere of judgment – and with this, the feelings of pleasure and displeasure – as both a ground that underlies the two spheres of theoretical and practical philosophy as well as a mediating link between them. In his discussion of the place of judgment and feeling in the critical system, Kant turns to an oft-used set of metaphorics: geographical and geopolitical.[6] He regularly turns to geographical metaphors when describing his system and the "place" of the faculties more generally. Kant consistently invokes: boundaries, surfaces, spheres, planes, domains, nomadism, resting places, horizons, and paths. He even goes so far as to describe David Hume as a "geographer of human reason," a title he most certainly would have used to describe himself (A760/B788). Here,

---

[6] For an insightful examination of a number of Kant's metaphors in the first *Critique*, see David W. Tarbet, "The Fabric of Metaphor in Kant's Critique of Pure Reason," *Journal of the History of Philosophy* 6, no. 3 (1968): 257–70. Only one author goes in-depth in analyzing the territory/domain discussion, however. Rudolf A. Makkreel treats this section of text adeptly in *Orientation and Judgment in Hermeneutics* (Chicago: University of Chicago Press, 2015); see esp. 63–69. He does not, however, develop his reading with an eye toward explicating the role of the third *Critique* in Kant's critical system.

as elsewhere, these metaphors do much heavy lifting, indeed, some of the only lifting, to help us understand how exactly judgment and feeling relate to the other faculties and the critical system. In his discussion, Kant defines territory, first, as the sphere "within which cognition is possible for us" (CJ 174). The territory, though, is not a sphere of legislation over the objects found there. Rather, Kant goes on, there are two domains within the territory where legislation over objects occurs: the theoretical and the practical, which are legislated over by the concepts of nature and freedom, respectively. But what is the relation of these two legislative domains, where determinative cognitive and practical judgments are made, to the broader, more inclusive sphere of judgment and feeling in which they are found?

The territory is the ground upon which the two legislative spheres of cognition and morality are founded. Kant writes that these two domains are "established" (*errichtet*) on the territory of judgment. Territory, as the sphere that contains "the set of objects of all possible experience," is the ground upon which their "legislation is exercised" (CJ 174). He goes on, "Understanding and reason thus have two different legislations on one and the same territory of experience" (CJ 174). The power of judgment, he has already told us, can be "annexed" (*angeschlossen*) to either domain (CJ 168). The German term with which he associates the Latin *territorium* is *Boden* or soil, further highlighting the grounding relation that territory has to the domains that are established on it. The territory of judgment is the entire sphere of objects that are possible for us – they become actual for us, that is, determined, when they are subject to the legislation of either the understanding or reason.

At the same time as the territory of judgment is the ground upon which the spheres of theory and practice are built, it also serves as an "intermediary" or middle term (*Mittelglied*) between them (CJ 168, 177). Kant continually refers the faculty of judgment and its feeling of pleasure as "between" cognition and desire. It is insofar as the power of judgment provides the "meditating concept" (*vermittelnden Begriff*) that it allows for the necessary transition between the two spheres. Kant's conception of the transition between the two spheres comes to light, then, insofar as we think of it quite distinctly as an *Übergang* – a way across. The transition between the theoretical and practical, between cognition and freedom, between knowledge and desire, is affected insofar as there stands a third, mediating thing between these two legislative domains that allows for us to go across from one to the other, and thus for them to be joined. In order for this to be possible, though, something about the third thing must be had in common with each of the other two spheres. There must be some homogeneity between each of the spheres and the territory between them. The problem with theoretical and practical spheres, as Kant articulates it, is that they are constituted by legislative regimes that are fundamentally incompatible – even at odds – with each other. There must, then, be some compatibility between each of these domains not with each other, but with a third sphere that lies between them and thus mediates their relation. As with articulated bones, then, the territory is akin to the space between the bones we name the joint, which allows the bones to maintain their independence yet be joined together into a functional whole.

The territory of judgment and the feeling of pleasure that functions as its "faculty of mind," serves, then, as the mediating link between the theoretical and practical domains. It does this, in part, in virtue of being the ground that also lies between them. In this, the territory of judgment contains the entirety of objects that are possible for us. Some of these objects become subject to and determined by the laws of the understanding and are annexed into the domain of cognition. Some of these objects become subject to and determined by the laws of reason, and are annexed to the domain of moral life. The last set of objects are those that remain out in the territory. These objects – principally the beautiful – are not determined by us, but remain in the sphere of judgment proper. That is, rather than be subject to a rule, it is mere judgment that we employ with these objects. One can say here that it is judgment all the way down, out in the territory; that is, it is mere judgment or judgment in its reflective capacity that brings these objects into the fold of experience as something that is possible for us.

In its pure state – as mere appearance or mere possibility of being for us –the pleasure of the faculty of judgment is enacted. Precisely when these objects appear in their pure possibility for us the faculty of judgment produces a pleasure. As no concept of nature or freedom is determined, we instead find ourselves in a much more indeterminate state: namely, a feeling.[7]

What is crucial about this feeling of pleasure is its ability to mediate between two other spheres in virtue of sharing a basic form or structure with each of them. By a basic or general form or structure, I mean to indicate that the elemental constituent parts of the judgment stand in the same relation; the feeling of pleasure is homologous with both the

---

[7] On why it must be a feeling, namely, a feeling of pleasure, see Melissa Zinkin, "Kant and the Pleasure of 'Mere Reflection,'" *Inquiry* 55, no. 5 (2012): 433–53.

theoretical and practical domains. For instance, in a determinate cognition the faculties involved in cognition (the understanding and imagination) are related to a representation insofar as they agree with or are in accord with it. In a practical judgment, reason judges something to be universally necessary. While the pleasure in a judgment of taste shares the mere form or general structure of these other two domains, though, it remains indeterminate – the relation is the same, but without a concept or law that determines it. In fact, we may do well to name it a kind of predeterminacy, as the pleasure of the judgment of taste suggests determinacy without achieving it. In this way, perhaps, Kant means it to be the ground or territory that is capable of being annexed into either legislative domain; it suggests the possibility, or embodies the mere appearance, of each domain without becoming either.

7.2 The Feeling of Pleasure: Cognitive Accord

If the feeling of pleasure that we find out in the territory must allow for a transition between domains on account of its homology with each, then the pleasure in the beautiful can be said to announce the *general form* or *structure of cognition*. The feeling of pleasure in the beautiful speaks to an accord between objects and our faculties of cognition. In this, it represents the pure or mere form of cognition: what we find out in the territory, while not determinable through a concept or principle, still appears to us as for us. The accord between objects in the territory – beautiful things – and our cognitive faculties can best be discerned in the third moment of the "Analytic of the Beautiful." In purposiveness without purpose, Kant brings together the purposive character of the object with the subjective purposiveness of our pleasurable representation of it. In this unity, Kant posits that the feeling we have in the beautiful is a pleasure in the agreement between the object and our faculties.

Kant claims that every judgment of taste "has nothing but the form of the purposiveness of an object (or of the way of representing it) as its ground" (CJ 221). An object is "purposive," on Kant's account, when "its possibility can only be explained and conceived by us insofar as we assume as its ground a causality in accordance in with ends, i.e., a will that has arranged it so in accordance with the representation of a certain rule" (CJ 221). Objects appear to us as objects, so the claim goes, insofar as we discern in them something distinctive about their form: their form cannot be conceived by us other than as deliberately brought into being through a will. A prior concept – conceived of by a will – is the ground and cause of the object coming into being as what it is. A comb, a glass, a house, for example, all appear to us as having their existence owed to a concept that was brought into being through a will. Those objects – human artifacts – will be determined through this concept and therefore will be annexed into the domain of knowledge.

Out in the territory of judgment, though, objects bear the mere form of purposiveness; they are purposive without a purpose. That is, they appear to us only *as if* they were brought into being through a will. No concept or purpose, however, is discernable in its appearance. In a way, these are not, strictly speaking, *objects*, as they have no purpose or conceptual ground. They are, we can say, things that are object-like. They suggest themselves as objects, but with no determinable purpose or concept. In this, what we find out in the territory is something that is purely possible. That is, what appears to us appears as possibly an object for our cognition. This is not to say that we do not have an empirical concept of what appears to us out in the territory. We can, of course, identify flowers and trees as such. But for Kant, the full determination of something – a true cognition of it – requires that we are able to place it in a longer chain of existence. Namely, we are able to determine something – at least in part – insofar as we can grasp its causality. Grasping something, for Kant, involves not only being able to name what it is, but, with this, being able to represent its ground and thereby bring it into the larger fold of experience.[8]

This purposiveness without a purpose in the object – "the determination of an object as a beautiful one" – Kant goes on to say "is combined with the feeling of pleasure ... [which is] nothing other than the subjective purposiveness in the representation of an object without any end" (CJ 221). Kant goes so far as to say that this subjective purposiveness is what constitutes (*ausmachen*) the feeling of pleasure in the beautiful. He insists on the identification of the feeling of pleasure with this subjective purposiveness: "The consciousness of the merely formal purposiveness in the play of the cognitive powers of the subject in the case of a representation through which an object is given is the pleasure itself." (CJ 222).

How, though, are we to understand subjective purposiveness? Above all, it means that the purpose lies in the subject and not in the object (as in an artifact of human creation). Yet, it is inextricably linked to the purposiveness without a purpose that Kant has already associated with the appearance of beautiful things. Since we do not cognize any objective purposiveness in

---

[8] This is why the territory of judgment is not one of necessity in the way the domain of cognition is; rather, it is identified with contingency.

the thing, he writes, "nothing remains but the subjective purposiveness of representations in the mind of the beholder, which indicates a certain purposiveness of the representational state of the subject" (CJ 227). In this we are reminded that, for Kant, a judgment of taste, strictly speaking, is not a claim about the object. Rather, it is a claim about our feeling as having a certain character, albeit as one that is necessarily linked to – even occasioned by – the thing we have encountered. The representational state of the subject to which Kant is referring in the judgment of taste is the free play of the imagination and understanding. Even more than a free play, though, Kant describes the relation of these two faculties as one of harmony or accord. This "relational attunement," as Gasché aptly names it, is in itself purposive without a purpose – as constituted by a feeling of pleasure, Kant writes, it seeks to maintain "the state of the representation of the mind and the occupation of the cognitive powers without a further aim" (CJ 222).[9] The feeling we have is one of contemplative lingering, with no aim other than its own state of being.

The accord that obtains between the imagination and the understanding reflects the accord that Kant believes we find between things as they appear out in the territory and our cognitive faculties. First, the harmony between the imagination and the understanding is one of agreement (*zusammen stimmen*). Whereas in a determinate cognition the imagination is subsumed under the understanding, in a judgment of taste the two faculties stand in a more open kind of relatedness. The feeling of pleasure we have in a judgment of taste is nothing other than the "animation of both faculties to an activity that is indeterminate but yet ... in unison" (CJ 219). It is, he goes on, the "sensation of the effect that consists of the facilitated play of both powers of the mind, enlivened through mutual agreement" (CJ 219). This accord between the imagination and understanding, and the pleasure in which the accord is manifest, second, betrays a deeper accord between things in the world and our cognitive faculties. The link between a purposiveness without a purpose as the formal quality of the thing is precisely what is represented in the free play. Thus, the feeling of pleasure in a judgment of taste also announces an accord between things in the world and our cognitive faculties. The pleasurable relation between the imagination and understanding, Kant writes, is an "agree[ment] with each other as is requisite for a **cognition in general** [*Erkenntnisse Überhaupt*]" (CJ 218). That such things in the world bring

---

[9] Rodolphe Gasché, *The Idea of Form: Rethinking Kant's Aesthetics* (Stanford, CA: Stanford University Press, 2003), 47.

us a contemplative, indeed cognitive, pleasure, expresses a kind of fittingness for these things and our ways of knowing.

The deeper accord expressed in the feeling of pleasure in a judgment of taste leads us to judge that there is a kind of prior harmony or underlying unity between nature and the faculties of human cognition. We judge what appears as beautiful as "aimed at correspondence with our power of judgment" and "as if selected for our own taste." Kant writes, "For the judgment of taste consists precisely in the fact that it calls a thing beautiful only in accordance with that quality in it by means of which it corresponds with our way of receiving it" (CJ 282). Hence Kant's claim in his notes that beautiful things "indicate that the human being belongs in the world" (AK 16:127). The pure possibility on display in the appearance of things out in the territory and the pleasure that constitutes our encounters with them suggest to us that the way things are is fit for our cognition.

In all of this, what emerges is that the feeling of pleasure we have in a judgment of taste is the feeling we have for the structure of cognition in general. Determinate cognition – knowledge – requires that a concept or rule be determinable in a representation of a given object. In this, a concept is fit for a representation and is able to grasp it fully. In a reflective judgment of taste, no concept is determined; rather, the feeling announces a more general fittingness of things in the world for our faculties. The feeling of pleasure suggests a more general – but also deeper and more grounding – agreement of the way that things are, and our way of knowing. Even though in the beautiful nothing is known, knowability, the possibility of knowing, is promised in the harmonious rapport between the things in the world and the agreement of the faculties it occasions. This agreement of the faculties is, at the same time, a more general and more grounding agreement that ultimately will make possible any determinate agreement found in a cognition.

7.3 The Feeling of Pleasure: Sensus Communis

If the feeling of pleasure is homologous with cognition, it also mirrors the mere form or structure of the moral demand. In the first, it shares a kinship with the theoretical sphere, and in the second, the practical. The name Kant gives the feeling of pleasure we find in the judgment of taste that captures its homology with the practical sphere is sensus communis. The sensus communis, as we shall see, reflects the structure of universality constitutive of the moral order; it does so, though, in mere form only. That is, there is no particular demand (be good!) given. It is universality and demand as such, in the same way that the feeling of pleasure in purposiveness without a purpose is the mere form of cognition.

What, for Kant, is the sensus communis? The term, as Kant certainly understood, has a long philosophical history. His very invocation of it and pains to distinguish his own appropriation of the term suggest as much. But what is the historical usage of the term that would have shaped his desire to use it at all? While the term avowedly has not only a long but also polysemic history, we can discern two broad understandings of it. When Paul Guyer, in a footnote to the introduction of the term in the text, references the Aristotelian and Cartesian traditions, he identifies Kant with the Cartesian use.[10] Interestingly, however, Guyer's description of the Cartesian use still seems to elide broader divergences within uses of the term. Namely, Guyer rightly takes common sense in an epistemological register for both the Aristotelian and Cartesian legacies. While the epistemological designation of the term has a long and rich philosophical trajectory, there is also a second use. The second historical trajectory of this term – which Kant himself references directly, if informally – is decidedly practical in character. These two uses of the term, I think, are both at play in Kant's appropriation of the idea of a sensus communis, and can lead us to a clearer understanding of this complicated yet integral concept in the text.

The epistemological register of the sensus communis is exemplified by the Aristotelian – principally the Thomistic – tradition. While Aristotle only mentions what comes to be called the sensus communis a handful of times, the concept and the problem to which it speaks have a key place in the Aristotelian commentaries. The problem Aristotle took the sensus communis to solve – a problem he inherits from Plato – is that of unifying the various physical senses of the human being. Put simply, it is this: when we perceive objects, something in us must coordinate all of our senses. We are able to perceive that *one* thing looks a certain way, feels a certain way, and makes a certain sound. We do not experience the sensory input in disperse multiplicity, but rather as unified in one object – the same thing is brown, hard, and dings when hit. In the Theaetetus, Socrates notes, "It would be a very strange thing, I must say, if there were a number of perceptions sitting inside us as if we were Wooden Horses, and there were not some single form, soul or whatever one ought to call it, to which all these converge."[11] What each sense senses must be brought together into a

---

[10] See CJ 238n47.
[11] Plato, "Theaetetus," in *Plato: Complete Works*, ed. John M. Cooper (Indianapolis, IN: Hackett Publishing, 1997), 184d.

unity with the other senses for us to experience the world as we do. While Aristotle addresses this issue in a few places, it is principally in *de Anima*, book III, that he addresses the need for something to unify what we perceive in each of our senses.[12] While the exact nature of the "common sense" that he identifies as doing this is up for debate, it is clear that the common sense is what, for him and subsequently for the Aristotelian tradition, brings unity to the otherwise independent senses. Descartes puts it simply, "[W]hen an external sense organ is stimulated by an object, the figure which it receives is conveyed at one and the same moment to another part of the body known as the 'common sense.'"[13]

The practical register of the sensus communis is exemplified by a more diverse – and divergent – lineage. We see the practical aspect in Roman Stoicism, in Vico, in Descartes's notion of good sense, and of course, in the Scottish Enlightenment. This meaning is closest, of course, to our own more colloquial usage of the term. Vico, for instance, argues, "Common sense is a judgment lacking all reflection, felt in common by a whole order, a whole people, a whole nation or the whole of mankind."[14] A plurality of uses of the term is in this register, but I think one crucial feature distinguishes it from the Aristotelian use. For the Aristotelian tradition, the common sense was related principally to the internal machinations of the mind; its purpose was to organize our perceptive capacities into a coherent whole, discerning a unity out of perceptual plurality. For the practical employment of the notion, the use is directed outward – it refers to a sense for how things are outside of you. The externality at stake may be one of a number of things, depending upon the trajectory or philosopher under examination: the way the world is, what other people think, social or communal customs and mores, what will be most efficacious, what is politically expedient, and so on. What these all share is that what is organized or coordinated is worldly in some way; that is, the sensus communis in its practical idiom coordinates us with things outside of ourselves. It is aimed, above all, at *praxis*; a person with common sense, in this idiom, has a good sense of what *to do* in any given situation.

Kant, I submit, actually inherits both of these ways of thinking about the sensus communis in his invocation of the idea. The preservation of the basic movements of each of these ways of thinking about the sensus

---

[12] For an extended treatment of the sensus communis in Aristotle, see Pavel Gregoric, *Aristotle on the Common Sense* (Oxford: Oxford University Press, 2007).
[13] René Descartes, *Rules for the Direction of the Mind*, in *The Philosophical Writings of Descartes*, Vol. 1 (London: Cambridge University Press, 1985), 41.
[14] Giambattista Vico, *Selected Writings* (Cambridge: Cambridge University Press, 1982), 163.

communis is, in part, what makes it such a complicated and almost mysterious idea in Kant's thought. In describing the sensus communis, too, Kant appeals to both of these lineages, leading the reader to some confusion about what he is really up to in these sections of the text. For Kant, the sensus communis is both a sense for the state of one's mind and, at the same time, a sense that other people will feel the same thing, have the same feeling about their own state of mind. In this, it is both a feeling that relates to one's internal state and also a feeling that casts itself out over the whole of humanity.

Kant first introduces the idea of a common sense (*Gemeinsinn*) in the third *Critique*, in the fourth moment of the "Analytic of the Beautiful." He invokes the idea of a common sense as the condition for the possibility of a judgment of taste – that something is *beautiful*, and not merely pleasing *to me*. It is the common sense that allows for the judgment of taste to bridge what, in the history of philosophy prior to Kant, was an ancient divide between two seemingly incompatible or incongruous aspects of experience. That is, in order to belong to the beautiful, it must be pleasing. Yet, pleasure typically is associated with what is merely subjective. To be beautiful, though, is a claim about something in the object that ought to be discerned by others, too. It is the union of both historical senses of the term that allows Kant to bridge these two otherwise irreconcilable features we attribute to beautiful things.[15]

The sensus communis, first, is a feeling of our own mental state; it is the pleasure we feel in the free play of our imagination and understanding. It is, he writes, "the effect of the free play of our cognitive powers" (CJ 238). And when he returns to the sensus communis in the "Deduction," it is a communal sense "if indeed one would use the word 'sense' of an effect of mere reflection on the mind: for there one means by 'sense' the feeling of pleasure" (CJ 295). And again, he calls it "the inner feeling of a purposive state of mind" (CJ 296). In one regard, then, the sensus communis refers us to our own mental state. It is a sense for our own state of mind – we feel ourselves, in our pleasure, to be having a certain kind of feeling. Here, Kant seems simply to be naming the pleasure described above as an accord between subject and object the sensus communis. In keeping with the Aristotelian tradition, too, Kant goes so far as to claim that the elements of the faculty of taste can be "unite[d] ultimately in the idea of a common sense" (CJ 240).

---

[15] For a lucid and detailed commentary on this issue in the text, see Brigitte Sassen, "Common Sense as the Answer to the Paradox of Taste," in *Kant und die Philosophie in weltbürgerlicher Absicht: Akten des XI Internationalen Kant-Kongresses*, Vol. 4 (Berlin: De Gruyter, 2013), 249–59.

The sensus communis, second, is a feeling that refers us to everyone else. What Kant means by this is crucial to understanding what is distinctive about the sensus communis and how it is homologous with the practical sphere. On the one hand, the sensus communis does not refer us to some universal *standpoint*. It is not distinguished in this way as a principally moral perspective. On the other hand, neither does it refer to cultural norms or mores. It is not empirically driven. Kant is quite clear that this is not the use of the term he has in mind: the common sense, he writes, "is essentially different from the common understanding that is sometimes also called common sense (*sensus communis*) since the latter judges not by feeling but always by concepts" (CJ 238). The sensus communis does refer us to a feeling that we take to be shared by others – it is, Kant says, a "common feeling." We may also say, however, that it is a feeling for what is common, what can be shared. When we make a claim about beauty, we are judging that this is the kind of thing others will feel pleasure in as well; the person of good taste is the one who has a good sense for what others will find beautiful, too.

The sensus communis thus has a particular kind of universality. Rather than attain a transcendent perspective as practical reason does, the standpoint of the sensus communis is attained "by putting oneself into the position of everyone else" (CJ 294); it "takes account (a priori) of everyone else's way of representing in thought, in order as it were to hold its judgment up to human reason as a whole" (CJ 294). This is not to say that there are principles or rules appealed to – on the contrary, it is universality per se to which we refer our own judgment. It is the fact that we share structures of experience that creates the conditions for the possibility to communicate in this way – not the presence of any specific concepts, principles, or ideas about what a human being is. To use a Gadamerian turn of phrase, the sensus communis is "concrete universality."[16] It is concretely universal in that the universality of it has an immanence to the human community. Rather than a vertical relation such as we have to the moral law, the universality of the sensus communis is horizontal – it is among human beings and refers precisely to the fact that we hold something in common. As a feeling for what is shared in itself it is not asymptotic, as the moral law or universal right may be seen to be. Rather, it grounds the possibility of community at all.

Even more than this, though, the sensus communis, in being a feeling for something being shared, brings with it a demand; it asserts that

---

[16] Hans-Georg Gadamer, *Truth and Method* (New York: Continuum, 1989), 21.

"everyone **should** agree with it" (CJ 239).[17] It is a peculiarity of this feeling that it is attended by such a demand. It takes shape as a demand because while subjective – it is a feeling, after all – it is also universal, insofar as it has its source in the free play of the cognitive faculties. We thus rightly expect that others will assent to the claim we make about its beauty.

If the sensus communis, in its epistemological register, is what concerns the unity in disparate senses, the sensus communis in its practical register discerns the unity of human beings. When Kant names the pleasure we take in the beautiful a sensus communis, he is suggesting that the pleasure is felt *as something shared*. In this, we feel ourselves displaced into the communal, into something common among all human beings. It is in this way that the pleasure in the beautiful is homologous with the practical sphere. The universality of the judgment of taste is really universality as such. It simply asserts that there is a universal, a shared, a common. Whereas the moral claim is a demand for universality, the judgment of taste presupposes such universality; the judgment of taste discerns and asserts the community of human beings – we have a sense for it. The demand for agreement, then, comes as if from below. We feel the demand as such, but are not subject to (or subjected by) it in the way we are the demand placed on us in practical life.

The feeling of pleasure in the judgment of taste is thus able to function as what mediates between the otherwise disparate spheres of cognition and morality. It does this insofar as it is a third, independent sphere that allows for a way across, between the two spheres. It allows for such a transition because it shares something with each of the two domains at issue, and can thus be accessed from either one (and annexed into either one). The pleasure we take in the beautiful, we saw, is homologous with the theoretical sphere insofar as it announces a general agreement of our faculties with things in the world. It is homologous with the practical sphere insofar as it announces the community of all human beings. While cognition and moral goodness both legislate and thus accomplish something – the determination of a representation, the bringing about of a community – the pleasure in the judgment of taste, in its homology with each domain, suggests the possibility of success in each domain. And, insofar as it is homologous with each domain, it can allow for space in which they are joined together, though not unified.

---

[17] This is why Kant associates the sensus communis with communicability.

8

*What Is It Like to Experience the Beautiful and Sublime?**

Paul Guyer

8.1 Two Views of Pleasure and Pain

Kant often writes of pleasure and displeasure or pain as two distinctive types of feeling, qualitatively or phenomenologically distinct from each other, of course, but qualitatively or phenomenologically identical across all of their own tokens or instances, such instances differing from each other only quantitatively in their intensity and/or duration and etiologically, that is, in their causal histories but not in their contents. A well-known passage in which he writes in this way about pleasure and displeasure – in fact, just about pleasure, although he initially does mention displeasure also – is the final section of the first "Moment of the Analytic of the Beautiful" in the *Critique of the Power of Judgment*, where he states that

> [t]he agreeable, the beautiful, and the good therefore designate three different relations of representations to the feeling of pleasure and displeasure, in relation to which we distinguish objects or kinds of representation from each other. The expressions appropriate to each of these, by means of which one designates the pleasure in each of them, are also not the same: **Agreeable** is that which everyone calls what **gratifies** him; **beautiful**, what merely **pleases** him; **good**, what is **esteemed**, **approved**, i.e., that on which he sets an objective value. (CJ 209–10)

This suggests that the difference among three main cases of pleasure lies not in any quality of the feeling of pleasure, which is the same in each case, but in the way in which that feeling is related to, specifically caused by, its object, and in the status of the judgment about the object that may be

---

* With apologies to Thomas Nagel. Nagel's title is invoked in a discussion of Kant's conception of the human experience of rationality by Birgit Recki, "Wie fühlt man sich als vernünftiges Wesen?" in *Pathos, Affekt, Gefühl: Die Emotionen in den Künsten*, ed. Bernhard Stumpfhaus and Klaus Herding (Berlin: Walter de Gruyter, 2004), 275–94. I am grateful to Katerina Deligiorgi for her helpful comments on an earlier draft of this chapter, even though I have deferred to her only in part, by allowing that a hybrid account of pain might work better than a similar account of pleasure.

147

made given the way in which it causes pleasure: an agreeable object is one that causes the feeling of pleasure solely through sensory stimulus, and on that basis one may say only that the object gratifies oneself (see also CJ 212); a good object is one that causes the feeling of pleasure by being subsumed under some concept of its purpose or end, and on that basis one may ascribe an objective value to it (CJ 207–8); and a beautiful object, on the account that Kant is about to develop, is one that causes the feeling of pleasure through the free play of imagination and understanding that it stimulates, and about which one can say with "a universal voice" that it ought to cause that pleasure in any properly situated subject even though beauty cannot be attributed to the object as if it were an objective property or value (CJ 213–16). This model of the feeling of pleasure has its advantages, above all that it explains Kant's conviction that our judgments of taste are not immune from error (CJ 237): if a judgment of beauty is or is based upon on our assessment that a feeling of pleasure that is qualitatively indistinguishable from all other feelings of pleasure has been caused in one way rather than another, by the free play of imagination and understanding rather than by mere sensory stimulation or by subsumption under the concept of an end, and if causal judgments are empirical judgments, as they are for Kant – "a causal relation ... (among objects of experience) can only ever be cognized *a posteriori*" (CJ 221) – then, since all empirical judgments are liable to error, so are judgments of taste.

On this model, then, Kant seems to treat the feeling of pleasure as it if were a single, phenomenologically distinctive sensation, like the sensation of red or the sound of an oboe, or even more particularly like the sensation of Harvard crimson or the sound of A at 440 Hz on an oboe; the feeling of pain would have to be some equally distinctive but appropriately opposed sensation. This is problematic because it seems implausible that there is a single way that all pleasures feel, and likewise problematic that there is a single way that all pains feel.

But there are also passages in which Kant writes as if pleasure and pain are not feelings at all, and therefore not a single way that all pleasures feel and not a single way that all pains feel, but rather as if pleasure and pain are more like behavioral dispositions than distinctive sensations. Thus, in the first draft of the introduction to the *Critique of the Power of Judgment*, Kant offers as a "transcendental" account (*Erklärung*) of pleasure that it "is a **state** of the mind in which a representation is in agreement with itself, as a ground, either merely for preserving this state (for the state of the powers of the mind reciprocally promoting each other preserves itself), or for producing its object" (AK 20:230–31); pain might correspondingly be described as a state of mind that disposes the mind toward its own cessation, if necessary by the removal or destruction of the object causing it. Now, by calling this account "transcendental" Kant might mean only that it is abstract or as he says "general" (*allgemein*) precisely in that it abstracts from the fact that pleasure and pain are distinctive feelings in order to focus upon their effects, namely that pleasure tends toward its own preservation while pain disposes us to try to stop it. But some passages more explicitly suggest that there is no distinctive way that pleasure and pain feel, rather that pleasure just consists in the disposition to remain in the state one finds pleasing and displeasure just is the disposition to exit that state – in either case, of course, a disposition that might be resisted, as when one knows that a particular pleasure is forbidden or that a particular pain must be suffered. One of the clearest of such passages occurs in Kant's lectures on anthropology, when he points out that when we are enjoying ourselves time passes quickly but that when we are not, it drags:

> The agreeable: everyone strives after it, and the idea of [the] uninterrupted comfort of life is called happiness. – Every discomfort or pain requires us to leave our present condition, and this is its definition. But comfort is the sensation that moves us always to prolong the condition we are in. Enjoyment: every moment we seek it and are driven to leave the condition we are in: hence it seems that we have pain incessantly. One says if time passed really quickly, one was really enjoying oneself. (AK 25:1316)

The crucial point here is that, when we are enjoying ourselves, we do not notice time passing, a fortiori do not experience or at least do not focus upon any special sensation of enjoying ourselves; we just go on doing what we were doing, and may retroactively and reflectively judge that we must have been enjoying ourselves, but do not even need to make such a judgment. When we are in pain or are displeased, we want and typically make efforts to exit that situation, and can hardly fail to notice that we are doing so, thus time seems to pass more slowly. But in neither case is it essential that there be a specific feeling of pleasure or pain.

I will need to say more about what I call Kant's dispositional rather than phenomenological account of pleasure and pain. But now I just want to pose the question I consider in this chapter, which is what Kant's accounts of the experiences of the beautiful and sublime look like if we interpret them along lines suggested by the dispositional rather than phenomenological accounts of pleasure and pain. I argue that interpreting Kant's accounts of the two chief forms of aesthetic experience along these lines allows us to make sense of much of Kant's text while also making his theory a more plausible model of our real-world aesthetic experience. I also argue that interpreting Kant's theory this way will not interfere with his explanation of the fallibility of judgments of taste, which I regard as a sine qua non for any sound theory of judgments of taste and not just for the interpretation of Kant. I also argue that one feature of Kant's dispositional account of pleasure and pain, when we consider it closely, blurs the line that Kant draws between the experiences of the beautiful and the sublime, but that this is not as bad as it might seem.[1]

First, a few more words about the phenomenological model of pleasure and pain.

8.2 The Phenomenological Model of Pleasure and Pain

That pleasure and pain are distinctive kinds of feeling or sensation, like sensations of colors or smells, was a sufficiently widespread view in Kant's time that he may have accepted it without much thought. Francis Hutcheson, with whose work Kant was well acquainted, treated pleasure and pain as sensations that are immediate responses to and accompaniments of other sensations or perceptions more broadly. For him, sensations are states of consciousness that are immediate in the sense of being caused by mechanisms of which we do not have to be aware, and pleasure and pain satisfy this criterion: "Many of our sensitive Perceptions are pleasant, and many painful, immediately, and that without any knowledge of the Cause of this Pleasure or Pain, or how the Objects excite it, or are the Occasions of it; or without seeing to what further Advantage or Detriment the Use of such Objects might tend."[2] He specifically applies this model to the experience of beauty: "This superior Power of Perception is justly called a Sense, because of its Affinity to the other Senses in this, that the Pleasure does not arise from any Knowledge of Principles, Proportions, Causes, or the Usefulness of the Object; but strikes us first with the Idea of Beauty," from which, he further claims, "it plainly appears, 'that some Objects are immediately the Occasions of this Pleasure of Beauty, and that

---

[1] The distinction between what I call phenomenological and dispositional accounts of pleasure is well established in the general literature on pleasure, with the dispositional approach going back at least to Gilbert Ryle in *The Concept of Mind* (London: Hutchinson, 1949). For an extensive discussion, see Leonard D. Katz, "Pleasure," *Stanford Encyclopedia of Philosophy*, June 17, 2016. But this distinction has not made its way into discussion of Kant's aesthetics. Consider the present chapter an initial exploration of the advantages of a dispositional rather than phenomenological approach of pleasure for the interpretation of Kant's aesthetics.

[2] Francis Hutcheson, *An Inquiry into the Original of Our Ideas of Beauty and Virtue* (1725), ed. Wolfgang Leidhold. Rev. ed. (Indianapolis, IN: Liberty Fund, 2008), treatise I, section I, paragraph VI, 20–21.

we have Senses fitted for perceiving it."[3] We have to have "Senses" or a sense "fitted for perceiving" beauty precisely because our pleasure in beauty is a kind of sensation, as is any other pleasure, although it is also what Hutcheson calls a "reflex" or second-order sensation, that is, one that is a response to other, first-order sensations or perceptions, simple sensations like those of colors but more interestingly the complex perception of uniformity amid variety.[4]

Closer to Kant's home, the Berlin academician and aesthetician Johann Georg Sulzer also employed a sensation model of pleasure and pain. In a Prussian Academy "Investigation of the Origin of Agreeable and Disagreeable Sentiments [*Empfindungen*]" delivered in 1751 and 1752, Sulzer took it for granted that "gratification and pain" (*Vergnügen* and *Schmerz*) are sentiments or sensations the instances of which are qualitatively identical although they differ quantitatively. In a statement that could have been a model for some of Kant's own, he wrote:

> I begin by tracing the ideas of gratification and pain back to simple concepts. Both sentiments are infinitely alterable in the different degrees of their strength, and as rivers at different removes from their sources carry different names, so they too receive different designations according to the degrees of their internal magnitude. One and the same sentiment, depending on whether it is stronger or weaker, is called agreeableness, gratification, joy, enchantment; as by contrast the words dissatisfaction, oppression, pain, suffering designate only one kind of disagreeable sentiment from its first to its final degree.

Sulzer continued to offer a causal account of the sentiments of pleasure and pain: "The origin of gratification is nothing other than what we call **comfortableness** [*aisance*]. This comfortableness begins with rest, with a kind of equilibrium in the soul; just as in contrast dissatisfaction begins with **coercion**."[5] Sulzer's expansion of this explanation anticipated Kant's dispositional model of pleasure and pain to an extent, and Sulzer also anticipated Kant's division of pleasures into those in the agreeable, beautiful, and good with his own division of "immediate gratifications" into "three different species," namely the "gratifications of the senses," the "gratifications of the heart," which "take their origin from the moral sentiments," and "the gratifications of the intellectual capacities," which

---
[3] Hutcheson, *Inquiry*, treatise I, section I, paragraphs XIII, XV, 25.
[4] Hutcheson, *Inquiry*, treatise I, section II, paragraph III, 28–29.
[5] Johann Georg Sulzer, "Untersuchung über der angenehmen und unangenehmen Empfindungen," section I, in Johann Georg Sulzer, *Vermischte Philosophische Schriften*, Vol. 1 (Leipzig: Wiedmanns Erben und Reich, 1773), 11.

are the basis for "the taste in the sciences and fine arts."[6] He in turn explained pleasure in beauty, along Hutchesonian lines, as dependent upon "unity in manifoldness, or the manifold brought back to unity."[7] But the point remains that he treated pleasure and pain each as a qualitatively uniform sensation, with their species and instances being differentiated by context and quantity but not by any internal quality or phenomenologically manifest feature.

One departure from this standard model is to be found in Hume, although in a passage in the *Treatise of Human Nature* with which Kant would not have been familiar while formulating his aesthetic theory. Hume clearly treated all cases of pleasure and pain as sentiments or sensations, thus the pleasurable response to beauty is also a sensation: "beauty like wit, cannot be defin'd, but is discern'd only by a taste or sensation," thus "all the effects of these qualities must be deriv'd from the sensations."[8] But at least once he suggested that there might be qualitative distinctions among kinds of pleasures:

> A good composition of music and a bottle of good wine equally produce pleasure; and what is more, their goodness is determin'd merely by the pleasure. But shall we say upon that account, that the wine is harmonious, or the music of a good flavour? In like manner, an inanimate object, and the character of a good person, both of them, give satisfaction; but as the satisfaction is different, that keeps our sentiments concerning them from being confounded, and makes us ascribe virtue to the one, and not to the other. Nor is every sentiment of pleasure or pain, which arises from characters and actions, of that *peculiar* kind, which makes us praise or condemn.[9]

But even here, Hume's text is open to the interpretation that we differentiate our responses to wine and actions, and to actions of rational and nonrational creatures, on the basis of contextual features, not on differences within feelings of pleasure or pain alone; in any case, it is clear that he too treats pleasure and pain as sensations. That is the standard model in Kant's time.

In moral philosophy, Kant treats pleasure and pain as sensations the instances of which may differ quantitatively and etiologically but not phenomenologically. His treatment is reminiscent of Sulzer's. The *Critique of Practical Reason* states that

---

[6] Sulzer, "Untersuchung," section I, 24.   [7] Sulzer, "Untersuchung," section I, 27.
[8] David Hume, *A Treatise of Human Nature*, ed. David Fate and Mary J. Norton (Oxford: Oxford University Press, 2000), book II, part I, section 8, paragraph 2, 195–96.
[9] Hume, *Treatise*, book III, part I, section 2, paragraph 4, 303.

[h]owever dissimilar representations of objects may be – they may be representations of the understanding or even of reason, in contrast to representations of sense – the feeling of pleasure by which alone they properly constitute the determining ground of the will (the agreeableness, the gratification expected from the object, which impels activity to produce it) is nevertheless of one and the same kind only insofar as it can always be cognized only empirically but also insofar as it affects one and the same vital force that is manifested in the faculty of desire, and in this respect can differ only in degree from any other determining ground. (CPR 23)

This might seem to apply only to (promised) pleasures taken as sufficient grounds for actions, in other words to nonmoral pleasures; but Kant makes it clear elsewhere that the difference between pleasure in nonmoral and moral cases of motivation is not any qualitative difference between the feelings of pleasure themselves, but only an etiological difference: namely that pleasure might be either "the cause or effect of ... desire"; if "the determination of the faculty of desire ... is caused and therefore necessarily *preceded* by ... pleasure" or the expectation of it, then "such pleasure is called *desire* in the narrow sense," but "if a pleasure can only follow upon an antecedent determination of the faculty of desire it is an intellectual pleasure, and the interest in the object must be called an interest of reason" (MM 212).[10] But in either case, the pleasure itself is presumed to be a feeling, and always qualitatively the same. "For this very reason pleasure and displeasure cannot be explained more clearly in themselves; instead, one can only specify what results they have in certain circumstances, so as to make them recognizable in practice" (MM 212). In the later terminology of G. E. Moore, Kant treats pleasure and pain as unanalyzable, because they are simple sensations, like the sensations of a color.

Such a conception of pleasure and displeasure then seems to inform Kant's aesthetic theory. In outline, Kant's theory appears to be that a harmonious free play between imagination and understanding, triggered in the simplest cases by the representation of the spatial and/or temporal form of objects, produces and manifests itself to consciousness in an unmixed feeling of pleasure, which, precisely because it has been produced by such a mechanism, involving only cognitive powers common to all human beings, can then be judged to be valid for all potential observers of the object, which is what is asserted by calling the object beautiful. The experience of the sublime, however, is more complex, and seems best

---

[10] For extensive discussion of the question of whether motivation (moral or not) proceeds by occurrent pleasure or the expectation of pleasure, see Iain P. D. Morrisson, *Kant and the Role of Pleasure in Moral Action* (Athens: Ohio University Press, 2008), chaps. 1–2.

characterized as a sequence of feelings of pain and pleasure: the initial experience of something overwhelmingly vast (in the case of the mathematical sublime) or physically threatening (in that of the dynamical sublime) is painful, in the first case because the effort to comprehend it exceeds the capacity of the imagination and in the second case simply because of the imagined harm; but then the feeling of pain is accompanied with one of pleasure as we somehow realize, in the first case, that our own power of reason is setting the imagination the task of comprehension in the first place, and, in the second, that our power to determine our wills by pure practical reason and its moral law is immune to physical threats. It might seem most natural to understand the experience of the sublime as a sequence of pain followed by pleasure, but Kant himself at least sometimes states that the two feelings occur "at the same time" (CJ 257).

A few passages will have to stand in for the many that suggest this picture. The account of the experience of beauty just given is suggested by this passage from the published introduction to the *Critique of the Power of Judgment*:

> [The] apprehension of forms in the imagination can never take place without the reflecting power of judgment, even if unintentionally, at least comparing them to its faculty for relating intuitions to concepts. Now if in this comparison the imagination ... is unintentionally brought into accord with the understanding ... through a given representation and a feeling of pleasure is thereby aroused, then the object must be regarded as purposive for the reflecting power of judgment. ... That object the form of which (not the material aspect of its representation, as sensation) is judged as the ground of a pleasure in the representation of such an object – with its representation this pleasure is also judged to be necessarily combined, not merely for the subject who apprehends this form but for everyone who judges at all. (CJ 190)

Kant's theory seems to be that when the imagination's play with the represented form rather than matter (e.g., shape rather than color; see CJ 225) satisfies the understanding's general demand for unity in its manifolds but without the application of any determinate concept (CJ 214), then a feeling of pleasure is produced, and the judgment of taste or beauty is then the judgment about the feeling of pleasure, that because that feeling has been produced in the way that Kant has described and in no other it may also be ascribed to others as what they too would feel should they also approach the object in a disinterested frame of mind and thus receptive to the free play of their own faculties with it. But since "no other consciousness of" the underlying state of mind, "the facilitated play of both powers of the mind," "is possible except through the sensation of the effect," namely the feeling of pleasure itself (CJ 219), and feelings of pleasure are all qualitatively identical, the judgment that a particular feeling of pleasure is due to the free play of the cognitive powers can only be made indirectly, by excluding other possible sources for it, e.g., a personal interest in the existence of the object (CJ 204–5). That is why judgments of taste, grounded as they are on the causal judgment that the feeling of pleasure is due to this particular cause, are "conditioned" and never certain (CJ 237, 289).

Kant's theory of the sublime is divided into his treatments of the mathematical and the dynamical sublime, and the former is much more detailed than the latter. It is based on the distinction between the "logical" or mathematical and the "aesthetic" comprehension of magnitudes: the former takes place by the reiteration of arbitrarily chosen units, and by this means magnitudes of any size can in principle be comprehended; but the latter is the attempt to take in a magnitude in a single representation or image, and in this case there are limits to the imagination. These limits are exceeded when we encounter something vast and apparently formless in nature, such as the ocean (rather than a mere bay) or the whole Alps (rather than an isolated peak), and since it is always unpleasant to be limited, we experience pain in the perception of such objects; but when we realize (somehow) that it is our own reason that is setting imagination the task of aesthetic comprehension in such cases, there is also a feeling of pleasure at the power of our own reason. Therefore Kant concludes that

> [t]he feeling of the sublime is thus a feeling of displeasure from the inadequacy of the imagination in the aesthetic estimation of magnitude for the estimation by means of reason, and a pleasure that is thereby aroused at the same time from the correspondence of this very judgment of the inadequacy of the greatest sensible faculty in comparison with ideas of reason, insofar as striving for them is nevertheless a law for us. (CJ 257)

Whether the two feelings, of pain and pleasure, are imagined to occur in tandem or in sequence, the point is that the experience of the mathematical sublime seems to consist precisely in these two feelings, and all the rest must be the philosopher's explanation of the etiology of those feelings. For as the simple, unanalyzable feelings that feelings of pleasure and pain are, like sensations of color, they cannot wear their own causal histories on their faces.

Kant does not refer so explicitly to simple feelings of pleasure and pain in his account of the dynamical sublime. He claims rather that overpowering objects in nature arouse fear in us, but can also allow "us to discover within ourselves a capacity for resistance of quite another kind" than mere physical resistance, by means of "which the mind can make palpable to itself the sublimity of its own vocation even over nature" (CJ 261–62). But he comes closer to speaking of a combination of feelings when he explicates this experience as one in which "[t]he **astonishment** bordering on terror, the horror and the awesome shudder, which grip the spectator in viewing mountain ranges towering to the heavens," is combined with the "calmness" of the mind, its feeling of being "superior to nature within us, and thus also that outside us, insofar as it can have an influence on our feeling of well-being" (CJ 269). Feelings of astonishment on the one hand and of well-being on the other might seem to be more complex feelings than simple feelings of pain and pleasure. But on classical accounts of the passions or emotions, they would differ from the simple feelings of pain and pleasure not qualitatively but contextually: in Hobbes, for example, the simple "motions" of "pleasure" or "joy" on the one hand and of "displeasure" or "payne" on the other are diversified by the kinds of hopes or expectations with which they are accompanied.[11] In his treatment of the sublime, Kant seems to be thinking along similar lines, of feelings of astonishment on the one hand and of well-being on the other as particular contextualizations of the basic feelings of pain and pleasure.

Kant makes no mention of the possibility of misjudgment about the sources and thus about the potential intersubjective validity of our feelings of pleasure and pain in the experience of the sublime. This may seem surprising, especially since Kant's explanation of the etiology of our feelings in the experience of the sublime seems highly speculative, and even if true it would seem to call for subjects undergoing the experience to make causal judgments about the origins of their feelings that could easily go awry.[12] How could one be sure, for example, that one was pleased by the immunity of one's pure reason and will from physical threats rather than by the mere fact of one's physical safety from those apparent threats (CJ 262)? But even apart from this epistemological problem, it might be felt that Kant's attempt to explicate the experience of the sublime in terms of the strictly phenomenological model of pleasure and pain is strained. So this may be the point at which to consider whether Kant suggests an alternative model for thinking about pleasure and pain in aesthetic experience.

---

[11] See Thomas Hobbes, *Leviathan* (1651), ed. Richard Tuck (Cambridge: Cambridge University Press, 1991), part 1, chap. 6, 40–41.
[12] For a critical assessment of Kant's account of the sublime, see Malcolm Budd, *The Aesthetic Appreciation of Nature* (Oxford: Clarendon Press, 2002), chap. III.

8.3 The Dispositional Model of Aesthetic Pleasure and Pain

What I have in mind by Kant's suggestion of a dispositional model of pleasure and pain is evinced by a passage such as this, from the beginning of the "Third Moment" of the "Analytic of the Beautiful":

> The consciousness of the causality of a representation with respect to the state of the subject, **for maintaining** it in that state, can here designate in general what is called pleasure; in contrast to which displeasure is that representation that contains the ground for determining the state of the representations to their own opposite (hindering or getting rid of them). (CJ 220)

A pleasurable state is one that disposes the one who has it to continue in that state, while an unpleasant state is a state that the subject is disposed to alter or exit. Kant refers to consciousness of these dispositions, so there is a suggestion that the subject who has one or the other of these dispositions is aware of that fact; but there is no suggestion here that there is a specific way that it always feels to be in one of these states or the other, that there is a specific, always identical way the disposition to continue in one's current state feels and a particular, likewise always identical way the disposition to alter one's state feels. On the simplest version of such an approach, to feel pleasure would just be to feel disposed to continue in one's state, and to feel pain would just be to feel disposed to alter it, whatever either of those states of mind might otherwise feel like. Perhaps the requirement of consciousness could even be satisfied retroactively, as when the person for whom time seems to pass quickly because he is so fully engaged with what he is doing may realize only afterward that he must have been pleased precisely because he was so fully engaged with what he was doing. Likewise, when "We **linger** over the consideration of the beautiful because this consideration strengthens and reproduces itself" (CJ 222), perhaps we become aware that our state is pleasurable only when we reflect on what has been going on – if we do.

Now it might be thought that Kant does not *exclude* that there is a distinctive way that it feels to be disposed to continue in one's state and likewise a distinctive way that it feels to be disposed to alter it: that there is a distinctive way all pleasure feels *and* that such a feeling is always accompanied with the disposition to continue feeling it, and mutatis mutandis for the case of pain. But that there are such phenomenologically distinctive manifestations of pleasure and pain would still be a strong claim to make, and Kant does not make it in a passage like that just quoted from the *Critique of the Power of Judgment*. Moreover, in the passage quoted from the *Anthropology Mrongovius* at the outset of this chapter, Kant said that it is the *definition* (his German uses *Definition*, not *Erklärung*) of discomfort or pain "that it requires us to leave our present condition" (AK 25:1316), and on Kant's theory of definition, according to which a proper definition must include everything essential to its concept and indeed everything essential to recognize an instance of its concept, anything left out of the definition would only be accidentally connected to its object. Thus, if there were a distinctive way in which pleasure or pain always feel, that would be an additional, synthetic claim, which would have to be based on empirical evidence – and Kant makes no attempt to provide such evidence. So we can suppose that at least sometimes he thought that the dispositional model of pleasure and pain was adequate.

Kant does make two additions to the basic model that we should note. The first is his characterization of pleasure as the feeling of *life*, or, we might say, the feeling of being alive. He uses this characterization in the first section of the "Analytic of the Beautiful," when he says that the representation of a beautiful object "is related entirely to the subject, indeed to its feeling of life, under the name of the feeling of pleasure or displeasure" (CJ 204). He repeats it in the anthropology lectures. Thus, in the *Anthropology Friedländer*, from 1775–1776, he states that "[t]he feeling of the promotion of life is enjoyment or pleasure. Life is the consciousness of a free and regular play of all the powers and faculties of the human being. The feeling of the promotion of life is what the feeling of pleasure is, and the feeling of the hindrance of life is displeasure" (AK 25:559). In the *Anthropology Mrongovius*, from the middle of the 1780s, thus closer to the time of the composition of Kant's critiques, he is recorded as saying that "[e]njoyment is the feeling of the promotion of life, pain is the feeling of the hindrance of life" (AK 25:1318). How is this characterization of pleasure and displeasure to be connected to the dispositional model? Through the idea that life is activity, thus that unhindered activity is pleasurable and hindered activity painful, and the further thought that as a matter of life itself one is disposed to continue in activity and to escape from hindrances to activity. Thus the promotion of life is pleasurable as the continuation of activity, and the hindrance to life painful as the hindrance to activity. Kant suggests all this when he states that "[f]reedom is the greatest life of the human being, thereby he exercises his activity without hindrance" (AK 25:560). Here is where Kant may well have been inspired by Sulzer, who had written that "[i]f dissatisfaction naturally arises from the hindered or disturbed activity of the soul, then the mere freedom of effect and the good success of applied powers seem to bring forth only satisfaction and calm, that is the origin or the element of gratification."[13] And all of this is why Kant ultimately locates the pleasure of beauty in the *free play* of our cognitive powers, because play is activity, free play is activity that can continue itself without any determinate concept or rule, and the disposition to continue in such a state is what makes it pleasurable. Thus, "if the mind has a sensation of a free play of its powers, then what produces this free play is an ideal enjoyment" (AK 25:560), that is, an aesthetic pleasure.

The second point to be noted here, however, is that when Kant is attempting to work out the details of this account, as far as he does, he also argues that "[i]n human beings, continuous enjoyment never occurs; rather pain and enjoyment must always alternate" (AK 25:1317). His thought, for which he credits Count Verri, could reach beyond Verri to Jean-Baptiste Du Bos.[14] This is that if we were in a continuous state of enjoyment it would be monotonous and boring, in other words would not feel like a state of activity at all, and would undermine our sense of being alive, therefore our pleasure. Activity has to overcome some sort of resistance in order to be felt as such. "If we were not driven by pain from one condition into another, we would always remain in one condition and do nothing" (AK 25:1317), indeed feel nothing, not even feel alive. The hindrance to activity might take various forms. In the obvious case, it is the need for physical labor, and Kant argues that we can feel pleasure in relaxing from physical labor that we could not feel if we did not have to undertake labor in the first place. But it can also take more abstract or in Kant's terminology "ideal" forms. Thus, the manifold of our intuitions can itself be a hindrance to our mental activity unless we can find a way to unify it, but if we do that by a determinate concept that is ready at hand, the activity will soon be over and boredom will threaten again, while if we somehow manage to do that without such a concept, our activity will be prolonged and with that our pleasure. Similarly, a vast manifold of representations can threaten to overwhelm our intellectual activity, while the representation of overwhelmingly powerful objects can threaten our

---

[13] Sulzer, "Untersuchung," 12.
[14] See Pietro Verri, *Del piacere e del dolore ed altri scritt* (Milan: Feltrinelli, 1964), translated into German in 1777; Jean-Baptiste Du Bos, *Critical Reflections on Poetry, Painting, and Music*, trans. Thomas Nugent, 3 Vols. (London: John Nourse, 1748). For discussion of Kant's response to Verri, see Susan Meld Shell, "Kant's 'True Economy of Human Nature': Rousseau, Count Verri, and the Problem of Happiness," in *Essays on Kant's Anthropology*, ed. Brian Jacobs and Patrick Kain (Cambridge: Cambridge University Press, 2003), 194–229.

life and thus all of our activity; but finding a way to represent such a manifold through our own theoretical reason or thinking of the possibility of the unhampered activity of our pure will in spite of the threat to our empirical will can seem like ways to maintain our activity and thus life itself in the face of these threats, and thus be pleasurable.

In other words, our experiences of the beautiful and sublime can be understood as pleasurable forms of mental activity in the face of potential hindrances to the continued possibility of such activity, without any requirement that unique, phenomenologically distinctive sensations of pleasure or of pain and pleasure, respectively, be part of these experiences. I believe that this model can make good sense of some of Kant's most characteristic descriptions of the experiences of the beautiful and the sublime. In the case of beauty, central passages from the section that Kant calls the "key to the critique of taste" (CJ 216) can be interpreted in this way. Here Kant states that "[t]he powers of cognition that are set into play by [a beautiful] representation are hereby in a free play, since no determinate concept restricts them to a particular rule of cognition. Thus the state of mind in this representation must be that of a feeling of the free play of the powers of representation in a given representation for a cognition in general" (CJ 217). Here Kant suggests that the subject is aware of the free play of her faculties, and if that is a form of activity that the subject is disposed to continue, as she is, then it will by definition be pleasurable, without any need to posit a phenomenologically unique sensation of pleasure. If the activity of comparing the representation of an object to one's cognitive faculties that Kant has described in section VII of the introduction to the *Critique of the Power of Judgment* (CJ 190) be equated with the "merely (aesthetic) judging of the object," then Kant's requirement that this judging "precedes the pleasure in" the object (CJ 218) can be considered to be satisfied by the conceptual priority of the disposition to continued activity to pleasure rather than by such judging causing a separate and distinct sensation of pleasure. Similarly, Kant's further statement that "the animation of both faculties (the imagination and the understanding) to an activity that is indeterminate but yet, through the stimulus of the given representation, in unison ... is the sensation whose universal communicability is postulated by the judgment of taste" (CJ 219) can also be interpreted on this model: the animation of the cognitive powers is their unhindered activity, and that comes with the disposition to its own continuation in which pleasure consists; thus in imputing this activity to others as universally communicable in a judgment of taste one is also imputing pleasure to them, as the judgment of taste does in speaking with its universal voice; but there is no separate and unique sensation of pleasure, and it is the sensation of "animation," not a separate sensation of pleasure, that is imputed to others. It may be noted that this model preserves the conceptual distinction between the judging of the object that leads to pleasure and the judgment about the universal communicability of the pleasure that constitutes the judgment of taste that has always been part of my interpretation of Kant.[15] It just does away with a separate sensation of pleasure intervening between the activity of judging the object and the disposition to continue that activity, on the one hand, and the judgment that the object has pleased by producing such a state and disposition that grounds the assertion of universal communicability in a judgment of taste, on the other.

Kant's thesis in the anthropology lectures that pleasure always presupposes some antecedent pain requires a refinement of this account of the experience of beauty, namely that there must be some sense of challenge from the manifold presented to harmonizing the imagination and understanding in the experience of it and then some sense of having overcome that challenge; moreover, an enduring experience of beauty would have to be one in which there is a continuing or repeated sense of challenge and a continuing or repeated sense of having overcome this challenge. This might in fact be a good way of explaining the difference between an aesthetic object whose beauty holds our interest and one whose beauty quickly fades or becomes cloying – to take an example from the realm of art, the difference between a work that only gradually reveals its beauty, like a late Beethoven quartet, and one that quickly becomes boring, like some piece of Telemann *Tafelmusik* endlessly repeated by your local public classical music station struggling to find some middlebrow market to stay on the air. I will say something more about the implications of this point at the end of the chapter. For the moment, I only want to emphasize that not only does it seem to fit much of our experience of art, it also does so without requiring the positing of a separate sensation of pleasure.

Let us now see how well this dispositional model of aesthetic pleasure fits Kant's account of the sublime. I have already argued that Kant does not refer to phenomenologically unique and distinct feelings of pleasure and pain in his account of the dynamical sublime. Here is a description of the experience of the mathematical sublime that also seems to omit the

---

[15] See Paul Guyer, "Pleasure and Society in Kant's Theory of Taste," in *Essays in Kant's Aesthetics*, ed. Ted Cohen and Paul Guyer (Chicago: University of Chicago Press, 1982), 21–54, and "One Act or Two? Hannah Ginsborg on Aesthetic Judgment," *British Journal of Aesthetics* (forthcoming).

assumption that there are such feelings: "the mind feels itself elevated in its own judging, if, in the consideration of such things" – that is, "shapeless mountain masses towering above one another in wild disorder with their pyramids of ice, or the dark and raging sea" – "without regard to their form, abandoning itself to the imagination and to a reason which, although it is associated with it entirely without any determinate end, merely extends it, it nevertheless finds the entire power of the imagination inadequate to its ideas" (CJ 256). All that we need to understand this passage is the idea that we have a continuing sense of the inadequacy of imagination to the demand of reason, which is by itself unpleasant, yet a continuing disposition to abandon ourselves to a reason that extends our consideration of such things, which is by definition pleasurable. We do not need to posit a separate sensation of pain preceding or accompanying a separate feeling of pleasure; we just need to imagine ourselves torn between the experience of the inadequacy of the imagination, which is painful, and the disposition to continue that experience precisely in order to get a sense of the power of our own reason, which is pleasurable. We can understand Kant's account of the experience of the sublime in terms of competing dispositions rather than competing sensations.

8.4 Conclusion

I offer three points in conclusion. First, I do not want to overstate the contrast between what I call the phenomenological and the dispositional accounts of pleasure and pain, each of which taken by itself might be too extreme. At least in the case of pain, there certainly are distinctive feelings of pain, and our overall state of mind can be described as a disposition to exit the state of suffering such feelings. Nevertheless, even if all toothaches feel more or less the same, differing from each other only in intensity and duration, a toothache does not feel the same as a burned tongue or a stubbed toe, so it might make more sense to think of pain as a family of distinctive types of sensations, all sharing the disposition to exit them. But although we – or at least Kant – might be tempted to think that pleasure and pain are analogous, it is not so clear that this analysis can hold in the case of pleasure: it still seems implausible to suppose that there is a distinctive way that the pleasure of listening to a beautiful opera feels and a different but equally distinctive way that the pleasure of looking at a beautiful painting feels, and that there is a family resemblance among these types of feeling (and perhaps with other kinds of pleasure as well). In particular, Kant's observation that when one is enjoying oneself one does not notice time passing at all continues to militate against the assumption that enjoying oneself necessarily involves noticing a distinctive sensation of pleasure, let alone one that is common to all cases of pleasure. To be sure, some cases of pleasure must involve distinctive sensations, for there is a characteristic way or range of ways that a good Bordeaux tastes, and a different way that a good Burgundy tastes, and each is enjoyable; but it is less plausible that there is a distinctive feeling of pleasure, whether always the same or not, *in addition to* the characteristic Bordeaux taste and Burgundy taste. So perhaps there is room for an account of pain that combines a phenomenological and a dispositional aspect, but it is less clear that this will be so for an account of pleasure.

Thus, at least in the case of pleasure, the dispositional model of aesthetic experience makes more sense of that experience than does what I called the phenomenological model. As with the pleasures of wine, to stay with Hume's example, there will no doubt be a variety of sensations involved in any positive aesthetic experience, and even some characteristic sensations – no doubt Siegfried's motif sounds a distinctive way, and Yves Klein blue looks a distinctive way. But this does not imply that there is a separate feeling of pleasure in aesthetic experience, whether common to all or varying in type among them. Do I really need to posit some distinctive sensation of pleasure that is common to my pleasant experience of Beethoven quartets, or common to my experience of Beethoven quartets and Shostakovich quartets or different between them, or common to my experience of music and painting or different between them? No, all I have to do is to suppose that in each case I find myself disposed to continue or repeat the experience, whatever particular sensations, in Hutchesonian terms first-order sensations, it involves. One of my own peak aesthetic experiences was the first time I saw Vermeer's *View of Delft* in the Mauritshuis. What I remember above all about that experience, now decades ago, is simply that I couldn't tear myself away from the painting – I didn't want my experience to end. Was I aware of a distinct sensation of pleasure, the same in that experience of the Vermeer as in my experience of Fabritius's *Goldfinch* a few moments earlier, or for that matter the same as in my experience of a nice glass of wine in the museum café an hour later? I don't think so. Likewise, I do not have to posit phenomenologically distinct sensations of pain and pleasure in my experience of the sublime; rather, in such an experience I just find myself torn between wanting to stop my experience of the inadequacy of the imagination and wanting to continue it so I can also continue to have a sense of the power of my own higher cognitive faculties. That is what the painfulness but pleasurableness of such an experience consists in.

Second, I suggest that the present approach can resolve an outstanding controversy in the interpretation of Kant's conception of aesthetic pleasure. Many have found troubling my earlier interpretation that Kant supposes the harmony of the faculties to be manifest only in a sensation of pleasure that is qualitatively identical to other feelings of pleasure, which thus does not wear its origin on its face and can only be assigned to its cause by an empirical judgment. They have proposed instead an "intentionalist" interpretation of the feeling of pleasure on which the sensation of pleasure in beauty does have a distinctive content that obviates the need for a separate causal judgment about its origin.[16] I sympathize with the queasiness about the idea of an entirely opaque sensation of pleasure, but have never been able to understand what sort of mental state a genuine sensation that yet has determinate intentional content is supposed to be – as a card-carrying Kantian, my view has been that determinate intentional content requires concepts and not just sensation. But this dispositional model of pleasure and pain allows us to sidestep this debate while preserving what I regard as one of the chief advantages of the opaque-sensation model, namely the room it leaves for the fallibility of aesthetic judgment. On the one hand, it allows for direct rather than merely inferential awareness of what Kant calls in one of his descriptions the animation of the cognitive powers and of the disposition to want to continue in that state, in the case of beauty, or of the dispositions to want both to leave and to continue in one's state, in the case of the sublime. On the other hand, it need make no claim about the infallibility of such awareness: one could be wrong in thinking that one's disposition to continue in one's state is due to the animation of the cognitive powers, as opposed, say, to some purely sensory mechanism, or even be wrong that one does want to continue in that state – as, say, when one is convincing oneself that one actually likes the music one is really listening to just to please a friend, when deep down one just wants the noise to stop. We need be no more infallible about what our dispositions and their real causes are than we would be about what our sensations and their real causes are.

Finally, to return to a point previously set aside, Kant's thesis in the anthropology lecture that all pleasure, thus even the pleasure in beauty,

---

[16] For example, Rachel Zuckert, "A New Look at Kant's Theory of Pleasure," *The Journal of Aesthetics and Art Criticism* 60, no. 3 (2002): 239–52, and Hannah Ginsborg, "Aesthetic Judging and the Intentionality of Pleasure," *Inquiry* 46 (2003): 164–81, reprinted in *The Normativity of Nature: Essays on Kant's Critique of Judgment* (Oxford: Oxford University Press, 2015), 94–110. The intentionalist approach was anticipated by Richard E. Aquila, "A New Look at Kant's Aesthetic Judgment," in *Essays in Kant's Aesthetics*, ed. Ted Cohen and Paul Guyer (Chicago: University of Chicago Press, 1982), 87–114.

presupposes some antecedent pain, might be thought to blur the distinction between the experiences of the sublime and the beautiful. That it is a complex experience involving both pain and pleasure seems to be precisely what is supposed to distinguish the sublime from the beautiful on Kant's account, the latter being an unalloyed experience of pleasure; so if the experience of the beautiful too turns out to require some element of pain, then the distinction collapses. But many have felt the need for a more complex set of distinctions than Kant makes – for example, Lord Kames distinguished between the beautiful, the sublime narrowly defined, and the "grand," the latter involving elements of both of the first two: for him, an object is not "intitled to the character" of "grandeur" "unless, together with its size, it be possessed of other qualities that contribute to its beauty such as regularity, proportion, order, or colour."[17] While the kind of challenge and therefore the element of pain that might be involved in the experience of beauty surely needs to be spelled out more fully, perhaps it can already be suggested that the experiences of the beautiful and the sublime are more like ranges on a continuum differing in the degree or intensity of the painful element of the experience rather than completely distinct kinds of experiences. Such a view might have some advantages, such as obviating the need for the rigid distinction between the experience of the sublime from nature and the merely beautiful representation of the sublime in art on which Kant sometimes insists (e.g., APV 243). Be that as it may, it is at least far from clear that a rigid distinction between the beautiful and the sublime is necessary, thus that it would be a defect in a model of these experiences that it does not allow for such a rigid distinction. And in any case, the thesis that pleasure always presupposes some pain might not be considered to be an indispensable feature of the basic dispositional model of pleasure and pain.

The dispositional model of pleasure and pain that Kant suggests in his transcendental definition of those states seems both truer to our actual experience than the phenomenological model employed by many of his contemporaries and often by Kant himself and to resolve difficulties in the interpretation of his aesthetic theory, such as the debate between opaque and intentionalist interpretations of the supposed sensation of pleasure and over the necessity for a rigid distinction between the beautiful and the sublime. For these reasons, it seems worthy of more of a hearing than it has hitherto received.

---

[17] Henry Home (Lord Kames), *Elements of Criticism*, Vol. 1, chap. IV; 6th ed., ed. Peter Jones (Indianapolis, IN: Liberty Fund, 2005), 151.

9

How to Feel a Judgment
The Sublime and Its Architectonic Significance*

Katerina Deligiorgi

Recent book-length vindications of the moral significance of the sublime, by Robert Clewis and Joshua Rayman, extend arguments from an established tradition of interpretation of Kant's aesthetics to motivate a revision of intellectualist interpretations of his ethics.[1] My aim in this chapter is not

---

* I thank Paul Guyer for prodding me to clarify, justify, and occasionally rethink some of the claims and arguments contained in an earlier draft of this chapter. I have sought to indicate some of the salient points of this discussion in the footnotes, but the most important debt has to do with enabling me to see more clearly what I wanted to say. I also thank Kelly Sorensen for helping me say it more clearly. Finally, I am thankful to Robert Clewis for his detailed and thought-provoking comments.

[1] Although they go about it in different ways, both Clewis and Rayman argue that the sublime can prepare us for morality (Robert R. Clewis, *The Kantian Sublime and the Revelation of Freedom* [Cambridge: Cambridge University Press, 2009], 3; Joshua Rayman, *Kant on Sublimity and Morality* [Cardiff: University of Wales Press, 2012], 33) and that it can reveal to us our freedom (Clewis, *The Kantian Sublime*, 3; Rayman, *Kant on Sublimity and Morality*, 65). They build on a tradition of interpretations that range from strongly moralist (Paul Crowther, *The Kantian Sublime: From Morality to Art* [Oxford: Clarendon Press, 1989]; Melissa McBay Merritt, "The Moral Source of the Kantian Sublime," in *The Sublime: From Antiquity to the Present*, ed. Timothy M. Costelloe [Cambridge: Cambridge University Press, 2012], 37–49), to moderately moralist, arguing for an indirectly moral role for the sublime (Henry E. Allison, *Kant's Theory of Taste: A Reading of the Critique of Aesthetic Judgment* [Cambridge: Cambridge University Press, 2001], and Paul Guyer, *Values of Beauty: Historical Essays in Aesthetics* [Cambridge: Cambridge University Press, 2005]). Rayman fits the former. Clewis would be somewhere in the middle since, although he makes a case for a distinctive *moral* type of sublime in Kant's work, he explicitly seeks to avoid moralizing the sublime in the third *Critique* (see Clewis, *The Kantian Sublime*, 134); also see Robert R. Clewis, "The Place of the Sublime in Kant's Project," *Studi Kantiani* 28 (2015): 149–68, which discusses the architectonic issues that also concern me here, but of which I was not aware at the time of writing this essay. Makkreel may be used as a contrast case, because he focuses on the relevance of the sublime to Kant's philosophy of mind and epistemology. See Rudolf A. Makkreel, *Imagination and Interpretation in Kant: The Hermeneutical Import of the Critique of Judgment* (Chicago: University of Chicago Press, 1990). For an even-handed treatment of the moral, psychological, and epistemic issues raised by Kant's discussion of the sublime throughout his work, see Kap Hyun Park, *Kant über das Erhabene: Rekonstruktion und Weiterführung der kritischen Theorie des Erhabenen Kants* (Würzburg: Königshausen and Neumann, 2009). Interpretations of Kant's ethics that challenge his perceived intellectualism also form by now an established tradition; see Barbara Herman, *The Practice of Moral Judgment* (Cambridge, MA: Harvard University Press, 1993); Paul Guyer, "Nature, Art, and Autonomy," in *Kant and the Experience of Freedom: Essays on Aesthetics and Morality* (Cambridge: Cambridge University Press, 1993), 229–74; Allen W. Wood, *Kant's Ethical Thought*

to add to the literature on the moral importance of the sublime, nor indeed to the revisionist trend in Kant's ethics. Rather it is to examine what this discussion reveals about the place of the sublime within the Kantian architectonic.

The architectonic question appears at first as a minor puzzle generated by the contrast between the important moral role of the sublime and its relatively marginal position in the third *Critique*. On one hand, as Henry Allison observes, the sublime "brings with it an awareness of our supersensible nature and vocation, in short, of our moral autonomy" and "puts us in touch (albeit merely aesthetically) with our 'higher self.'"[2] On the other hand, it is scarcely mentioned outside the "Analytic of the Sublime," a section that looks like a mere afterthought.[3] Solutions to the puzzle include reconstructions of the analytic of the sublime, aiming to disclose its internal cohesion and structural connection with the rest of the *Critique*, or refusal to grant significance to its brevity and organizational oddities.[4]

In this chapter I take a different path. Kant's treatment of the sublime in the third *Critique* shows the strain of accommodating a knotty topic. For a start, the sublime eludes placement within a taxonomy of emotions: it encompasses a number of feelings and yet it also names a specific aesthetic feeling, which, though aesthetic, is not a feeling of pure delight, since it combines pleasure with displeasure.[5] Furthermore, the sublime is also a judgment.[6] The judgment exactly matches the dual character of the feeling

---

(Cambridge: Cambridge University Press, 1999); Robert B. Louden, *Kant's Impure Ethics: From Rational Beings to Human Beings* (Oxford: Oxford University Press, 2000); Alix Cohen, *Kant and the Human Sciences: Biology, Anthropology, and History* (New York: Palgrave Macmillan, 2010). I discuss this tradition sympathetically in Deligiorgi, *The Scope of Autonomy: Kant and the Morality of Freedom* (Oxford: Oxford University Press, 2012).

[2] Allison, *Kant's Theory of Taste*, 335–36, 343.
[3] Allison, *Kant's Theory of Taste*, 303–5; also see Clewis, *The Kantian Sublime*, 62.
[4] Park, *Kant über das Erhabene*, 118–68; Rayman, *Kant on Sublimity and Morality*, 54.
[5] For a systematic attempt at such a taxonomy see Kelly D. Sorensen, "Kant's Taxonomy of the Emotions," *Kantian Review* 6, no. 1 (2002): 109–28. His essay shows that distinctions that work reasonably well for other Kantian emotions, including various inclinations, affects, and feelings, do not work well for the sublime. One example is that the sublime is neither unconnected with reason, nor *quite* "reason-produced," as Sorensen acknowledges (Sorensen, "Kant's Taxonomy," 126n); as Clewis put it helpfully, in correspondence with me, reason may not be sufficient in this case, but it is necessary. Another is that the sublime is an aesthetic feeling and it is not, because it is not just a feeling of passive delight; it is more like a stirring, a movement between pleasure and displeasure (Sorensen, "Kant's Taxonomy," 120).
[6] My original formulation was that "the feeling is also a judgment," which as Paul Guyer points out opens up a debate about the one-act versus two-act interpretation of aesthetic judgment (see Hannah Ginsborg, *The Role of Taste in Kant's Theory of Cognition* [New York: Garland Publishing, 1990]; and Paul Guyer, *Kant and the Claims of Taste*, 2nd ed. [Cambridge: Cambridge University Press, 1997]), which as I now hope to have made clear is not my concern at this point. My interpretation given in section 2 is at variance with both the one-act and the two-act readings.

by combining "purposiveness" and "contrapurposiveness." To say of something, "This is sublime," is not to sort the object categorically, as in ordinary cases of predication – instead, it is to reflect on the mental state of pleasure and displeasure generated by the encounter with the object; "purposive" and "contrapurposive" are technical terms aiming to say something about this process of reflection. Finally, and perhaps more strikingly, this kind of reflection reveals to the experiencing subject that the content of her judgment is a priori determined by reason: while the judgment refers to the object, the "this" in "This is sublime" is really about the subject's moral vocation.

In what follows, I seek to trace a path through these complex matters, for the purpose of finding out why this topic, which, as Kant himself acknowledges, "seems far-fetched and subtle, hence excessive for an aesthetic judgment" (CJ 262), matters for Kant and what its accommodation within the architectonic tells us about his conception of system. The argument is presented as answers to a series of questions: "What is the sublime?" "What is the sublime about?" "Why does the sublime matter?"

9.1 What Is the Sublime?

The question, "What is the sublime?" asks what the term "sublime" stands for. Ordinarily such questions are taken as requests for definition. In the present context, however, such requests are bound to mislead, because the sublime is not detachable from Kant's theory of aesthetic judgment.[7] The theory contains an analysis of the feelings characteristic of aesthetic responses to certain objects and also of the judgments that express and are warranted by such feelings. So to understand Kant's use of the term "sublime" we need to understand the feeling of the sublime, its corresponding judgment, and the relation between the two.

9.1.1 The Feeling of the Sublime

Confronted with certain "objects of nature" (CJ 245), objects of immeasurable magnitude or might, human beings experience a range of feelings,

---

[7] The point was originally made forcefully in Paul Guyer, "Kant's Distinction between the Sublime and the Beautiful," *Review of Metaphysics* 35, no. 4 (1982): 753–83. My approach will be therefore methodologically internalist; that is, I am interested in the use and role of "the sublime" within Kant's systematic writings. For important work documenting Kant's indebtedness to his German rationalist contemporaries and British empiricist predecessors see Susan Meld Shell and Richard Velkley, *Kant's Observations and Remarks: A Critical Guide* (Cambridge: Cambridge University Press, 2012); Rayman, *Kant on Sublimity and Morality*, chaps. 2 and 3.

including astonishment "bordering on terror," "horror," and "shudder" (CJ 269).[8] Given Kant's description of such encounters, it seems more natural to speak of feelings in the plural rather of *the* feeling of *the* sublime. So the first issue that needs clarification is the relation between these various feelings and the feeling of the sublime.

Useful in this context is a brief comparison with Kant's earliest writing on the topic, his *Observations on the Feeling of the Beautiful and the Sublime* (1764). In that work, Kant identifies the sublime with a range of feelings, from dread and shudder to melancholy and quiet admiration of "a beauty spread over a sublime prospect" (OBS 209). Some of these feelings, as well as the examples Kant uses of the nonnatural objects that arouse them, such as St. Peter's in Rome (OBS 210; CJ 252), make their way into the third *Critique*. Importantly, however, most of the content of the *Observations* finds its place in the *Anthropology*.[9] In the latter work, Kant calls the various feelings that convey the experience of the sublime "physical feelings," such as the "*shuddering* that comes over children when they listen at night to their nurses' ghost stories" (APV 264).[10] I take "physical" in this context to be an indication that such items belong to empirical psychology or at least to descriptive phenomenology.[11] I want to propose that the development of Kant's treatment of the sublime, from the early to the later

---

[8] I will be talking throughout of objects of nature. This is not to ignore the obvious references to nonnatural objects that Kant also discusses; it is rather that I have my doubts about their centrality to the experience. For arguments to that effect see Allison, *Kant's Theory of Taste*. Neither of these points, however, is intended as a denial of the existence of artistic sublimity.

[9] The material that is included in the *Anthropology* includes some of the discussion of feelings of the sublime as well as the discussion of the two sexes and of different nationalities (compare for example OBS 209 and APV 243).

[10] The empirical feelings of the sublime are responses to a whole range of perceptual qualities, including those Emily Brady calls "multi-sensory," such as "darkness, obscurity, greatness, massiveness, the tremendous, towering, dizzying, shapeless, formless, boundless, blasting, thundering, roaring, raging, disordered, dynamic, tumultuous, and so on. ... Sublime qualities cause intense, mixed emotional responses characterized by feelings of being overwhelmed and anxious, combined with excitement and pleasure" (Brady, *The Sublime in Modern Philosophy: Aesthetics, Ethics, and Nature* [Cambridge: Cambridge University Press, 2013], 187).

[11] Also see CJ 258 as well as Kant's use of the term "physiological" to refer to Burke's analysis of the sublime (CJ 277). The link between physiology and empirical psychology is warranted by Kant's association of empirical psychology with the study of pain (*Schmerz*) and pleasure (*Lust*) (CJ 266); see also Guyer, "Nature, Art, and Autonomy," 259; though my distinction between physical pleasure and pain and positive and negative sensations is at variance with Guyer, *Kant and the Claims of Taste*, 104–05. In fact, we disagree about the importance of the distinction between a plurality of feelings and the feeling of the sublime, which I consider quite significant. I understand empirical psychology very broadly, here, to include the empirical study of sense modalities and the transcendental study of sensibility, the "capacity [*Fähigkeit*] (receptivity) to acquire representations through the way in which we are affected by objects" (A19/B33). So I take the reference to "empirical psychology" and "rational physiology" in A848/B876 for example to be also about the study of sense modalities. Ameriks notes that Kant becomes rather pessimistic about the prospects

works, is marked by a clear separation between feelings (in the plural) and feeling (in the singular) and that this separation matters conceptually as well as methodologically. Physical feelings describe the *felt* quality of the sublime – they answer "What is it like?" questions. As such they continue to have a role in the discussion of the sublime in the third *Critique*, since the felt quality of the experience still has a place in the analysis of the sublime. However, in the latter work, Kant is centrally interested in answering a question that cannot be settled by description and so is not suited to empirical psychology (CJ 266); this is a "What is it?" question. Kant's answer is that the sublime is a feeling that combines pleasure (CJ 244, 267) and displeasure (CJ 259).

Although the tradition from which Kant draws also notes this feature of the sublime – Hume calls it an "opposition" – what is distinctive in Kant's account is the way he uses the basic character of the feeling to refer the analysis to a basic model of mind, specifically the human ability to feel.[12] The characterization of the feeling of the sublime as a feeling with a dual valence reveals its special relation to the human ability to feel as such; the sublime is interesting because it illuminates the human "faculty of feeling" (MM 212). In the third *Critique*, the reference to this faculty or ability (*Vermögen*) is unobtrusively signaled by the use of "feeling" (*Gefühl*) in the singular.[13] "Feeling," in this context, is a receptive ability concerned with subjective sensations of pleasure (*Lust*) and displeasure (*Unlust*) (CJ 206). The feeling of the sublime has a special relation to this ability because it engages it fully, combining pleasure and displeasure. To gauge the significance of this relation,

---

of the scientific study of psychology (Karl Ameriks, *Kant and the Fate of Autonomy: Problems in the Appropriation of the Critical Philosophy* [Cambridge: Cambridge University Press, 2000], 46) though he does seem to return to the topic in the *Anthropology*; see APV 153–61. For a more optimistic and systematic vindication of the place of human sciences in the Kantian context see Cohen, *Kant and the Human Sciences*.

[12] David Hume, *A Treatise of Human Nature*, ed. L. A. Selby-Bigge (Oxford: Clarendon Press, 1949), 435.

[13] See too the schematic presentation of the powers of mind in the first introduction (AK 20:245–46). It is important to note that, despite the appearance of a very tight systematic set of relations between the different powers of the mind, their basic character and empirical manifestations, associated ideas, principles, and judgments, the various distinctions Kant draws are often context specific and help illustrate specific points he seeks to raise in the context of his argument. A good example of this is the use of "feeling" (*Gefühl*) in the "Orientation" essay to speak of how one necessarily feels the difference between left and right and how this feeling helps one's geographical orientation (OT 135). On the faculty of feeling see Sorensen, "Kant's Taxonomy," 114; Clewis, *The Kantian Sublime*, 34; Park, *Kant über das Erhabene*, 67. The textual evidence is not by itself conclusive concerning this argument about feelings (psychological and physiological) and feeling (the topic of a transcendental enquiry); see for example the title of the 1764 work, in which "feeling" is in the singular (I thank Clewis for encouraging me to clarify this point).

I consider two sets of contrasts Kant draws: first, between objective and subjective sensations, and second, between affects and passions.

Objective sensations are informative about objects, paradigmatically colors such as the "green" of the meadows (CJ 206). The classification of colors under objective sensations does not mean that Kant believes that color is an intrinsic property of objects; as he writes in the first *Critique*, "things like colors, taste, etc., are correctly considered not as qualities of things but as mere alterations of our subject" (A29/B45). The point he seeks to make is that colors have "reality in appearance" (A169/B211), which is to say that color is characteristic of a *way* in which we perceive the world, namely by sight (see AK 29:856). The sensation is objective because color perception allows us to establish reliable connections to our environment. So the characterization "objective" captures the role of perception in establishing such connections, which is compatible with color being a secondary quality or alteration of our subject, as Kant puts it (A29/B45; also see AK 23:21).[14]

Subjective sensations, the domain of the faculty of feeling, differ from objective sensations because they tell us nothing about the "constitution of the object" (CJ 207). Neither, however, do they inform us about the subject (CJ 206). The denial of a cognitive role to pleasure and displeasure is puzzling, because, if one feels pleasure, one at least knows that much about oneself, namely that one is feeling it. That is to say, pleasure and displeasure are at least perceptions of somatic alterations. Kant appears to accept this elsewhere where he describes the feeling of pleasure and displeasure "as a receptivity belonging to inner sense" (CPR 58). I suggest that the denial of a cognitive role to subjective sensations in the third *Critique* can be seen as a refinement of the earlier claim rather than a rejection of it. The refinement would consist in a claim about sense modalities, namely that we would be wrong to model subjective sensations, perceptions of pain and pleasure, in parallel with objective ones, perceptions of colors or sounds, because, very simply, there is no distinctive sense modality associated with the sensation of

---

[14] Kant envisages the possibility of a relation between objective and subjective sensations. Colors and sounds, he says, can be, and often are, associated with feelings and also ideas. For example, the song of the bird "proclaims joyfulness and contentment with its existence. At least this is how we interpret nature, whether anything of the sort is its intention or not" (CJ 302). In this tradition of interpretation of nature belong certain color/feeling/idea associations: the white color of the lily charms us and also arouses ideas of innocence and, more abstractly, the "seven colors, in their order from red to violet" (CJ 302) are linked with feelings and ideas ranging from sublimity to tenderness. I use "associate" and "link" because there is not enough in what Kant says here to commit him to a better-defined relation between objective and subjective sensations and then both of these with ideas. I take the point of these remarks to be that pure aesthetic judgment such as he is expounding and defending in this context does not preclude such empirical associations and, by extension, the existence of layers of aesthetic experience that come with particular aesthetic traditions.

pleasure or displeasure. The basic thought then is that in the case of subjective sensations there is *no* characteristic mode of perception through which we establish a reliable connection to the environment.[15] Whatever its plausibility with respect to physical pain and pleasure, this negative thesis may be reasonably maintained in the context of the analysis of the sublime, where pain and pleasure are explicitly described as states of mind (CJ 266).[16] Despite the fact that its cognitive role is at the very least uncertain, the feeling of the sublime is of interest to the transcendental philosopher because it promises to yield more, on reflection, than is given by merely remarking on the dual valence of the feeling; to put it differently, and anticipating somewhat, the dual valence of the feeling is a stepping stone for a more full revelation concerning the feeling, experiencing, judging subject.

Let us now turn to the contrast between affects and passions.[17] Kant places the former within the purview of feeling and the latter within the purview of the *Begehrungsvermögen* or faculty of desire (CJ 272; also see MM 408); he offers anger as example of an affect (*Affekt*) and hatred as example of passion (*Leidenschaft*).[18] Kant then explains that passions are morally more significant because more pernicious. Affects influence how we act of course, but their effects are short lived. They are "stormy and transitory" (APV 265) and they make us lose our ability to exercise control over ourselves and reflect calmly about what to do (MM 408). Passions, by contrast, "are not thoughtless," they can "co-exist with rationalizing"

---

[15] To put it more technically: all sensations are alterations of the subject, but some (e.g., colors) are properties of objects, whereas others (pleasure and displeasure) are just a "property of the subject" (CPR 58; also see APV 239–40). This does not mean that alterations of the subject, such as pains for example, may not be informative; it is just that Kant is likely interested in establishing – consistent with his antidogmatic idealism – a link between the phenomenal character of experience and the mode of presentation of the object.

[16] See for example the description of pleasure (*Lust*) as "a state of mind [*Zustand des Gemüths*] in which a representation is in agreement with itself either for preserving this state itself . . . or for producing its object" (AK 20:231–32).

[17] The distinction between feeling and emotion, which is an important topic in contemporary philosophy and marked usually by differentiating between the felt quality of an emotion or mood and its cognitive content, is absent in Kant. I say usually because there is no agreement in the contemporary literature about the nature of emotions and feelings; see Laura Sizer, "What Feelings Can't Do," *Mind and Language* 21, no. 1 (2006): 108–35, for a review of the relevant debates as well as an original argument about how best to mark the distinction. Two terms, translated as "emotion," *Rührung* (e.g., CJ 253) and *Gemütsbewegung* (e.g., APV 266), range in meaning from emotional turmoil to feeling moved in some way. It is generally treacherous to seek to find an equivalent to "emotion" as in current use in aesthetics and philosophy of mind. For an attempt at a systematic taxonomy of emotions in Kant, see Sorensen, "Kant's Taxonomy."

[18] The faculty of desire is mainly discussed in the *Metaphysics of Morals* (MM 211–13) and extensively in the *Lectures on Metaphysics*; see AK 29:893–94, 29:1012–13, 28:676. It also features in the *Critique of Practical Reason* (CPR 21) and the *Critique of the Power of Judgment* (CJ 178–79 and 178n); its pragmatic and empirical study is contained in the *Anthropology*.

(APV 265), and for this reason, they are "cancerous sores for pure practical reason" (APV 266). Passions can derail in lasting ways our faculty of desire.

Though brief, this discussion is significant. First, it reinforces the earlier conclusion about "pleasure" and "displeasure" being states of mind. The parallel with affects helps us understand "pleasure" and "displeasure" as terms for positive and negative subjective sensations of the faculty of feeling, which, in current usage, would be called positive and negative emotions to distinguish them from physical pain and pleasure. Second, and more importantly, the faculty of desire, presented here as subject to passions and indeed to all kinds of empirical prompts, which are determined by some object whose reality is desired (see CPR 21), is also determinable a priori through the moral law. Although it would have struck Kant's empiricist predecessors as an absurdity, Kant argues that the faculty of feeling too is determinable a priori. Kant aims to show this through transcendental analysis of the sublime, which starts with an examination of the form of judgment that corresponds to or expresses the feeling of the sublime.

9.1.2 The Judgment of the Sublime

The feeling of the sublime describes the engagement of the faculty of feeling, through negative and positive sensations, by some object that challenges the feeling subject's cognitive abilities. The feeling is of interest to the transcendental philosopher not because of its dual character – there may well be other feelings that similarly engage the faculty of feeling. Rather the interest lies in discovering the grounds of the experience or *how* something that challenges the subject of this experience yet affords them pleasure. We have so far considered the subjective responses to some object in terms of feelings and states of mind. Just like other experiences Kant discusses, these aesthetic responses are also things we can identify and about which we are in a position to say something. However, we are not seeking to describe what we encounter, in terms of its color or shape. We rather seek to identify and communicate an encounter that arouses negative and positive subjective sensations. The form of the judgment exactly replicates the negative and positive sensations that constitute the feeling: it is a judgment that unites contrapurposiveness and purposiveness.[19]

---

[19] I am not discussing here Kant's reasons for associating purposiveness with pleasure and contrapurposiveness with displeasure; I have done so in some detail in Deligiorgi, "The Pleasures of Contra-purposiveness: Kant, the Sublime and Being Human," *The Journal of Aesthetics and Art Criticism* 72, no. 1 (2014): 25–35.

A thorny issue that has arisen in the context of interpretations of Kant's analysis of the beautiful but that can also arise here is whether Kant's account commits him to the existence of two judgments, a judging act (*Beurteilung*), which generates the feeling, followed by a further properly reflective judgment (*Urteil*) that takes propositional form, or whether a single judgment can account for the complexity of the experience.[20] Since there is agreement on the complexity of the experience, a contextualist way around this issue that does not commit us to a temporal order between its different elements might be useful. *What* we are talking about is settled by the context of the inquiry: so if we ask someone who witnessed "flashes of lightning and crashes of thunder" or "a lofty waterfall" (CJ 261), "What did it feel like?" the answer will contain feelings. If we ask about the basic character of the feeling, e.g., "So was it pleasurable or not?" the answer will be that it combines pleasure and displeasure. Now, all this imaginary dialogue presupposes that our interlocutor has a use for the term "sublime"; we are in conversation with someone who can identify their experience of flashes of lightning and crashes of thunder as an experience of something sublime. So when they recall or relate the experience, they are able to make a judgment, the judgment "This is sublime."

The judgment "This is sublime" picks out, and makes it possible to communicate to others, the experience of the encounter of the object (the "this") that arouses the feeling. On an empiricist construal, the judgment of the sublime would be a way of "calling" the feeling one has sublime (CJ 261), communicating nothing more than empirical subjective states. On a rationalist construal, the judgment is possible on condition that we possess a rule that is applied to the experienced particular, placing it under the concept "sublime." Kant proposes a "reflective" answer. We are not just saying how we feel about things, nor do we have a rule we apply to our cognitions. The judgment is reflective because it requires reflection and it is also aesthetic because it engages our senses and our subjective sensations. A simple way of understanding what Kant might be saying here is that we gain access *to* the judgment *through* the feeling.[21] Using Kant's vocabulary,

---

[20] The controversy concerns the judgment of taste: Guyer, *Kant and the Claims of Taste*, 106–47, champions the two-act reading, which is disputed by Allison, *Kant's Theory of Taste*, 98–118. On the complexity of aesthetic experience see Karl Ameriks, *Interpreting Kant's Critiques* (Oxford: Clarendon Press, 2003), 324–43.

[21] Lest the idea of "access" appear too metaphorical, I believe that the model can work for mere sensations such as pain that are not the topic here. The feeling of pain in my thumb, which pains immediately (that is, I am not inferring the presence of the pain), can reasonably be described also as consisting in a relation insofar as it tells me that there is possibly something wrong with my thumb. This access model does not address the controversy mentioned earlier directly; it is rather an

we can say that we gain access to the unity of contrapurposiveness and purposiveness through the particular way our capacity to feel is engaged by some objects.

The unity of judgment is effected by the use of the term "sublime." But given that, on Kant's account, we do *not* have at our disposal a definition of the term that we can use as a rule to judge the particulars confronting us, we have to ask: What makes our use of the term apt in the specific circumstances in which we apply it? Kant's answer to this question involves reflection on the nature of the experience. We are within our rights to use the term when the object experienced confronts us with our inability to deal with it – either because it is immeasurable or because it is threatening – in other words, when the object is experienced as contrapurposive. Yet at the same time, for "sublime" to apply, there must be pleasure in the experience, which secures the purposive element in the judgment of the sublime. Reflection, now, takes the form of an inference. The object is the source of the negative emotion. The negative emotion is accompanied by a positive one. The positive emotion cannot have its source in the object, for the object is consistently and unambiguously experienced as contrapurposive. So the pleasure must come from the subject's ability to draw on resources that are elicited by the object and the frustration it causes, yet are not in or of the object.[22]

Reflection on the experience – the feelings, the feeling, the form of the judgment – leads us to the central question in Kant's analysis of the sublime, "how can we designate with an expression of approval that which is apprehended in itself as contrapurposive?" (CJ 245); how is "the very same violence that is inflicted on the subject by the imagination ... judged as purposive **for the whole vocation** of the mind"? (CJ 259). Reflection on the form of the judgment of the sublime enables us to focus our search on an idea of purposiveness and ask where this idea comes from. In other words, reflection is directed to the content of the judgment, "What is the sublime about?" Getting an answer to that question will enable us fully and finally to answer what makes the use of the term sublime apt. Before we turn to this, we need to address a final point about the relation between feeling and judgment.

---

attempt to get around it. To address the controversy, a more detailed exposition would be required and this exceeds the scope and aims of the present chapter.

[22] There are a number of issues, including the purity or otherwise, and dependence or otherwise of the judgment of the sublime, that I do not address here because they are not essential to the main topic of the chapter; for extensive treatment see Park, *Kant über das Erhabene*.

On the account given here, feeling gives us access to a judgment and through it to some cognitive content. This appears to contradict Kant's claim that subjective sensations do not "serve for any cognition at all, not even that by which the subject **cognizes** itself" (CJ 206). The way to reconcile the present account with this claim is to say that subjective sensations have no cognitive content themselves; they are merely indicative of something, namely that we are in a condition of receptivity to some content that we can reflectively retrieve. At the same time, through engaging feeling in this specific way, objects make accessible to the subject of the experience some content that becomes reflectively available to the subject. Feeling then works in two ways: it is a condition for receptivity and also a sign of receptivity *to* content.

9.2 What Is the Sublime About?

One way of answering the question, "What is the sublime about?" is by pointing at some object of outer sense, the "this" in the judgment, "This is sublime." However, there is also a clear inward direction to the analysis of the experience of the encounter with certain objects, though "inward" should not be understood as concerned with the felt quality of the experience, but rather with the resources the subject brings to the experience and that explain the pleasure taken in it. We encounter here another thorny issue about the kind of analysis we are engaging in, that is, whether we reconstruct a series of causal steps or, alternatively, give an account of what our feelings and thoughts are about.[23] On the account presented here, a causalist reconstruction would start with the objects of nature as causes of the "physical" feelings, which lead to awareness of the engagement of our faculty of feeling, that is, awareness of a concurrently negative and positive mental state, which then prompts the thought, "This is sublime," which pushes the subject to search for the explanation for the experience.[24] On the intentionalist alternative, the same path is followed but under the aim of properly locating what our experience is about. Either way, it seems that

---

[23] See Clewis, *The Kantian Sublime*, 59; Guyer, *Kant and the Claims of Taste*, 88; Allison, *Kant's Theory of Taste*, 54. The two issues are related; if we perform two acts of judgment then one has causal precedence over the other, and problems with either part of this conditional can motivate the intentionalist or one-act reading. At the same time the contextualist way around the original problem is neutral with respect to the choice between causalism and intentionalism.

[24] Kant himself uses liberally causalist vocabulary, including when describing the causes of pleasure and displeasure and locating them in either senses or the understanding (CPR 22–23; also see APV 239–40).

the answer to the question, "What is the sublime about?" points simultaneously in two different directions: one is toward some object of the outer senses, and the other is toward some object of thought. This is the issue that I address here.

Some authors split the difference by saying that the former is the proximate cause of the feeling but not the real cause of it, citing in support Kant's idea of "subreption" (CJ 257), a self-incurred deception consisting in the fallacy of attributing to the object something that does not belong to it; we make a false inference calling the object sublime because it is the encounter with the object that arouses the feeling of the sublime.[25] I do not think that either a hierarchy of causes or a deepening awareness of what the judgment is about can solve what looks like a structural oddity. We have a set of contents that are, ostensibly, *all* we experience and judge sublime, then we have another set that make good our use of the term sublime but that are somewhat mysterious since they are not what we experience. The oddity is that we have two different sets of contents that are of a different order to one another, yet are joined together in one experience.

Kant talks about the object of the sublime as "an object (of nature) **the representation of which determines the mind to think of the unattainability of nature as a presentation of ideas**" (CJ 268). One way of interpreting this is that the object of the outer sense is supplanted by another object: our consciousness, as Kant says earlier, "of being superior to nature within us and thus also to nature outside us" (CJ 264). Some commentators indeed take this path, arguing that the pleasure we take in becoming aware of our moral vocation trumps the displeasure occasioned by the object; contrapurposiveness is thus subsumed under purposiveness for the judgment of the sublime.[26] I think this option is unattractive because it undermines the basic character of the feeling of the sublime, which is of pleasure and of displeasure, not of pleasure overwhelming the displeasure. This basic character of the feeling is, as we saw, replicated in the form of the judgment of the sublime, which is a unity of contrapurposiveness and purposiveness.

---

[25] See Clewis, *The Kantian Sublime*, 14f. Clewis uses causalist vocabulary here though he is in favor of the intentionalist interpretation. The account of the content of the judgment I give is neutral between the two options.

[26] See Merritt, "The Moral Source of the Kantian Sublime." Clewis, in "The Place of the Sublime in Kant's Project," acknowledges the contrapurposiveness but concludes that it has to be a kind of contrapurposive purposiveness.

A simple and I think quite intuitive way of holding onto the duality of the feeling is to distinguish between the subject's sensitivity to features in the environment, which gives us the feeling and the form of the judgment, and the *ground* for the judgment. When asking about the ground for the judgment we ask in virtue of what something experienced as contrapurposive nonetheless arouses a positive subjective sensation. The question concerning ground is not about the valence of the experience and its objects, but rather about what makes the application of the term "sublime" apt. Posing the question in terms of the source of the pleasure in the experience leads to a dead end: the object or "this" we term "sublime" is contrapurposive. Importantly, Kant does not think that we are going to get very far either, if the search for ground becomes a search for some psychological mechanism that, when appropriately aroused, produces such and such feelings. The right way to put the ground question is: *for whom* is such a judgment, and so feeling, possible?

Kant's answer does not hold any surprises. For Kant, the sublime has moral significance. The judgment of the sublime is possible *for* a finite moral being. It is in virtue of our moral vocation that we judge the frustrating and threatening objects of nature as sublime. This fits the duality of the feeling and the unity of the judgment while it also makes sense of Kant's claims that the object that arouses the feeling is "improperly" called sublime (CJ 264) and that "sublimity is not contained in anything in nature" (CJ 264). What makes the use of the term sublime in the judgment, "This is sublime" apt is not a rule, it is a relation between an object and a subject capable of "judging nature without fear" because of the sort of subject they are.

By turning the question around, and asking us to reflect on *for whom* the object is sublime, Kant invites us to consider not just conditions of receptivity, which include the possession and deployment of various capacities, but also a distinct responsiveness condition, which gives us the ground of the experience: the subject's identity as a moral being. This identity has a form of purposiveness because it is about the fitness of the subject for moral ends; it is not about this or that end, but an overall judgment of fitness to ends that exceed natural ends.[27] So it is then that "in our aesthetic judgment nature is judged as sublime not insofar as it arouses fear, but rather because it calls forth our power (which is not part of nature) to regard those things about which we are

---

[27] Also see Tom Hanauer, "Sublimity and the Ends of Reason: Questions for Deligiorgi," *The Journal of Aesthetics and Art Criticism* 74, no. 2 (2016): 195–99.

concerned (goods, health and life) as trivial" (CJ 262). And this is what finally makes good the a priori determination of the faculty of feeling, the rational idea of our moral vocation.[28] We are now in position to answer the question, "What is the sublime about?" The sublime is about the experience that such a subject, as specified in the foregoing analysis, has of the object that arouses the feeling of the sublime, as given in the earlier section and that gives rise to a certain type of self-knowledge.

The experience of the sublime affords us a unique sort of moral self-knowledge.[29] Outside the third *Critique*, Kant treats moral self-knowledge in two forms. The first is theoretical-deductive moral self-knowledge, which is available to any human being who is able to go from the general premise, "All rational beings are subject to the moral law," to the particular premise, "I am a rational being," and conclude, "I am subject to the moral law."[30] Kant presents another form of moral self-knowledge as a practical task for human beings. The first command of all duties to oneself is the "command [to] '*know* (scrutinize, fathom) *yourself*,' not in terms of your natural perfection ... but rather in terms of your moral perfection in relation to your duty. That is, know your heart – whether it is good or evil" (MM 441).[31] The experience of the sublime gives us yet a different form of moral self-knowledge: the subject of the experience is uniquely identified as a particular, because of their susceptibility to certain sensations. At the same time, the experience of such a subject reveals that it is in virtue of their moral vocation that they can stand before the object of nature overwhelmed yet not annihilated.

9.3 Why Does the Sublime Matter?

On April 26, 1336, Francesco Petrarca writes to his friend, Francesco Dionigi da Bordo San Sepolcro, "Today I ascended the highest mountain

---

[28] Also see: "the majesty of the law ... rouses a *feeling of the sublimity* of our own vocation that enraptures us more than any beauty" (R 23n).
[29] Park argues that at best we can speak of self-feeling not self-knowledge (Park, *Kant über das Erhabene*, 117), but it is possible here to use "knowledge" in the sense of "cognition" which is cognitively less demanding than in common philosophical usage (see Ameriks, *Kant and the Fate of Autonomy*, 44).
[30] For a discussion of the limitations of the inferential model of self-knowledge, see Owen Ware, "The Duty of Self-Knowledge," *Philosophy and Phenomenological Research* 79, no. 3 (2009): 671–98.
[31] The task to know oneself is part of what is required in order to become "better human beings" (R 45). See Jens Timmermann, "Autonomy and Moral Regard for Ends," in *Kant on Moral Autonomy*, ed. Oliver Sensen, (Cambridge: Cambridge University Press, 2012), 212–24.

in this region, which, not without cause, they call the Windy Peak" (36).[32] Petrarca explains that, in undertaking this ascent, inspired by the writings of classical historians and cosmographers, he was seeking to satisfy a long-held desire. Curious and determined, he set off early one morning up the steep "and almost inaccessible pile of rocky material" (38). After a long and arduous climb, in the company of his brother and a servant, he reaches the summit: "I stood there almost benumbed" (41). The numbness is a result not just of the physical intensity of the exertion, but also the shock of the exposure to the "unusually open and wide view" (41). Feeling momentarily without resources to respond to the experience, Petrarca weeps over his imperfection. At the same time, looking around to see "what I had intended to see in coming here" (43), he admires "every detail, now relishing earthly enjoyment, now lifting up my mind to higher spheres" (44). Moving from numbness to enjoyment and from feelings of inadequacy to feelings of elation, the account leaves the reader in no doubt that the journey up the mountain is spiritual as well as physical: "mortal men lack counsel who, neglecting the noblest part of themselves in empty parading, look without for what can be found within" (45). Petrarca's account of his experience has a jagged feel to it, as he intersperses references to classical and Christian sources with descriptions of his emotions, descriptions of the striking landscape, recollections of personal struggles and affections. In response to the strong emotions that "rouse a storm" (46) within him, Petrarca turns to God, guided by Augustine, whose *Confessions* is the one book he carries with him. Although he does not explicitly cite this line from the *Confessions*, "interior intimo meo et superior summo meo" (3.6.11), he presents his relation to God as to someone intensely intimate and unreachably high. The concluding lesson is that "we ought to exert our strength to get under foot not a higher spot of earth but the passions which are puffed up by earthly instincts" (46).

Although Petrarca does not use the term "sublime," his account of his ascent reflects many of the themes of the Kantian sublime, the overwhelming object, the contrasting emotions, the reflective character of the experience, and, finally, the attainment of moral self-knowledge.[33] In drawing this parallel I do not seek to make a point about scholarly influence, but

---

[32] All references are to Ernest Cassirer, Paul Oskar Kristeller, and John Herman Randall Jr., eds. *The Renaissance Philosophy of Man: Petrarca, Valla, Ficino, Pico, Pomponazzi, Vives* (Chicago: University of Chicago Press, 1948). The translation is by Hans Nachod. "Windy Peak" is a translation of Mont Ventoux, which in popular etymology was considered to derive its name from its wind-lashed peaks.

[33] In contrast to the Petrarcan account, in the Kantian one, God does not feature prominently; Kant simply draws a parallel between the experience of moral self-awareness and the virtuous man's

rather about the broad lineaments of a tradition, a certain way of thinking about human beings and their place in the world.[34] The question that exercises Kant, and also Petrarca, is how human beings can orient themselves in the world. For some, the question is senseless or misleading: human beings find their place in the world qua natural beings; there is nothing more to add to this, and in particular, there is no need for metaphorical ascent. But for this other tradition, to which Kant belongs and that stretches at least as far as Petrarca, orientation is an issue because the moral vocation of human beings has a transcendent character and finding one's way is troublesome, because the right path is not obvious. Coming now to the specific expression of the orientation question that concerns us here, that is, in the context of experiencing and being overwhelmed by nature, it is precisely because of the transcendent character of the moral vocation of human beings that feelings matter. That is to say: the human moral vocation is not a piece of metaphysical knowledge; reason in its theoretical employment fails us in this regard, while in its practical employment it presupposes and helps us realize our moral vocation. To say that a feeling gives access to such content is to say that such content is nonetheless humanly available. I now justify this link to the topic of orientation by returning to the architectonic question raised at the start of the essay and examining the systematic position of the sublime.

It is customary to think of the Kantian system as establishing a rigid separation of domains – theoretical and practical, a priori and a posteriori, passive and active – and of the boundaries between these domains as strictly policed by interdictions about what can be known and how. The discussion of the sublime suggests a less rigid organization, and perhaps, a more modest system.[35] A philosophical concept within Kant's aesthetic theory, the sublime functions as a bridging concept between some of these domains without offending against the interdictions that police their boundaries. For example, the experience of the sublime permits moral self-knowledge without granting us acquaintance of our noumenal self nor a revelation of our true moral character; it does something else: it sets off a

---

relation to God (CJ 260–61). Essential to Kant's account is the transcendence of the moral law, which fits the sublime's "resistance to the interest of the senses" (CJ 267). Readers who are unconvinced by Kant's anti-naturalist ethical message will find his analysis of the sublime unconvincing; see, for example, Jane Forsey, "Is a Theory of the Sublime Possible?" *The Journal of Aesthetics and Art Criticism* 65, no. 4 (2007): 381–89.

[34] Regarding the reception and influence of Petrarca's work in German-speaking lands, see Frank L. Borchardt, "Petrarch: The German Connection," *Studies in Romance Languages* 3 (1975): 418–31.

[35] The designation "modest" comes from Ameriks, *Kant and the Fate of Autonomy*, whose concern is not with flexibility, but rather with the restricted scope and non-absolute basis of Kant's system.

train of reflection on an experience we can have as embodied particulars who are moral beings and also capable of awareness of their moral vocation. The architectural role of the sublime then is as a bridging concept, a role that is of a piece with the overall unifying ambition of the third *Critique*.[36] Taking this point a bit further, I take the very existence of such a bridging concept as an indication that there is sufficient flexibility in the system, or perhaps sufficient confidence in its conception, to allow for the sort of border crossing that is needed to accommodate the sublime.

But a further question arises now, namely, why might Kant consider it important or worthwhile to try to accommodate the sublime in the first place? It is one thing to have in view a model of unity that is effected not through some foundational concept or method, but rather through border-crossing concepts that help stitch the whole together, and quite another to give the sublime such a role. To address this question, we need to move beyond recognition of the architectural role of the sublime and to its specific contribution to the Kantian architecture.

Beyond the pull exerted by the immediate context of aesthetic debates about the sublime and the beautiful, to which Kant is certainly responding in the third *Critique*, another force is at work, as I suggested by the reference to Petrarca. This force is not tradition, but rather the force of the urgency of the orientation question. Kant takes this up directly in a short essay in which he criticizes Moses Mendelssohn's view that philosophers should seek to hew closely to common sense (OT 133). Kant's positive argument does not concern philosophers only. It is an argument about the orientation of human reason morally through rational belief. Importantly, such rational belief also comes with strong antidogmatic maxims for the guidance of one's reason, in particular the maxim of thinking "in community with others" (OT 144–45).[37] Interestingly, Kant introduces the topic of orientation by reference to the feeling of left and right, which he says, helps orient us geographically. The point is interesting because it suggests an attractive parallel with the feeling of sublime: the latter helps orient us morally. So in answer to why it matters that the sublime be accommodated in the system, the answer, given in the language of the "Orientation" essay, is pretty straightforward: the sublime addresses a "need" of reason for moral orientation (OT 140 and 140n).

---

[36] Thanks to Paul Guyer for reminding me not to overlook the broader unifying purpose of the third *Critique*.

[37] I discuss this in Deligiorgi, *Kant and the Culture of Enlightenment* (Albany: SUNY Press, 2005), 64–69 and 77–85. Also see Nicolas Osborne, *Opinion, croyance, savoir: Recherches sure la pragmatique kantienne de la pensée* (PhD diss., University of Lille, 2016).

I conclude by linking Kant's responsiveness to the orientation question to his conception of system. A system, he writes, is "the unity of the manifold cognitions under one idea" (A832/B860). As such, system is to be contrasted with "mere aggregates of cognitions" (A835/B863). Systematicity then is a response to another need of reason, which appears as a demand for unity of thought and of cognitions: "the unity of reason is the unity of a system" (A680/B708). It is a matter of debate just how ambitiously such unity is to be construed, especially when comparing the first with the third *Critique*.[38] Alongside this concern with unity, however, Kant makes a point of ascribing a yet more ambitious role to his architectonic, his "art of systems." He draws a distinction between scholastic and cosmopolitan conceptions of philosophy. The former, he writes, aims at the logical perfection of cognition without taking into account moral ends of humanity; the latter, by contrast, seeks to relate "all cognition to the essential ends of human reason" (*teleologia rationis humanae*) (A838–39/B866–67). From the vantage point provided by this distinction, we can see that, while Kant is deeply engaged in the theoretical-scholastic project of showing how cognitions can be unified, he discerns a further focus of unity that gives a humanistic-cosmopolitan purpose to philosophy. Philosophy is guided by the good, or, to put it in Kantian language, by the idea of humanity's essential ends. The third *Critique* addresses both concerns about the unity of cognition and concerns about the unifying end that should guide thought. Architecturally, the sublime allows us to consider a model of unity that is achieved through bridge-building and border-crossing concepts, and most importantly, it serves the cosmopolitan end of the system: it is a feeling that gives us access to moral self-knowledge.

---

[38] See Thomas E. Wartenberg, "Reason and the Practice of Science," in *The Cambridge Companion to Kant*, ed. Paul Guyer (Cambridge: Cambridge University Press, 1992); Paul Guyer, *Kant on Freedom, Law, and Happiness* (Cambridge: Cambridge University Press, 2000); and Guyer, *Kant's System of Nature and Freedom: Selected Essays* (Oxford: Oxford University Press, 2005). Although answering this question is beyond the scope of this chapter, it is worth noting that Guyer's ambitious reading of the demand for unity especially in the third *Critique* is compatible with flexibility within and even modesty of the system itself.

10

The Feeling of Enthusiasm*

Robert R. Clewis

Kant defines enthusiasm as "the idea of the good with affect" (CJ 271) and as "the participation in the good with affect" (*die Theilnehmung am Guten mit Affect*; CF 86; cf. MM 408f.). This may strike readers today as a rather odd definition. Exactly what kind of a feeling is Kantian *Enthusiasmus*?[1] The meaning of Kant's concept of enthusiasm differs somewhat from its ordinary English counterpart, which means an exalted state of excitement or intense, eager enjoyment or approval. Since Kant calls enthusiasm an "affect" (*Affekt*) and an affect *hinders* the attainment of ends and goals set by agents, enthusiasm is not really an eagerness to achieve a goal, as contemporary readers might think. Although Kantian enthusiasm is an

---

* I am grateful to Kelly Sorensen for his suggestions on an earlier draft of this chapter. I am also grateful for the comments and questions from the audience at the philosophy department of the University of Pavia, where I read a version of the chapter in June 2016, and I thank Serena Feloj and Luca Fonnesu in particular.

[1] The topic of this chapter is *Enthusiasmus*/Enthusiasm, not *Schwärmerei* (fanaticism). On translating these terms as "enthusiasm" and "fanaticism," respectively, see Clewis, *The Kantian Sublime and the Revelation of Freedom* (Cambridge: Cambridge University Press, 2009), 4f., and especially Rachel Zuckert, "Kant's Account of Practical Fanaticism," in *Kant's Moral Metaphysics: God, Freedom, and Immortality*, ed. Benjamin Lipscomb and James Krueger (Berlin: Walter de Gruyter, 2010), 293–97. Kant distinguishes *Enthusiasmus* and *Schwärmerei* at OBS 252n and "General Remark," CJ 275. While the *Cambridge Edition* of Kant's writings typically glosses *Schwärmerei* as "enthusiasm," this archaic use of the latter risks confusing readers today (for whom "enthusiasm" means something like enjoyable excitement or approval), and just as significantly, it hides Kant's crucial distinction between *Enthusiasmus* and *Schwärmerei*. The archaic translation has given rise to considerable conceptual confusion and misunderstanding among scholars (for examples, see Clewis, *The Kantian Sublime*, 5n10) and still continues to do so: a recent example is Robert Doran, *The Theory of the Sublime from Longinus to Kant* (Cambridge: Cambridge University Press, 2015), 199–200, 267. In a 2012 translation of the Mrongovius lecture on anthropology and in *The Kantian Sublime*, I therefore used "enthusiasm" for *Enthusiasmus* and "fanaticism" for *Schwärmerei*. Like Hume and (at times) Shaftesbury, Locke condemns "enthusiasm" in a sense close to Kantian *Schwärmerei* (hence not in the sense of enthusiasm discussed in the present chapter). See John Locke, *An Essay Concerning Human Understanding*, ed. Peter H. Nidditch (Oxford: Clarendon Press, 1975), 697–706, IV.xix; Anthony Ashley Cooper (3rd Earl of Shaftesbury), "A Letter concerning Enthusiasm," in *Characteristics of Men, Manners, Opinions, Times*, ed. John M. Robertson (Indianapolis, IN: Bobbs-Merrill, 1964), 4–28.

"interested" or interest-based feeling in that it involves an engagement or determination of the will, and although it can have motivational force, the meaning of Kant's term differs from, and is arguably more obscure than, its English counterpart. Its obscurity would seem to derive in large part from its status as an affect.

Although there is insufficient space to delve into the concept's notable history, it is worth recalling that Kant contributes to the development of a concept found in authors ranging from Plato and Aristotle to Shaftesbury, Voltaire, and Diderot, up to card-carrying "postmodern" authors such as Jean-François Lyotard.[2] In his post-Platonic analysis of music, songs, and poetry in *Politics* (book 8), Aristotle defined enthusiasm as an *emotion of the ethical part of the soul*. Kant's definition of enthusiasm as a person's *sympathy or participation in the good with affect*, intentionally or not, takes up this ethical and psychological dimension. Unlike most of his Greek and even modern predecessors, Kant dissociates enthusiasm from artistic creation, musical and poetic genius, and/or divine inspiration. Kant conceives of enthusiasm more in anthropological and moral terms than in terms of inspired poetry, music, or songs. At a general level, one could say that his account goes in the same direction as his anthropocentric turn in theoretical philosophy, in which the Copernican revolution in philosophy involves stepping away from the theocentric perspectives of Leibniz, Wolff, and Newton, and in the same direction as his turn in ethics, in which reason, rather than a divine being, is the ground or source of morality and the moral law. Enthusiasm does not come from the gods or the divine, for Kant, but from reason in conjunction with the imagination and sensibility. On the one hand Kant's account in the third *Critique* gives the impression that enthusiasm is a state of mind of individuals, rather than a group phenomenon (part of "mob" psychology), but on the other hand, in *The Conflict of the Faculties* a peculiar instance of enthusiasm is characterized as a "universal" and communal feeling shared by spectators in response to a monumental historical event perceived to be striking, stirring, and rare: the French Revolution.[3]

---

[2] Jean-François Lyotard, *L'Enthousiasme: La critique kantienne de l'histoire* (Paris: Editions Galilée, 1986). Jean-François Lyotard, *Enthusiasm: The Kantian Critique of History* (Stanford, CA: Stanford University Press, 2009).

[3] On the individual/group distinction, see Zuckert, "Kant's Account of Practical Fanaticism," 294. I suspect that a Platonic conception of enthusiasm as a feeling communicated and transmitted to others without the check of reason forms the background to Kant's account more than he may have realized.

In the following, I characterize and comment on Kant's account of enthusiasm in the *Observations on the Feeling of the Beautiful and Sublime* (1764), the lectures on anthropology (which Kant gave between 1772 and 1796), *Critique of the Power of Judgment* (1790), *Anthropology from a Pragmatic Point of View* (1798), and an essay in *The Conflict of the Faculties* called "An Old Question Raised Again: Is the Human Race Constantly Progressing?" (written ca. 1795–1796 but published in 1798). This wide range of texts alone should indicate that Kant's reflections on enthusiasm do not amount to mere afterthought, a fleeting philosophical blip. While not at the center of his epistemology, aesthetics, or ethics, the concept of enthusiasm was clearly of philosophical interest to Kant over a period spanning several decades.

I begin by looking at the third *Critique*'s account (Section 10.1). Subscribing to the position that feelings can have cognitive content (Section 10.2), I propose that the content of the feeling is an imaginative representation of a rational idea of the morally good. I characterize the more ordinary cases of Kantian enthusiasm (Section 10.3), which come primarily from Kant's essays and lectures on anthropology. I call these ordinary instances of enthusiasm described throughout the pre-Critical writings and student notes "paradigmatic" or typical enthusiasm, to distinguish them from the rather atypical kind of enthusiasm felt in response to the establishment of the first French Republic. I then examine this remarkable instance of enthusiasm: though an affect, it functions as a sign of moral progress in Kant's philosophy of history (Section 10.4). This leads me to a brief comparison of paradigmatic enthusiasm with other Kantian feelings (Section 10.5).

I conclude by claiming that enthusiasm remains profoundly ambiguous in Kant's account, with a deeply problematic side stemming from its nature as an affect, yet still capable of functioning as a symbol of moral progress and after all an imaginative-sensible response to the morally *good*. Since Kant had a lifelong interest in the topic, the feeling of enthusiasm deserves to be classified as an important Kantian feeling.

10.1 The Critical Account

It seems natural to commence a characterization of the feeling of enthusiasm by examining a *Critique*. In the *Critique of the Power of Judgment*, Kant defines enthusiasm as the "idea of the good with affect," that is, as an affective response elicited by an imaginative engagement with the idea of the morally good. One could say it is a kind of imaginative-intellectual pleasure, though it should not be confused with the feelings of respect and (though this relation is more complicated) sublimity. The crucial passage is worth quoting in full. Just after claiming that morality ("the morally good"), when judged aesthetically, must be represented not so much as beautiful as sublime, Kant writes:

> Conversely, even that which we call sublime in nature outside us or even within ourselves (e.g., certain affects) is represented only as a power of the mind to soar [*schwingen*] above **certain** obstacles of sensibility by means of moral principles, and thereby to become interesting.
>
> I should like to dwell a little on the last point. The idea of the good with affect is called **enthusiasm**. This state of mind seems to be sublime, so much so that it is commonly maintained that without it nothing great can be accomplished. Now, however, every affect* is blind, either in the choice of its end, or, even if this is given by reason, in its implementation; for it is that movement of the mind that makes it incapable of engaging in free consideration of principles, in order to determine itself in accordance with them. Thus it cannot in any way merit a satisfaction of reason. Nevertheless, enthusiasm is aesthetically sublime, because it is a stretching of the powers through ideas, which give the mind a momentum that acts far more powerfully and persistently than the impetus given by sensory representations. But (what seems strange) even **affectlessness** (*apatheia, phlegma in significactu bono*) in a mind that emphatically pursues its own inalterable principles is sublime, and indeed in a far superior way, because it also has the satisfaction of pure reason on its side. (CJ 271f.; cf. MM 408f.)

Before we examine how enthusiasm can be "aesthetically sublime" and why affectlessness (*apatheia*) is said to be sublime in a "far superior" way, we must attend to the beginning of this passage. Kant expresses a desire "to dwell a little on the last point." What is that point? It is that some affects are seen as instances of the "sublime" in "nature . . . within ourselves," that is, within human sensibility. Enthusiasm is presumably one of those affects that is represented as a power of the mind to "soar" above obstacles of sensibility by means of "moral principles." Despite the reference to moral principles (or the "idea of the good"), enthusiasm should be distinguished from moral feeling and respect, not least because enthusiasm is an affect. The nature of "affects" is explained in a notable footnote:

> Affects are specifically different from **passions**. The former are related merely to feeling; the latter belong to the faculty of desire, and are inclinations that make all determinability of the faculty of choice by means of principles difficult or impossible. The former are tumultuous and unpremeditated, the latter sustained and considered; thus indignation, as anger, is an affect, but as hatred (vindictiveness), it is a passion. The latter can never,

in any circumstances, be called sublime, because while in the case of an affect the freedom of the mind is certainly hampered, in the case of passion it is removed. (CJ 272n; cf. APV 251, MM 408)

What we call sublime within ourselves (certain affects) is represented as a power (*Macht*) of the mind. It "becomes interesting" because it demonstrates the ability to rise above sensibility by means of rational moral principles.[4] This leads Kant to consider the view that enthusiasm is "aesthetically sublime."[5]

If enthusiasm is the affect described in the passage above, and it is thus represented as a power of the mind to soar above obstacles of sensibility, what would those obstacles be? The familiar, troubling inclinations and modifications of sensibility broadly construed are certainly good candidates. Just before the beginning of the block quote, Kant wrote that "human nature does not agree with that good of its own accord, but only through the dominion that reason exercises over sensibility" (CJ 271). In addition, perhaps one should not exclude the possibility that being phlegmatic or lacking feeling in a *negative* sense can also be an obstacle, just as phlegm can have a positive, moral sense, in which case it is an advantageous natural gift (APV 254).

Kant "dwells a little" at this point in order to claim that *enthusiasm* is an instance or example of the mind's soaring above sensibility. It may be tempting to read this claim as referring not to enthusiasm but to the moral feeling of respect or to some purely rational or reason-caused feeling.[6] Such an alternate reading would claim that only the moral feeling of respect (respect for the "morally good") "soars" above sensibility and that enthusiasm is to be *contrasted* with such superiority of reason. But such a reading does not seem accurate: it seems clear that Kant is discussing enthusiasm here, since he refers to certain "affects."

---

[4] I suggest that we understand Kant's claim that enthusiasm is "interesting" as similar to his claim that natural beauty is interesting or merits our intellectual interest (CJ § 42). According to the latter, the experience of natural beauty can be taken as a sensible hint or sign that nature is amenable to our ends or at least will not thwart our aims and efforts, above all our efforts to be moral (i.e., the highest end of nature; CJ 435). While this is not the same reason he finds enthusiasm interesting, surely Kant is exhibiting an analogous intellectual "interest" here.
[5] On the Kantian sublime, see Chapter 9, by Katerina Degligiorgi, in this volume. See also Clewis, *The Kantian Sublime*, chap. 2 (56–125); "What's the Big Idea? On Emily Brady's Sublime," *Journal of Aesthetic Education* 50, no. 2 (2016): 104–18; and "The Place of the Sublime in Kant's Project," *Studi Kantiani* 28 (2015): 149–68.
[6] I will not pursue the differences between respect, the moral feeling, and other moral feelings (cf. MM 399–403), but use the term "moral feeling of respect" broadly. I also leave aside the issue of what motivates the moral agent – the moral law, a feeling of moral respect, or some combination or alternative.

In the next paragraph, Kant calls enthusiasm "aesthetically sublime." To the extent that we recognize the dominance of *sensibility* in it, enthusiasm is not sublime: generally, if sensibility dominates reason, a feeling cannot be sublime. But enthusiasm is called "aesthetically sublime" because it shares a stretching of the mental powers and faculties (including imagination) also present in the sublime, even if enthusiasm qua affect lacks reason's reflection and does not appear to involve an act of judgment.[7] That enthusiasm has the structure of the sublime is clear from Kant's explanation: "it is a stretching of the powers through ideas." This gives "the mind a momentum that acts far more powerfully and persistently than the impetus given by sensory representations."[8] In this stretching through ideas, there is a *free play* between the faculties, namely, imagination and reason, whereby the imagination is expanded by the possibilities on which it reflects.[9] The free play between imagination and reason is a crucial component of Kant's transcendental-philosophical explanation of enthusiasm.

If enthusiasm has a stretching (yet, qua *affect*, without reason's reflection and judgment) similar to the one present in the sublime, then it would presumably be pleasant, just as the sublime is a "negative pleasure" (CJ 245). It is easy to see why enthusiasm would be pleasant. From a transcendental-philosophical perspective, i.e., at the level of explanation if not that of psychological awareness and phenomenology, the imaginative expansion and mental "stretching" is the principal source of the pleasure.[10] The exercise creates an expansion of the imagination, which is pleasing, even exhilarating.[11] Another source of pleasure arises from the fact that the enthusiast is imaginatively responding to and engaging with an idea of the *good*.

---

[7] It is worth recalling that in marginal notes from the 1760s Kant wrote that enthusiasm is the passion of the *sublime* (AK 20:43).

[8] Frierson reads this as an indication of the motivational force or "efficacy" of the enthusiasm. Patrick Frierson, *Kant's Empirical Psychology* (Cambridge: Cambridge University Press, 2014), 223. This seems right, even if Kant's claim eventually needs to be squared with his claim that enthusiasm seems *aesthetically* sublime.

[9] Frierson emphasizes the role of the unbounded exercise of imagination in the construction of intuitions that are supposed to satisfy our moral demands, in the process of which reason momentarily loses control; Frierson, *Kant's Empirical Psychology*, 224f. James Kirwan, in *The Aesthetic in Kant: A Critique* (London: Continuum, 2004), 90f., offers a sensualist reading of enthusiasm, in which sensuousness (in the affect) dominates sensuousness (sensibility).

[10] Kelly Sorensen prompts me to consider whether the pleasure and reflection are extrinsic, or instead intrinsic, to enthusiasm qua affect. I think that the pleasure and a kind of reflective activity are intrinsic components of enthusiasm; but the reflection is of or by imagination, not reason. Thus, I would distinguish the reflective activity of imagination (in enthusiasm) from that of reason and/or the power of judgment, in a judgment (*Urteil*) of the sublime. Reflection, moreover, should not be confused with *reflexivity* (i.e., self-awareness).

[11] With respect to the sublime (not enthusiasm), this source of the pleasure is elaborated in Clewis, "A Theory of the Sublime Is Possible," *Wassard Elea Revista* 4 (2016): 45–68, esp. 60–61.

A puzzle arises at this point. Kant thinks that enthusiasm is *aesthetically* sublime, but he also denies that it is *truly* sublime, or at least not as sublime as *apatheia* (since affects, unlike experiences of the sublime, do not have the satisfaction of reason on their side). With this move, Kant appears to have asserted a contradiction. How can enthusiasm be both aesthetically sublime and *not* sublime (or at least not *very* sublime)?

The contradiction arises from an equivocation, and it disappears when one realizes that there are two senses of the sublime at work. The first is the familiar sense of the "aesthetic" feeling[12] of the sublime, where "aesthetic" is understood in a sense similar to the one in which the "Analytic of the Beautiful" is devoted to an examination of beauty. The feeling of enthusiasm has a stretching similar to that of the sublime in this sense: despite their crucial differences, both enthusiasm and the sublime can be characterized as a stretching of the mental powers through ideas of reason in conjunction with imagination, or as involving a play between the faculties of reason and imagination.

However, "sublime" sometimes just means "superior" to the sensible, that is, raised above inner or outer nature.[13] Here the sublime simply means elevation over or superiority to sensibility (inner nature). So construed, sublimity just *is* the fact that the rational faculty is independent of nature. Employing this sense, for instance, Kant refers to the sublimity of our nature and of our moral vocation, spiritual capacity, moral predisposition, and susceptibility to determination by pure rational principles and the moral law.[14] This sense has little to do with aesthetic *feeling* (in the third *Critique* sense) as such, and has no necessary connection to it. Enthusiasm is *not* sublime in this sense, since it is an affect. The enthusiast experiencing an affect is in the throes of sensibility; reason is not in control. To this extent, enthusiasm does not have the satisfaction of reason on its side. For this reason, Kant claims *apatheia* is far superior to enthusiasm in sublimity. In other words, the diminished view of enthusiasm derives from this second sense of "sublime." It leads Kant to suggest that *apatheia* "in a mind that emphatically pursues its own inalterable principles is sublime."

---

[12] Kant uses the term "sublime" quite widely: feelings, judgments, experiences, ideas, and reason are variously described as sublime, albeit in different senses. The fact that Kant is not clear about the sublime's referent (reason, faculty of the supersensible, ideas of infinite power or magnitude, idea of humanity, idea of freedom) is unimportant for the present argument. It seems uncontroversial to claim (as I do here) that the sublime is a feeling.

[13] I thank Oliver Sensen for this point; see Sensen, *Kant on Human Dignity* (Berlin: Walter de Gruyter, 2011), 196f.

[14] See Clewis, "The Place of the Sublime," 158. Examples of this sense can be found at: CPR 7, 87, 117; CJ 262; and MM 435.

If we do not make the foregoing distinction between these two senses of sublimity, this passage can lead to absurdities. How could *apatheia* be sublime if the sublime involves intense feeling and *apatheia* (affectlessness) does not? The answer is not that *apatheia* necessarily involves an intense feeling of the sublime; this would be contradictory. A better answer is that the *apatheia* stimulates the feeling of the sublime in observers who aesthetically judge and appreciate *apatheia*, similar to how one might be impressed by a person fulfilling a (supererogatory) duty, especially at great self-sacrifice or even peril.[15] There is another, compelling and not necessarily exclusive explanation. Like freedom and our determinability by rational and moral principles, *apatheia* is called sublime in the sense of necessarily involving elevation over sensibility. "Sublime" is not being used in its "aesthetic" sense: *apatheia* is "sublime" in the second, perhaps simpler, sense of the word (elevated, raised).[16]

Kant's claim that it is "commonly maintained" that "nothing great" can be accomplished without enthusiasm also merits comment. Examining the common opinions or beliefs, Kant's method here is reminiscent of Aristotle's consideration of received *endoxa*. What is the origin of the common view here? The slogan that without enthusiasm nothing great can be accomplished was frequently repeated throughout the eighteenth century.[17] It derives both from modern philosophers such as Shaftesbury and Rousseau, and strikingly, from Kant himself. (Later, Ralph Waldo Emerson cited the view approvingly, in the last paragraph of his 1841 essay, "Circles.")

---

[15] Kant's own examples: soldiers obeying orders stoically, going to their deaths, while following the principles of war ("displaying all the virtues of peace, gentleness, compassion") and rules of engagement, with "reverence for the rights of civilians." The "object of the greatest admiration" is "someone who is not frightened, who has no fear, thus does not shrink before danger but energetically sets to work with full deliberation." They display the "incoercibility" of their minds by danger (CJ 262f.). An extreme instance of this is when such a person faces death without fear. Representations of such courageous confrontations, especially in art forms such as tragedy (as Schiller and Schelling explored in their discussions of sublimity) and in films such as Stanley Kubrick's *Barry Lyndon* and *Spartacus* and Mel Gibson's *Braveheart* seem intended to elicit the sublime.

[16] The present explanation thus expands my treatment of how Kant uses the word "sublime" and adds to the account in Clewis, *The Kantian Sublime*, 234, where I claim that moral *apatheia* can *elicit* the sublime. But, as Sorensen suggested to me, both of the following claims can be true: (a) affectlessness can arouse an affect in observers and spectators, and (b) affectlessness is "sublime" in the sense of "superior." Sorensen offers an interpretation affirming (a) and maintains that a state or condition of affectlessness can arouse or elicit an affect, admiration (*Bewunderung*): "reason can *produce* an affect in attending to the *absence* of affect." Kelly D. Sorensen, "Kant's Taxonomy of the Emotions," *Kantian Review* 6, no. 1 (2002): 123.

[17] Zuckert, "Kant's Account of Practical Fanaticism," 296.

Whereas in the cited passage Kant seems to deny, or at least doubt, the truth of the claim that nothing great could be accomplished without enthusiasm, Kant once considered it to be *true*.[18] Kant asserted a version of the claim: "This two-sided appearance of fantasy in moral sensations that are in themselves good is enthusiasm, and nothing great has ever been accomplished in the world without it (EH 267).[19] Eventually, however, Kant came to doubt the truth of the claim. For instance, the Friedländer transcription of the anthropology lecture (1775–1776) states, with a hint of skepticism: "One is wont to speak highly of enthusiasm, that it does many great things, and that all the great changes in the world are to have originated from enthusiasm, not from cold judgment, but from intuition" (AK 25:530, cf. 621). The Mrongovius transcription (1784–1785) develops this notion that cold judgment or reason should be the source of great changes, i.e., that reason should provide a rational principle (identified, in the contemporaneous *Groundwork*, as the moral law) by which to discern and even motivate courses of action. "Nowadays enthusiasm is praised so much, but one must intuit principles not with affect, but with cold reason" (AK 25:1287). Hence, when Kant says it is "commonly maintained," he could have in mind not only writers such as Shaftesbury or Rousseau, but himself.

Although he calls enthusiasm "aesthetically sublime," Kant never characterizes it as a judgment (*Urteil*) of the sublime. Why does he choose not to characterize enthusiasm as a pure or impure judgment of sublimity? An important conceptual reason is that, in the typical case, enthusiasm is "interested" whereas in judgments of the sublime the appreciator is disinterested: the satisfaction in the sublime is represented as "without interest" (CJ 247). Enthusiasm typically gives rise to an action, or at least to a desire based on a determination of the will. Unlike pure aesthetic feeling (i.e., beauty and sublimity), enthusiasm has motivational power, or at least involves an interested response to an idea of the good.

After stating that affects are imprudent because they do not have the guidance of reason, and that it would be wrong to foster affects intentionally, Kant states in the (1798) *Anthropology* (book III, "On the Faculty of Desire"):

---

[18] The claim itself seems to be false. For reasons, see Clewis, *The Kantian Sublime*, 40.
[19] The passage continues (slightly modified): "Things stand quite differently with the fanatic (visionary, raver) [*Fanatiker* (*Visionär*, *Schwärmer*)]," making a strong case for translating *Schwärmerei* as "fanaticism" (and reserving "enthusiasm" for *Enthusiasmus*).

> Nevertheless, reason, in representing the morally good by connecting its ideas with intuitions (examples) that have been imputed to them, can produce an enlivening of the will (in spiritual or political speeches to the people, or even in speeches to oneself). Reason is thus enlivening the soul, not as effect but rather as cause of an affect with respect to the good, in which reason still always handles the reins, and an enthusiasm of good resolution is produced – an enthusiasm which, however, must be attributed to the faculty of desire and not to affect as a stronger sensible feeling. (APV 253f.; translation modified)

This passage is puzzling, since Kant is unclear about whether the feeling in question is an affect ("as cause of an affect") or it is not ("attributed ... not to affect").[20] This lack of clarity, however, does not justify modifying the claim that for Kant enthusiasm is an affect. But there is another peculiarity: even if it is an affect, the feeling described here is far more *positive* than the description in the anthropology transcriptions and the third *Critique*. Reason, *while holding the reins*, causes enthusiasm by representing an idea of the good in intuitions and examples, thereby animating the will. It is thus an enthusiasm of "good resolution." The enthusiasm is "interested" in the sense that it is "an enlivening of the will." Yet reason appears to be in control. This is admittedly difficult to reconcile with Kant's claim that enthusiasm is an affect, since that would seem to rule out control by reason.

Since affects belong to feeling (sensibility) (MM 407; CJ 272f), and enthusiasm is an affect, enthusiasm is a feeling rather than a desire. But the above-quoted passage is found in the section, "On the Faculty of Desire." What is going on here? Enthusiasm is a feeling that (like the agreeable) engages the will, and therefore is linked to desire; this is what is meant by claiming that it has motivational force. But it is also an affect. In other words, the text seems unclear about whether enthusiasm belongs to the faculty of sensibility or desire, because enthusiasm is an affect that can eventually motivate.[21] As Frierson puts it, enthusiasm is a "practical" feeling.[22] In this context, it is useful to recall that Kant once wrote (in the 1760s) that enthusiasm is a *passion* (AK 20:43). Based on his later

---

[20] In *The Kantian Sublime* (3f., 42, 169–73) I resolved this by distinguishing "practical" from "aesthetic" enthusiasm, as well as at least five different senses of interest, which bear on how to conceive of the "practical." In some senses, aesthetic enthusiasm is "interested," while in others it is not. For a nuanced account of a relation between the idea of reason and the exercise of imagination that ultimately issues in volition and action, see Frierson, *Kant's Empirical Psychology*, 223–27.
[21] That some affects can be desires and feelings is usefully illustrated by Sorensen's figure 3 in "Kant's Taxonomy of the Emotions," 118.
[22] Frierson, *Kant's Empirical Psychology*, 227.

accounts, I think Kant's considered, mature view is that it is an affect that can *lead to* or become a passion (see also APV 269).

Even if enthusiasm is a response to the morally good, deliberately inculcating it is still unquestionably prohibited since it is an affect (CPR 155), as I noted elsewhere.[23] In claiming this, Kant adopts a negative view of enthusiasm. Kant notes that it is popular to try to shape minds through "melting, tender feelings" or "high-flown, puffed-up pretensions" (one could say, through *bathos*, or the "false sublime"), which make the heart languid instead of strengthening it, rather than "by a dry and earnest representation of duty." He continues:

> It is altogether contrapurposive to set before children, as a model, actions as noble, magnanimous, meritorious, thinking that one can captivate them by inspiring an enthusiasm [*durch Einflößung eines Enthusiasmus*] for such actions. For, since they are still so backward in observance of the commonest duty and even in the correct judging of it, this is tantamount to soon making them fantasizers. But even with the instructed and experienced part of humankind this supposed incentive has, where it is not a prejudicial effect on the heart, at least no genuine moral one, though this is what one wanted to bring about by means of it. (CPR 157)[24]

It is not that the feeling is immoral per se, but that it does not help educators achieve the ends of moral education: it has no genuinely moral effect. Of course, if such feelings are used improperly, it could create moral confusion in children and even adults. In similar fashion, Kant writes in the *Metaphysics of Morals*: "A good example (exemplary conduct) should not serve as a model, but only as a proof that it is really possible to act in conformity with duty" (MM 480).

---

[23] My recognition of this point was not sufficiently noted by Melissa McBay Merritt, who wrote: "According to Clewis, *Enthusiasmus* can play a legitimate and benevolent role in our moral development." See Merritt, "Review of Robert R. Clewis, The Kantian Sublime and the Revelation of Freedom," *British Journal for the History of Philosophy* 18, no. 3 (2010): 528. Yet I had written on page 140: "Kant is wary of using feeling in moral education, since it can lead to flighty fancifulness and sentimentality." Likewise: "In moral education Kant is critical of replacing firm, resolute states of mind with tenderhearted ebullitions, in short, with oversensitivity (CPR 155n; CJ 273), *and I am not suggesting that enthusiasm be used in this way*" (emphasis added); Clewis, *The Kantian Sublime*, 198. Likewise: "I am not suggesting that enthusiasm can or should replace the moral feeling of respect in Kant's account of moral agency" (197). "I am not claiming that enthusiasm is a *necessary* condition of acting from a priori, moral motives" (196). Her review also misidentifies the contents of the final two chapters (528), and for some reason interprets me as endorsing what she calls the "enthusiastic admiration of exemplars" (her words, not mine) (530). For what I actually wrote, see Clewis, *The Kantian Sublime*, 85.

[24] I also quoted this passage in Clewis, *The Kantian Sublime*, 179.

10.2 Conceptual Content: Freedom

It is beyond the scope of this chapter to give a proper account of the cognitive content of feelings.[25] I will simply assume that feelings can have cognitive or conceptual content of some kind. If so, what would be the conceptual content of enthusiasm? According to the account found in the third *Critique* (CJ 272), the conceptual content of the feeling would be the idea of the morally good and corresponding representation or intuition provided by the imagination, or perhaps more precisely, it would be the play between this idea and an imaginative representation. What makes enthusiasm an affect is that (as Frierson observes) "the activity of reason misfires into an overabundance of imagination, which in turn inspires intense feelings that preclude rational choice." The feeling "arises from the efforts of *imagination* to reach the ideal posed by reason."[26] The role of an unbounded imagination distinguishes enthusiasm from a rational reflection on a moral idea, i.e., from respect and other moral feelings.

Is Kant ever specific about which idea is in play here? He describes the conceptual or intellectual content in various ways over the four decades in which he discussed enthusiasm. Yet even in the early accounts in the *Observations* and lectures, the content is a "principle" or "idea." In the third *Critique*, it is the idea of the "morally good" (CJ 272) and perhaps even the idea of God (CJ 274). In formulations from the 1790s, Kant understands "the good" broadly to include moral-political ideas (e.g., a republic). In the *Anthropology*, Kant calls it the idea of freedom.[27] (This does not mean that it must be this particular idea, but that it can be.) This identification of the content as freedom fits nicely into Kant's conceptual framework, since, like other moral-political ideas, political freedom can be

---

[25] The literature on this topic is vast. For a useful overview, see Jenefer Robinson, *Deeper than Reason: Emotion and Its Role in Literature, Music, and Art* (Oxford: Oxford University Press, 2005).
[26] Frierson, *Kant's Empirical Psychology*, 226f.
[27] In my discussion in *The Kantian Sublime* of what it meant for the sublime and enthusiasm to "reveal" or be an experience of freedom, I paid attention to the necessary Kantian strictures about experiencing freedom, and these strictures still apply. While I still accept the core of my earlier account, my aim here is more modest: to cast freedom (the good) as enthusiasm's *conceptual content*, while being agnostic about *revealing* freedom. For a defense of the latter, see Clewis, *The Kantian Sublime*, and Sorensen, "Kant's Taxonomy of the Emotions." In this 2002 article on sublimity, astonishment, and enthusiasm, Sorensen claims that "emotions can reveal our supersensible vocation as moral beings" and that the sublime plays the positive role of making us "aware of our noumenal freedom" (Sorensen, "Kant's Taxonomy of the Emotions," 124, and 128n22, respectively).

construed as a species of the good in a broad sense (leaving aside the debate about the priority of the right and the good).

Kant's aesthetic theory seems to imply that there can be a free play involving imaginative reflection with this idea, in other words, that there can be a play between the faculties of imagination and reason (the source of the moral idea) or between the specific imaginative intuitions and the idea of reason.[28] This would explain why the imagination is expanded: it is (pleasantly) stretched by the imagined possibilities on which it reflects. This reveals another specific difference between enthusiasm and the sublime (at least on one reading of the sublime). The conceptual content is not, as it is with sublimity, the agent's own agency or rational *powers*, i.e., theoretical reason (in the mathematical sublime) and practical reason (in the dynamical sublime).[29] Rather, it appears to be a play between the imagination and a moral idea (political freedom, the republic, justice, friendship) or corresponding attempt to realize that idea in the course of history.

Although Kant does not characterize it this way, it seems plausible to claim that enthusiasm is a response to some actual or concrete event or object, not just to an idea of reason, whereby an enthusiast judges an object or event to be good. If so, this could be articulated in terms of the more general formula:

> An agent is enthusiastic about X because (only if) the agent judges X to be good.[30]

This reveals why enthusiastic agents can get into trouble or produce harm. A person can be wrong about what is good, i.e., (1) wrong about whether X is in fact good (good for oneself, for others, and so on), or (2) can attempt to achieve and instantiate X in the wrong way, or employ the wrong means to realize or attain X. The latter, for Kant, was a crucial fault and shortcoming of the French revolutionaries in the late 1780s and 1790s, as we will see. Employment of the wrong means is also a problem in the case of religious *Enthusiasmus*, which incites people to act in ways they would not typically act (possibly for the worse), making them harder for the authorities to control (CJ 275). To avoid such outbreaks of

---

[28] Hence in Clewis, *The Kantian Sublime*, 191–94, I call enthusiasm a *dependent* (adherent) feeling, on analogy with dependent beauty, since the perceiver imaginatively attends to the conceptual content (the good) in the object or event.

[29] Yet, as noted (see n. 12), Kant is not always clear about what actually is sublime.

[30] Note that the implication does not go in the reverse direction ("if").

religious enthusiasm, the "momentum of an unbounded imagination" would need to be moderated (CJ 274).

Perhaps it would have been better if Kant had defined enthusiasm not as the response to the *good* with affect, but as a response to the *perceived* good. This is compatible with (1) above: one's perception could still be misguided or misinformed. Kant's definition of enthusiasm (a response to the morally good with affect) masks part of the shortcomings displayed by enthusiasts, for the problem is not simply that enthusiasm is an affect. The enthusiast can also be wrong about what is in fact good. This feature of enthusiasm is made possible by its cognitive elements.

If one wanted to stay with *Kant's* definition of enthusiasm as the idea of the good with affect, however, one could offer the following explanation, which is a way to account for (2) above: the good is properly identified (by reason), but the unbound imagination produces an intuition that obstructs or gets in the way of the proper implementation of means to that end (the rational ideal), while producing an affect.

10.3 Paradigmatic Enthusiasm in Kant's Lectures and Essays

Up to this point, my discussion has been based on the Critical account. But the concept of enthusiasm did not just suddenly become interesting to Kant from out of nowhere, without a trace. He did not just mention enthusiasm in passing. Rather, there are descriptions of enthusiasm throughout the pre-Critical writings and student notes. To distinguish these from the enthusiasm described in the next section, these instances can be called *paradigmatic* or typical cases.

Kant's pre-Critical work, *Observations on the Feeling of the Beautiful and Sublime*, despite having a title suggesting that it is a work in aesthetic theory, is largely about the sociological and anthropological differences between men and women and various peoples and nations. When Kant began to offer a course on anthropology in 1772–1773, it is thus unsurprising that much of this material was included in or covered by the new anthropology course. Enthusiasm, for instance, is discussed in the course.

In the *Observations*, Kant distinguishes fanaticism from enthusiasm. Fanaticism (*Fanaticism*), Kant writes (employing personification), "believes itself to feel an immediate and extraordinary communion with a higher nature" (OBS 251n).[31] In contrast, enthusiasm "signifies the state

---

[31] The fact that Kant uses the cognate (*Fanaticism*) in his characterization of *Schwärmerei* provides still more support for translating the term as "fanaticism."

of the mind that is inflamed beyond the appropriate degree by some principle [*Grundsatz*], whether it be by the maxim of patriotic virtue, or of friendship, or of religion, without involving the illusion of a supernatural community" (OBS 251n). In its "degenerate" form, the "fervor for freedom" inclines to enthusiasm (OBS 221). The fanatic or visionary (*Visionär*) is a "deranged" person who presumes to have immediate inspiration and familiarity with heavenly powers (EH 267).[32]

In the lectures on anthropology, Kant offers several descriptions of enthusiasm, at times taking the opportunity to criticize the textbook he adopted in the course, Alexander Baumgarten's *Metaphysica*: "The author [Baumgarten] conflates enthusiasm with fanatics [*Schwärmern*] or visionaries" (AK 25:1287).[33] A lecture transcription from 1775/76 (Friedländer) states: "The fantast fancies he sees objects of this world, but the enthusiast believes he sees objects of the spirit world ... Enthusiasm is a fantasizing in regard to objects of the understanding, for example enthusiasm of the virtue of patriotism, when an ideal is taken for something real" (AK 25:528). "As noble as is the enthusiast, so base is the fanatic. The enthusiast has after all a true archetype as his object, but the fanatic follows absurdities and figments of the mind ... All fanatics have no correct philosophy, but the enthusiasts indeed do, only they follow their correct concepts with complete affect" (AK 25:531). Whoever "gives way" to the ideal of patriotism "with affect," where the ideal cannot be attained, "is enthusiastic" (AK 25:530). The lecture transcription cites Rousseau as an example of an enthusiast who, for the sake of his ideals of universal benevolence and love of humanity, gave up chances at actual friendship and community with others. Still, "such enthusiasts are not malicious people, but they are touched with principles of benevolence toward the entire human race, and since they cannot find such, they become misanthropes, for example, Rousseau" (AK 25:530). In the

---

[32] Peter Fenves acknowledges the difference between the fanatic and the enthusiast: "Kant, like other German writers of the eighteenth century, never tired of trying to distinguish a thoroughly repugnant *Schwärmerei* from an *Enthusiasmus* without which 'nothing great in the world could take place.'" Fenves, *Raising the Tone of Philosophy*, ed. Peter Fenves (Baltimore: Johns Hopkins University Press, 1993), xi.

[33] According to the Academy editors, Kant is referring to *Metaphysica* section X "Praesagitio" (Anticipation) of part III (Psychology) (*Metaphysica* §§ 610–18), where Baumgarten mentions prophecy and divination. The interesting issues of how Kant made use of and commented on Baumgarten's *Metaphysica*, and the extent to which the lectures can or should be interpreted as illustrating Kant's dialectical interaction with the assigned textbook, are beyond the scope of this chapter. For Kant's university teaching and his relation to his textbook authors, see the essays in the collected volume, *Reading Kant's Lectures*, ed. Robert R. Clewis (Berlin: Walter de Gruyter, 2015).

Mrongovius lecture from the mid-1780s, a slight shift appears, as enthusiasm is called a "passion":

> Whoever habitually occupies himself with the idea of the good in fantasy is a fantast. For whoever is so taken in by the idea of a perfect good *up to the point of passion* that he forgets that this is a mere idea and believes that it could actually be realized, is such a fantast in the good, or enthusiast. Thus there are enthusiasts of patriotism, friendship, etc.[34] (AK 25:1262, cf. 1373; emphasis added)

How does the concept of enthusiasm develop in the 1790s? In the published *Anthropology* (1798), which came to press about five years after the Reign of Terror of 1793–1794, Kant criticizes loving freedom too much or in the wrong way. In the section, "On the Inclination to Freedom as a Passion," Kant describes how nomadic or tribal peoples appear to value "outer" or external freedom, sometimes leading to a violent passion.

> Thus it is not only the concept of freedom under moral laws that arouses an affect, which is called enthusiasm, but the mere sensible representation of outer freedom heightens the inclination to persist in it or to extend it into a violent passion, by analogy with the concept of right. (APV 269)

The contrast between the affect (enthusiasm) and violent passion is significant. The former enthusiasm is an *affect* involving an imaginative play with a rational (moral) concept, the idea of the good or "the concept of freedom under moral laws." With a violent *passion*, there is only an *analogy* with the concept of right. By contrast, genuine enthusiasm is oriented toward the actual right (cf. CF 86).

The aforementioned passage at APV 269 sheds light on another passage in APV, where Kant discusses an enthusiasm that shakes "everything" and goes "beyond all bounds" as it did in revolutionary France. The revolutionaries (not the spectators) possessed a reprehensible passion, not just a strong affect (which after all would inhibit the choice and implementation of ends). The affable, friendly inclination of the French encourages benevolence toward others and even a general love of humanity ("universal philanthropy according to principles"), making the French likeable on the whole. But, Kant continues,

---

[34] Someone, presumably the transcriber (Mrongovius), here later inserted in reddish ink: "Enthusiasts of freedom 1793." While not written by Kant himself, it agrees with Kant's account in the *Anthropology*.

> The other side of the coin is a vivacity that is not sufficiently kept in check by considered principles, and to clear-sighted reason it is thoughtlessness not to allow certain forms to endure for long, when they have proved satisfactory, just because they are old or have been praised excessively; and it is an infectious spirit of freedom, which probably also pulls reason itself into its play, and, in the relations of the people to the state, causes *an enthusiasm that shakes everything and goes beyond all bounds*. (APV 313f.; italics modified)

Readers may be tempted to interpret the claim in APV that enthusiasm "goes beyond all bounds" as a mere repetition of the claim in the *Critique of the Power of Judgment* that in enthusiasm qua affect the imagination is "unreined" ("General Remark," CJ 275). However, in light of the deadly violence of the Reign of Terror, it is more likely what "shakes everything" is a violent *passion* rather than an affect.

It is likely that the Reign of Terror affected Kant's characterization of enthusiasm. The characterization of enthusiasm in *Anthropology* counts more as a modification than a mere repetition of Kant's familiar views concerning enthusiasm. For instance, in a lecture from 1784–1785, about five years before the beginning of the French Revolution, Kant is reported to have made a claim nearly identical to the one found in the third *Critique*. "With enthusiasts, the power of imagination is no doubt unreined, that is, without limits, but not unruled. With the dreamer, the power of imagination is unruled" (AK 25:1262, cf. 1287). Later in the same lecture (Mrongovius), the characterization of enthusiasm is repeated: "If the melancholic has a great deal of understanding, he becomes an enthusiast; if he has little understanding, he becomes a fantast [*Phantast*] or fanatic [*Schwärmer*]. With the enthusiast, the power of imagination is unreined; with the fantast, it is unruled. I can still tame the former, for it is mere exaggeration of the rules, but not the latter, for it is without all rules" (AK 25:1373).

At the same time, the political events in France led Kant to characterize enthusiasm in a more *positive* light, too. According to a draft of "An Old Question Raised Again: Is the Human Race Constantly Progressing?" (R8077, ca. fall 1795–fall 1797) a feeling of "enthusiasm" is felt by "mere spectators of the revolution" sympathizing "with affect" and with "lively participation" (AK 19:604). The "universal" yet "forceful" participation (*Theilnehmung*) in the "highest cosmopolitan good" could even "approach the most powerful moral incentive" (AK 19:612). In the published version, to which we now turn, Kant clarified that, though enthusiasm cannot be a *moral* incentive per se, it is oriented toward the moral-political good or right (*Recht*), and he further interpreted enthusiasm for an actual republic in Europe as evidence of a moral predisposition in humanity.

10.4 An Exceptional Case: Enthusiasm for a Republic

This exceptional instance of the feeling is felt in response to what Kant considered a remarkable event in history, the establishment of the first French Republic.[35] This instance stands apart in the Kantian corpus. As much as he faults the French people for (passionate, practical) enthusiasm in *Anthropology*, Kant also admires the enthusiastic response felt around the world and above all in other European nations. In "An Old Question Raised Again,"[36] enthusiasm is described as a sublime mental movement that is both disinterested and has universal validity. In section 6, "Concerning an Occurrence in Our Time Which Demonstrates This Moral Tendency of the Human Race," Kant identifies this "occurrence" in the following passage:

> It is simply the way of thinking of the spectators which reveals itself *publicly* in this play [*Spiele*] of great revolutions [*Umwandlungen*], and manifests such a universal yet disinterested participation [*uneigennützige Teilnehmung*] for the players on the one side against those on the other, even at the risk that this partiality could become very disadvantageous for them if discovered. Owing to its universality, this way of thinking demonstrates a character of the human race at large and all at once; owing to its disinterestedness, a moral character of humanity, at least in its predisposition, a character which not only permits people to hope for progress toward the better, but is already itself progress insofar as its capacity is sufficient for the present.
>
> The revolution ... finds in the hearts of all spectators (who are not engaged in this play themselves) a wishful *participation* [*Teilnehmung*] that borders closely on enthusiasm, the very expression of which is fraught with danger; this participation, therefore, can have no other cause than a moral predisposition in the human race. (CF 85)

Kant reads this rare enthusiasm as a sign of a moral tendency or predisposition in humanity, and thus as the basis for hope in moral-political progress for human beings. This feeling is clearly an extraordinary instance of enthusiasm. It fits into his broader philosophical aims in a way that ordinary enthusiasm does not. It helps him articulate an account of how morality, which he takes to be the "final end" of nature (CJ §§ 83–84), can

---

[35] I agree with Frierson that this instance of enthusiasm is the "exceptional" rather than paradigmatic case (Frierson, *Kant's Empirical Psychology*, 227n13). I adopted a similar position in *The Kantian Sublime* (20, 169) and there called it "aesthetic" enthusiasm, highlighting its disinterestedness.
[36] For background on this text, see Clewis, *The Kantian Sublime*, 2n2.

be actualized in the natural order.[37] Here, the spectators feel enthusiasm in response to a concrete event unfolding in history, an event, Kant thinks, that will not easily be forgotten: such enthusiasm takes on symbolic import.

Despite Kant's interpretation of this instance of enthusiasm, his characterization of the feeling is consonant with that of the third *Critique*. Kant uses the language of exaltation (*Exaltation*) and of being stretched (*gespannt werden*). He describes the "zeal and grandeur of soul" (*Eifer und der Seelengröße*) (CF 86f.). The concepts of exaltation and grandeur were used throughout the eighteenth-century aesthetic and rhetorical tradition to describe or explain the experience of the sublime. Kant's reference to "being stretched" should sound familiar to readers of the third *Critique*. The description is reminiscent of the characterization of enthusiasm in the *Critique of the Power of Judgment* (CJ 272).

Some commentators have questioned whether the onlookers are actually feeling enthusiasm rather than something only "bordering" closely on it. But they are perhaps being misdirected by the phrase, "borders closely." It seems quite clear that the spectators are actually feeling enthusiasm. Kant characterizes this wishful participation as the "passionate participation in the good" (*Teilnehmung am Guten mit Affect*), which is nearly identical to the definition of enthusiasm in the third *Critique*. More explicitly, Kant makes a reference to "genuine" enthusiasm. He even defines it: "genuine enthusiasm always moves only toward what is ideal and indeed, to what is purely moral" (CF 86). In a footnote to this passage, Kant again mentions enthusiasm and refers to "such an enthusiasm – for upholding justice for the human race" (CF 86n). So there is actually little room for doubt.

Unlike the enthusiasm discussed in the *Observations* and anthropology lectures, this instance of enthusiasm is described as universal and disinterested ("universal yet disinterested participation"), namely, as possessing two of the "big four" features of a pure aesthetic judgment. (The other two are "purposiveness without a purpose" and "necessity.") Kant claims that the feeling is required of all disinterested spectators of the events ("the hearts of all spectators").[38] This is quite remarkable, and it suggests that

---

[37] See also Kant's discussion of creating a bridge from nature to freedom (CJ 175, 195; AK 20:244), in which aesthetic feelings and experience are to play a role.

[38] For these reasons, in Clewis, *The Kantian Sublime* (cf. 20), I claimed that *this particular instance* of enthusiasm, which like the sublime involves a stretching of the powers "through ideas," counts as an experience of the sublime. There are crucial differences between *paradigmatic* enthusiasm and the sublime (such as: qualifying as a judgment, the role of reason, nature of the reflective activity). Paradigmatic enthusiasm cannot be an instance of the sublime in the full Kantian sense of an aesthetic judgment of sublimity.

enthusiasm plays a far more important role in Kant's philosophy broadly construed than one would expect, if one limited one's reading to the third *Critique* alone. This symbolic use of enthusiasm in Kant's philosophy of history, which employs language from his aesthetics, justifies calling enthusiasm a significant Kantian feeling.

But Kant's characterization leads to a puzzle: how can enthusiasm be *disinterested*, as it states in this passage, if it is based on an interest and gives rise to actions, i.e., if it has motivational power? It is crucial to keep in mind the various senses of "disinterestedness."[39] The puzzle can be resolved if one keeps in mind that these spectators are disinterested in some senses, but not in others. They are disinterested in the sense that they are not directly involved in the events. They are not so much active contributors to the revolution as they are well-wishing onlookers. The spectators are neither the French nobility and aristocracy, nor the peasants and revolutionaries. The enthusiasts are not exactly passive, for they are actively reading, observing, discussing, and hoping – contributing by way of *feeling*, as it were. As observers and spectators, their "enthusiasm" does not exactly have the same motivational force as it does for the revolutionaries themselves (whom I think are best characterized as being passionate in Kant's sense of the term). They are not actively contributing in the sense of soldiers or partisans, nor even participating through "softer" means (e.g., providing resources or materials). But they are not impartial (in this sense they *are* "interested"), for they want the republicans to win. In the passage cited above, Kant ascribes "partiality" to the onlookers. One might call them "partial spectators" looking on from a distance. They want the good and the right to be realized in the world. They are rooting for the republic to be established; in this sense they are *not* indifferent to the "existence" of the "object" (to adopt the terms from CJ 205), namely, the republic in France. They have a rationally based desire to see the republic established, and they express this even at great risk to their own lives and well-being; hence the expression of their enthusiasm even runs *against* their personal interests (thereby creating another parallel with the sublime, which overrides or threatens self-interest).

But what is so special about this event? If we do not interpret the establishment of the French Republic in its historical-political context, it is easy to overlook that it was the first attempt of its kind in continental Europe, and that Kant saw it in its novelty. There were no other European events by which to compare it – indeed, like the sublime it could have been

---

[39] In Clewis, *The Kantian Sublime* (146f., 189), I distinguished five senses of disinterestedness.

perceived as being great "beyond all comparison" (CJ 250). It is meaningful to the spectators that these moral-political ideals are enacted for the first time, enlivening the imagination with thoughts of future possibilities. Kant's observers see the establishment of the Republic as a historical event with consequences that could spread far beyond the single nation-state in which the events occurred. Kant claims that the event, and the response to it, will never be forgotten. It was not the violence and blood that had symbolic import, but the fact that the revolution was seen as a concrete first step toward setting up republics across Europe, and, Kant might have hoped (as *Perpetual Peace* suggests), a league of European states.

The reference to "a character which not only permits people to hope for progress toward the better, but is already itself progress insofar as its capacity is sufficient for the present" brings out the temporal character of this instance of enthusiasm. The modality of the feeling seems to be above all *futural*, even if it is obviously connected to and based on present events and opportunities. The spectators are not enthusiastic about the past as such, but about emerging possibilities – reflection on which the imagination, the faculty of possibility, plays an active role. Like hope, enthusiasm is oriented toward the future.

10.5 Comparison with Other Feelings

I now briefly compare and contrast (paradigmatic) enthusiasm with other Kantian feelings of pleasure and displeasure. Like the agreeable and the moral feeling of respect, and unlike the sublime, enthusiasm is "interested," in that it engages and determines the will; it can be based on prior desires and interests as well as cause them and lead to actions. Like hope, the feeling has a *positive* valence since enthusiasm is a response to the morally good through an expanded imagination, even if (from the perspective of practical reason) enthusiasm qua affect involves a reprehensible loss of rational control.

Like the moral feeling of respect, and unlike the agreeable, it is a response to the morally good, hence is a kind of intellectual-imaginative pleasure, albeit one unquestionably distinct from the moral feeling. Unlike the agreeable, enthusiasm involves an imaginative play with ideas of reason. Like the sublime, it is a stretching of the mental powers through ideas in which the imagination is expanded, an intense and stirring (*rührend*) feeling and emotion. But unlike the sublime, it is not a *pure aesthetic* feeling or *judgment* (in the third *Critique* senses), and it lacks the reflection on one's rational powers that seems to be (on one reading) a necessary component of the sublime.[40] Unlike moral feelings and respect for the moral law, enthusiasm is not a purely rational feeling, but rather involves an unbounded, expanded imagination; technically, enthusiasm lacks moral worth and does not merit the satisfaction of reason. As an affect, enthusiasm involves an overpowering sensibility, in which the imagination is "unreined."

The "unboundedness" of the imagination might perhaps be seen as another specific difference from the sublime: one might be tempted to claim that in enthusiasm the imagination is (or feels) unbounded, whereas in the sublime it is not. However, I do not think this point is as clear as it has struck most commentators, who tend to overlook this aspect of the Kantian sublime. (Lyotard is an exception here.) In the sublime, too, the imagination is active, stretched, and expanded. Moreover, the sublime is an intense, moving, stirring feeling. But is the sublime also an affect? In the rhetorical-aesthetic tradition, with which Kant was to a significant extent familiar, the sublime was indeed characterized as an affect, rapture, and transport, a kind of *ekstasis*. Following (if not exactly agreeing with) writers such as Edmund Burke, even Kant uses "astonishment" to present his account of the feeling of the sublime.[41] "The astonishment [*Verwunderung*] bordering on terror ... [is] not actual fear, but only an attempt to involve ourselves in it by means of the imagination, in order to feel the power of" imagination ("General Remark," CJ 269).[42] In the second *Critique*, Kant uses the term amazement (*Erstaunen*), an affect, to capture the responses to conventional elicitors of the sublime. "Something that comes nearer to this feeling [respect] is admiration [*Bewunderung*], and this as an affect, amazement, can be directed to things also, for example, lofty mountains, the magnitude, number, and distance of the heavenly bodies, the

---

[40] Or at least, the *potential* to so reflect seems to be necessary, even if it is not always realized in particular experiences of the sublime.
[41] Cf. Burke: "Astonishment ... is the effect of the sublime in its highest degree." Edmund Burke, *A Philosophical Enquiry into the Origin of Our Ideas of the Sublime and Beautiful* (part II, § 1), in *The Sublime: A Reader in British Eighteenth-Century Aesthetic Theory*, ed. Andrew Ashfield and Peter de Bolla (Cambridge: Cambridge University Press, 1996), 131–44, 132.
[42] Astonishment is an affect, namely an "affect" in the representation of "novelty" that "exceeds expectation" (CJ 272; cf. CJ 365 and APV 261). Although this would seem to imply that some feelings of the *sublime* could count as affects, I doubt that Kant would claim that the sublime is an affect (he never explicitly characterizes it that way). The claim that the sublime is an affect (unlike the more modest claim that the affect, astonishment, can issue from, or spin out of, the experience of the sublime) would appear to put into question the sublime's rational basis, the role of reflection, and its status as a judgment. Kant would have wanted to avoid such implications.

strength and swiftness of many animals, and so forth" (CPR 76). But since it is time to conclude, I will not pursue this point further.[43]

10.6 Conclusion

For Kant, paradigmatic enthusiasm is problematic and deeply *ambiguous* (which is not to say that Kant's description is vague). Throughout the Kantian corpus, enthusiasm is dual natured.

On the positive side, Kant defines enthusiasm as an imaginative response to the morally good, i.e., a sensible-imaginative play with an idea of reason: enthusiasm is "aesthetically sublime." From a teleological perspective (and keeping in mind Kant's Critical strictures regarding teleological claims), one could say that enthusiasm is one of the means that nature uses (or *appears* to use) in order to achieve the good. It helps bring about or cause "great" movements or effects. Enthusiasm perhaps functions in some ways like the drive for honor.[44] The latter leads us to want to appear to be good or honorable, which has the fortuitous outcome that we pursue the course of action that is in *accordance* with morality, even if we do so for amoral or prudential reasons (thus, for Kant, acting without moral worth).

Moreover, in one remarkable and exceptional instance, enthusiasm acts as a moral sign of progress in Kant's teleological reading of history. As an imaginative response to ideas of the moral or political good, it possesses positive features that make it far preferable to delirium or fanaticism (*Schwärmerei*).

On the negative side, enthusiasm, qua affect, merits censure, for reason momentarily loses control while the enthusiast is in the throes of affect. The decisive feature here is not enthusiasm's status as a feeling, since feelings per se are neither immoral nor moral, but its status as an affect. Without the constraints of reason, enthusiasm can in principle lead agents to commit immoral or unjust acts. As I have noted here and in *The Kantian Sublime and the Revelation of Freedom*, Kant clearly warns against employing the feeling of enthusiasm in moral education, since it replaces respect for the moral law with sentimental feeling and fantasy.[45]

---

[43] Sorensen writes that astonishment is an affect that appears "related" to the feeling of the sublime. Sorensen, "Kant's Taxonomy of the Emotions," 128n22.
[44] On the drive for honor, see Alix Cohen, "From Faking It to Making It: The Feeling of Love of Honor as an Aid to Morality," in Clewis, *Reading Kant's Lectures*, 243–56.
[45] The negative side is evident at CJ 273; APV 202; APV 314. See especially MM 408f. (translation modified): "It is only the apparent strength of someone feverish that lets a lively participation [*Anteil*] even in the good rise to the point of affect, or rather degenerate into it. An affect of this kind is called enthusiasm."

Kant thought and wrote about enthusiasm from the relatively early and middle stages of his philosophical career until its very end – he published a characterization of enthusiasm in 1764, continued to discuss it in his lectures on anthropology beginning in 1772, and wrote on the topic well into the 1790s, devoting a passage to it in a *Critique* published in the first year of that decade, and further commenting on it in the *Anthropology* and *The Conflict of the Faculties* as the eighteenth century drew to a close. Kant therefore maintained a lifelong interest in the topic, and enthusiasm deserves to be classified as an important Kantian feeling.

11

*Sympathy, Love, and the Faculty of Feeling**
Kelly Sorensen

Everything good in Freud is already there and better in Nietzsche, Ken Gemes tells me. I don't disagree. But I am tempted by a bolder claim: everything good in Nietzsche is already there and better in Kant – or so I want to claim about the cases of sympathy and love, at least. Kant, like Nietzsche, is masterfully suspicious about sympathy and the attitudes that often accompany it. Both thinkers recognize the self-aggrandizement and darker mental states often lurking alongside sympathy, revealed when we undertake a careful archaeology of our mental states.

Kant's diagnosis of, and his various prescriptions for, the problems with sympathy and love are superior to Nietzsche's, I believe. I advance both an offensive case, with Kant on the attack against deficient forms of sympathy and love, and a defensive case, interpreting Kant as a friend of better forms of these emotions. I focus disproportionately on sympathy, at the expense of love, and more on Kant, at the expense of Nietzsche.

The offensive case is the one I have been suggesting: Kant is masterfully suspicious about whether certain kinds of sympathy and love are as admirable as they may seem to be. These kinds of sympathy and love may instead be surface expressions of deeper attitudes and commitments that are morally unflattering for the agent who has them. Besides Allen Wood, too few Kantian apologists have pressed the offensive case. I aim to do so here.

The defensive case is a version of the strategy, familiar over the last few decades, of showing that Kant is not the stereotypical cold Prussian fish of some twentieth-century Anglo-American scholarship. What is new here are arguments about the various ways in which Kant does, and with

---

* I thank Robert Clewis for thorough and helpful comments on this chapter. For additional comments, I thank Ryan Davis, Ken Gemes, Kate Norlock, Gudrun von Tevenar, and audiences at the 2016 Rocky Mountain Ethics Congress and the 2016 Lehigh University Philosophy Conference. My deepest appreciation goes to Allen Wood for the conversations that led to this chapter.

no significant modification of his views *could*, morally characterize and encourage sympathy.

11.1 The Offensive Case: Problems with Sympathy and Love

On the conventional interpretation, Kant does not think much of sympathy, compassion, or love. He does not fully trust them. And that conventional interpretation is mostly – but only mostly – correct. Let us start with Kant's mistrust, saving the forms of sympathy and love he trusts for the next section. Kant's mistrust is compelling when better understood.

Kant uses a variety of words – *Sympathie, Teilnehmung, Mitfreude, Mitleid, Mitleidenschaft, teilnehmende Empfindung* – for the conceptual territory associated with the English term "sympathy" (a territory already disputed among etymologists of English).[1] Nevertheless, a reasonable starting definition is this: "*Sympathetic joy [Mitfreude]* and *sadness [Mitleid] (sympathia moralis)* are sensible feelings of pleasure or displeasure (which are therefore to be called 'aesthetic') at another's state of joy or pain (shared feeling, sympathetic feeling)" (MM 456). Note that these sensible feelings are "aesthetic" in the sense that they are not tied to a desire or intention. Note also that sympathy may have a positive or a negative valence, according to the object of the feeling. When it has a negative valence, "compassion" functions as a near synonym (but see the distinctions in this area Kant makes in MM 456–57).

(1) One problem with sympathy is that it might not be available as a "mainspring" or incentive for some morally important action.[2] The sorrowing philanthropist of the *Groundwork* has become "overclouded by his own grief, which extinguished all sympathy [*Teilnehmung*] with the fate of others" (G 398). Kant's main aim in this case is less about sympathy and more about showing what he thinks "common rational cognition" entails about the nature of morality, as the title of the first section of the *Groundwork* indicates. There is no claim here that sympathy is never valuable, and no claim that one should endeavor to act without sympathy. But still, sympathy's sometime motivational unavailability – its

---

[1] See various essays in *Sympathy: A History*, ed. Eric Schliesser (New York: Oxford University Press, 2015).

[2] "We must distinguish between measuring-rod and mainspring. The measuring-rod is the principle of discrimination; the mainspring is the principle of the performance of our obligation" (AK 27:1422; quoted in Paul Guyer, *Kant and the Experience of Freedom* [Cambridge: Cambridge University Press, 1993], 339).

disappearance when an agent would benefit from its help – stands out. That is one mark against it.

(2) Second, sympathy is not an adequate moral "measuring-rod." Tuned as it is to the pains and struggles of others, sympathy may guide us to aid even others who are at pains – at pains to harm, lie, cheat, and steal. As a "principle of discrimination," sympathy is unreliable. Feelings like sympathy do "little" to "furnish a uniform standard of good and evil" (G 442).

(3) The third problem – a family of problems, really – will take more time to explore. For a start, note that sympathy can coexist all too easily with corrupt attitudes toward others. Kant readily imagines a world where everyone "prates about sympathy [*Teilnehmung*] and benevolence" and even sometimes acts sympathetically and benevolently, but "also cheats where he can, sells the right of human beings or otherwise infringes upon it" (G 423). Flawed in its own way, a world of rugged individualists would nevertheless be better than this woeful world of sporadic sympathy, he says. Kant's derisive tone here is striking, especially when the case says little against sympathy and benevolence besides that they can live alongside flagrant mistreatment of others.

His negative tone is better understood in light of his additional views about popular sentiments like sympathy, compassion, and love. In some cases, these sentiments not only coexist easily with corrupt attitudes toward others; they can even help *express, reflect, promote, and hide* those corrupt attitudes.

This is a startling claim. How could it be the case? Allen Wood is a helpful exegete of what he calls Kant's "shrewdly bleak vision" here.[3] We might begin, Wood suggests, by noticing that sympathy – negatively valenced sympathy, at least – is typically felt in regard to someone weaker than oneself (APV 263). In most reactions of sympathy, there is already a sort of hierarchy, or at least asymmetry, built into the relation between the sympathizer and the object of his sentiments. To admire sympathy is to admire an attitude of the strong toward the weak.

By itself, this may seem little cause for worry, since the sympathizer usually is in fact in a more fortunate position than the sympathizee. But note that the sympathizer can easily become engaged by *his own* sympathy: there you are, in distress and pain, and here I am, offering you the magnanimous gift of my sympathetic attention and care, the sympathizer expresses. Baked into that experience is the sympathizer's interpretation of

---

[3] Allen W. Wood, *Kant's Ethical Thought* (Cambridge: Cambridge University Press, 1999), 269–75.

Sympathy, Love, and the Faculty of Feeling 211

himself as superior, or at least in a superior position. The sympathizer's baked-in superiority might be explicit in his thoughts, or it might not be. Either way, the encounter with the object of sympathy then becomes something quite different than the pure, other-directed matter it first seemed. Instead of pure care for the other in distress, what is expressed is the self-indulgence of the sympathizer. Think about what bothers Milan Kundera about kitsch in art:

> Kitsch causes two tears to flow in quick succession. The first tear says: How nice to see children running on the grass!
> The second tear says: How nice to be moved, together with all mankind, by children running on the grass!
> It is the second tear that makes kitsch kitsch.[4]

The second feeling of the sympathizer's experience – the self-indulgent part about how nice it is to be sympathetic – felt either together with other agents (as Kundera's second tear is) or simply by the sympathizer alone, is one thing that makes deficient sympathy deficient. This is a "one thought too many" argument that Kantians can deploy. We can more accurately call it a "one *feeling* too many" argument, since again although the sympathizer might not be thoughtfully aware of this second self-focused feeling, this feeling takes the sympathizer's own sympathy as its object.[5]

The self-indulgence of sympathy is a problem because it is a species of the genus problem of self-conceit (*Eigendünkel*) – a propensity in human nature that worries Kant repeatedly. Self-conceit is what morality strikes down (CPR 73). We have a propensity, at least when thrown together in social groups and in the context of scarce resources, to compare ourselves with others – and further, a delusional propensity to want ourselves to come out well in the comparison. We like to think well of ourselves, and there is moral peril in doing so. Kant's claims here are largely empirical, but they are neither surprising nor controversial.[6] Many of the moral vices Kant most worries about – envy, ingratitude, malice, arrogance – stem from this sort of propensity for delusional comparison of self with others (MM 458–68). (As Wood notes, Kant's claims here are very strongly influenced by his reading of Rousseau. I can almost hear my Rousseau

---

[4] Milan Kundera, *The Unbearable Lightness of Being* (New York: Harper and Row, 1984), 251.
[5] Might some second-order pleasure at one's own sympathy, if not too much, be a good thing? Thomas Hurka argues so in *Virtue, Vice, and Value* (New York: Oxford University Press, 2001). But Hurka would concede that it does not take much second-order pleasure at one's own sympathy for it to be a bad thing.
[6] For example, see the growing empirical literature concerning "moral self-licensing": individuals who think of themselves as more sympathetic and virtuous than other people are more likely to allow

scholar colleague in the next building, reading this chapter and saying, "Actually, what is good in Nietzsche and Kant is already there and better in Rousseau." But more on that another time.)

Reasoning about the moral law strikes down this propensity. When I am "before a humble common man in whom I perceive uprightness of character . . . *my spirit bows*, whether I want it or whether I do not and hold my head ever so high, that he may not overlook my superior position" (CPR 76–77). Strutting and pretending I am superior, nevertheless when I reason about the moral law, my attention shifts away from a comparison of myself with another person toward instead a comparison of myself and my conduct with the demands of morality: "[The humble common man's] example holds before me a law that strikes down my self-conceit when I compare it with my conduct" (CPR 77).[7]

Sympathy is vulnerable to this self-conceit. This is not to say that all sympathy takes a deficient, self-indulgent form. Kant certainly does not think that it does, as we will see below. But he would think that there is a standing danger that morally useful sympathy will transform into its self-indulgent form. The human propensity to self-conceit can transform morally useful sympathy into something deficient. So sympathy needs constraint and oversight – it needs morality as a chaperone. People in the throes of sympathy and compassion might pretend they do not need moral constraint and chaperoning, but this is a pretense that is itself all the more self-indulgent.[8]

There is still more to say about this third family of problems with sympathy. Return to this characterization of the all-too-common experience of the sympathizer: there you are, in distress and pain, and here I am, offering you the magnanimous gift of my sympathetic attention and care. I noted above the one-feeling-too-many deficiency embedded in this experience and the self-conceit and self-indulgence often associated with it. But a further problem is the sympathizer's sense of his aid as a *magnanimous gift* on his part. Again, this sympathizer's particular experience of his aid might be explicit in his thoughts, or it might not. Either way, he is vulnerable to treating what is in fact a moral duty to the suffering poor as instead an exercise of his generous whim.

---

themselves to later indulge in unsympathetic and vicious behavior. See Anna C. Merritt, Daniel A. Effron, and Benoît Monin, "Moral-Self-Licensing: When Being Good Frees Us to Be Bad," *Social and Personality Psychology Compass* 4, no. 5 (May 2010): 344–57; and Daniel A. Effron and Paul Conway, "When Virtue Leads to Villainy: Advances in Research on Moral Self-Licensing," *Current Opinions in Psychology* 6 (2015): 32–35.

[7] See also Wood, *Kant's Ethical Thought*, 136–39.   [8] Wood, *Kant's Ethical Thought*, 274.

> Many people take pleasure in doing good actions but consequently do not want to stand under obligations toward others. If one only comes to them submissively, they will do everything: they do not want to subject themselves to the rights of people, but to view them simply as objects of magnanimity. It is not all one under what title I get something. What properly belongs to me must not be accorded to me merely as something I beg for. (AK 19:145)[9]

Kant's shrewd observation is that we tend to enjoy priding ourselves on what we prefer to interpret instead as our bountiful sentiments of sympathy and generosity. One way morality strikes down this self-conceit is painful and not self-celebratory: it reminds us that aid to others is often simply morally demanded of us, whether we want to offer it or not. In cases where institutional injustice creates inequality, "does a rich man's help to the needy, on which he so readily prides himself as something meritorious, really deserve to be called beneficence at all?" (MM 454).[10] Similarly, does a well-off person's sympathetic aid, which he so readily experiences as a magnanimous gift, really deserve to be considered a magnanimous gift?[11] Is it not morally corrupting, Kant believes, to entertain and endorse varieties of sympathy and sympathetic aid, in oneself and presumably in others too, that falsely inflate the moral excellence of the self and bury the demandingness and constraining nature of morality? Kant says that sympathy's directional tendency toward weaker beings tends to track our duty to protect them – that is, of course, nice news about sympathy; but the duty to protect others is a moral *duty* nonetheless (APV 263).

This moral psychological archaeology displays Kant's masterful capabilities of suspicion. When we turn to the case of love, we see the same "shrewdly bleak vision." Love, however wonderful, might at times be motivationally unavailable as a "mainspring" for moral action. And again like sympathy, love can be an unreliable "measuring-rod," since love might guide us to aid and protect those who harm, lie, cheat, and steal.

Love is subject to sympathy's complicated third set of problematic tendencies, too. Love's structure is such that it often takes as its object someone weaker or under our power – someone we do not necessarily need

---

[9] Quoted in Wood, *Kant's Ethical Thought*, 8.   [10] Quoted in Wood, *Kant's Ethical Thought*, 8.
[11] Instead we have *duties* to help others. And, if we can make it out in the right way, others have rights to our aid (maybe *collective* rights, given that Kant thinks of the duty to aid others as an imperfect duty, where no particular case of aid is morally required); see Robert N. Johnson, "Duties to and Regarding Others," in *Kant's Metaphysics of Morals: A Critical Guide*, ed. Lara Denis (Cambridge: Cambridge University Press, 2010), 192–209).

to respect. "We love everything over which we have a decisive superiority, so that we can toy with it, while it has a pleasant cheerfulness about it: little dogs, birds, grandchildren" (R1100 AK 15:490). Wood's translation of his favorite passage relevant to this view reads like a Nietzschean aphorism: "Love, like water, always flows downward more easily than upward" (AK 27:670).[12]

The problem with these deficient forms of love, using an interesting metaphor Kant employs, is that they pull us too close to the object of love:

> In speaking of laws of duty (not laws of nature) and, among these, of laws for human beings' external relations with one another, we consider ourselves in a moral (intelligible) world where, by analogy with the physical world, *attraction* and *repulsion* bind together rational beings (on earth). The principle of **mutual love** admonishes them constantly to *come closer* to one another; that of the **respect** they owe one another, to keep themselves *at a distance* from one another; and should one of these great moral forces fail, "then nothingness (immorality), with gaping throat, would drink up the whole kingdom of (moral) beings like a drop of water" (if I may use Haller's words, but in a different reference). (MM 449)

Love is a "great moral force," Kant says. But love that draws us too close to one another, without the cooperation of respect, that other great moral force, can become obsequious, suffocating, adhesive, demeaning, and paternalistic. (Importantly, Kant also suggests here that respect that draws us too distant from one another, without the cooperation of love, is equally dangerous.) Someone might express love for me by making my (non-immoral) ends their own; but I must not "demand that another throw himself away in order to slave for my end" (MM 450), and I should not welcome even another's gratuitous gift of slavish devotion to my ends – I should not welcome this gift for my own self-respect, and because it is difficult for the lover to avoid feeling superior to a being like me who is so distrusted to achieve my own ends.[13]

Like sympathy, love also needs moral constraint and oversight – it needs morality as a chaperone. Paul Guyer shows why in his waggish response

---

[12] The two passages in this paragraph are quoted in Wood, *Kant's Ethical Thought*, 272.
[13] See also Marcia Baron, "Love and Respect in the Doctrine of Virtue," in Mark Timmons, ed., *Kant's Metaphysics of Morals* (Oxford: Oxford University Press, 2002), 391–407; Christine Swanton, "Kant's Impartial Virtues of Love," in *Perfecting Virtue: New Essays on Kantian Ethics and Virtue Ethics*, ed. Lawrence Jost and Julian Wuerth (Cambridge: Cambridge University Press, 2011), 241–60.

to an objection I mentioned above: Bernard Williams's "one thought too many" argument. Williams imagines a man on a cruise who hears two people overboard and calling for help, one of whom is his wife; if the man stops and reflects about whether morality allows him to favor his wife and throw the lone available life preserver to her, he has, Williams says, "one thought too many." But Guyer claims that Williams cheats in this example by telling us too little about other relevant matters. Suppose the man is on a cruise with his wife but has been eyeing a younger, prettier woman. The man hears two people overboard calling for help, one of whom is his wife, and the other the younger woman. In the way Williams seems to endorse, the man acts immediately *from love* and so throws the lone life preserver – to the younger woman. Guyer says, correctly, that we should call this *one thought too few*.[14]

Why Kant's views about sympathy and love evoke Nietzsche should be clearer now. In each case something that is first taken as especially worthy turns out to be, under careful suspicion, something crucially different. Sentiments can obscure what they are really about. They can turn out to be less other-regarding after all, instead associated with, and even enabling and expressing, attitudes of hidden superiority. And for both Kant and Nietzsche, power and dominance do important explanatory work. Sympathy and love always flow downward more easily, from someone who presumes to have power or advantage over another, and who enjoys expressing that power in a way she might not otherwise be able to. Many adhering to the Judeo-Christian ethic, these weak people, Nietzsche says in *On the Genealogy of Morality*, they too want to be powerful; but unable or unwilling to express power now and in this life, they do so instead in a hidden, sometimes deferred manner. Nietzsche notes the self-focus of Aquinas's Christians in heaven, looking down upon the suffering of those in hell, so that their own enjoyment of heaven is greater.[15] This antisympathy is the kind of deeper attitude that can lurk behind putative Christian sympathy.

So what is good in Nietzsche's analysis about certain kinds of sympathy and love is already there in Kant. Kant has a neglected case for suspicion about the tendencies of sympathy and love. In section 2, I claim that it is not only there, but better.

---

[14] Guyer, *Kant and the Experience of Freedom*, 393.
[15] Friedrich Nietzsche, *On the Genealogy of Morality*, trans. Maudemarie Clark and Alan Swensen (Indianapolis, IN: Hackett, 1998), I: 15.

11.2 The Defensive Case: The Importance of Sympathy and Love

While Kant is correct to regard many varieties of sympathy and love with suspicion, he also articulates important morally positive roles for other varieties. Loyal Kant exegetes of the last several decades have often made defensive cases for sympathy and love in Kant's thought. This has been a necessary development, given the caricature of the cold Kant that prevailed before. I echo some of the positive roles noted by others, then argue for the existence of some roles less often noted.

(1) First, Kant claims that sympathy can serve as a substitute during moral development. Sympathy can be unavailable as a mainspring for performing a moral action – but so can reason, in its own, more patterned and predictable way, when an agent is young and immature. For Kant, moral development and strength of character are long-term achievements; it takes time to develop the strength to oppose counter-moral inclinations. During that development, sympathy can stand in "*provisionally*, until reason has achieved the necessary strength" (APV 253).[16]

(2) Second, sympathy gives information to deliberating agents. Sympathy helps an agent perceive morally relevant factors in the circumstances at hand.[17]

(3) More fundamentally, Kant also thinks that the "moral endowment" of love of one's neighbor is one of four preconditions for all moral behavior. "There is no obligation to have these [four preconditions] because they lie at the basis of morality, as *subjective* conditions of receptiveness to the concept of duty," and they are "antecedent predispositions on the side of *feeling*," Kant says (MM 399).[18] But he does think there are obligations associated with these preconditions, including a duty to cultivate sympathy, as indicated in this passage:

> But while it is not in itself a duty to share the sufferings (as well as the joys) of others, it is a duty to sympathize actively in their fate; and to this end it is therefore an indirect duty to cultivate the compassionate [*mitleidige*] natural

---

[16] Quoted in Wood, *Kant's Ethical Thought*, 270.
[17] See Nancy Sherman, *Making a Necessity of Virtue: Aristotle and Kant on Virtue* (Cambridge: Cambridge University Press, 1997), and "Reasons and Feelings in Kantian Morality," *Philosophy and Phenomenological Research* 55, no. 2 (June 1995): 369–77; see also Paul Guyer, "Moral Anthropology in Kant's Aesthetics and Ethics: A Reply to Ameriks and Sherman," *Philosophy and Phenomenological Research* 55, no. 2 (June 1995): 379–91, and Wood, *Kant's Ethical Thought*, 36.
[18] Paul Guyer argues for a certain relationship among these four preconditional feelings in Guyer, "Moral Feelings in the Metaphysics of Morals," in *Kant's Metaphysics of Morals: A Critical Guide*, ed. Lara Denis (Cambridge: Cambridge University Press, 2010), 130–51.

(aesthetic) feelings in us, and to make use of them as so many means to sympathy [*Teilnehmung*] based on moral principles and the feeling appropriate to them. – It is therefore a duty not to avoid the places where the poor who lack the most basic necessities are to be found but rather to seek them out, and not to shun sickrooms or debtors' prisons and so forth in order to avoid sharing painful feelings one may not be able to resist. For this is still one of the impulses that nature has implanted in us to do what the representation of duty alone might not accomplish. (MM 457)

Kant thinks that there is no duty to share the sufferings of others, since, for instance, in cases where I cannot help another person, my suffering at his suffering would only "increase the ills in the world." To return briefly to the offensive case above, this "would be an insulting kind of beneficence, since it expresses the kind of benevolence one has toward someone unworthy, called *pity*; and this has no place in people's relations with one another" (MM 457). As harsh as this view may seem at first, Kant's proto-Nietzschean suspicion about pity here is worth taking seriously: pity, like deficient varieties of sympathy and love, easily tends to be self-indulgent and associated with ugly interpersonal power asymmetries. Pity lacks respect.[19]

The passage also indicates Kant's view of sympathy (or as we will see below, one kind of sympathy) as something communicable by contagion, in sickrooms and debtors' prisons. And the passage returns us to the first positive role I listed for sympathy, as a morally useful impulse, implanted in us by nature, when reason is not yet at sufficient strength. It is tempting to understand sympathy here as merely a temporary developmental moral crutch. But that view would neglect Kant's long-game views about moral development. As Guyer argues, Kant's specific claims that

> sympathetic feelings are the means that nature has implanted in us to promote benevolence rather suggest that sympathetic feelings are the means *through* which the general representation of duty naturally and ordinarily works to move us to beneficent actions – they are not safeguards in case the representation of duty fails to work, but the means through which the representation of duty normally works.[20]

---

[19] Sympathetic pity also tends to be temporary and behaviorally ineffectual, compared to respect, Elizabeth Anderson argues, noting that nineteenth-century American white abolitionists tended to promote the former in behalf of slaves, and black abolitionists (like Frederick Douglass) the latter. See Anderson, "Moral Bias and Corrective Practices: A Pragmatist Perspective," in *Proceedings and Addresses of the American Philosophical Association* 89 (2015): 21–47, esp. 32–38.

[20] Guyer, "Moral Feelings in the Metaphysics of Morals," 147. See also Guyer, *Kant and the Experience of Freedom*, 390.

So sympathy is not just a substitute for the immature; it remains a core element in the everyday, lived moral life of the human agent.

(4) It might be easy to suppose that Kant endorses sympathy and love of neighbor because they are often gentle feelings – feelings that pose less of a threat to moral reflection and deliberation. But intriguingly, Kant also cautiously endorses a subset of powerful feelings that at least temporarily impede reflection. He calls these particular feelings "affects" (*Affekten*), a technical term he consistently uses across various texts for a class of feelings that are sudden, short lived (MM 408; CJ 272n), and overwhelming, "like water that breaks through a dam" (APV 252). The power of an affect is less about its strength and more about its eclipsing of reflection: "it is not the intensity of a certain feeling that constitutes the affected state, but the lack of reflection in comparing this feeling with the sum of all feelings (of pleasure or displeasure)" (APV 253–54).

Even though affects do "momentary damage to freedom and dominion over oneself" (APV 267), Kant nevertheless thinks some of them can play a positive moral role. And remarkably, he even thinks reason itself can foster and cause affects; reason can and sometimes must let itself be impeded. Consider the case of courage. "Courage as affect ... can also be aroused by reason," Kant writes, for circumstances where one needs the kind of emotional surge that would enable one to run into a burning building and rescue a child, "the courage, in doing what duty commands, not to shrink even from the loss of life" (APV 259). And Kant offered other cases of reason-caused affects as early as 1790 in the *Critique of the Power of Judgment*. One is "enthusiasm" (*Enthusiasmus*). While some might think that reasoning about the moral law offers nothing more than a "cold, lifeless approval and no moving force or emotion [*Rührung*]," Kant says that it is "exactly the reverse" – reasoning about the moral law instead can generate a powerful affect, something of a natural by-product of moral reasoning (CJ 272–74). The experience of the sublime in the third *Critique*, a moment of fear and displeasure at something like a crushing waterfall, followed by the pleasure of discovery of one's own internal indomitability in the face of these forces, might be another reason-caused affect, although Kant does not explicitly categorize it as such (CJ 259–61).[21]

---

[21] Robert R. Clewis questions whether the experience of the sublime is an affect in Chapter 10, "The Feeling of Enthusiasm," in this volume. See also Clewis, *The Kantian Sublime and the Revelation of Freedom* (Cambridge: Cambridge University Press, 2009). Katerina Deligiorgi would agree with Clewis; on her characterization, recognizing one's rational agency is part of the experience of the sublime, and this seems incompatible with the nature of an affect. See Deligiorgi, "The Pleasures of Contra-purposiveness: Kant, the Sublime and Being Human," *The Journal of*

Sympathy is also not explicitly named by Kant as an affect, but it is not hard to imagine it taking that form, since he does count joy and sadness as affects.[22] Certain experiences of sympathy can have the features of reason-caused affects. The person who goes to "sickrooms and debtors' prisons" may feel a sudden burst of fellow-feeling – the sort that enables him to persist in treating the stinking wound. Reason might be impeded by this burst of fellow-feeling, but agents have reason to seek out this particular rational impediment – to seek out exactly these experiences. So Kant can endorse as morally positive even intense, powerful, reason-inhibiting, sympathetic feelings.

(5) For a better understanding of sympathy in Kant, we should look more closely at the geography of faculties from which sympathy can arise. For most of his career, Kant characterized the human mind as consisting of three faculties or capabilities: cognition, desire, and feeling (of both pleasure and displeasure). The faculty of cognition dominates his attention in the first *Critique*, with the faculties of desire and feeling receiving more focus beginning with the second *Critique*. The faculty of feeling, the topic of this volume, is still a neglected topic in the literature about Kant. Human action occurs through the cooperation of these three faculties: the faculty of cognition represents an object or state, and when this representation is accompanied by pleasure or displeasure from the faculty of feeling, a desire arises for that object or state. So the cooperation of the three faculties is the regular functioning of the human mind, and it is worth noting that no action without feeling is possible on Kant's theory of action. But the desire that arises in this way is not sufficient for action, since an agent may not regard the desire as a ground for choice. Only when the agent takes up this desire under a maxim (whether consciously or only unconsciously such that a maxim could be retroactively constructed later by the agent in explaining her action) does human action occur.[23]

Each of the three faculties includes higher and lower forms or subfaculties. The lower subfaculties are characterized by their passivity and

---

Aesthetics and Art Criticism, 72, no. 1 (2014): 25–35. I make the case for reason-caused affects in Kant at greater length in Kelly D. Sorensen, "Kant's Taxonomy of the Emotions," *Kantian Review* 6 (2002): 109–28. A failure to acknowledge the positive moral role of reason-caused affects explains some of the problems in Melissa McBay Merritt, "Review of Robert R. Clewis, The Kantian Sublime and the Revelation of Freedom," *British Journal for the History of Philosophy* 18, no. 3 (2010): 529–32.

[22] Julian Wuerth, *Kant on Mind, Action, and Ethics* (Oxford: Oxford University Press, 2014), 226.
[23] Wuerth, *Kant on Mind, Action, and Ethics*, 231–32.

receptiveness, and the higher subfaculties by their activity and spontaneity. For instance, "The *lower* faculty of cognition is a power to have representations so far as we are affected by objects. The *higher* faculty of cognition is a power to have representations from ourselves," and the "*lower* faculty of pleasure and displeasure is a power to find satisfaction or dissatisfaction in the objects which affect us. The *higher* faculty of pleasure and displeasure is a power to sense a pleasure and displeasure in ourselves, independently of objects," and so on for the faculty of desire (AK 28:228–29).[24] Interestingly, as Julian Wuerth points out, the lower subfaculties are never completely passive: "Even in the case of sensibility we need to be active to a degree in receiving the impression of foreign objects in order for these impressions to inhere in us."[25]

> [T]hat substance suffers (passive) whose accidents inhere through another power. How is this passion possible, since it was said earlier that it is active insofar as its accidents inhere? Every substance is active insofar as its accidents inhere, but also passive, insofar as they inhere through an external power, this is not self-contradictory. E.g., a representation of a trumpet sound inheres in me through an external power, but not alone, for had I no power of representation, then it could be sounded forever and I could not have a representation. From the union of one substance with another an effect comes about, namely the representation of the trumpet sound. We can never be merely passive, but rather every passion is at the same time action. ... A merely suffering substance is a contradiction; otherwise it could not have any accidents. (AK 29:283)[26]

An interesting question in light of this passage arises: What happens when the lower subfaculties encounter and represent the cry of a suffering person – the kind of cry about which an agent might feel sympathy? There must be some activity even in the lower subfaculty's representation of the pain; that is what makes it possible for us to hear sounds, in a way that rocks and posts do not.[27] Beyond that, Kant offers little explicit guidance here.

The most primitive representation of the cry of a suffering person would be simply as a sound, with no positive or negative valence. A less primitive representation of the cry represents it as the cry of some sort of animal, or more specifically as the cry of a human being. We can imagine additional kinds of representational specificity: the cry as negative and bad, as suffering rather than joy, as a cry of physical pain or instead emotional grief, and so on.

---

[24] Quoted in Wuerth, *Kant on Mind, Action, and Ethics*, 211–12.
[25] Wuerth, *Kant on Mind, Action, and Ethics*, 212.
[26] Quoted in Wuerth, *Kant on Mind, Action, and Ethics*, 213.
[27] A post is Kant's contrast case in AK 28:52. See Wuerth, *Kant on Mind, Action, and Ethics*, 213.

The lower subfaculty of sensibility certainly represents the sound as a sound. Does the lower subfaculty of feeling join a feeling of pain to this representation? If so, this is primitive sympathy in the Kantian framework. If not, then a feeling of pain joins in only further along the spectrum of representational specificity, as the higher subfaculties of cognition and of feeling do their work, and the most basic kind of sympathy in the Kantian framework appears instead among the operations of the higher subfaculties.

Consider the former possibility. This kind of primitive sympathy, or at least the capacity to feel it, might be the ur-sympathetic feeling that Kant characterizes as "unfree" and "*communicable* (since it is like receptivity to warmth or contagious diseases), and also compassion [*Mitleidenschaft*], since it spreads naturally among human beings living near one another" (MM 456–57). This is at least part of what should happen when one visits sickrooms and debtors' prisons. As we saw above, Kant thinks well of it. Within the garden of morally positive categories in Kant – obligation, moral worth, moral merit, etc. – this morally positive feeling grows there as well. And as part of the "gradual reformation of sensibility" (R 47) necessary to the achievement of good moral character, agents should develop and strengthen their capacity to be moved by this communicable ur-sympathy.

Consider now the latter possibility. In the same passage just noted, Kant calls this higher kind of sympathy "the *capacity* and the *will* to *share in others' feelings* (*humanitas practica*)." It is "*free*, and is therefore called *sympathetic* (*communio sentiendi liberalis*); it is based on practical reason" (MM 456–57). How we represent the pain of others matters – it is not all one under what representation pain falls. Here, the feeling of pain at another person's pain is joined with cognitively rich representations: the pain represented is the state of pain in another human, rational agent. And here is also where Kant would insist on certain representations as morally dangerous and others as morally commendable, depending on details about the representations. One morally dangerous representation portrays the pain as residing in an inferior. By contrast, a representation of pain in a fellow, like person whose ends are thwarted is a morally commendable representation. Another morally dangerous representation represents the pain as merely an object of the magnanimous generosity of one's excellent, benevolent self. By contrast, a representation of pain in another person that it is a duty to address is a morally commendable representation.[28]

---

[28] These more commendable representations need not carry the entire Kantian apparatus along with them.

With sufficient moral development, when one visits sickrooms and debtors' prisons, one might produce not just "communicable" sympathy, but this richer kind of sympathy, through the cooperation of the higher subfaculties of cognition and feeling – one might feel along with the sick and imprisoned while regarding them as equals with thwarted ends, as equals with a claim on other agents. One might thereby guard against the transformation of sympathy into the less admirable forms discussed earlier – and avoid having a self-conceited "one feeling too many." That is how morality chaperones us: by helping us represent the pain of another as the pain of an equal.

11.3 Conclusion

With the considerations above in mind, we can now bring the offensive and the defensive cases together, and return to the claim that what is good in Nietzsche about sympathy and love is already there and better in Kant.

First, consider what constitutes and constrains a well-lived human life. For Nietzsche, it is good for life to exercise capacities and powers in the world – or at least good for rare and gifted beings to do so. For Kant, by contrast, the good of the exercise of capacities and powers in the world is associated with and constrained by other valuable exercisers of those same capacities and powers. Nietzsche is less interested in such constraints. Kant's egalitarianism about moral status – the demand that all rational agents regard each other as having the same fundamental moral protections and dignity and worth – is something we should be loath to give up. A lesson from Kant is that one can hold wise suspicions about deficient forms of sympathy and love without giving up this egalitarianism about moral status.

Second, Nietzsche criticized Schopenhauer for a view of sympathy on which the self dissolves into the other person and asserted that valuing the self is fundamental to any worthwhile form of altruism.[29] But Kant's worries come from the other direction: the "dear self" always all too readily attempts to make itself and its inclinations central (G 405–8). Kant's worries are more weighty than Nietzsche's. The worst things that people do to one another are better explained by too much focus on the self, not too little. Both Nietzsche and Kant would agree that rationalized self-justification is a common and unadmirable human tendency (G 405). But

---

[29] Bernard Reginster, "Sympathy in Schopenhauer and Nietzsche," in *Sympathy: A History*, ed. Eric Schliesser (New York: Oxford University Press, 2015), 254–85.

Kant's account is better because its suspicion rightly identifies self-focus as the deficiency at the core of bad sympathy and bad love.

Nietzsche's views about sympathy, love, and pity are complex, and there is much more to say about them; for instance, Nietzsche locates the core deficiency of sympathy instead in the misguided view of a well-lived life that it suggests.[30] Sympathy's defenders often support a utilitarian account of well-being in which diminished suffering in a life is best. Instead, for Nietzsche, pain and suffering are inextricably tied up with the goods of achievement and developing one's talents. Kant is considerably less interested than Nietzsche in the grand achievements of a few great individuals. But Kant does believe that we – each and all of us, at all levels of native capabilities – are under an obligation to develop our talents (G 422–23; MM 392), and he is under no illusion that this is a painless endeavor. And he is under no illusion that well-being is valuable to an individual who did not struggle to be worthy of it. So Kant can agree that a fixation on sympathy neglects the realities of a well-lived life. But he can do so without the callousness toward human suffering that so often erupts in Nietzsche's work.

In the end, the claim that Kant's account of sympathy and love is better than Nietzsche's is less important than the virtues of the account itself. It is an account on which sympathy and love occupy important parts of the geography of morality, but take up no more space than they merit, especially given human proclivities to self-deception and a hunger for superiority over others. It is an account that requires less apology than many defenders of Kant have thought, in part because its suspicious view of these human proclivities is so plausible and increasingly empirically supported. For Kant, the kinds of sympathy and love worth suspecting are those that hide and bury self-conceit. And the kinds of sympathy and love most worth wanting are constrained by normative facts about the equal worth of other rational agents, representing those other agents as like beings whose thwarted aims makes claims on oneself – why would we not most want *these* kinds of sympathy and love?

---

[30] I thank Ken Gemes for critical comments here. See Gudrun von Tevenar, "Nietzsche's Objections to Pity and Compassion," in *Nietzsche and Ethics*, ed. Gudrun von Tevenar (Oxford: Peter Lang, 2007), 263–82.

12

Respect, in Every Respect*

Diane Williamson

"All respect for a person is properly only respect for the law."

(G 401n)

"Our own will, insofar as it were to act only under the condition of its being able to legislate universal law by means of its maxims – this will, ideally possible for us, is the proper object of respect."

(G 440)

"[D]uties to one's fellow human beings arising from the respect due to them are expressed only negatively."

(MM 464)

"Although there is nothing meritorious in the conformity of one's actions with right (in being an honest human being), the conformity of right of one's maxims of such actions, as duties, that is **respect** for right, is meritorious."

(MM 390)

Kant refers to respect in a variety of senses: respect for the moral law, respect for persons, the negative duty of respect, the positive duty of respect, etc. Similarly, commentators have variously referred to Kant's two, three, four, or more accounts of respect.[1] When taken out of context, as I have intended to above, Kant's various comments about respect might lead his readers to believe that he lacks a coherent philosophy of this concept. Nevertheless, when we fully understand the different senses he employs and the way they work together, we can better appreciate the way

---

* I would like to thank Rachel Zuckert for her helpful comments on this chapter.
[1] Darwall makes a distinction that helps us make sense of Kant's philosophy between two different kinds of respect; Stephen Darwall, "Two Kinds of Respect," *Ethics* 88, no. 1 (October 1977): 36–49. Klimchuk argues that there are three compatible accounts of respect in Kantian moral theory; Dennis Klimchuk, "Three Accounts of Respect for Persons in Kant's Ethics," *Kantian Review* 8, no. 1 (March 2004): 38–61. Singleton draws attention to both a broad account of respect and a narrow account of respect with two senses of the term in each; Jane Singleton, "Kant's Account of Respect: A Bridge between Rationality and Anthropology," *Kantian Review* 12, no. 1 (March 2007): 40–60.

his theory of respect advances our understanding of feeling as well as the fact that it is a radically progressive moral and political ideal.

I begin this chapter by establishing that Kant holds that respect for the moral law is indeed a feeling. I suggest that formulating his theory of respect allowed him to fully develop his theory of feeling. I then develop Geiger's suggestion that the feeling of respect encompasses a great variety of moral feelings.[2] I attempt to systematize this variety by correlating each sense in which we can understand the term "respect" with each kind of duty. The duties involved in respecting humanity (positive self-respect, negative self-respect, negative other-respect, and positive other-respect) help us understand the variety of the ways in which we must act respectfully in the Kantian sense. Positive self-respect entails cultivating moral consciousness as well as the various feelings that it entails; it is therefore the broadest sense of the term that encompasses all the other feelings and duties related to respect.

After we have canvassed this variety of senses in which Kant uses the term "respect," and I have begun to show that they are all related, I return to a more common debate in Kant scholarship regarding respect. I argue that neither respect for the moral law nor respect for humanity is foundational for Kant's account; instead, these two different types of respect amount to the same thing. Kant's theory of respect is unified amid so much diversity because at its heart its purpose is to merge two different common senses of the term: respect as a behavior (*observantia*) and respect as a feeling (*reverentia*). This merger is what allows Kant's theory of respect to be essential to his moral philosophy and radical politically.

12.1 Respect as a Feeling

Many theorists of respect are slow to call respect a feeling. They are even less likely to consider it within the context of the faculty of feeling. Stephen Darwall, for example, calls respect an "attitude"; Carl Cranor holds that it can sometimes involve an "evaluative point of view."[3] In the second *Critique* Kant makes a distinction between pathological and practical feeling; in the *Anthropology* he makes a distinction between sensuously and intellectually wrought feelings. If there is a difference between these two classifications, it is related to the fact that earlier in his writings Kant

---

[2] Ido Geiger, "Rational Feelings and Moral Agency," *Kantian Review* 16, no. 2 (June 2011): 283–308.
[3] Stephen Darwall, "Two Kinds of Respect," 37; Carl Cranor, "Toward a Theory of Respect for Persons," *American Philosophical Quarterly* 12 (October 1975): 303–19.

seems to be leaning toward holding that respect is the only feeling of its kind. Later, in the *Metaphysics of Morals*, for example, there seems to be a greater variety of moral feelings.

It is essential for Kant's theory of moral motivation that respect be characterized as a feeling because it is the bridge between pure reason and desire that makes pure reason practical. Kant consistently characterizes respect as the effect that moral understanding has on sensibility. As such, respect does nothing to aid in our comprehension of the moral law; it is merely the effect the moral law has on us sensibly (MM 212).

The question of why and how thoughts can affect us sensibly is interesting and particularly important in the case of the feeling of respect. If there were no essential, conceptual connection between consciousness of the moral law and the physical feeling of respect, it might seem that moral feeling is an arbitrary biological coincidence. While in the *Groundwork* Kant argues that it is "beyond the power of human reason" to answer the question of how this causation is possible (G 460), in the second *Critique* he holds that this connection can be rationally understood. He there argues that the effect of morality on feeling can be cognized a priori (CPR 72), saying that it is

> the first and perhaps also the only case where we have been able to determine a priori from concepts the relation of a cognition to the feeling of pleasure or displeasure. (CPR 73)

The fact that we can cognize the necessity of respect a priori entails that respect for the moral law is indeed necessary (CPR 73). The moral law necessarily acts as an incentive to action because it presents itself as a value that strikes down selfishness. In the second *Critique*, Kant almost consistently holds that the effect of the moral law on sensibility is purely negative.[4] Nevertheless, the effect of the moral law is still characterized as a feeling and it is still positive in the sense that it is a cause of action. Additionally, following his discussion of Epicurus in the context of the highest good, Kant describes the effect of virtue as "self-satisfaction," which is closely related to joy (CPR 116–17).[5]

---

[4] Geiger notes that Kant employs a strictly narrow understanding of respect in the second *Critique* because there he focuses on the pure comprehension of the moral law: "Had Kant had here in mind a detailed conception of our moral duties and of our various moral failings, the affective depiction of respect would be richer" (Geiger, "Rational Feelings and Moral Agency," 292). Geiger later suggests that the expanded notion of respect in the *Metaphysics of Morals* is due to the more empirically oriented applicatory nature of that work (Geiger, "Rational Feelings and Moral Agency").

[5] Clewis discusses the positive-negative structure of respect. See Robert R. Clewis, *The Kantian Sublime and the Revelation of Freedom* (Cambridge: Cambridge University Press, 2009).

Jane Singleton argues that respect for the moral law is not a feeling at all; it is not the same as *reverentia*.[6] She agrees with Philip Stratton-Lake that respect is not the effect on sensibility from the moral law but simply describes instead our consciousness of the moral law.[7]

In the second *Critique*, we do indeed see the importance of stressing that moral pleasure is an effect of moral comprehension and that moral choice is determined not by pleasure but by the moral law. Even still, Kant there labels respect a sensation, and he argues that the important distinction between moral feeling and pathological feeling is that the former comes from moral comprehension:

> Here there is in the subject no *antecedent* feeling that would be attuned to morality, since all feeling is sensible whereas the incentive of the moral attitude must be free from any sensible condition. Rather, sensible feeling, which underlies all our inclinations, is indeed the condition of that sensation which we call respect. But the cause that determines this sensation lies in pure practical reason, and hence this sensation, because of its origin, cannot be called *brought about pathologically* but must be called *brought about practically*. (CPR 75)

Moral motivation and the practicality of pure reason are affected by respect's bridge between pure reason and sensibility:

> [I]t must be noted that, as far as respect is an effect on feeling and hence on the sensibility of a rational being, it presupposes this sensibility and hence also the finitude of such beings on whom the moral law imposes respect. (CPR 76)

Fully formulating the way that understanding can cause an effect on sensibility, as Kant does in the case of the feeling of respect, quite possibly allowed him to see the variety of possible ways that understanding can affect pleasure or pain – although each of these effects might not be similarly discoverable a priori. It seems reasonable to speculate that the fact that Kant went on to write a *Critique of the Power of Judgment*, which corresponds to the faculty of feeling, focusing on other intellectually caused feelings, when he did not stipulate this necessity at the time of writing the second *Critique*, can be explained at least partially by his changing view of feeling in the second *Critique*.

Kant is clear about the fact that respect for the moral law is a feeling. Next I demonstrate that this feeling is not uncommon, nor does it always take the form of pure awe and fear. When we act immorally, we feel self-

---

[6] Singleton, "Kant's Account of Respect."
[7] Philip Stratton-Lake, *Kant, Duty, and Moral Worth* (London: Routledge, 2000).

abhorrence, for example (MM 380). Similarly, positive self-respect involves multiple feelings; Kant gives the examples of disgust and horror, but we can see that any "moral feeling" involves a variety of different feelings. Nor is moral feeling necessarily distinct from affect, which Kant describes as "precipitate" and "rash." The essential factor making moral feeling legitimate is that reason leads the way, or else moral feeling devolves into enthusiasm (MM 408).

12.2 Four Duties of Respect

In the *Groundwork* Kant uses four examples to help him outline the four different types of duties, viz., perfect duties to oneself, perfect duties to others, imperfect duties to oneself, and imperfect duties to others. He touches on these four examples in giving both of the first two formulations of the categorical imperative. The second formulation of the categorical imperative involves the notion of respect: "Act in such a way that you treat humanity, whether in your own person or in the person of another, always at the same time as an end and never simply as a means" (G 429). To treat humanity in this way is to treat it with respect. His four examples (suicide, lying, developing one's talents, and charity) are shown to be ways in which we must treat humanity as an end, i.e., respectfully, and avoid treating it merely as a means.

A brief reminder of these examples of the four different types of duties in light of the duty to respect humanity may be helpful (MM 429–30). First, he argues that one ought not commit suicide because doing so would be using oneself (rational humanity) as a means to ending suffering. Second, he argues that lying uses another as a means to one's own end that the other does not also hold. Third, we should develop our capacities because our actions should positively "harmonize" with the end of humanity. Fourth, we should promote the happiness of others, again, in order to positively promote the end of rational humanity.

My argument here is that these four different types of duties correspond with four different types of respect. In outlining the sense of the term proper to each of these duties, I suggest a correlation between these duties and the four affective preconditions of morality that Kant canvasses in the "Doctrine of Virtue" (moral feeling, conscience, love, and self-esteem).[8] Nevertheless, even if these affective preconditions of morality cannot

---

[8] My main evidence for this correlation is the way they are presented in the text. Kant introduces the four affective forms of sensibility to duty immediately after he lays out the four different kinds of duties (MM 398–99).

convincingly be seen as corresponding with the four different types of duties, we can still see that feelings accommodate the consciousness and fulfillment of these duties.

Positive self-respect, corresponding to the positive duties to oneself, is the most important and most expansive form of respect because it includes the cultivation of moral consciousness and respect for the moral law as well as the development of a virtuous disposition overall, including all kinds of moral feelings. If we are to divide Kant's notions of respect into broad and subsidiary accounts, positive self-respect is the broadest, and it includes the necessity of all of the other forms of respect. When we understand the extent of its breadth, we appreciate the fact that Kant's theory of respect is truly systematic and comprehensive.[9]

12.3 Positive Self-Respect

Kant divides our duties to ourselves into those regarding the body (or one's animality) and those regarding the soul (or one's rationality and morality) (MM 419).[10] Regarding the former, we have a duty to help ourselves develop and thrive physically; regarding the latter, we have a duty to develop our mental capacities and strive for moral perfection.

Positive self-respect underlies the recognition and fulfillment of these duties. It is based in the internal connection between respect for the moral law and respect for humanity because it involves promoting our moral prosperity (MM 419). We must appraise ourselves highly – indeed, sublimely – because of our capacity for moral reasoning and consciousness. Of course, all rational beings have this capacity, and so – and this part is perhaps the most difficult – one must value herself "on a footing of equality with them" (MM 435).

Moral feeling is the aesthetic concept that corresponds with the duty of self-perfection (MM 399–400). It is here described as the way we are moved affectively by our comprehension of the moral law. In other words, perfecting ourselves morally involves cultivating the feeling of respect for the moral law. Kant's description of "moral feeling" in this section shares much of the same language with his explanation of respect for the moral

---

[9] Singleton, by contrast, argues that Kant does not have a unified account of respect. Singleton, "Kant's Account of Respect," 41.
[10] Later he uses the more common threefold distinction between animal, person, and human (MM 434–35).

law in the second *Critique*.[11] One slight difference is that now the feelings that follow from our actions are also included: "the susceptibility to pleasure or displeasure merely from the consciousness of the agreement or disagreement of our action with the law of duty" (MM 399). Like respect, Kant uses the term "moral feeling" in a variety of ways, and we can see that here it plays both a broad role, in implying all possibly moral feelings, and a narrow sense of the effect on our consciousness of the moral law.[12] In the broad sense, "[Moral feeling] is a moral perfection, by which one makes one's object every particular end that is also a duty" (MM 387).

With regard to the positive duty of self-respect – the perfecting of the self and developing a virtuous disposition – Kant writes "not every obligation of virtue is a duty of virtue" (MM 410). He notes that there is only one obligation of virtue, which is to comprehend the moral law and act only out of respect for it. This obligation extends to both duties of right and duties of virtue. Duties of virtue, on the other hand, involve specifically the ends of self-perfection and the happiness of others, and "respect for law as such," while an obligation of virtue, does not specify particular duties (MM 410). Additionally, acting out of respect for duty, not merely according to duty, is virtuous because it involves the internal and positive action of adopting morality as an end for oneself. Similarly, the obligation to respect the moral law is not a narrow obligation (although we are tempted to think of it as such) because we cannot know for sure whether it has been successfully fulfilled. Instead, the obligation is to "strive with all one's might" to purify the will and act out of pure respect for morality (MM 393). For this reason, Kant characterizes moral feeling as the highest form of self-perfection: "the greatest perfection in a human being is to do his duty from duty" (MM 398).

Positive self-respect is "narrow and perfect" in quality but "wide and imperfect in degree" because of the foundational importance Kant places on self-transparency. Additionally, Kant's reverence for honesty, which is often dismissed as being overly simplistic, makes more sense when we consider, similarly, the foundational role that virtue and duties to oneself

---

[11] "Every determination of choice proceeds from the representation of the possible action, through the feeling of pleasure or displeasure in taking an interest in the action or in its effect, to the deed; and here the sensitive condition (the affection of the internal sense) is either a pathological or a moral feeling ... the latter is that which can only follow the representation of the law" (MM 399).

[12] Although it is beyond the scope of this chapter to provide this argument in its entirety, Kant often identifies respect for the law with moral feeling (see for example MM 387). In the *Groundwork* he explains that moral feeling is the interest we take in moral laws: "the subjective effect that the law exercises upon the will" (G 460). This "causality of reason" "infuse[s] a feeling of pleasure ... in the fulfillment of duty" (G 460).

play in his moral theory. "The first command of all duties to oneself," he writes, is to "*know ... yourself*" (MM 441). Without this honest self-scrutiny there can be no discovery of the moral law within oneself and hence no morality at all. Additionally, without the personal commitment to live a morally upright life (virtue or the positive obligation of self-respect), one can (and does) easily lie to oneself about one's righteousness. No authority keeps morality alive in the world except for the self-wrought feeling of respect. (That thought is itself both terrifying and amazing.)

12.4 Negative Self-Respect

Negative self-respect involves refraining from harming the self physically, psychologically, or morally. Dividing up duties into negative and positive terms is not always a clear-cut task, and Kant's presentation of positive self-respect is interwoven with his presentation of negative self-respect (e.g., with the vice of servility) because one avoids damaging one's self-respect by positively furthering one's rational humanity. In human psychology these maxims are intimately related. We can refer to the negative duty not to deprive oneself of the means of fulfilling one's true needs (become avaricious), or we can refer to the positive duty to promote one's true needs (physical self-perfection). Similarly, we can refer to the positive duty to know oneself or the negative duty not to lie to oneself. The basic idea of respecting humanity in oneself and others must be rationally comprehended overall, and the particular actions required by a particular situation must be determined (as either a negative or positive duty) in that context.

The feeling of self-esteem relates to negative self-respect. Perhaps contradictorily, Kantian self-esteem involves both consciousness of this "sublime moral predisposition" in oneself and the humility or the feeling of one's insignificance in comparison with the moral law (MM 435).

The interesting discussions in the literature on self-respect usually focus on negative self-respect.[13] Stark holds that external factors, like social institutions or misfortune, can impair one's self-respect and that "[s]ocieties create individuals with limited self-respect by creating individuals with limited rationality." In some instances then, respecting ourselves might not be psychologically possible, and moralizing self-respect may be

---

[13] Building on Hill, Dillon adds considerably to the cast of characters *lacking* in self-respect, including "The Self-Absorbed" and "The Complacent." Thomas E. Hill Jr., "Servility and Self-Respect," *The Monist* 57, no. 1 (January 1973): 87–104; Robin S. Dillon, "How to Lose Your Self-Respect," *American Philosophical Quarterly* 29, no. 2 (April 1992): 125–39.

no more than "victim-blaming."[14] Nevertheless, we should maintain that there are duties of self-respect just as we must maintain that there are duties to respect others, even in the face of this apparent determinism.

Carol Hay agrees that "oppression" is a "part of a structural and systemic network of social institutions," but her argument overall is that, out of self-respect, oppressed people have the duty to resist their oppression.[15] Hay is worried about these tools of oppression, like sexual harassment, because they restrict the autonomy of the oppressed; oppression restricts "the quantity and quality of choices available."[16] Indeed, oppression can lead to what Amartya Sen calls "adaptive preferences" that undermine self-respect. Oppressive societies can lead the oppressed to internalize their negative and limited roles, even to the point of failing to desire basic goods, like education or food. I agree with Hay that "our capacity for practical rationality [is] a human capacity, as susceptible to harm as many other human capacities."[17] She outlines a sample of the types of psychological harm that result from oppression, like self-deception, weakened intelligence, and weakness of will.

If damaged rationality could negate the duty to respect oneself, it could also negate the obligation to be respected by others. One's very status as a moral being would be annulled. We must reject the conclusion, I think, that oppression negates the duty of self-respect, but doing so is less difficult, it seems, if we consider real examples of oppressed people who nevertheless have a strong sense of right and wrong as well as self-respect. Oppression does not always weaken one's respect for the moral law and for oneself; it sometimes strengthens it.

Even still, the negative duties of self-respect are bound to sound dogmatic because they are not pragmatic counsels of prudence, whereby one can decide for himself what makes him happy, but instead they are internal moral commands that are nevertheless discussed (by Kant and other moralists) externally. If one grants the premise that a human being has a sublime calling because she is able to grasp morality and make it actual in the world, then even the prudish-sounding dictates, like not to masturbate, can seem plausible. The premise of these duties is that it is possible to treat oneself merely as a means just as it is surely possible to

---

[14] Cynthia A. Stark, "The Rationality of Valuing Oneself: A Critique of Kant on Self-Respect," *Journal of the History of Philosophy* 35, no. 1 (January 1997): 75–77.
[15] Carol Hay, *Kantianism, Liberalism, and Feminism: Resisting Oppression* (New York: Palgrave Macmillan, 2013), 3.
[16] Hay, *Kantianism, Liberalism, and Feminism*, 98.
[17] Hay, *Kantianism, Liberalism, and Feminism*, 123.

treat other people merely as a means. Granted, it is a bit counterintuitive that such is possible.

The fact that it is possible (and blameworthy) to treat oneself as a mere means is even more puzzling when we consider certain, perhaps many, cases in which we normally treat ourselves as a means to promote our long-term physical health, for example. I exercise in order to elongate my lifespan and also in order to preserve my rational capacities, for example. Am I thereby using myself as merely a means? Herein lies the essential difference between using myself as a means and using others merely as a means. When I use others merely as a means, it does not matter if I intend a good end – their own moral improvement, for example – because I am not able to set ends for others. Let us say that I hide my friend's cigarettes against his will. I certainly may have a good intention here, but doing so still fails to fully respect him as a person because it does not fully acknowledge his ability – indeed, his right – to set his own ends. What if I were to hide my cigarettes from myself (or to ask someone else to)? Kant's answer here is complex. If my goal is to perfect myself, either physically or mentally, then deceiving myself in this case does not entail using myself *merely* as a means. If, on the other hand, there were some way in which doing this action were merely for pleasure (or some other superficial goal), then we would be able to say that I would be using myself merely as a means and hence failing to sufficiently respect myself. It is rather odd to think that I must respect (within reason) others' rights to set whatever ends they choose for themselves but that I myself am not allowed this much latitude. After all, my necessary end is my self-perfection, not my happiness.

12.5 Negative Other-Respect and Positive Other-Respect

Negative respect for others is the sense of the term perhaps most commonly associated with Kantian respect, i.e., refraining from dishonesty, coercion, etc. Nevertheless, when we take negative other-respect out of the context of respect broadly construed, as the comprehension of all of our moral duties implied in positive self-respect, confusion about the nature of these duties results. Sharon Anderson-Gold argues, for example, that duties of respect to others are primarily expressed negatively.[18] Melissa Seymour Fahmy argues that, as a duty of virtue, the duty

---

[18] Sharon Anderson-Gold, "Privacy, Respect and the Virtues of Reticence in Kant," *Kantian Review* 15, no. 2 (July 2010): 28–42.

of respect must correspond to some end but that there is no clear candidate for what this end is.[19]

In the "Doctrine of Virtue" Kant discusses love and respect (which are "united by the law into one duty") (MM 448). Here he is using the term "respect" in the sense of negative other-respect. Previously, he used the term in the sense of positive self-respect, making it clear that all of the other duties of virtue follow from developing respect for oneself in the form of a moral consciousness and a virtuous disposition. Now the term is being used in a much narrower sense.

We can count his comments about love here as related to his notion of positive other-respect. The duties of negatively respecting others include the commands to avoid arrogance, defamation, and ridicule. The duties to positively respect others include beneficence, gratitude, and sympathy. These two sets of duties negatively correlate with each other: the opposite of arrogance is beneficence; the opposite of defamation is gratitude; and the opposite of ridicule is sympathy. In a later passage, Kant identifies respect with negative, juridical duties to others, and love with positive, virtuous duties to others:

> All moral relations of rational beings, which involve a principle of the harmony of the will of one with that of another, can be reduced to *love* and *respect*; and insofar as this principle is practical, in the case of love the basis for determining one's will can be reduced to another's *end*, and in the case of respect, to another's *right*. (MM 488)

Therefore, love and respect (in this narrow sense) correlate with our positive and negatives duties to others.[20] As Kant writes, "[t]hese feelings can be considered separately ... and they can also exist separately ... But they are basically according to the law always combined in one duty" (MM 448). We can account for this combination with the fact that the law is to respect humanity and that respect has both a positive and a negative sense.

Positive respect for others involves promoting the happiness of others. The happiness of others is a necessary end of virtue, and as such, there is

---

[19] It cannot be the duty to promote the happiness of others, she argues, because love, not respect, corresponds that end. She dismisses the duty of self-perfection because duties of respect are other regarding (Melissa Seymour Fahmy, "Understanding Kant's Duty of Respect as a Duty of Virtue," *Journal of Moral Philosophy* 10, no. 6 [2013]: 726). Instead, the humanity of others or others' self-esteem are better candidates.

[20] An example of respect used in the broader sense in relation to love comes in the second *Critique*: "For as a command [*Love God above all and your neighbor as yourself*] it does demand respect for a law that orders love" (CPR 83).

latitude in our choice of the way we are to act to promote it. Nevertheless, it is not quite accurate to hold that "[r]espect is something we owe to all others; love is not."[21] While it is not possible to be beneficent to all people, for example, the object of the maxim of charity is humanity as such, not simply "loved ones," and we can imagine cases in which ignoring the neediness of strangers, simply because they are not one's chosen recipients of beneficence, would not reveal a universalizable maxim.

While it seems clear enough that love is the affective precondition that corresponds with our positive duties to others, that leaves only conscience to correlate with negative other-respect. Nevertheless, it is fitting to link the feeling of conscience with the negative duties of other-respect because negative duties of other-respect entail all of the duties laid out in the doctrine of right and conscience is an internalized version of the external lawgiver.

While it is surely possible to limit the meaning of respect in Kantian philosophy to perhaps negative other-respect or negative self-respect, such an interpretation would inevitably result in yet another sense of the term springing up in Kant's text, and the interpreter would then need to address the relationship between these different uses. Just as the duty to cultivate moral consciousness is primary in Kant's philosophy, respect for the moral law similarly entails the other senses of the term. Nevertheless, respect for the moral law is not distinct from respect for rational humanity, as I now demonstrate.

12.6 Respect for the Moral Law and Respect for Humanity

Within Kant scholarship there is debate about whether respect for the moral law or respect for persons is primary. In this section I argue that they are both primary because they amount to the same thing. Therefore, to hold that self-respect is based in respect for morality, as Hill does, is not quite accurate as a reading of Kant.[22]

Hill characterizes the duty of self-respect as a duty "to morality" rather than a duty to oneself: "The essentially Kantian idea here is that morality, as a system of equal fundamental rights and duties, is worthy of respect, and hence a completely moral person would respect it in word and manner

---

[21] Stephen Darwall, "Kant on Respect, Dignity, and the Duty of Respect," in *Kant's Ethics of Virtue*, ed. Monika Betzler (Berlin: De Gruyter, 2008), 195–96. Darwall denies that love and respect can be characterized as positive and negative duties.
[22] Hill, "Servility and Self-Respect."

as well as in deed."[23] It surely must be the case that a moral person respects morality, but the question remains: "Why?" and "What does it mean to respect morality?"

Evidence for his interpretation that respect for the moral law is foundational for respect for persons comes primarily from the *Groundwork*'s presentation of the first formulation of the categorical imperative, and it ignores the presentation of the second formulation of the categorical imperative that equates respect for the moral law with respect for rational being. In the footnote in which Kant writes "all respect for persons is properly only respect for the law" it is not likely that he is referring to respect for persons in the full moral sense (G 401n). It is more likely, looking at the text, that he is referring to appraisal respect for persons in Darwall's sense. The full text runs thusly:

> All respect for persons is properly only respect for the law (of honesty, etc.) of which the person provides an example. Since we regard the development of our talents as a duty, we think of a man of talent as being also a kind of *example of the law* (the law of becoming like him by practice), and that is what constitutes our respect for him. (G 401n)

This piece of text ought not lead to the conclusion that respect for humanity is grounded in respect for the moral law. Instead, this footnote seems to be saying that respect for moral merit is grounded in our understanding of morality. In this same footnote he writes, "Respect is properly the representation of a worth that thwarts my self-love" (G 401n). Any kind of absolute worth would thwart self-love and could thereby be an object of respect.[24] The argument in the main text – the deduction of the first formulation of the categorical imperative – is that if we exclude all determination by hoped-for effects of action, the will can only be determined by principle – or "objectively the law and subjectively pure respect for this practical law" (G 400). The purpose of this argument is to introduce the first formulation of the categorical imperative as the only possible moral law, following analytically from the very idea of moral goodness. If, as this argument runs, the will is either determined by the representation of the moral law or by inclination (an a posteriori desire for

---

[23] Hill, "Servility and Self-Respect," 104, 99.
[24] Further confirmation for my interpretation comes in the concluding sentence of the footnote: "All so called moral *interest* consists solely in *respect* for the law" (G 401n). Of what could moral interest consist if not respect for the law? Perhaps in etiquette or religion – any practice or artifact that has the tendency to morally edify. Kant's point here is that these "so called" "moral" authorities that we "respect" because of some kind of appreciation of their "greatness" do not actually deserve our reverence unless they are legitimately grounded in a sound comprehension of the moral law.

a particular state of affairs), then this argument is not well suited for ruling out rational being as an irreducible object of respect. The point here is that morality commands a priori (and that only one possible law can do that). The argument does not run the other way around, viz., that the moral law is the only possible object of respect.

Paul Formosa is correct that Kant closely associates the idea of respect with the idea of dignity; both dignity and respect are accorded because of the possession of autonomy. Kant writes, "the word 'respect' alone provides a suitable expression for the esteem which a rational being must have for [dignity]" (G 436). Formosa even goes so far as to argue that the third and fourth formulations of the categorical imperative mean the same thing as "always treat persons with respect."[25]

If we hold with Hill that respect for rational being rests in respect for the moral law, we must also hold that respect for the moral law rests in respect for rational being because, according to the presentation of the second formulation of the categorical imperative, rational being is the ground of the moral law (G 428). Rational being has absolute and inherent value, just like morality itself, and rational being is therefore itself a sublime object: "For not insofar as he is subject to the moral law does he have sublimity, but rather has it only insofar as with regard to this very same law, he is at the same time legislative and only thereby subject to the law" (G 440). Herein lies the reason that the first and second formulations of the categorical imperative (in fact, all of the formulations of the categorical imperatives) express the same idea. When Kant writes that "a righteous act elevates the soul" it is a moot point whether one thinks of the righteous act qua righteous or qua act because it is the *righteous act* – the real demonstration of morality – that elevates the soul (G 441).

Kant often argues that the concept of a moral law is inseparably linked to the concept of a free being because only the moral law prescribes actions that are determined by pure reason. In a similar passage in the second *Critique*, Kant notes that the moral law is holy and that humanity must also be taken to be holy. Autonomy is here described as having absolute moral worth and being a limiting condition for all choice. When we appreciate the equivalence of rationality and the moral law as objects of respect, we can appreciate the value of all people:

---

[25] Paul Formosa, "Dignity and Respect: How to Apply Kant's Formula of Humanity," *Philosophical Forum* 45, no. 1 (Spring 2014): 51.

This idea of personality, which arouses respect and which the sublimity of our nature (as regards its vocation) puts before our eyes while at the same time drawing attention to the lack of our conduct's adequacy to this idea and thereby striking down self-conceit, is natural and easily discernable even to the commonest human reason. (CPR 87)

Similarly, Kant writes that the "pure moral law itself" allows us to "discern the sublimity of our own supranatural existence" (CPR 88).

In some passages, Kant states that respect is based on merit, e.g.: "Respect is a tribute that one cannot refuse to pay to merit" (CPR 77).[26] These passages might be taken to suggest that humanity *only* deserves respect if it manifests morality. Darwall, in a later piece, for example, challenges the interpretation that all people deserve equal respect.[27] In the *Metaphysics of Morals* Kant brings up the question of how we should treat "human beings who are in a state of moral purity or depravity" (MM 468). He does not answer it.[28] It would be nice if Kant were to clearly distinguish between the respect that is owed to every human being – what Darwall calls recognition respect – regardless of their actions and the meritorious respect owed only to the virtuous (appraisal respect). Kant does refer to meritorious respect often enough: "we think of a man of talent as being also a kind of *example of the law* (the law of becoming like him by practice), and that is what constitutes our respect for him" (G 401n). Nevertheless, to my knowledge, he never straightforwardly suggests that it is morally permissible to treat an immoral person without respect.

12.7 Respect, a Radical Notion

The merger between respect for the moral law and respect for persons allows for a radically egalitarian moral and political ideal. Traditionally

---

[26] Klimchuk's third account of respect is that we have a duty to respect only those people who behave virtuously, but he makes sense out of these of Kant's comments with a distinction between "respect-for" (which is similar to Darwall's appraisal respect) and "respect-as" (recognition respect). Klimchuk, "Three Accounts of Respect for Persons in Kant's Ethics," 40.

[27] Darwall, "Kant on Respect, Dignity, and the Duty of Respect."

[28] Bunch argues that Kant's comments regarding the effects of one's behaving in a degrading way, being to throw away one's humanity, are compatible with the notion that we can never forfeit human dignity. To throw away one's humanity is to fail to claim it, on Bunch's account. He argues that when we treat ourselves like a thing we give others no choice but to do likewise; it is not that they are therefore morally permitted to do so (Aaron Bunch, "Throwing Oneself Away: Kant on the Forfeiture of Respect," *Kantian Review* 19, no. 1 [March 2014]: 86). Respect for humanity is owed because of the "predisposition to the good in all human beings and for the ideal that governs it" (Bunch, "Throwing Oneself Away," 88).

(and even commonly today), the notion of respect is connected to authority. We often say that certain people are owed respect because they stand in a position of authority over us. Children are told they must respect their elders because they ought to obey them. Students are told to behave respectfully toward their teachers because the latter are in a position of power. Oftentimes, respect refers to a behavioral stance that prudentially forms in reaction to a feared person. In the eighteenth century the social distinctions granting deferential treatment were more numerous than they are today due to a legalized class hierarchy. The peasantry owed the nobility respect, for example, regardless of whether the latter were truly "noble." Critical of these quasi moral obligations, Kant cites Fontenelle:

> '*Before a prominent man I bow, but my spirit does not bow*' ... Before a lowly plain man in whom I perceive righteousness of character in a certain measure that I am not conscious of in myself *my spirit bows*, whether I want it to or not and whether I hold my head ever so high to keep him from overlooking my preeminence. (CPR 76–77)

Darwall's distinction between recognition respect and appraisal respect is somewhat helpful in this regard. If we tease apart his "two kinds of respect" a bit further, we can get a better sense of the social and political context informing Kant's vision of human equality. Darwall's motivation, looking to Kant, is to explain the fact that we are both obligated to respect everyone simply because we recognize that each is a person (recognition respect) and also obligated to respect some people more than others because we appraise their moral achievements more highly (appraisal respect).[29] He is right about that. We can also see that recognition respect is related to behavioral choices and appraisal respect is related to the detached feeling of awe or admiration. Most commonly, as I noted above, we speak about recognition respect in the sense of recognizing that a person occupies a certain social position or role, that of police officer or father, for example, and we speak of them deserving respect because of this position. This type of respect primarily entails certain behaviors that follow from understanding the socially correct ways of treating this type of person, as Darwall notes. Similarly, appraisal respect need not be a moral notion. Any appraisal of a person's greatness might entail respect.

Kant's theory of respect is a merger between respect as a behavior and respect as a feeling (*observantia* and *reverentia*). In other words, Kant is well aware of the fact that in his day – and we can see that the same is true even

---

[29] An example of Kant using the term in both these ways comes at MM 448.

for us still – force is used or implied to compel respect. His moral theory seeks to replace this hierarchical, coercive obedience with egalitarian, moral motivation inherent to the thing we respect, by means of a feeling of admiration, awe, obligation, etc. We comprehend the moral law and we *feel* reverence.[30] We then act dutifully out of our own feeling of the need for obedience not because we fear punishment or social shunning.[31] For example, when Kant writes that "only the law itself can be an object of respect and hence a command" he means that there is no other source of legitimate authority (G 400).

Nevertheless, for Kant, recognition respect for persons is not based in *recognition* respect for the moral law. Such a ground would seem to make moral obligation rather hollow. After all, we must demand to know the nature of the power the moral law wields. Instead, recognition respect for persons should be based in appraisal respect of their *capacity* for morality – we are awed by the moral capacity of humanity. Or we might hold what amounts to the same thing, that our recognition respect for others is based in appraisal respect for the moral law within us – our awe for the transcendent value of morality in which we participate. Kant's goal, with which anyone familiar with his theory of moral motivation will feel comfortable, is to ground moral obedience in morality itself. Such a task risks making this authority arbitrary and groundless, but the feeling of respect – the effect of our comprehension of the moral law on our sensibility – motivates us and makes the authority of morality real for us. Perhaps then it is more correct to say that recognition respect and appraisal respect, or respect as a rational comprehension and respect as a feeling, must be united. Without the moral recognition, the feeling might be inappropriate, but without the feeling, the recognition might seem externally forced. Kant notes that the feeling of respect gives felt authority to the moral law while the rational law itself can be recognized as objectively necessary:

---

[30] Kant writes, "I am not bound to *revere* [*verehren*] others (regarded merely as human beings), that is, to show them *positive* high esteem. The only reverence [*Achtung*] to which I am bound by nature is reverence for the law as such (*revere legem*); and to revere the law, but not to revere other human beings in general (*reverential adversus hominem*) or to perform some acts of reverence for them, is a human being's universal and unconditional duty towards others, which each of them can require as the respect originally owed others (*observantia debita*)" (MM 467–68). In the next paragraph Kant explains the reason that the treatment befitting various social distinctions does not belong in the *Metaphysics of Morals*.

[31] The distinction I am drawing attention to here is closely related to the distinction Kant often makes between practical and pathological feeling. See for example G 399.

And thus respect for the law is not an incentive to morality; rather, it is morality itself regarded subjectively as an incentive inasmuch as pure practical reason – by rejecting, in contrast to self-love, all of self-love's claims – imparts authority to the law, which now alone has influence. (CPR 76)

In other words, Kant's theory of respect brings together thought and feeling, recognition and appraisal. It involves both duty and esteem. It unites respect for morality with respect for persons, including self-respect. It grounds his theory of moral consciousness and virtuous affectivity, and it paves the way for a political theory whereby all legitimate authority is ultimately grounded democratically in individuals.

13

*Is Kantian Hope a Feeling?**

Rachel Zuckert

Kant famously identifies three (later four) major questions to be addressed by reason. Two of these questions are frequently discussed, recognizably central philosophical questions: What can I know? What ought I to do? But Kant's third question is unusual: What may I hope Or, more properly: What am I permitted to hope? (Was darf ich hoffen?)[1] This question is not frequently discussed in philosophy (or elsewhere), and it is unclear what sort of question or issue, or corresponding answer, is envisioned by it. Why are hopes of central interest to reason? What does philosophy have to offer concerning hope, specifically concerning (as it sounds) permission to hope? Kant's own understanding of this question and his answers to it are likewise not as easily identifiable as his responses to the other questions: his two first *Critiques* (along with the *Groundwork* and other works) respectively aim to answer the questions concerning human knowledge and moral obligations, while the *Anthropology* (like all his works generally) speaks to the global question concerning human nature. By contrast, Kant mentions hope infrequently, and never provides an explicit analysis of what it is or what its philosophical significance – its centrality to reason's interests – might be.

There are, of course, Kantian arguments and doctrines that appear to be within the purview of hope, and Kant does so characterize them, if without much comment. Kant argues that we may and should believe in God's existence and in our own immortality, so that we may believe that our ultimate moral aims – to perfect our own virtue and to realize the highest good, the proportionate union of virtue and happiness – are achievable, that we may (in short) hope to be happy, succeed in improving ourselves,

---

* I am grateful to Katalin Makkai, Lissa Merritt, Sasha Newton, Sally Sedgwick, Ken Seeskin, and Helga Varden for helpful discussion of the topics of this essay, and to the editors of this volume, especially Diane Williamson, for comments on an earlier draft. All errors are of course mine.
[1] A805/B833 and AK 11:420. Kant's fourth question is "What is the human being?"

and enjoy a blessed afterlife. He argues that we may interpret human history as having been politically progressive, and thus understand historical forces as potentially supporting the realization of further, not yet accomplished moral and political goals (as well as maintaining achieved progress). And, in the third *Critique*, Kant suggests that we may and ought to judge nature as "purposive" for us, as amenable to scientific investigation and explanation, and (again) as amenable to the realization of our moral and political purposes; we may take it, in other words, that nature is in some rather undefined sense friendly to us, that it will accommodate, not thwart, our highest aims.

All of these arguments concern subject matters about which it would be common, in ordinary usage, to claim to be hopeful: historical progress, the afterlife, achieving one's cognitive or moral goals generally. But in another way it is not clear whether Kant's discussions fit our ordinary conception of hope. For the tentatively positive attitudes toward such subject matters – which he is aiming, in some way, to defend – are not obviously or explicitly, for Kant, affective states or feelings. Indeed, he tends to describe such attitudes in more cognitive terms: an "idea" of history as progressive, a "regulative principle" guiding judgment of nature as purposive, "postulates" or "belief" (*Glaube*, also translated as "faith") in immortality and in God's existence.

In this essay, I am concerned with this latter question: Is Kantian hope to be understood as an emotional state – a feeling?[2] This question is clearly pertinent to the theme of this volume, and, as I just suggested, connects Kant's discussions of hope to our everyday understanding of hope as an emotional response or attitude – particularly if one answers it in the affirmative, as I shall. It also allows for more specific formulation of the puzzlement one might have concerning Kant's question: if hope is a feeling, it seems even less likely to be of central interest to reason, less amenable to philosophical treatment or justification, and more a matter of empirical psychology or personal attitude than a cognitive state or attitude like ideas, beliefs, or principles might be. And so, in thinking about

---

[2] As far as possible, I use "feeling" (*Gefühl*), rather than "emotion" or "affect," as the term for the general class of affective states, so as to accord with Kant's usage. Kant uses "affect" (*Affekt*) to refer to one specific, problematic form of feeling that can overwhelm thought and prevent deliberation (CJ 272n); he refers briefly and (in an evaluative register) somewhat ambivalently to "emotion" (*Rührung, berührt sein*, or *Bewegung des Gemüts*) in the context of discussing aesthetic responses (CJ 273–74, 264ff.). As I shall not here be concerned with Kant's criticism of over-powerful feeling, however, I use "emotional" and "affective" as neutral and general terms to serve as adjectival versions of "feeling."

Kantian hope as a feeling, we may begin to think about the larger questions raised by his surprising third question. In particular, I will suggest that, on Kant's view, philosophical reason is neither to produce hope nor (directly) to justify it – it does not convince us *to* hope. Rather, reason opens the way to (permits) and provides specific, thought-through content for the pre-reflective, felt orientation to the world that is hope. That pre-reflective orientation, in turn, comprises one aspect of what it is to be a human being on Kant's conception, that is, to be a sensible being furnished with reason: hope is a felt recognition of the vulnerability and dependence of a finite rational being, important to reason precisely in its acknowledgment of that which lies beyond reason, that upon which finite reason depends.

I focus my discussion on a central case of such hopeful attitudes in Kant's philosophy (though with an eye to the broader category), namely that concerning the realizability of the highest good. I begin with a brief reminder of Kant's arguments on this point.

13.1 Hope and the Moral Proof of God's Existence

As I indicated, Kant provides little explicit discussion of hope. Following his introduction of the third question, however, he claims that "all hope concerns happiness" (A805/B833) and proceeds to present the first version of his "moral proof" of God's existence in the critical philosophy. This line of argument is later presented more extensively (and with some modifications) in the "Dialectic" section of the *Critique of Practical Reason*, in the form of an antinomy of practical reason. I sketch the latter, as it represents Kant's worked-out version of the argument, in accord with his mature moral philosophy.[3]

Kant begins in the second *Critique* with the idea of the highest good, an idea that reason is driven to formulate in its search for ultimate conditions.[4] Like many of the ideas of theoretical reason, the highest good is the idea of a totality, here the ultimate, complete end of all action, which combines all of our ends, or, specifically, virtue and happiness, the two

---

[3] In the first *Critique*, Kant suggests that the moral law is motivational for us only if it is backed up by "threats and promises" (of happiness or its denial), a position that Kant later rejects in favor of the view that the moral law motivates us directly, not through "incentives of fear and hope" (A811/B839, CPR 129). In both earlier and later critical texts, the moral proof is conjoined with reasoning concerning the immortality of the soul, which, for reasons of space, I largely omit from discussion here.

[4] See A308/B364–65, A322/B379; CPR 110.

basic ends of all human action. (All moral actions aim to follow the moral law or realize virtue, while happiness is the sum of the satisfaction of all other ends, those of sensible desire.) Since we are finite rational beings, we necessarily aim at both, and thus our complete end must include both. More specifically, Kant contends that the highest good is a world in which all are happy in proportion to (or as conditioned by) their virtue.[5]

The antinomy of practical reason concerns the possibility of realizing this end. We are morally obliged to aim to realize the highest good, to make the world "match" our idea of it. Thus, Kant argues, it must be possible to do so: "ought," famously, "implies can"; if we are duty bound to will the highest good as our end, we must be able to realize it. But – so the opposing, antithesis argument goes – the highest good appears not to be possible. For it combines two heterogeneous elements (virtue and happiness), which must therefore be understood to be in a causal relation (CPR 111–12). The cause combining the two must, specifically, be intentional action, for we are here concerned with an end, a state of affairs to be brought about through action.[6] Thus one must hold *either* that aiming at happiness will bring about virtue, *or* that aiming at virtue will bring about happiness. Neither of these seems to be possible, however. Virtue can never be the result of aiming at happiness: agents are virtuous *only if* they aim to follow the moral law for its own sake, not as a result of aiming at something else (happiness). But it also appears that aiming at virtue cannot bring about happiness. For, Kant argues, in moral action we think *only* of the lawfulness (morality) of our actions. In order to become happy, by contrast, we must have knowledge of natural laws and the physical ability to bring about our sensibly desired ends (CPR 113). Thus it does not appear that acting morally as such could bring about happiness. If the highest good is impossible (as this reasoning suggests), then it can be no rational end for action.[7]

---

[5] CPR 111. For differing views on the character of this combination within the highest good, see Andrews Reath, "Two Conceptions of the Highest Good in Kant," *Journal of the History of Philosophy* 26, no. 4 (1988): 593–619, and Stephen Engstrom, "The Concept of the Highest Good in Kant's Moral Theory," *Philosophy and Phenomenological Research* 52, no. 4 (1992): 747–80.

[6] Kant does not state this premise explicitly, but it is presupposed by his line of argument, as summarized in the following.

[7] Here I largely follow Lewis White Beck, *A Commentary on Kant's Critique of Practical Reason* (Chicago: University of Chicago Press, 1960), 248ff. This argument has of course been subject to much discussion; for a recent treatment, see Kyla Ebels-Duggan, "The Right and the Good, and the Threat of Despair: (Kantian) Ethics and the Need for Hope in God," in *Oxford Studies in the Philosophy of Religion*, Vol. 7, ed. Jonathan L. Kvanvig (Oxford: Oxford University Press, 2016), 81–109.

This antinomy raises a serious problem, Kant contends: unless we can show that the highest good is somehow realizable, the moral law will be shown to be "itself false" because it directs us to pursue "imaginary ends" (CPR 114). Kant accordingly argues that there *is* a way to understand the highest good as realizable: though aiming at virtue does not itself bring about happiness, it might do so "mediately (by means of an intelligible author of nature)" (CPR 115). As the moral, omniscient and omnipotent "author" of nature, God can not only recognize virtue (as residing in human intention), but also arrange natural laws such that virtue might bring about happiness. (Or, a view more present in the first than in the second *Critique*: God may allocate rewards and punishments in the afterlife, as a "consequence" of virtue, or lack thereof, in this life [A811/B839; but see also CPR 128].) Therefore, Kant concludes, the moral agent ought to believe in – "postulate" – the existence of God in order consistently to commit to realizing the highest good.

Kant's language of "postulating" is meant to reflect his view that this argument does not amount to objective proof, but rather is a practical argument, establishing the "subjective" necessity of faith: not that God exists, but rather that the moral agent ought to believe in the existence of God in order to sustain her in striving to bring about the highest good. The argument is practical, then, in that it identifies a presupposition for action (pursuing an end).[8] It is "subjective" not in the sense of being idiosyncratic, arbitrary, or ungrounded (quite the contrary, as we all ought to will the highest good, and thus all ought to believe), but in that it concerns the state of mind, the attitude, of the subject – *she* ought to *have* such beliefs – and in that it comprises a *possible* way to think about the world (or agency), not a definitive claim to know its character.[9]

What, now, does this line of thought have to do with hope? Though Kant does not provide a worked-out analysis, as noted above, his claim that all hope concerns happiness in the first *Critique* and his continuing association of hope and happiness in the later account (e.g., CPR 130) give us some indications (some of which are slightly misleading, as I note in a moment). First, this claim suggests that hope is an attitude of expectation concerning desirable outcomes, i.e., concerning objects (in the widest sense) that are good, and are to be attained or brought about in the future; "happiness" is, for Kant, a blanket term for (nonmoral)

---

[8] See Allen W. Wood, *Kant's Moral Religion* (Ithaca, NY: Cornell University Press, 1970), chap. 1 on the practical character of this argument.
[9] CPR 145–46.

things going well (the state where everything goes according to one's "wish and will," as Kant puts it [CPR 124]). Happiness is, moreover, a positive outcome over which we do not have (total) control: here, on Kant's view, we are vulnerable, subject to the pushes and pulls of fortune, requiring the collaboration of "nature" (that which is outside us, "not within our power" [CPR 128n]).[10] Thus, to put these two points together, I suggest that hope is an attitude of tentative positive expectation: not a view that a good outcome is guaranteed, certain, but rather that it could happen, might happen, if all things go well (one could say: if it all goes happily), in ways we cannot ourselves control.

Such tentativeness helps us also to understand the relation between reason, belief, and hope on Kant's account. Our representation of this object of hope – the highest good – is formulated by reason. Moreover, as Andrew Chignell has argued, hope appears to have some rational constraints; for example, we cannot hope for that which is logically impossible (contradictory).[11] Nor, Kant's "moral proof" suggests, can we hope for that which appears really impossible (in Kantian terms), that is, for an outcome that we cannot, even tentatively, think could happen, even could be caused to happen within sensible reality, in accord with natural causal laws. For, as noted above, Kant suggests that God might be thought to arrange natural laws so that *they* will operate to promote the highest good.[12] We do not, of course, *know* that the world has been so ordered by God, on Kant's view – nor, therefore, that the highest good is really possible in this way. Rather, we ought merely to believe, on subjective practical grounds, that God exists, and so also that the realization of the highest good is really possible. The belief does not, moreover, concern a fully worked-out explanation (much less a guarantee) of how in fact the outcome might be produced – it does not allow us to predict or control it – but just a general way of thinking of things such that the outcome might be (thought of as) possible (CPR 145–46).

---

[10] Katrin Flikschuh also emphasizes that (in Kant) hope concerns that over which we have no control – or, as she puts it, in which we "trust," or even to which we "cede control" – in "Hope as Prudence: Practical Faith in Kant's Political Thinking," in *Internationales Jahrbuch des Deutschen Idealismus/International Yearbook of German Idealism*, Vol. 7, ed. Fred Rush, Jürgen Stolzenberg, Paul W. Franks, and Lars-Thade Ulrichs (Berlin: Walter de Gruyter, 2009): 107, 111–12.

[11] Andrew Chignell, "Rational Hope, Moral Order, and the Revolution of the Will," in *Divine Order, Human Order, and the Order of Nature*, ed. Eric Watkins (Oxford: Oxford University Press, 2013), 199–207.

[12] So Chignell also concludes, at least concerning Kant's view, though he defends a more permissive view of rational hope himself, and suggests that the latter may be more appropriate concerning objects of hope like continued moral improvement in the afterlife (Chignell, "Rational Hope," 209, 211). It is indeed hard to see how to construe such an object as really possible within the sensible world.

Hope is, to return to my earlier formulation, tentative expectation: it concerns something good, aimed at, but not entirely within one's powers, thought to be really possible on the basis of some non-dispositive grounds. In sum: the structure of Kant's account is that a certain belief (here: that God exists) allows us to hope that a certain outcome (here: happiness, in proportion to virtue) could come about. Reason formulates the idea of that outcome and elaborates the facilitating belief, or (more broadly) an account suggesting how the outcome might be possible.

Kant's discussions of hope in other contexts – historical progress, moral self-improvement, and (occasionally) scientific progress in finding new laws of nature (e.g., TP 309–10; CPR 123–24; CJ 188) – also seem (mutatis mutandis) to fit this description, as I discuss only briefly now. In these cases, too, hope concerns positive outcomes envisioned by reason, for which we are to strive: the fulfillment of cognitive goals (finding new laws of nature, in accord with reason's "idea" of a complete, systematic science[13]), moral goals (perfect virtue), or moral-political goals (republican government or peace). (Thus, contra Kant's assertion, quoted above, *not* all hope concerns happiness.) In these cases also, we need the "collaboration" of nature or of a power beyond ourselves for that outcome to be realized, Kant argues. If we are to realize our scientific ambitions, nature has to be empirically law governed, in ways discernible by us; Kant emphasizes the contingency of such a "fit" of empirical natural particularity to our cognitive desiderata (CJ 183). If we are to bring about international peace (or other, less ambitious political improvements), we need the collaboration of untold other people over the arc of human history (TP 309). And, perhaps somewhat problematically, Kant also argues that moral perfection is both required of us and beyond our own abilities: we cannot make ourselves perfectly virtuous, because we are finite rational wills, because there is always a chance of slipping or relapse, of privileging self-interest over the claims of morality. If we are to strive nonetheless for perfect virtue – as morality requires – and hope that we may achieve it, Kant therefore argues, we must invoke God's grace or God's merciful judgment (in taking endless striving for virtue, over the course of an immortal existence, to amount to perfect virtue). Only so, he claims, may we see our striving as not in vain, as able to bring about (or contribute to bringing about) goals that lie beyond itself.[14]

---

[13] Kant articulates reason's role in formulating this idea, and the related regulative principles for natural scientific investigation, in the appendix to the Dialectic of the *Critique of Pure Reason*.

[14] E.g., R 75–76. This argument is problematic because Kant often emphasizes elsewhere that virtue *is* within our powers – by contrast to happiness (or, say, fulfilling all of our natural scientific aspirations) – and so may be both required of and imputed to us. Kant's own discomfort with this

Is Kantian Hope a Feeling? 249

These are, then, outcomes that are desirable, and identified as such by reason, and Kant appears in these cases, too, to take it as a philosophical task to give an account (more or less extensive in the different cases) of how these outcomes might be really possible:[15] to articulate justifiable beliefs or assumptions that might allow us to see them so, not (again) to show that such outcomes are guaranteed, nor even definitively known to be really possible. In the *Critique of the Power of Judgment*, Kant argues that it is justified to assume ("subjectively") that nature is "purposive for our understanding" (so that we may justifiably hope to achieve our scientific aims) (CJ 184). As just mentioned, Kant argues that we ought to believe in the immortality of the soul or in God's grace to support our striving for perfect virtue: if we were to have infinite time (for self-improvement), or to receive supplemental grace, we may hope to achieve perfect virtue (if in ways that we do not fully understand). And Kant's more extensive philosophical accounts of history are aimed to give us some way of thinking about history and collective human action – perhaps a belief, or a global, systematic interpretation ("idea") concerning the character of history – that can give us some tentative sense that our ambitious political goals might be realizable, even if they far transcend any person's abilities, and flout the evidence of much sad and terrible historical fact (see TP 309).

So, in sum, the objects of hope on Kant's view are taken (in or by the attitude of hope) to be: desirable objects or outcomes of action that cannot be brought about by oneself alone, and the future existence of which can be believed, tentatively, to be really possible, not guaranteed or certain. Insofar as the ideas of these objects are formulated by reason, and hope for the realization of them is supported by rationally articulated beliefs, however, one may wonder (again) whether hope is properly understood as a feeling. Are such objects, conceived by pure reason, truly objects of *feeling* – of sensible responsiveness? Can Kant claim so, given the sharp divide he often makes between reason and sensibility?[16] Or should we

---

line of argument is manifested, I think, in his discussions of grace and his unwillingness to allow that we might receive moral credit for results of God's grace, rather than our own efforts (R 143).

[15] Kant seems to assume that these objects of hope are logically possible, but one might wonder whether the perfection of an (essentially) imperfect (i.e., finite) will might in fact fail to accord with this rational standard.

[16] I should note that the consensus position in current scholarly discussion is that Kant's conception of morality, i.e., practical rationality, does not rule out or absolutely oppose sensibility, though of course there are many different views concerning how reason and sensibility are to be related or combined. See, for example, Jeanine Grenberg, "Feeling, Desire, and Interest in Kant's Theory of Action," *Kant-Studien* 92, no. 2 (2001): 153–79, and for a representative range of positions, Alix Cohen, ed., *Kant on Emotion and Value* (London: Palgrave Macmillan, 2014). I take my discussion here to be consonant with, if different in focus from, these discussions.

conceive of Kantian hope (for happiness, perfect virtue, and so forth) in fact as belief, a tentative cognitive attitude concerning the likelihood of a desired outcome? I turn now to consider such questions.

13.2 Rational Objects of Feeling

We may note first that, given the above discussion, there is at least space in Kant's view for a distinction between belief and hope, and so also for hope to be a feeling: belief concerns – affirms on subjectively sufficient practical grounds – a proposition, namely that God exists (or that nature is purposive, history progressive, and so forth). Hope, by contrast, concerns a desirable (positively evaluated and aimed-at) object or outcome – the realization of the highest good, peace, or systematic science – and is a tentative expectation of the future existence of this object. One might in turn characterize this tentative expectation in propositional, assertoric terms, as a further belief: I believe that the highest good might be realized, someday. But, I will suggest, one need not do so, and in fact, for Kant, this tentative expectation is better characterized in terms of feeling. (To my knowledge, Kant himself does not commit himself on this point, though he does refer to a "feeling" of hopelessness [R 71], and, as noted above, pairs hope with fear, the latter of which is a feeling on his view.) I will argue, specifically, that the (often) pure rational or supersensible content or object of the hopeful attitude does not weigh against considering it to be a feeling, and, more positively, that the nature of feeling comes closest to describing the role of this attitude in Kant's systematic conception of human life and thought: as (quasi-)motivational and subjectively, personally orienting, and as a passive, temporally located state of the empirical subject.

To begin, we may note that Kant himself, in early metaphysics lectures, articulates difficulties with conceiving of feelings for or about rationally conceived objects. In discussing moral feeling, or the subjective incentive to act in accord with the moral law, Kant writes that it is difficult to understand such a feeling, for

> [o]ne is to cognize the good through [reason], and yet have a feeling of it. This is obviously something that cannot be properly understood ... I am supposed to have a feeling of that which is not an object of feeling, but rather which I cognize objectively through [reason]. Thus there is always a contradiction hidden in here. For if we are supposed to do the good through a feeling, then we do it because it is agreeable. But this cannot be for the good cannot at all affect our senses. (AK 28:257–58 [1770s])

Though Kant's focus here is moral feeling, the main problem he raises seems relevant to rational hope as well: feeling concerning rationally conceived objects (or rational representations) fits ill with Kant's conception of human faculties as correlated to, or even defined by, the type of object with which they are concerned, or the type of representation that they provide.[17] On Kant's view, reason is, of course, a faculty that formulates a priori propositions or ideas, for example, that of the highest good. Feelings, by contrast, are sensible states of human beings, empirically known, present at particular temporal moments in a subject's mental life, and "pathological" – passive or affected, not spontaneously produced. They would seem correspondingly, Kant suggests here, to concern particular sensible objects or states of affairs. A feeling "of" an a priori representation or its object (e.g., the highest good) thus appears incomprehensible, a contradiction in terms – it is a "feeling" of that which is "not an object of feeling," a sensible apprehension of the nonsensible, of that which "cannot affect our senses."[18]

I suggest, however, that Kant's mature account of the nature of feeling – most basically, pleasure or displeasure – in the *Critique of the Power of Judgment* allows him to conceive of such purportedly "contradictory" feelings, to address his own challenge of how to conceive of feeling for rational objects as at once recognizably sensible and yet also directed toward or responsive to the non-sensible. Pleasure, Kant writes, is the "consciousness of a representation's causality directed at the subject's state so as to *keep* him in that state" (CJ 220); displeasure, correspondingly, is the consciousness of a representation's causality that "prompts" the subject to "*leave*" his state (APV 230).[19] These definitions are not immediately perspicuous, but they have two significant aspects for our purposes. First, on this definition, feelings are intentional states: they are "consciousness" of *another* representation (as having an effect on me).[20] In accord with this

---

[17] This "matching" of faculty to type of representation is perhaps most explicit in Kant's introduction of his distinction between understanding and sensibility (et al.) at A19/B33f.

[18] Kant expresses similar concerns about moral feeling, though with less explanation, at G 460 and CPR 80 and 83. Kant, and commentators following him, have sometimes wished to claim that respect is a special case, a rational feeling or a non-sensible feeling, or the like. This move seems, however, question begging; better (on my view) for Kant to recognize, and work out how to account for, the fact that, in general, feeling may both be sensible and have rational objects.

[19] I use Kant's language from the *Anthropology* as it is less obscure than that provided in the *Critique of the Power of Judgment*.

[20] This claim is perhaps somewhat dubious concerning simple sense pleasures or pains, but I shall not concern myself with that problem here, because Kantian hope – like other feelings such as joy, anger, fear – does seem (often) to be directed intentionally at some object or state of affairs, as represented under certain descriptions, i.e., as good for certain reasons.

intentional definition of feeling, Kant in the third *Critique* distinguishes among three sorts of pleasure (and, presumably, corresponding displeasures) – the agreeable, aesthetic pleasure, and pleasure in the good – by distinguishing among three sorts of representation that may be the object of feeling (sensation, form, or conceptual judgment). As thus intentional, it would appear, such responsiveness may also be *to* – or be feeling *about* – rational representations, such as laws, ideas, or judgments.

This intentional state is, however, still understood as sensible, as quite distinct from a purely cognitive attitude such as a belief in (affirmation or assertion of) the propositional content of the relevant representation. That is (this is the second important point): insofar as pleasure and displeasure are understood as "consciousness of ... causality ... so as to maintain" or "leave" one's current state, they retain distinctive characteristics of sensibility, specifically evaluative (affective) sensibility. As consciousness of the effectual character of representations ("causality") *on me*, feelings are identified as belonging to me, as related to (or concerning) my own individual, empirical current and future states.[21] Feeling is, in other words, here understood as itself a temporally occurrent mental state of the individual, empirical subject and as consciousness of another representation likewise temporally located and individuated (as part of my own mental life). Moreover, feeling on this understanding is passive, brought about by and dependent on something else (the other representation); it is a way in which the subject is affected, rather than active. Most generally, feeling so understood is a fact or a consciousness of a fact about the subject – a state in which one finds oneself, to which one is given (to use somewhat Heideggerian formulations) – rather than a judgment that the subject might affirm or deny.

Feelings so understood are also, however, states that are prima facie good or bad for the subject, or from the subject's point of view, or, more properly, they identify (are the "consciousness of") *other* representations as prima facie good or bad. Such prima facie goodness or badness (for the subject) is, again, glossed not as a judgment, but as a motivational tendency or as effectual, a "causality" on the subject to remain in or leave its state – as a positive or negative affective orientation, as it were an "impulse" or push to action.

---

[21] I here build on the discussions of Kant on pleasure in Zuckert, "A New Look at Kant's Theory of Pleasure," *The Journal of Aesthetics and Art Criticism* 60, no. 3 (2002): 239–52, and *Kant on Beauty and Biology: An Interpretation of the Critique of Judgment* (Cambridge: Cambridge University Press, 2007).

Kant's reference to causality in these definitions is, in sum, an attempt to capture the subjective and temporal locatedness and the passivity of sensibility (in general), as well as the evaluative/motivational character of feeling in particular, as a specific, i.e., affective, mode of sensibility. Such (felt) intentional consciousness is no mere assertion of some propositional content, connected to other judgments or propositions logically (e.g., inferentially). Rather, it is explicitly and consciously my own state of mind, and presents its intentional object (the representation, the causality of which I am conscious) as effectual on – as mattering to – me. So Kant responds to the problem, the potential contradiction, he raised in the passage from the metaphysics lectures quoted above: we cannot sense the rational, the non-sensible; indeed, that would be a contradiction. But we can *feel* (sensibly, as a passive or "given" state, with motivational valence) the effect of a rational (non-sensible) representation on ourselves. To take the most famous, widely discussed example: in the feeling of respect, I do not just represent the moral law rationally, but rather am sensibly (passively, subjectively, emotionally) aware of that representation as effectual upon me – that it matters to me (individually), that it has a "hold on" me (as empirical subject), that I am moved by it, that it could lead me to act in accord with its dictates.

Kant's third *Critique* definition of feeling allows him, then, to hold that (sensible) feeling may concern rational representations. We may understand Kantian hope, in particular, as a feeling about, in response to, rationally formulated ideas such as the highest good or historical progress. And we also have some reason to do so: not only because we commonsensically take hope to be an affective state, but also, as I will now argue, because (Kantian) hope shares the characteristics of feeling just outlined, namely subjective "location," subjective evaluative and (what I call) quasi-motivational tenor, and passivity.

13.3 The Feeling of Hope

As noted above, Kant (not unusually) understands hope to concern states of affairs taken to lie in the future; he correspondingly emphasizes in some of his discussions of hope that in this attitude we take noumenal entities or states of affairs – the condition of the immortal soul, our own intelligible moral character – *as* future states, even though of course on his view noumena are not, properly speaking, temporally determined. Hope thus represents a certain (as it were) insertion of such objects – or, more properly, the representation of such objects – into the temporal arc of lived experience, as had by actual, individual, empirical subjects.[22] This emphatic future orientation in hope is perhaps a reason why it is centrally (though, as noted above, not exclusively) concerned with happiness: happiness too, on Kant's view, is "not a possession but a progression," a pursuit temporally stretching out over the course of one's life, a project reaching toward the future (AK 28:1090).

As also mentioned above, hope is certainly an evaluative attitude for Kant, and arguably a subjectively evaluative one. It is positively valenced in two related senses: it concerns a desirable (i.e., positively evaluated) object of action or outcome, and it is positively inclined toward (hopeful about, as it were) the potential realization of that object or goal. It seems plausible to think, moreover, that these positive orientations are "bought into" by the individual subject who hopes: she personally, as the individual empirical subject that she is, here and now, takes both the object and the future (as including the existence of that object) to be good. Thus there is some (perhaps vague) sense in which hope can be seen as subjective, not in the sense, again, of being arbitrary, but in the sense of being located in and mattering to an individual subject as such.

Hope is not, however, subjectively evaluative in the sense of being a directly motivational attitude on Kant's view, and in fact ought not to be: one should not act morally *out of* (motivated by) hope for one's thereby merited happiness.[23] Yet hope is on Kant's view related to motivation, to the subject's commitment to the pursuit of her cognitive or moral goals, if more indirectly. For, as we have seen, Kant argues that if one lacks hope that one's pursuit of one's goals will be supported by external factors – whether nature, other people, or God – that one requires for success but that are beyond one's control, one will lose the confidence, the vigor, to strive for one's goals, to do what one can do oneself. Without hope, the

---

[22] Kant's use of "future" language is particularly striking in the first *Critique* – see A800/B828, A803/B831, A811/B839, A827/B855–A830/B858 – and in the *Religion* (e.g., R 68–69). I would distinguish this suggestion from the view proposed by Daniel Guevara and Paul Guyer that feeling (they are both concerned with respect rather than hope) might be the phenomenal appearance of something noumenal. (See Paul Guyer, *Kant and the Experience of Freedom: Essays on Aesthetics and Morality* [Cambridge: Cambridge University Press, 1993], 354–55; Daniel Guevara, *Kant's Theory of Moral Motivation* [Boulder, CO: Westview Press, 2000], 108.) My suggestion is more straightforward: feelings (indeed phenomenal) can concern *representations* of noumenal entities. These representations can also play a role in one's phenomenal life, one's lived experience. Indeed, feelings register a certain sort of role for such representations – their effects on the subject, the subject's consciousness of being moved by them. This should not be understood (I think) as a consciousness of being moved by noumena.
[23] For discussion of difficulties on this point, however, see Lara Denis, "Autonomy and the Highest Good," *Kantian Review* 10, no. 1 (2005): 33–59.

future is closed off, and the subject will see no reason to act, to do her part in bringing about the best of ends. Hope is, then, not itself a motivation: it is not, or should not be, itself the reason, or (perhaps better) the "impulse," to do something. But it is (on Kant's view) needed to *support* motivation, to orient the subject to the world such that she can and will pursue her ends. Hope is, then, at least "quasi-motivational": not itself a motivation, but connected to and supportive of the subject's motivation to act.

More generally, Kantian hope for the realization of the highest good is supposed to have effects in, on, for the subject – give her a certain orientation in the world, support her commitment to her goals, help her perform actions – and not logical consequences, roles in inference, or the construction of doctrine.[24] Indeed, Kant tends to warn against too much argument, or the elaboration of doctrine, about the objects of hope and the beliefs (or faith) supporting them: better to be moved to act, strive to realize moral ends, than try to figure out how exactly God's grace or the machinery of realizing the highest good might work.[25]

Kantian hope is, then, at least *like* feeling in being both subjectively located and subjectively evaluative: it is temporally determined as part of the subject's arc of experience, and is a component of personal motivation or commitment. Hope is also, I think, importantly passive – a central characteristic of sensibility on Kant's view – though this point is somewhat more complicated to work out, as I proceed to do now.

In general, Kant tends to conceive of feelings as passive for familiar reasons: it is not "up to you" whether you feel something or not; feelings are effects of other things impinging upon one, or (in the terms I used above) they are facts about the subject – just "given" or "there" – rather than judgments made by her, in accord with reasons. Unlike most feelings, however, Kantian hope seems not to be produced by the impingement of some external objects upon one: hope may be our "given" state, we may simply "find ourselves" hoping – as indeed, I believe, is Kant's view – but this fact is not to be explained by the causal influence of some external object or situation. Indeed, hope not only concerns ideas that are produced, spontaneously, by reason (such as God's grace, the highest good, and historical progress), but also seems to be the subject matter of arguments concerning how to conceive of the world such that it might be justified, as we have seen. So again one might think that Kantian hope is not (very)

---

[24] See CPR 143: it is the "subjective effect" of belief and hope that matters. See also AK 28:1117.
[25] See, for example, Kant's discussion of Job in MPT 265–67.

passive, more the result of argument than of being affected, more a reasoned attitude than a feeling.

Or, more moderately, one might suggest that hope is (what I call) a self-wrought feeling like respect or aesthetic pleasures in the beautiful and the sublime. In those cases, one *is* affected (moved) by certain representations – of the moral law, purposive form, or infinity. The feeling itself is passive, and perhaps also a consciousness *of* one's passivity, of *being* affected (the representation of the moral law affects me). Yet this affection is also *self-affection*: one is moved by one's *own* active, spontaneous, rational self-legislation, or the active, free play of one's cognitive faculties. Such feeling is, to return to the definition of feeling above, a "consciousness" of the causality of a representation on one – in that sense one is passive, affected – but one is also, importantly, the author of that representation.

Though plausible, these lines of thought seem to me to misread the intended import of Kant's arguments concerning hope, and the tenor of his question, "What may I hope?" The phrasing of this question suggests that human beings *already* hope, or have tendencies to do so. Reason, then, is to establish which objects are proper or permissible for that preexisting attitude – the "what" that is its focus, and the "may" that governs or restricts it – not to *produce* it. Correspondingly, Kant's arguments in support of belief in the existence of God, the immortality of the soul, and historical progress are – as has often been remarked, and as I emphasized above – rather weak.[26] They do not even definitively establish the real possibility of the objects of hope, but just provide us with a "way of thinking" about the world, with tentative (subjective, practical) grounds for belief. Such accounts could not – and, I am suggesting, are not meant to – convince someone of some conclusion, nor to persuade someone who feels no hope to do so. Rather, they have more modest, modifying aims: to ward off "crafty hope" and "wild despair," to use Kant's language (R 160 and 71); that is, not to produce hope, but to prevent the corruption or loss of preexisting hope.

I now expand a little on these permissive and protective functions of philosophical reason, with respect to hope. First, Kant's language of permission in his question (what I *may* [*darf*] hope) indicates, I suggest, that he takes there to be not just theoretical rational conditions on our conception of the objects of hope (as both logically and really possible, as I have discussed), but also moral conditions for or restrictions on hope.

---

[26] For discussion of worries concerning the weakness of these arguments, see Andrew Chignell, "Belief in Kant," *Philosophical Review* 116, no. 3 (2007): 323–60.

Most centrally for Kant, it is not morally permissible to hope that one will receive salvation from God without engaging in moral striving (R 71). That would be a corruption of hope – "crafty hope" – for hope properly concerns that which lies outside our control, and not that which we are called upon, by practical reason, to do ourselves (become worthy of salvation).[27] This criticism of "crafty hope" might be seen, in turn, as an instance of a more general function of reason with respect to hope that I have already mentioned, namely to clarify the character of its object(s): what *are* the truly desirable outcomes of action (according to practical reason), which "things" are to be tentatively expected (hoped) to go well?

Kant's answer to this question in the broadest terms is, of course, the highest good – an object that may well seem likely to arouse not hope but despair. For, as Kant emphasizes, not only is it difficult to conceive how the highest good might come about (as discussed above), but experience does not seem to support even a tentative expectation of such an outcome. Rather, we frequently see good people suffer and the evil prosper (MPT 261). And the same may be said of historical progress, a conception not unambiguously supported (to say the least) by empirical historical fact. More generally, insofar as hope on Kant's conception is a feeling about a potentially rather complex set of ideas and judgments (about objects judged as good and possible in the future), it may be corrected or modified by judgments or redescriptions of those objects, even thereby transformed into its opposite, despair.[28]

I suggest again here, in response to the possibility of despair, that Kantian philosophical reason is invoked not to produce but to sustain hope: it provides an alternative way of conceiving of the world, such that it may be understood as more, or (potentially) other, than it has been seen to

---

[27] See also CPR 127–29, where Kant praises the Christian over the Stoic conception of the relationship between morality and happiness precisely on the grounds that it makes a firm distinction between the two, and thus between that which is within and that which is outside our powers (between that which we are required to do and that for which we hope). Not coincidentally, I think, in claiming that virtue can bring its own "contentment" (happiness) with it, the Stoic view underemphasizes human vulnerability and finitude.

[28] On this point, Kant's view touches upon a currently often-discussed question concerning the rationality of emotion, i.e., whether emotions are themselves judgments and, therefore, rational or irrational (as [in]correct or [un]justified judgments). Though I cannot discuss this question here, I believe that Kant's view entails a qualified affirmative answer to it (at least about hope). That a subject has a certain feeling (or not) is a matter of fact (dependent upon her temperament or given, natural dispositions, how representations affect her), not of judgmental correctness: either I do or do not feel hopeful about the future. Yet insofar as feelings concern a representation of an object as judged, they may be justified or not: my pleasure in spinach, represented as good for health, is justified if that judgment is true of spinach. Likewise, hope that the highest good will be realized is justified only if I can judge the world somehow to be (possibly) so.

be empirically – so that one may not come to, but *continue to* hope. Kant describes the burden of his arguments thus: "I do not need to prove this presupposition [of historical progress]; it is up to my adversary to prove [his] case" (TP 309). In the surrounding text, Kant emphasizes the claims of duty: we must aim to bring about moral ends, and so must believe that they are possible. But this statement (as well as his subsequent ad hominem argument against Mendelssohn as a hopeful moral agent) also suggests that morally contributing hopefulness is the default condition, an affective reliance upon and trust in support for one's dutiful action (not just the requirement to act morally itself). Kantian philosophical reason must, then, not prove its case, but merely remove impediments to this hopefulness, redescribe the world such that it does not get corrupted or overridden by despair.

So, in sum, I propose that, on Kant's view, hope is not the product of philosophical reason – of its conceptions of God, grace, historical progress, and so forth – whether as cognitive attitude or self-wrought feeling. Like the self-wrought feelings, hope is a feeling of being affected (moved) by certain rationally articulated representations. But hope is more passive than such feelings: it is not created, brought about, by our cognitive activity. Rather, we are furnished naturally with a feeling that "things will go well," or (perhaps better) with a disposition to have such feelings.[29] Reason can clarify what the objects of such feeling could be, place moral conditions upon it, and ward off conceptions of the world that might override or curdle it. Reason may, correspondingly, show how appropriately clarified versions of such feeling contribute to rational ends, and therefore that it can and should be part of a moral life. But the formulation of such ideas or arguments, the proposal of mere "ways of thinking," does not produce hope; hope is rather given, a fact, a disposition we have, not an attitude or conclusion to which we can be brought by reasoning (or will).

Hope is, I suggest moreover, not just passive, but appropriately so. For hope is a felt consciousness *of* our passivity or vulnerability; it concerns, precisely, outcomes beyond our control, and our need of support from that which is beyond us, for our aims to be accomplished, our desires to be fulfilled. It is the emotional stance, one might say, of a healthy animal that trusts in its place in the world, in the world's fit to its desires or requirements, as it needs to do.

This proposal brings us back of course to the questions with which I began: If hope is a naturally given feeling, a passive, subjective, quasi-

---

[29] I am grateful to Helga Varden for conversation on these points.

motivational orientation to the world, why is it, how can it be, a central subject matter for philosophical reason, on Kant's view? Some of the answer to this question surely lies in the metaphysical (religious) character of the objects of hope and of the beliefs enlisted in its support: hope concerns rationally formulated ends, and to sustain it, Kant's accounts suggest, we are driven to transcend experience, to deploy pure rational ideas, to look to the supersensible. But I wonder whether hope might also be central for Kant precisely because it instantiates and identifies a limit to reason, because it marks the ways in which human reason is finite, even vulnerable, reliant on support from outside itself, both within and without the human being. So, to modify slightly my previous suggestion, hope is perhaps better understood as the affective stance of the healthy *rational animal*, which – as rational – sets ends beyond the given and beyond itself, which therefore conceives of the future and of its own insufficiency, and which in turn – as animal – needs to hope, to feel that such ends might be realizable, that it will be furnished with the support it needs.

Bibliography

Allison, Henry E. *Kant's Theory of Freedom*. Cambridge: Cambridge University Press, 1990.
  Kant's Theory of Taste: A Reading of the Critique of Aesthetic Judgment. Cambridge: Cambridge University Press, 2001.
  Kant's Transcendental Idealism. New Haven: Yale University Press, 2004.
Altman, Matthew C., ed. *The Palgrave Kant Handbook*. London: Palgrave Macmillan, forthcoming.
Ameriks, Karl. *Interpreting Kant's Critiques*. Oxford: Clarendon Press, 2003.
  Kant and the Fate of Autonomy: Problems in the Appropriation of the Critical Philosophy. Cambridge: Cambridge University Press, 2000.
Anderson, Elizabeth. "Emotions in Kant's Later Moral Philosophy: Honour and the Phenomenology of Moral Value." In *Kant's Ethics of Virtue*, edited by Monika Betzler, 123–46. Berlin: de Gruyter, 2008.
  "Moral Bias and Corrective Practices: A Pragmatist Perspective." *Proceedings and Addresses of the American Philosophical Association* 89 (2015): 21–47.
Anderson-Gold, Sharon. "Privacy, Respect and the Virtues of Reticence in Kant." *Kantian Review* 15, no. 2 (July 2010): 28–42.
Aquila, Richard E. "Is Sensation the Matter of Appearances?" In *Interpreting Kant*, edited by Moltke S. Gram, 11–29. Iowa City: University of Iowa Press, 1982.
  "A New Look at Kant's Aesthetic Judgment." In *Essays in Kant's Aesthetics*, edited by Ted Cohen and Paul Guyer, 87–114. Chicago: University of Chicago Press, 1982.
Aristotle. *Nicomachean Ethics*. Translated by Terence Irwin. 2nd ed. Indianapolis, IN: Hackett, 1999.
Ashfield, Andrew, and Peter de Bolla, eds. *The Sublime: A Reader in British Eighteenth-Century Aesthetic Theory*. Cambridge: Cambridge University Press, 1996.
Banham, Gary. *Kant's Practical Philosophy: From Critique to Doctrine*. London: Palgrave Macmillan, 2003.
Baron, Marcia. *Kantian Ethics Almost without Apology*. Ithaca, NY: Cornell University Press, 1999.

"Kantian Ethics and the Claims of Detachment." In *Feminist Interpretations of Immanuel Kant*, edited by Robin May Schott, 145–72. University Park, PA: Pennsylvania State University Press, 1997.

"Love and Respect in the Doctrine of Virtue." In *Kant's Metaphysics of Morals: Interpretative Essays*, edited by Mark Timmons, 391–407. Oxford: Oxford University Press, 2002.

Beck, Lewis White. *A Commentary on Kant's Critique of Practical Reason*. Chicago: University of Chicago Press, 1960.

Early German Philosophy: Kant and His Predecessors. Cambridge, MA: Harvard University Press, 1969.

Betzler, Monika, ed. *Kant's Ethics of Virtue*. Berlin: De Gruyter, 2008.

Borchardt, Frank L. "Petrarch: The German Connection." *Studies in Romance Languages* 3 (1975): 418–31.

Borges, Maria. "Physiology and the Controlling of Affects in Kant's Philosophy." *Kantian Review* 13, no. 2 (2008): 46–66.

Brady, Emily. *The Sublime in Modern Philosophy: Aesthetics, Ethics, and Nature*. Cambridge: Cambridge University Press, 2013.

Brandt, Reinhard. "The Deductions in the *Critique of Judgment*." In *Kant's Transcendental Deductions*, edited by Eckhart Forster, 177–91. Stanford, CA: Stanford University Press, 1989.

Breitenbach, Angela. "Understanding, Knowledge, and the Touchstone of Truth." In *Proceedings of the 12th International Kant Congress*, edited by Violetta L. Waibel and Margit Ruffing. Berlin: de Gruyter, forthcoming.

Broadie, Alexander, and Elizabeth M. Pybus. "Kant and Direct Duties." *Dialogue* 20, no. 1 (1981): 60–67.

Budd, Malcolm. *The Aesthetic Appreciation of Nature*. Oxford: Clarendon Press, 2002.

Bunch, Aaron. "Throwing Oneself Away: Kant on the Forfeiture of Respect." *Kantian Review* 19, no. 1 (March 2014): 71–91.

Burke, Edmund. "A Philosophical Enquiry into the Origin of Our Ideas of the Sublime and Beautiful (1759)." In *The Sublime: A Reader in British Eighteenth-Century Aesthetic Theory*, edited by Andrew Ashfield and Peter de Bolla, 131–43. Cambridge: Cambridge University Press, 1996.

Cassirer, Ernest, Paul Oskar Kristeller, and John Herman Randall Jr., eds. *The Renaissance Philosophy of Man: Petrarca, Valla, Ficino, Pico, Pomponazzi, Vives*. Chicago: University of Chicago Press, 1948.

Chignell, Andrew. "Belief in Kant." *Philosophical Review* 116, no. 3 (2007): 323–60.

"Rational Hope, Moral Order, and the Revolution of the Will." In *Divine Order, Human Order, and the Order of Nature*, edited by Eric Watkins, 197–218. Oxford: Oxford University Press, 2013.

Clewis, Robert R. *The Kantian Sublime and the Revelation of Freedom*. Cambridge: Cambridge University Press, 2009.

"The Place of the Sublime in Kant's Project." *Studi Kantiani* 28 (2015): 149–68.

"A Theory of the Sublime Is Possible." *Wassard Elea Revista* 4 (2016): 45–68.
"What's the Big Idea? On Emily Brady's Sublime." *The Journal of Aesthetic Education* 50, no. 2 (2016): 104–18.
ed. *Reading Kant's Lectures*. Berlin: Walter de Gruyter, 2015.
Cohen, Alix. "From Faking It to Making It: The Feeling of Love of Honor as an Aid to Morality." In *Reading Kant's Lectures*, edited by Robert R. Clewis, 243–56. Berlin: Walter de Gruyter, 2015.
Kant and the Human Sciences: Biology, Anthropology, and History. New York: Palgrave Macmillan, 2010.
"Kant on Doxastic Voluntarism and Its Implications for the Ethics of Belief." *Kant Yearbook* 5 (2013): 33–50.
"Kant on Emotions, Feelings and Affectivity." In *The Palgrave Kant Handbook*, edited by Matthew C. Altman. London: Palgrave Macmillan, forthcoming.
"The Ultimate Kantian Experience: Kant on Dinner Parties." *History of Philosophy Quarterly* 25, no. 4 (2008): 315–36.
ed. *Kant on Emotion and Value*. London: Palgrave Macmillan, 2014.
Cohen, Ted, and Paul Guyer, eds. *Essays in Kant's Aesthetics*. Chicago: University of Chicago Press, 1981.
Cooper, Anthony Ashley (3rd Earl of Shaftesbury). "A Letter concerning Enthusiasm." In *Characteristics of Men, Manners, Opinions, Times*, edited by John M. Robertson, 5–42. Indianapolis, IN: Bobbs-Merrill, 1964.
Costelloe, Timothy M. *The Sublime: From Antiquity to the Present*. Cambridge: Cambridge University Press, 2012.
Cranor, Carl. "Toward a Theory of Respect for Persons." *American Philosophical Quarterly* 12 (October 1975): 303–19.
Crowther, Paul. *The Kantian Sublime: From Morality to Art*. Oxford: Clarendon Press, 1989.
Darwall, Stephen. "Kant on Respect, Dignity, and the Duty of Respect." In *Kant's Ethics of Virtue*, edited by Monika Betzler, 175–200. Berlin: De Gruyter, 2008.
"Two Kinds of Respect." *Ethics* 88, no. 1 (October 1977): 36–49.
Deimling, Wiebke. "Kant's Pragmatic Concept of Emotions." In *Kant on Emotion and Value*, edited by Alix Cohen, 108–25. New York: Palgrave Macmillan, 2014.
Deligiorgi, Katerina. *Kant and the Culture of Enlightenment*. Albany: SUNY Press, 2005.
"The Pleasures of Contra-purposiveness: Kant, the Sublime and Being Human." *The Journal of Aesthetics and Art Criticism* 72, no. 1 (2014): 25–35.
The Scope of Autonomy: Kant and the Morality of Freedom. Oxford: Oxford University Press, 2012.
Denis, Lara. "Autonomy and the Highest Good." *Kantian Review* 10, no. 1 (2005): 33–59.
ed. *Kant's Metaphysics of Morals: A Critical Guide*. Cambridge: Cambridge University Press, 2010.

Denis, Lara, and Oliver Sensen, eds. *Kant's Lectures on Ethics: A Critical Guide*. Cambridge: Cambridge University Press, 2015.
Dennett, Daniel C. *Freedom Evolves*. New York: Penguin, 2004.
Descartes, René. "Rules for the Direction of the Mind." In *The Philosophical Writings of Descartes*, Vol. 1, translated by John Cottingham, Robert Stoothoff, and Dugald Murdoch, 9–77. Cambridge: Cambridge University Press, 1985.
DeWitt, Janelle. "Respect for the Moral Law: The Emotional Side of Reason." *Philosophy* 89, no. 1 (2014): 31–62.
Dillon, Robin S. "How to Lose Your Self-Respect." *American Philosophical Quarterly* 29, no. 2 (April 1992): 125–39.
Doran, Robert. *The Theory of the Sublime from Longinus to Kant*. Cambridge: Cambridge University Press, 2015.
Du Bos, Jean-Baptiste. *Critical Reflections on Poetry, Painting, and Music*. Translated by Thomas Nugent. 3 Vols. London: John Nourse, 1748.
Düsing, Klaus. "Beauty as the Transition from Nature to Freedom in Kant's *Critique of Judgment*." *Noûs* 24, no. 1 (March 1990): 79–92.
Dyck, Corey W. *Kant and Rational Psychology*. New York: Oxford University Press, 2014.
Ebels-Duggan, Kyla. "The Right and the Good, and the Threat of Despair: (Kantian) Ethics and the Need for Hope in God." In *Oxford Studies in the Philosophy of Religion*, Vol. 7, edited by Jonathan L. Kvanvig, 81–109. Oxford: Oxford University Press, 2016.
Effron, Daniel A., and Paul Conway. "When Virtue Leads to Villainy: Advances in Research on Moral Self-Licensing." *Current Opinions in Psychology* 6 (2015): 32–35.
Engstrom, Stephen. "The Concept of the Highest Good in Kant's Moral Theory." *Philosophy and Phenomenological Research* 52, no. 4 (1992): 747–80.
Esser, Andrea. *Eine Ethik für Endliche, Kant's Tugendlehre in der Gegenwart*. Stuttgart: Frommann-Holzboog, 2004.
Fahmy, Melissa Seymour. "Active Sympathetic Participation: Reconsidering Kant's Duty of Sympathy." *Kantian Review* 14, no. 1 (2009): 31–52.
  "Understanding Kant's Duty of Respect as a Duty of Virtue." *Journal of Moral Philosophy* 10, no. 6 (2013): 723–40.
Falkenstein, Lorne. "Was Kant a Nativist?" *Journal of the History of Ideas* 51, no. 4 (1990): 573–97.
Fenves, Peter, ed. *Raising the Tone of Philosophy: Late Essays by Immanuel Kant, Transformative Critique by Jacques Derrida*. Baltimore: Johns Hopkins University Press, 1993.
Ferrarin, Alfredo. *The Powers of Pure Reason: Kant and the Idea of Cosmic Philosophy*. Chicago: University of Chicago Press, 2015.
Fichte, Johann Gottlieb. *System of Ethics*. Translated by Daniel Breazeale and Günter Zöller. Cambridge: Cambridge University Press, 2005.

Sämmtliche Werke. Edited by I. H. Fichte (1845–1846). Berlin: Walter de Gruyter, 1971.
Flikschuh, Katrin. "Hope as Prudence: Practical Faith in Kant's Political Thinking." In *Internationales Jahrbuch des Deutschen Idealismus/ International Yearbook of German Idealism*, Vol. 7, edited by Fred Rush, Jürgen Stolzenberg, Paul W. Franks, and Lars-Thade Ulrichs, 95–117 (Berlin: Walter de Gruyter, 2009).
Formosa, Paul. "Dignity and Respect: How to Apply Kant's Formula of Humanity." *Philosophical Forum* 45, no. 1 (Spring 2014): 49–68.
Forsey, Jane. "Is a Theory of the Sublime Possible?" *The Journal of Aesthetics and Art Criticism* 65, no. 4 (2007): 381–89.
Forster, Eckhart. *Kant's Transcendental Deductions*. Stanford, CA: Stanford University Press, 1989.
Frierson, Patrick R. *Freedom and Anthropology in Kant's Moral Philosophy*. Cambridge: Cambridge University Press, 2003.
    "Kantian Feeling: Empirical Psychology, Transcendental Critique, and Phenomenology." *Con-textos Kantianos* no. 3 (2016): 353–71.
Kant's Empirical Psychology. Cambridge: Cambridge University Press, 2014.
Gadamer, Hans-Georg. *Truth and Method*. New York: Continuum, 1989.
Gasché, Rodolphe. *The Idea of Form: Rethinking Kant's Aesthetics*. Stanford, CA: Stanford University Press, 2003.
Geiger, Ido. "Is the Assumption of a Systematic Whole of Empirical Concepts a Necessary Condition of Knowledge?" *Kant-Studien* 94, no. 3 (2003): 273–98.
    "Rational Feelings and Moral Agency." *Kantian Review* 16, no. 2 (June 2011): 283–308.
George, Rolf. "Kant's Sensationism." *Synthese* 47 (1981): 229–55.
Ginsborg, Hannah. "Aesthetic Judging and the Intentionality of Pleasure." *Inquiry* 46 (2003): 164–81.
    "Kant's Aesthetics and Teleology." *Stanford Encyclopedia of Philosophy*, February 13, 2013. https://plato.stanford.edu/archives/fall2014/entries/kant-aesthetics.
The Normativity of Nature: Essays on Kant's Critique of Judgment. Oxford: Oxford University Press, 2015.
    "Reflective Judgment and Taste." *Noûs* 24, no. 1 (1990): 63–78.
The Role of Taste in Kant's Theory of Cognition. New York: Garland Publishing, 1990.
    "Why Must We Presuppose the Systematicity of Nature?" In *Kant and the Laws of Nature*, edited by Michela Massimi and Angela Breitenbach. Cambridge: Cambridge University Press, forthcoming.
Goy, Ina. "Immanuel Kant über das moralische Gefühl der Achtung." *Zeitschrift für philosophische Forschung* 61 (2007): 337–60.
Gram, Moltke S., ed. *Interpreting Kant*. Iowa City: University of Iowa Press, 1982.

Gregor, Mary J. "Critique of Practical Reason: Introduction." In *The Cambridge Edition of the Works of Immanuel Kant: Practical Philosophy*, translated and edited by Mary J. Gregor, 135–36. Cambridge: Cambridge University Press, 1996.
Laws of Freedom. Oxford: Blackwell, 1963.
Gregoric, Pavel. *Aristotle on the Common Sense*. Oxford: Oxford University Press, 2007.
Grenberg, Jeanine. "Feeling, Desire, and Interest in Kant's Theory of Action." *Kant-Studien* 92, no. 2 (2001): 153–79.
Kant's Defense of Common Moral Experience: A Phenomenological Account. Cambridge: Cambridge University Press, 2013.
Grier, Michelle. *Kant's Doctrine of Transcendental Illusion*. Cambridge: Cambridge University Press, 2001.
Guevara, Daniel. *Kant's Theory of Moral Motivation*. Boulder, CO: Westview Press, 2000.
Guyer, Paul. "Beauty, Freedom, and Morality: Kant's *Lectures on Anthropology* and the Development of his Aesthetic Theory." In *Essays on Kant's Anthropology*, edited by Brian Jacobs and Patrick Kain, 135–63. Cambridge: Cambridge University Press, 2003.
"Editorial Notes." In *The Cambridge Edition of the Works of Immanuel Kant: The Critique of the Power of Judgment*, edited by Paul Guyer, 351–97. Cambridge: Cambridge University Press, 2000.
Kant. New York: Routledge, 2006.
Kant and the Claims of Taste. 2nd ed. Cambridge, MA: Harvard University Press, 1997.
Kant and the Experience of Freedom: Essays on Aesthetics and Morality. Cambridge: Cambridge University Press, 1993.
Kant on Freedom, Law, and Happiness. Cambridge: Cambridge University Press, 2000.
"Kant's Distinction between the Sublime and the Beautiful." *Review of Metaphysics* 35, no. 4 (1982): 753–83.
Kant's System of Nature and Freedom: Selected Essays. Oxford: Oxford University Press, 2005.
"Moral Anthropology in Kant's Aesthetics and Ethics: A Reply to Ameriks and Sherman." *Philosophy and Phenomenological Research* 55, no. 2 (1995): 379–91.
"Moral Feelings in the Metaphysics of Morals." In *Kant's Metaphysics of Morals: A Critical Guide*, edited by Lara Denis, 130–51. Cambridge: Cambridge University Press, 2010.
"Nature, Art, and Autonomy." In *Kant and the Experience of Freedom: Essays on Aesthetics and Morality*, 229–74. Cambridge: Cambridge University Press, 1993.
"Notes." In *The Cambridge Edition of the Works of Immanuel Kant: Notes and Fragments*, edited by Paul Guyer, 545–625. Cambridge: Cambridge University Press, 2005.

"One Act or Two? Hannah Ginsborg on Aesthetic Judgment." *British Journal of Aesthetics* (forthcoming).

"Pleasure and Society in Kant's Theory of Taste." In *Essays in Kant's Aesthetics*, edited by Ted Cohen and Paul Guyer, 21–54. Chicago: University of Chicago Press, 1982.

"Reason and Reflective Judgment: Kant on the Significance of Systematicity." *Noûs* 24, no. 1 (1990): 17–43.

Values of Beauty: Historical Essays in Aesthetics. Cambridge: Cambridge University Press, 2005.

ed. *The Cambridge Companion to Kant*. Cambridge: Cambridge University Press, 1992.

ed. *The Cambridge Companion to Kant's Critique of Pure Reason*, Cambridge: Cambridge University Press, 2010.

Hanauer, Tom. "Sublimity and the Ends of Reason: Questions for Deligiorgi." *The Journal of Aesthetics and Art Criticism* 74, no. 2 (2016): 195–99.

Hay, Carol. *Kantianism, Liberalism, and Feminism: Resisting Oppression*. New York: Palgrave Macmillan, 2013.

Hegel, G. W. F. *Elements of the Philosophy of Right*. Edited by Allen W. Wood. Translated by H. B. Nisbet. Cambridge: Cambridge University Press, 1991.

Herman, Barbara. *The Practice of Moral Judgment*. Cambridge, MA: Harvard University Press, 1993.

Hill, Thomas E., Jr. "Servility and Self-Respect." *The Monist* 57, no. 1 (January 1973): 87–104.

Hobbes, Thomas. *Leviathan*. 1651. Edited by Richard Tuck. Cambridge: Cambridge University Press, 1991.

Home, Henry (Lord Kames). *Elements of Criticism*. 6th ed. Edited by Peter Jones. Indianapolis, IN: Liberty Fund, 2005.

Horstmann, R.-P. "Why Must There Be a Transcendental Deduction in Kant's *Critique of Judgment*?" In *Kant's Transcendental Deductions*, edited by Eckart Förster, 157–76. Stanford, CA: Stanford University Press, 1989.

Hume, David. *A Treatise of Human Nature*. Edited by David Fate and Mary J. Norton. Oxford: Oxford University Press, 2000.

A Treatise of Human Nature. Edited by L. A. Selby-Bigge. Oxford: Clarendon Press, 1949.

Hurka, Thomas. *Virtue, Vice, and Value*. New York: Oxford University Press, 2001.

Hutcheson, Francis. *An Inquiry into the Original of Our Ideas of Beauty and Virtue*. 1725. Edited by Wolfgang Leidhold. Rev. ed. Indianapolis, IN: Liberty Fund, 2008.

Irwin, Terence. *The Development of Ethics*. Vol. 1. Oxford: Oxford University Press, 2007.

Jacobs, Brian, and Patrick Kain, eds. *Essays on Kant's Anthropology*. Cambridge: Cambridge University Press, 2003.

Johnson, Robert N. "Duties to and Regarding Others." In *Kant's Metaphysics of Morals: A Critical Guide*, edited by Lara Denis, 192–209. Cambridge: Cambridge University Press, 2010.
Jost, Lawrence, and Julian Wuerth, eds. *Perfecting Virtue: New Essays on Kantian Ethics and Virtue Ethics*. Cambridge: Cambridge University Press, 2011.
Katz, Leonard D. "Pleasure." *Stanford Encyclopedia of Philosophy*, June 17, 2016. https://plato.stanford.edu/entries/pleasure.
Kemp Smith, Norman. *A Commentary to Kant's Critique of Pure Reason*. New York: Palgrave Macmillan, 2003.
Kirwan, James. *The Aesthetic in Kant: A Critique*. London: Continuum, 2004.
Kleingeld, Pauline. "The Conative Character of Reason in Kant's Philosophy." *Journal of the History of Philosophy* 36, no. 1 (1998): 77–97.
Klimchuk, Dennis. "Three Accounts of Respect for Persons in Kant's Ethics." *Kantian Review* 8, no. 1 (March 2004): 38–61.
Korsgaard, Christine. "Fellow Creatures: Kantian Ethics and Our Duties to Animals." In *The Tanner Lectures on Human Values*, edited by Grethe B. Peterson. Vols. 25/26. Salt Lake City: University of Utah Press, 2004.
  Self-Constitution: Agency, Identity, and Integrity. Oxford: Oxford University Press, 2009.
  The Sources of Normativity. Cambridge: Cambridge University Press, 1996.
Kühn, Manfred. *Kant: Eine Biographie*. München: C. H. Beck, 2003.
Kumar, Apaar. "Kant's Definition of Sensation." *Kant Studies Online*, 2014. www.kantstudiesonline.net.
Kundera, Milan. *The Unbearable Lightness of Being*. Translated by Michael Henry Heim. New York: Harper and Row, 1984.
Lipscomb, Benjamin, and James Krueger. *Kant's Moral Metaphysics: God, Freedom, and Immortality*. Berlin: Walter de Gruyter, 2010.
Locke, John. *An Essay Concerning Human Understanding*. Edited by Peter H. Nidditch. Oxford: Clarendon Press, 1975.
Louden, Robert B. *Kant's Impure Ethics: From Rational Beings to Human Beings*. Oxford: Oxford University Press, 2000.
Lyotard, Jean-François. *L'Enthousiasme: La critique kantienne de l' histoire*. Paris: Editions Galilée, 1986.
  Enthusiasm: The Kantian Critique of History. Stanford, CA: Stanford University Press, 2009.
Makkreel, Rudolf A. *Imagination and Interpretation in Kant: The Hermeneutical Import of the Critique of Judgment*. Chicago: University of Chicago Press, 1990.
  Orientation and Judgment in Hermeneutics. Chicago: University of Chicago Press, 2015.
Massimi, Michela, and Angela Breitenbach, eds. *Kant and the Laws of Nature*. Cambridge: Cambridge University Press, forthcoming.
McCarty, Richard. "Kantian Moral Motivation and the Feeling of Respect." *Journal of the History of Philosophy* 31, no. 3 (1993): 421–35.
  Kant's Theory of Action. Oxford: Oxford University Press, 2009.

Menzel, Randolph, and Julia Fischer, eds. *Animal Thinking: Contemporary Issues in Comparative Cognition*. Cambridge, MA: MIT Press, 2010.

Merritt, Anna C., Daniel A. Effron, and Benoît Monin. "Moral-Self-Licensing: When Being Good Frees Us to Be Bad." *Social and Personality Psychology Compass* 4, no. 5 (May 2010): 344–57.

Merritt, Melissa McBay. "The Moral Source of the Kantian Sublime." In *The Sublime: From Antiquity to the Present*, edited by Timothy M. Costelloe, 37–49. Cambridge: Cambridge University Press, 2012.

——— "Review of Robert R. Clewis, The Kantian Sublime and the Revelation of Freedom." *British Journal for the History of Philosophy* 18, no. 3 (2010): 529–32.

Michalson, Gordon, ed. *Kant's Religion within the Boundaries of Mere Reason: A Critical Guide*. Cambridge: Cambridge University Press, 2014.

Morrisson, Iain P. D. *Kant and the Role of Pleasure in Moral Action*. Athens: Ohio University Press, 2008.

Mudd, Sasha. "Rethinking the Priority of Practical Reason in Kant." *European Journal of Philosophy* 24, no. 1 (2016): 78–102.

Nagel, Thomas. "What Is It Like to Be a Bat?" *Philosophical Review* 83, no. 4 (1974): 435–50. Reprinted in Thomas Nagel. *Mortal Questions*. Cambridge: Cambridge University Press, 1979.

Nietzsche, Friedrich. *On the Genealogy of Morality*. Translated by Maudemarie Clark and Alan Swensen. Indianapolis, IN: Hackett, 1998.

Osborne, Nicolas. *Opinion, croyance, savoir: Recherches sure la pragmatique kantienne de la pensée*. PhD diss., University of Lille, 2016.

Park, Kap Hyun. *Kant über das Erhabene: Rekonstruktion und Weiterführung der kritischen Theorie des Erhabenen Kants*. Würzburg: Königshausen and Neumann, 2009.

Paton, H. J. *The Categorical Imperative: A Study in Kant's Moral Philosophy*. London: Hutchinson and Co., 1947.

Plato. "Theaetetus." In *Plato: Complete Works*, edited by John M. Cooper, 157–234. Indianapolis, IN: Hackett Publishing, 1997.

Rauscher, Frederick. "The Appendix to the Dialectic and the Canon of Pure Reason: The Positive Role of Reason." In *The Cambridge Companion to Kant's Critique of Pure Reason*, edited by Paul Guyer, 290–309. Cambridge: Cambridge University Press, 2010.

Rayman, Joshua. *Kant on Sublimity and Morality*. Cardiff: University of Wales Press, 2012.

Reath, Andrews. "Kant's Theory of Moral Sensibility: Respect for the Moral Law and the Influence of Inclination." *Kant-Studien* 80 (1989): 284–302.

——— "Two Conceptions of the Highest Good in Kant." *Journal of the History of Philosophy* 26, no. 4 (1988): 593–619.

Reath, Andrews, and Jens Timmermann, eds. *Kant's Critique of Practical Reason: A Critical Guide*. Cambridge: Cambridge University Press, 2010.

Recki, Birgit. "Wie fühlt man sich als vernünftiges Wesen?" In *Pathos, Affekt, Gefühl: Die Emotionen in den Künsten*, edited by Bernhard Stumpfhaus and Klaus Herding, 275–94. Berlin: Walter de Gruyter, 2004.

Reginster, Bernard. "Sympathy in Schopenhauer and Nietzsche." In *Sympathy: A History*, edited by Eric Schliesser, 254–85. New York: Oxford University Press, 2015.
Reimarus, Hermann Samuel. *Allgemeine Betrachtungen über die Triebe der Thiere*. Bohn: Hamburg, 1760.
Rescher, Nicholas. *Kant and the Reach of Reason: Studies in Kant's Theory of Rational Systematization*. Cambridge: Cambridge University Press, 2000.
Robinson, Jenefer. *Deeper than Reason: Emotion and Its Role in Literature, Music, and Art*. Oxford: Oxford University Press, 2005.
Rohlf, Michael. "The Transition from Nature to Freedom in Kant's Third *Critique*." *Kant-Studien* 99, no. 3 (2008): 339–60.
Rotenstreich, Nathan. "Morality and Culture: A Note on Kant." *History of Philosophy Quarterly* 6, no. 3 (1989): 303–16.
Ryle, Gilbert. *The Concept of Mind*. London: Hutchinson, 1949.
Sassen, Brigitte. "Common Sense as the Answer to the Paradox of Taste." In *Kant und die Philosophie in weltbürgerlicher Absicht: Akten des XI Internationalen Kant-Kongresses*, Vol. 4, 249–59. Berlin: De Gruyter, 2013.
Schapiro, Tamar. "Desires as Demands: How the Second-Person Standpoint Might Be Internal to Reflective Agency." *Philosophy and Phenomenological Research* 81, no. 1 (2010): 229–36.
  "Foregrounding Desire: A Defense of Kant's Incorporation Thesis." *The Journal of Ethics* 15, no. 3 (2011): 14–67.
  "The Nature of Inclination." *Ethics* 119, no. 2 (2009): 229–56.
  "On the Relation between Wanting and Willing." *Philosophical Issues* 22, no. 1 (2012): 334–50.
  "What Are Theories of Desire Theories Of?" *Analytic Philosophy* 55, no. 2 (2014): 131–50.
Schiller, Friedrich. *On the Aesthetic Education of Man*. Mineola, NY: Dover Publications, 2004.
Schliesser, Eric, ed. *Sympathy: A History*. New York: Oxford University Press, 2015.
Schott, Robin May. *Cognition and Eros: A Critique of the Kantian Paradigm*. Boston: Beacon Press, 1988.
Sensen, Oliver. *Kant on Human Dignity*. Berlin: Walter de Gruyter, 2011.
  ed. *Kant on Moral Autonomy*. Cambridge: Cambridge University Press, 2012.
Shell, Susan Meld. "Kant's 'True Economy of Human Nature': Rousseau, Count Verri, and the Problem of Happiness." In *Essays on Kant's Anthropology*, edited by Brian Jacobs and Patrick Kain, 174–229. Cambridge: Cambridge University Press, 2003.
Shell, Susan Meld, and Richard Velkley. *Kant's Observations and Remarks: A Critical Guide*. Cambridge: Cambridge University Press, 2012.
Sherman, Nancy. *Making a Necessity of Virtue: Aristotle and Kant on Virtue*. Cambridge: Cambridge University Press, 1997.
  "Reasons and Feelings in Kantian Morality." *Philosophy and Phenomenological Research* 55, no. 2 (1995): 369–77.
Singleton, Jane. "Kant's Account of Respect: A Bridge between Rationality and Anthropology." *Kantian Review* 12, no. 1 (March 2007): 40–60.

Sizer, Laura. "What Feelings Can't Do." *Mind and Language* 21, no. 1 (2006): 108–35.
Sommerlatte, Curtis. "Empirical Cognition in the Transcendental Deduction: Kant's Starting Point and His Humean Problem." *Kantian Review* 21, no. 3 (November 2016): 437–63.
Sorensen, Kelly D. "Kant's Taxonomy of the Emotions." *Kantian Review* 6, no. 1 (2002): 109–28.
Stark, Cynthia A. "The Rationality of Valuing Oneself: A Critique of Kant on Self-Respect." *Journal of the History of Philosophy* 35, no. 1 (January 1997): 65–82.
Stratton-Lake, Philip. *Kant, Duty, and Moral Worth*. London: Routledge, 2000.
Stumpfhaus, Bernhard, and Klaus Herding, eds. *Pathos, Affekt, Gefühl: Die Emotionen in den Künsten*. Berlin: Walter de Gruyter, 2004.
Sturm, Thomas. *Kant und die Wissenschaften vom Menschen*, Münster: Mentis Verlag, 2009.
Sulzer, Johann Georg. *Vermischte Philosophische Schriften*. Vol. 1. Leipzig: Wiedmanns Erben und Reich, 1773.
Swanton, Christine. "Kant's Impartial Virtues of Love." In *Perfecting Virtue: New Essays on Kantian Ethics and Virtue Ethics*, edited by Lawrence Jost and Julian Wuerth, 241–60. Cambridge: Cambridge University Press, 2011.
Tarbet, David W. "The Fabric of Metaphor in Kant's Critique of Pure Reason." *Journal of the History of Philosophy* 6, no. 3 (1968): 257–70.
Timmermann, Jens. "Autonomy and Moral Regard for Ends." In *Kant on Moral Autonomy*, edited by Oliver Sensen, 212–24. Cambridge: Cambridge University Press, 2012.
Velkley, Richard. *Being After Rousseau: Philosophy and Culture in Question*. Chicago: Chicago University Press, 2002.
Verri, Pietro. *Del piacere e del dolore ed altri scritt*. Milan: Feltrinelli, 1964.
Vico, Giambattista. *Selected Writings*. Cambridge: Cambridge University Press, 1982.
Von Tevenar, Gudren, ed. *Nietzsche and Ethics*. Oxford: Peter Lang, 2007.
"Nietzsche's Objections to Pity and Compassion." In *Nietzsche and Ethics*, edited by Gudrun von Tevenar, 263–82. Oxford: Peter Lang, 2007.
Waibel, Violetta L., and Margit Ruffing, eds. *Proceedings of the 12th International Kant Congress*. Berlin: de Gruyter, forthcoming.
Ware, Owen. "The Duty of Self-Knowledge." *Philosophy and Phenomenological Research* 79, no. 3 (2009): 671–98.
Wartenberg, Thomas E. "Reason and the Practice of Science." In *The Cambridge Companion to Kant*, edited by Paul Guyer, 228–48. Cambridge: Cambridge University Press, 1992.
Willaschek, Marcus. "The Primacy of Practical Reason and the Idea of a Practical Postulate." In *Kant's Critique of Practical Reason: A Critical Guide*, edited by Andrews Reath and Jens Timmermann, 168–96. Cambridge: Cambridge University Press, 2010.
Williams, Bernard. *Moral Luck*. Cambridge: Cambridge University Press, 1981.

Williamson, Diane. *Kant's Theory of Emotion: Emotional Universalism*. New York: Palgrave Macmillan, 2015.
Wolff, Christian. *Psychologia Empirica*. 2nd ed. Frankfurt and Leipzig: Renger, 1738.
Wood, Allen W. "The Antinomies of Pure Reason." In *The Cambridge Companion to Kant's Critique of Pure Reason*, edited by Paul Guyer, 245–65. Cambridge: Cambridge University Press, 2010.
   "The Evil in Human Nature." In *Kant's Religion within the Boundaries of Mere Reason: A Critical Guide*, edited by Gordon Michalson, 31–57. Cambridge: Cambridge University Press, 2014.
   Fichte's Ethical Thought. Oxford: Oxford University Press, 2016.
   "The Final Form of Kant's Practical Philosophy." *Southern Journal of Philosophy* 36 (1997): 1–20.
   Formulas of the Moral Law. Cambridge: Cambridge University Press, 2017.
   The Free Development of Each: Studies on Freedom, Right, and Ethics in Classical German Philosophy. Oxford: Oxford University Press, 2014.
   Kantian Ethics. Cambridge: Cambridge University Press, 2008.
   Kant's Ethical Thought. Cambridge: Cambridge University Press, 1999.
   "Kant's History of Ethics." In *Kant's Lectures on Ethics: A Critical Guide*, edited by Lara Denis and Oliver Sensen, 120–37. Cambridge: Cambridge University Press, 2015.
   Kant's Moral Religion. Ithaca, NY: Cornell University Press, 1970.
Wuerth, Julian. *Kant on Mind, Action, and Ethics*. Oxford: Oxford University Press, 2014.
Yovel, Yirmiyahu. *Kant and the Philosophy of History*. Princeton, NJ: Princeton University Press, 1980.
Zammito, John H. *The Genesis of Kant's Critique of Judgment*. Chicago: Chicago University Press, 1992.
Zinkin, Melissa. "Kant and the Pleasure of 'Mere Reflection.'" *Inquiry* 55, no. 5 (2012): 433–53.
   "Respect for the Law and the Use of Dynamical Terms in Kant's Theory of Moral Motivation." *Archiv für Geschichte der Philosophie* 88, no. 1 (2006): 31–53.
Zuckert, Rachel. *Kant on Beauty and Biology: An Interpretation of the Critique of Judgment*. Cambridge: Cambridge University Press, 2007.
   "Kant's Account of Practical Fanaticism." In *Kant's Moral Metaphysics: God, Freedom, and Immortality*, ed. Benjamin Lipscomb and James Krueger, 291–317. Berlin: Walter de Gruyter, 2010.
   "A New Look at Kant's Theory of Pleasure." *The Journal of Aesthetics and Art Criticism* 60, no. 3 (2002): 239–52.

Index

a priori principles, 5, 15, 20, 107–20
aesthetic feeling. *See also* beauty, *See* aesthetic judgment
aesthetic judgment, 30, 98, 107, 109–13, 117–18, 123–24, 126–28, 130, 138–41, 160–61, 167–68, 171, 202, 252
    fallibility of, 150, 164
    a priori principles of, 129
    as reflective, 141
    universality of, 146, 160
affect, 2, 7, 26–27, 31, 38, 171, 184, 187, 189, 192–93, 205–6, 218–19, 228
    as contrasted with passion, 172, 187, 199
    as sublime, 187
Allison, Henry, 31, 125, 167
Anderson-Gold, Sharon, 233
anger, 2, 38, 172, 187, 251
animality, 5, 62, 67–69, 86, 92–93, 96, 99, 101, 229
    healthy, 258
    as rational, 72
    rationality of, 69
animals, 5, 36, 39, 67–68, 70, 80–83, 85, 88–90, 92, 95, 99
    cognition of, 90
    as determined, 70
    faculties of, 88
Antinomy
    Third, 52–54, 62
Aquila, Richard, 30
Aquinas, Thomas, 215
Aristotle, 98, 106, 142–43, 185, 191
Augustine, 180
autonomy, 4, 52, 64, 167, *See also* freedom

Baumgarten, Alexander Gottlieb, 91, 124
beauty, 2, 6, 29, 38, 110–11, 124, 126, 130–31, 133, 137–39, 141, 144, 147–50, 152, 160–61, 164, 190, 192
    as related to sublimity, 165
Beck, Lewis White, 107

belief, 247, 250, 252
benevolence, 210
boredom, 159

categorical imperative, 97, 228, 236–37
categories of freedom, 51
categories of the understanding, 53
Chignell, Andrew, 247
Churchland, Patricia, 89
Clewis, Robert, 166
cognition
    drive for, 14
    empirical, 2, 10
    faculty of, 1, 3, 13, 134
        higher, 116–17, 119, 121, 220
        lower, 116, 220
    as limited to experience, 48
    a priori principles of, 119
    moral, 3
    regulative principles of, 10
color, 171
compassion, 208–12, 221
concupiscence, 77, 100
cosmopolitanism, 200
courage, 218
Cranor, Carl, 225

Darwall, Stephen, 225, 238–39
Descartes, 143
desire, 2, 4–6, 14, 25, 99–100
    definition of, 33
    faculty of, 1–4, 13, 35, 74, 76, 98
        higher, 5, 33, 96, 101, 120
        lower, 5, 33, 75, 96, 101
    as intellectual, 33, 100
    a priori principles of, 119
    as sensible, 77
    harmony of, 40, 53, 85, 106
    manifold of, 63
    multiplicity of, 60
    role in motivation, 103

Index

despair, 257
determinism, 2, 50, 52, 91
DeWitt, Janelle, 92–95, 98–99, 103–4
displeasure. *See* pleasure and pain
Du Bos, Jean-Baptiste, 159
duties, 7, 39–40, 105–6, 213, 224, 226–35
   four types, 228
   to onself, 179
   of virtue, 97, 230, 234

embodiment, 3, 6
Emerson, Ralph Waldo, 191
emotion, 2, 4, 25–26, 28, 30, 36–40, 71–72, 78, 84, 156, 167, 175, 204, 218, 243,
   See also affect
   cognitivist theories of, 40
empirical psychology, 4, 42–45, 91, 114, 116, 129, 169, 243
empiricism, 1
enthusiasm, 2, 6, 26, 184–207, 218, 228
   as an affect, 193
   as disinterested, 203
   and moral education, 194, 206
   as sublime, 188–90, 192, 196
   temporality of, 204
Epicurus, 226
evil, 101–2

Fact of Reason, 51
faculties
   free play of, 7, 111, 127–28, 139–41, 144, 146, 153, 155, 159–60, 189–90, 196, 256
   organization of, 134
   three, 1, 5, 13, 28, 107–9, 114–17, 119, 121, 123, 128, 219
Fahmy, Melissa, 233
fanaticism, 46, 48, 65, 184, 192, 197–200, 206
feeling
   cognitive account of, 71–73
   as determination of value, 74
   as intuition, 45–46
   as judgment, 78, 81
   as passive, 255
   as perception, 31
   a priori principles of, 109–15, 123, 126, 128–29
   as receptive, 51
   as related to desire, 31–34, 103
   as sensibly determined, 61
   as subjective, 30, 124, 170–71
   as tracking information, 27
   cognitive content of, 16–17, 28, 84, 98, 171, 176, 186, 195, 252
   faculty of, 1–5, 76, 107, 219
      higher, 2, 117, 220
      lower, 2, 14, 86, 220
   in contrast to cognition, 27–31, 37
   in relation to desire, 32, 78
   noncognitive account of, 69–71
   pathological, 227
   rational, 17, 20, 205, 251
   role in action, 219
feeling of reason's need, 2–3, 10, 12, 14–15, 17, 19–20, 22–23
feminist critiques of Kant, 93–94
Feuerbach, Ludwig, 88
Fichte, Johann Gottlieb, 95, 100
five senses, the, 1
Formosa, Paul, 237
freedom, 4, 7, 24, 50, 68, 79, 84, 86, 89–90, 92, 96, 158, 195, 198, 200, 237
   causality of, 59
   as compatible with determinism, 52–54, 92
   concepts of, 58
   passion for, 199
   relationship to nature, 131–33
French Revolution, 7, 185, 196, 198–203
Frierson, Patrick, 43–44, 193

Geiger, Ido, 225
Ginsborg, Hannah, 31
God, 50, 100, 180, 184, 195, 234, 242–59
Guyer, Paul, 11, 17, 23, 30, 107, 109, 113, 116, 123, 125, 142, 214, 217

happiness, 149, 244–45, 248, 254
Hay, Carol, 232
Hegel, Georg Wilhelm Friedrich, 100
Highest Good, 8, 46, 50, 226, 242, 244–47, 250–51, 253–55, 257
Hill, Thomas, 235, 237
Hobbes, Thomas, 156
hope, 2, 8, 204, 242–59
   crafty, 257
   as like respect, 256
human nature
   duality of, 67–68, 95, 132, 181
   as finite, 78
Hume, David, 135, 152, 163, 170
Hutcheson, Francis, 31, 104, 150–51
hypochondria, 36, 38
hypothetical imperatives, 120

ideas of reason, 9–11, 14–15, 17, 20–24, 51, 122, 155, 190, 196, 204, 244–50
immortality, 51
impartiality, 97–98
incentives of pure practical reason, 112
inclination, 4, 14, 18, 27, 67–68, 78, 82, 99–101
incorporation thesis, 68, 80
inner sense, 4, 42–45, 52, 57–59, 61, 66, 75, 171

instinct, 68, 70, 79–87, 89, 99–100
intellectual feeling, 8, 60, 225, 231, 256, 258
intellectual pleasure, 2, 115, 126, 187, 204, 227, 251
intelligible self, 61–62, 64
intuition, 46, *See also* feeling: as intuition

Jacobi, Carl Gustav Jacob, 95
jealousy, 38
joy, 36
judgment, 5
  as association, 81
  as between cognition and desire, 136
  definition of, 120
  determinative, 5, 120–21
  as a part of feeling, 37, 174
  as an intermediate faculty, 117
  as part of feeling, 99
  a priori principles of, 117, 120–21, 126–27
  reflective, 5, 120, 122, 126, 128, 154
    pleasure of, 127
    a priori principle of, 125
    as related to feeling, 123

Kleingeld, Pauline, 12
Korsgaard, Christine, 92, 96
Kundera, Milan, 211

Leibniz, Gottfried Wilhelm, 49
life
  definition of, 127
  feeling of, 27, 34–37, 40, 124, 158
  promotion of, 4, 27, 40, 73
love, 7, 25, 38, 105, 198, 208, 210, 213–16, 218, 222–23, 228, 235
  criticism of, 215
  as related to respect, 234

Maimon, Salomon, 95
Mendelssohn, Moses, 182
misogyny, 5
Moore, G.E., 153
moral cognition, 4, 6–7, 25–27, 37–38, 40–66
moral education, 7
moral fanaticism, 47–48
moral feeling, 19, 24, 26, 39, 42, 104–5, 228–29, 251
  intellectualist interpretations of, 41
  temporality of, 42–49
moral law, 4, 7, 10, 18–20, 24, 37–66, 71, 86, 104–5, 112, 115, 119, 126, 145, 154, 173, 179, 181, 185, 192, 205, 218, 226, 231, 235–38, 244, 246, 256, *See also* moral feeling
  as object of mystery, 47
  respect for, 226–27, 229–30, 232, 235–37, 240, 253
  schematism of, 50
  striking down conceit, 212
  sublimity of, 190, 218, 231
moral psychology, 26, 43, 103
moral sense theory, 1, 25, 31, 104
motivation, 2–4, 8, 18, 25–26, 40–41, 67, 69, 75–76, 103, 226, 255
  as related to feeling, 32

Nagel, Thomas, 91
Nietzsche, Friedrich, 7, 208, 212, 214–15, 222

O'Neill, Onora, 97
opium, 36

pain. *See* pleasure and pain
Paralogisms, 63
passion, 2, 7, 27, 38, 71, 102, 156, 193, 199, 220
  as contrasted with affect, 172, 187, 199
Petrarca, Francesco, 180
pity, 38
pleasure and pain, 2, 4–6, 14–16, 18, 28–29, 31, 37, 69, 98–99, 111–12, 117
  of animals, 70
  as bridge between theoretical and practical philosophy, 137
  casuse of, 126
  cognitive content of, 171
  definition of, 4, 6, 13, 32–35, 73, 127–28, 157–58, 251–52
  as determined a priori, 118
  in the feeling of sublimity, 170, 174
  intellectual. *See* intellectual pleasure
  judgment of, 76, 78
  as link between theoretical and practical philosophy, 135
  as necessarily related, 164
  from overstimulation, 35
  perception of, 220–21
  a priori principles of, 123–24
  as related to desire, 103
  as related to the other faculties, 36
  two accounts of, 147–65
practical cognition, 69
  as like theoretical cognition, 50, 54–57, 63
practical philosophy. *See* practical reason
practical reason, 3–4, 6, 9, 22, 25, 27, 39, 53, 72, 104, 112
  as like theoretical reason, 95
  pure, 154

Index

relationship to theoretical reason, 131–38
precritical period, 1, 197
progress, 186, 200–1, 204, 206, 243, 248–49, 253–54, 257
prudential reason, 7, 80
purposiveness, 6, 15, 39, 122–23, 125–28, 138, 168, 173, 177–78, 218, 243, 249
   and contrapurposiveness, 173, 175, 177
   pleasure of, 125, 128, 138
   without a purpose, 139–40, 142, 202

rational agency, 21
rationalism, 1, 49
Rawls, John, 97
Rayman, Joshua, 166
reason
   practical. *See* practical reason
   theoretical. *See* theoretical reason
recognition respect, 238–40
Reinhold, Carl Leonhard, 92, 95–96, 108–28
respect, 2–4, 7, 10, 17–18, 24–25, 39, 42–43, 53, 73, 104–6, 126, 187, 224–41, *See also* moral feeling
   accounts of, 224–25
   appraisal, 236, 238–40
   as a bridge, 227
   as compared with enthusiasm, 204
   for oneself, 38, 214, 225
   for rational being, 65
   recognition, 238
   as related to sympathy, 214
   in relation to love, 214
   for self, 228–33
   as special, 60, 115, 128, 226
   as sublime, 188
ridicule, 106, 234
Rousseau, Jean-Jacques, 133, 159, 191–92, 198, 211

sadness, 2, 36, 38, 209, 219
Schapiro, Tamar, 93, 96
schematism, 42, 50, 54–58, 60
Schopenhauer, Arthur, 222
Schulze, Gottlob Ernst, 95
self-conceit, 7, 102, 211–12, 223, 238
self-esteem, 38, 228, 231, 234
self-love, 73, 75–76, 80, 82, 236, 241
Sen, Amartya, 232
sensation, 6, 28–29, 171, 176
   as an element of cognition, 29
sensus communis, 6, 131, 141–46
Sidgwick, Henry, 92, 96
Singleton, Jane, 227
Socrates, 142

Stark, Cynthia, 231
Stoicism, 71, 143
Stratton-Lake, Philip, 227
sublimity, 2–3, 6, 147, 149–50, 153, 155–56, 160–83, 187–92, 194–96, 202–6, 218, 232, 256
   of *apatheia*, 187, 190–91
   as a bridging concept, 182–83
   dynamical, 155, 161, 196
   early writings on, 169
   of enthusiasm, 201–3, 206
   judgment of, 168, 173–79, 192
   mathematical, 155, 161, 196
   moral importance of, 178–79
   of the morally good, 187
   as morally important, 179–82
   of rational being, 237
   as related to beauty, 165
Sulzer, Johann Georg, 151, 158
sympathy, 7, 25–26, 38, 85, 105, 185, 208–23, 234
   as perceptive, 216
   criticism of, 209–13, 215, 217
   in moral development, 216
   primitive, 221
systematicity, 3, 9–11, 14, 22–23, 125, 131, 183
   of philosophy, 108, 129, 134
   pleasure of, 15, 17

teleology, 5, 107, 109, 122, 125, 183, 206
temporality. *See* moral feeling: temporality of
Tetens, Johann Nicolas, 91
theoretical philosophy. *See* theoretical reason
theoretical reason, 3–4, 6, 9, 15, 22
   feeling of, 10
   relationship to practical reason, 131–38
Transcendental Aesthetic, 57
transcendental idealism, 9, 52
transcendental psychology, 1
transcendental unity of apperception, 4, 43, 54, 62–65
Typic of Pure Practical Judgment, 53

understanding, 4
unity, 3, 9, 11, 14, 23, *See also* systematicity
   of consciousness, 53, 63
   of psyche, 68
universality, 3, 6, 111–12, 114, 118, 131, 145, 148, 160, 201–2
universalizability, 98
unsocial sociability, 5, 101–2

Verri, Count, 159
Vico, 143

virtue, 25–26, 105–6, 230–31, 233, 242, 244–45, 248, *See also* duties, of virtue
feeling of, 226

will, 42, 51, 53, 66, 154, 193
Williams, Bernard, 97, 215

Wolff, Christian, 31
Wood, Allen, 208, 210–11, 214
Wuerth, Julian, 220

Zammito, John, 12
Zuckert, Rachel, 31